Explorations in Truth, the Human Condition and Wholeness

Will Barno

PAGE PUBLISHING, INC.
New York, NY

First originally published by Page Publishing, Inc. 2015

ISBN 978-1-63417-671-2 (pbk)
ISBN 978-1-63417-672-9 (digital)

Printed in the United States of America

In the still of the night
In the world's ancient light
Where wisdom grows up in strife.
My bewildered brain
Toils in vain
Through the darkness
On the pathways of life . . .

We live and we die . . .

We eat and we drink, we feel and we think,
Far down the street we stray.
I laugh and I cry and I'm haunted by
Things I never meant nor wished to say.
The midnight rain follows the train
We all wear the same thorny crown
Soul to soul, our shadows roll . . .

I heard definite noise
I've felt transient joys
I know they're not what they seem
In this earthly domain, full of disappointment and pain . . .

And I owe my heart to you
And that's saying it true
And I'll be with you when the deal goes down.

—Bob Dylan, "When the Deal Goes Down"

Well I'm grinding out my life
Steady and sure
Nothing more wretched
Then what I must endure . . .

The more I die the more I live . . .

I pay in blood but not my own.

—Bob Dylan, "Pay in Blood"

Deep in the city of the saints and . . .
Pearls before pigs and dung becomes jewels
I sit down with tigers, I sit down with lambs
None of them know who exactly I am

I've got this thing in my heart
I must give you today
It only lives when you
Give it away.

—Bruce Cockburn, "When You Give It Away"

Contents

Section 2

Preface

There once was a note, pure and easy,
Playing so free, like a breath rippling by.
The note is eternal. I hear it, it sees me,
Forever we blend it, forever we die . . .
I listened and I heard music in a word . . .

The simple secret of the note in us all

—The Who, "Pure and Easy"

I watch and I wait
And I listen while I stand
To the music that comes
From a far better land . . .

—Bob Dylan, "Cross the Green Mountain"

In my long career as an alcohol and drug counselor, music has been the most influential of all the arts to the tens of thousands of clients I have been privileged to work with. Music inspires "inner experiences" in nearly everyone I've counseled. Bob Dylan's drummer, Mickey Jones, from their 1966 world tour, said, "You don't listen to music, you experience it."

Inner experiences are more significant to those at or past midlife—thirty-five years old or so—for whom this book is written. The first half of life is primarily motivated by the accumulation of external experiences while achieving independence and some modicum of autonomy in the world. The second half entails a subtle but persistent shift in our motivations from the external world toward inner experiences, which sustain our equilibrium and prepare us for our departure from this life. I would venture to say music is one of the most frequent vehicles by which we are transported into domains of the inner life or soul. Music that combines its tones with poetry has been embraced by almost everyone at every time in every culture. Music is a universal language that stirs and transports us from the mundane world of ordinary life into the spheres of soul and spirit.

The marriage of music and poetry goes back into ancient history before the advent of the written word. Epics, tragedies, and traditions were relayed and transmitted through song by itinerating bards and sages who traveled from town to town, singing tales of laments and wisdom in poetic verse. The melodies assisted the bard's memory and enhanced the poetic sagas. The performers also embellished basic themes by spontaneously creating their own interpretations, which came directly from their unconscious minds. These songs were passed down for each new generation to incorporate. They protected and nurtured traditions and myths, which sustained people's relationship to their psyche and the outer world, and therefore their beliefs, attitudes, and behaviors/practices within the cultural context. The world of poetry and song conveyed a vision that was intimately tied to traditions, which furnished meaning and purpose to the largely illiterate masses. The Psalms were of this genre, and though we no longer have most of the melodies, the scope and depth of human experiences found therein articulate of their poetic and psychological profundity.

The works we will be surveying in this book, Homer's epics *The Iliad* and *The Odyssey* and the book of Job are rooted in poetry and are inexorably linked in the collective consciousness of the Western mind. They were in all probability expressed in song at their most primitive stages. The written word has largely replaced these oral traditions and melodies, and the fact we can rarely experience these traditions in the same ways robs us of how the unconscious mind must have awakened awe and wonder at the hearing of these and many other tales sung so long ago.

I have chosen to use lyrics to introduce sections in this work that capture a merging of inspiration and rational thought that uniquely enhance that which is disclosed herein. I have been influenced by a variety of artists who have spoken to me throughout most of my life. These lyrics speak directly from musicians that, for me, carry on these ancient traditions by communicating through symbolic imagery, precious truths. Sadly, I can't provide the music here nor unpack the extraordinary inner experiences these compositions have incarnated within my psyche. I have chosen to quote primarily lyrics from present-day bards who personify for me a marriage between poetry and music that span fifty-plus years, from the 60s to the present. My pantheon includes primarily four: Bob Dylan, Bruce Cockburn, Van Morrison, and Leonard Cohen. These poet-musicians have cobbled together collective archetypal material from the inner depths of their souls and created a plethora of songs throughout their five-plus decades, which continue to endure. These particular artists seem to have remained creative through the disparate stages in their lives, which is no easy task for any artist. They all seem to have remained willing to live authentic lives by wrestling with the unconscious and thereby maintaining their creativity over many years. I also add three others who reside at the periphery of my pantheon—Bruce Springsteen, Jackson Browne, and Neil Young—who also have endured since the sixties. At this writing, all seven are still alive and continue to produce masterpieces of melodic poetry. In addition to my personal pantheon of modern-day musicians, I'm compelled to include many other artist who have birthed archetypal truths within me and many others over these many years.

As I alluded to earlier, all the arts allow us to approach truths and principles, which live on within the inner life of modern humans. All the arts reflect, like myths, the universal archetypes of human experience. Creativity stems from the ability to tap into the unconscious mind. It appears a few are born with an elastic portal between the conscious and unconscious minds from which they commandeer perceptions obscure to the majority of humanity. Dylan has talked about how his music and lyrics "come to him" from some other place. Most creative people acknowledge an ability to tap into something beyond themselves by which they were "enlightened." Those so gifted seem to encapsulate insights that inch unconscious contents to the surface of consciousness. No artist is consciously aware of the full implications of these hidden fountains and springs the unconscious spontaneously stirs up in their music and/or lyrics.

When music and poetry are combined, the experience is enhanced by its capacity to induce emotional archetypal states. A sense of wonder and mystery is evoked by the archetypes whenever they are stimulated. As we shall discuss at length, the language of poetry, music, dreams, and myths links us to our psyche or soul. Music passionately links people in every culture to the inner life—the heart and soul. Like each of the arts, I consider music and poetry capable of animating and conducting us not only to and from the unconscious, but also to higher levels or states of consciousness. They stimulate the unconscious archetypes, which grip us from within and force us out of the ordinary world of space and time. In my experience, poetic music shepherds us into tantalizing and temporary flavors of what joy, peace, and unity/wholeness might *feel* like. However, in the experience of wonder and joy, a fine line exists between these "mystical states" and fanaticism. We are imbued with rational capabilities, which use the language of poetry and description to convey these experiences in the world of space and time. All art forms are expressions of our consciousness in time and space, and yet ironically, artists provide "aesthetic interpretations of reality which allows for the temporary suspension of the traditional sense of time and space" (Diane Apostolos-Cappadona from her introduction to Mircea Eliade's *Symbolism, the Sacred, and the Arts*, edited by her, the Crossroads Publishing Company, 1986). All the arts, literary or visual, afford a temporary suspension of time and space, which permits us to peer into the nature of reality as both our emotions and intellects are stimulated. Our conscious vision of the world is built upon the inspiration and imagination of the unconscious mind. Art reflects the creative capacities, needs, and longings of the unconscious mind. Art is full of myths and symbolisms, which, as we shall discuss, are transformative in nature. We will be exploring myths and symbols throughout this work, and I will provide ample examples of how ordinary men and women grow and mature through this process. Traditionally, mythology contained collective beliefs about every aspect of human conduct where meaning and purpose merged. Today, we are again recognizing that myths contain reality in that they convey truths projected from within our inner life. They reflect our collective projections of what resides within our inner life in the forms of beliefs, attitudes, and practices/behaviors. They are evoked by existential situations life has presented us with and the demands to adapt to life experiences, adaptations that relate to both external and internal "reality."

Anyone interested in making relations to their psyche need only retrieve music or the art form that has carried the archetypes from their past, then the energy of the archetypes will often return with force, gripping you where you need it and stimulating the changes latent in your psyche. Like nature and all the arts, music ferries us into landscapes of possibilities and experiences that stir our imaginations and transform our souls. One can term these "mystical experiences" in the sense they convey emotional experiences that stir our souls. Some of these "mystical" experiences are highly charged emotionally with a sense of joy. Music is often referred to as soulful. As I said earlier, music and poetry give the impression of evoking latent soulful and spirit cravings and experiences that point beyond our mundane daily existence. Artists seem able to communicate soul to soul and touch the inner life of others. Art can mediate mystical experiences that cannot be described in words nor shaped by our will. They seem to appear when we least expect them and then vanish as quickly, leaving us with doubts that they ever really happened. I think this is due to the fact they communicate something beyond normal, everyday experiences. In addition, *they also* represent everyday experiences with all their responsibility and attention to duty, responsibility, and accountability. Art both captures our imaginations and our needs to live in the real world. Don't doubt these communications; we all have them! If our intuition grasps their significance, they will transport us to pearls lying dormant within. This is where faith and hope intersect with our rational capabilities. Intuition is an experience unto itself and is part of the process our mind goes through in unraveling experience. In fact, intuition is that part of our psyche that networks us with spirit.

Some of the lyrics I have chosen are direct in their communication while others are short parables and/or paradoxes to challenge conventional thought and are meant to make you ponder and puzzle out for yourselves your own truths, for in the end we are all responsible for ourselves. Have fun with it and imagine what lyrics you might have chosen to make a parable or emphasize a given text. I also listen to the blues, jazz, and classical music for these have supplied me with ample inspiration and truth over the years. Obviously, I cannot quote instrumental music, but instrumental music is a primary tool of meditation. Words can and do get in the way of higher states of consciousness, and therefore, instrumental music provides a salvo to many troubled psyches. In fact, silence and solitude are of more importance in experiencing these higher levels or states of consciousness than anything auditory. Nevertheless, from classical to modern configurations, music and poetic utterances have long reflected our imaginations and a link to those unique landscapes of the heart. It is also important to note that listening to the music presented here will enhance your appreciation of the epitaphs due to the poets' extraordinary abilities to express their poetry in musical form, where they punctuate certain words and phrases with meaningful melodies and thereby offer subtle variations in nuance. I dedicate this to all the wearied folks whose strength lies in the strings and cords, which bind them to truth.

> There's a dream where the content is visible.
> Where the poetic Champions compose . . .
>
> —Van Morrison,
> "Queen of the Slipstream"

Introduction

In the ebb and flow of dying and birth
In wounded streets and whispered prayer
The dance is the truth and it's everywhere.

—Bruce Cockburn,
"Everywhere Dance"

But I know what is wrong.
And I know what is right.
And I'd die for the truth
In My Secret Life . . .

—L. Cohen,
"In My Secret Life"

What's the true nature of being human and our relation to the world and death? What makes us tick, and what does experience teach us? What motivates us and why? Is it possible to live without illusions? What is the truth, and how does it free us from what ails us? What is the nature of "being,"[1] and how does one become authentic? What are the secrets of the inner life, which propel us toward enlightenment? How do we overcome our wounds and brokenness to experience heal-

---

1.   This is one of the traditional definitions of philosophy, which is of "being" and its concern with the study of "truth" or "reality."

ing, health, and wholeness and the joy and serenity it engenders? How do we affirm all the complexities and paradoxes inherent in life and death and fashion a lifestyle that honors these truths? Answering these riddles is what this book is about. Socrates said the unexamined life is not worth living, so let us begin to examine the human condition and our lives in particular.

To find some answers to these puzzling queries, we must venture inward, where our consciousness encounters external reality and the unconscious mind. There we will find many contradictions and paradoxes that only those willing to endure these will ever begin to find any satisfactory answers. In the alchemy of *subjective experiences*, consciousness is capable of cultivating an authentic and genuine inner life. Kierkegaard, the great Danish philosopher and proponent of the inner life, defines truth as follows: "Truth is subjective. It is an objective uncertainty held together in an appropriation process of the most passionate inwardness, the highest truth attainable for an existing individual" (*Unscientific Postscript*, p. 182). Kierkegaard was champion of the inner life like few others. When Kierkegaard disparages objectivity, he does so in the context where an existing individual gets caught in the net of unrelated and insignificant facts. The objective facts can pilfer sanity and bombard our consciousness with platitudes by the millisecond. In contrast, he proclaims that one of the few objective truths is that life is riddled with uncertainty, and to find, understand, and grasp truth, we must examine and excavate that which lies within our psyche or soul while simultaneously appropriating these truths passionately with our attitudes, behaviors, and beliefs (*psyche* is the Greek word that means "soul"). Recognizing the primacy of subjective experiences does not rule out the possibility of universal principles or truths, nor does it deny science as a valid pursuit of the truth. In fact, science has taught us much about the human condition, and *there are accessible and attainable truths the mind can affirm through our beliefs and actions.*

What Kierkegaard is driving at is that so-called objective truth is meaningless unless it is applied by subjective and conscious beings who live in the real world where paradoxes, contradictions, death, confusions, limitations, obligations, creativity, conflicts, morality, relationships, feelings, will, possibilities, tragedies, responsibilities, etc., transpires, and often with *brutal force.* Our quest includes inducing truths from the natural world and confirming truth or reality by experience. Consciousness, with the aid of the unconscious mind and external experiences, is capable of embracing truth as it has emerged historically in the evolution of human's consciousness, engendering self-knowledge and wisdom. Truth cannot be defined objectively; it is up to the individual to seek, experience, and apply truth. Abstract concepts and deductions are of little value without our subjective participation in the experience of life with the additional capability to act upon truth. Only within a person can truth subsist, acquire stature or form, and become visible. A healthy balance is achieved where priorities are fashioned and truth is lived and valued. We must *be and do.* Thought and life must be wedded through our attitudes, beliefs, and actions/practices. Our consciousness entertains possibilities and free will. Our freedom is limited (sometimes by our own choice), but there always exist choices within each set of circumstances that we come across. Truth involves finding a synthesis of understanding and will, knowledge and actions, and insight and behavior amidst the many paradoxes that are inherent within the human condition.

On the other hand, subjective experiences devoid of rational concepts and common sense engender superstition and ignorance. For the individual, truth is generated by trial and error; all the while trafficking with and beyond the five senses into obscure and nether regions and landscapes of our inner life. We can then puzzle together truths or principles, which uncover our deepest inner motivations and dynamics. The point of emphasis is therefore *self-knowledge* and the inner experiences it engenders. We organize the world through our conscious perceptions and, therefore, create our philosophy and our beliefs, which become subjective lenses through which we perceive and interpret experience.

Einstein said all knowledge or truth comes from experience. From experience comes the need to interpret experience. Between experience and its interpretation comes the field of epistemology, the study of how we know what we know. What is the truth, and how do we know it? Alas, there are no universally accepted theories that tell us how or what we know. As we will explore in chapter 3, the basic conclusions of quantum physics supports the fact we don't know how or what we really know. Uncertainty with a dash of choice seems of the foundational tenets/truths that are imbedded within the universe. Hence, Kierkegaard was ahead of his time when asserting truth is subjective and an objective uncertainty. Uncertainty contains the realm of possibility and free will. The world is not a completely preprogrammed machine. Many experiences we encounter in the world shake us out of the delusion of certainty and call us to operate outside the lines of convention and false security. Classical physics, rationalism, and predestination make assumptions based on a world where there is little or no choice. However, quantum physics and common sense exposes this deception; we are not puppets on a string. Tomorrow is not determined and locked in a cage like some domestic bird. Choices do count. We create our tomorrows by what we believe and choose today. We choose our beliefs and attitudes—whether we are open-minded or closed, are dominated by self-pity or hope, whether we reach out to others or are centered on self. *Out of our choices we create ourselves.* We are not controlled by scientists, gurus, computers, or any other forms of delusion unless we choose to be. Granted, there are still many inherent limitations and weaknesses that stand outside our control and therefore are determined by fate. For instance, our need for love, food, and water to survive; our upcoming death; living in space-time; gravity; certain personality characteristics; etc. However, we always have choices in how we respond to these external and internal limitations or fate.

It seems our destiny is a conjunction and harmony of fate/events and our entire personality. Emerson said, "The secret of the world is, the tie between person and event. Persons make event, and event person . . . He thinks his fate alien, because the copula is hidden. But the soul contains the event that shall befall it, for the event is only the actualization of its thoughts . . . Nature magically suits the man to his fortunes, by making these the fruit of his character . . . Thus events grow on the same stem with persons; are sub persons" (Ralph Waldo Emerson, *The Conduct of Life*, 962-4,967-8, from the Library of America, 1983 by Literary Classics of the United States, Inc., New York, NY).

Events are subpersons! We are, in part, what happen to us and how we deal with what happens to us as persons. Our fates and the choices we make as persons seem to be inexorably linked! To grasp this concept in more depth, we will have to venture into the astonishing and uncanny world of quantum mechanics.

As we turn inward, we discover the human condition is laden with a glut of existential needs: to bestow and be loved (accepted, understood, respected, appreciated, and forgiven); to feel our life has worth or purpose, meaning, and direction; to feel safe and secure; and to experience serenity and joy. However, countless superficial and false roads line our consciousness and personal journeys and can lead us astray from facing both collective truths encountered by everyone and unique truths specific to each of us. The way in which we covenant with our inner life either enlightens our way as we become more open, compassionate, humble; accepting, detached, etc.; or these inner contracts and choices lead us toward the darker facets and features of our nature: selfishness; dishonesty and self-deception; arrogance and the thirst for power and/or control; fear; irresponsibility; and the blaming and hatred of our fellow sojourners and pilgrims through this mortal and moral universe.

Truth with a capital *T* cannot be adequately defined in its entirety, nor can it ever be lived in wholeness, completeness, or totality. However, I will be arguing we can make an approach to understanding and living truth and experiencing enlightenment. Though I affirm truth has the power to guide and define our everyday functioning within the human condition (navigating relationships, feelings, values, conflicts, fears, sufferings, mortality, meanings, directions, and problems), we will never grasp or experience truth in its entirety. We can delve with passion in seeking truth, but never will any of us have a corner on its market. In addition, all truths that can be understood will always be greater than that which can be demonstrated in a person's life; therefore, wisdom/ understanding always comes before holiness/wholeness.

It is interesting to note that holiness and wholeness derive from the same root word: *health*. Therefore, health implies holiness and wholeness. Carl Jung recognized that by its very nature, the individual psyche or soul seeks wholeness. This is achieved through a union of

17

the contents of the conscious and unconscious minds. It is through this union and the struggles it engenders that truth is uncovered and exposed. To realistically expect healing and progress, we must therefore venture into the inner realms of truth where consciousness encounters the mysteries of external experiences and the contents of our unconscious mind.

To experience wholeness and health, we need to make truth a companion and a moral compass through our life's journey. However, intrinsic weaknesses within our consciousness conspire against wholeness, and all our knowledge can be a barrier to understanding and living truth. Emerson put it thus when describing truth in the context of the fields of philosophy, science, and religion:

> We are now so far from the road of truth, that religions dispute and hate each other and speculative men are esteemed unsound and frivolous. But to sound judgment, the most abstract truth is the most practical. Whenever a true theory appears, it will be its own evidence. Its test is that it will explain the phenomenon. (Emerson, Library of America, 7.)

Are there theories of the human condition that explain the phenomenon? I believe this is the case with regards to the *perennial philosophy*. Briefly, the perennial philosophy runs through the various wisdom traditions throughout history and contains a threefold unifying belief system or theory of being; that is existence is made up of matter, psyche or soul, and spirit. It promotes the belief that we need to accept and harmonize or balance all aspects of being rather than reducing and restricting being and experiences. One starts with thesis and antithesis, and we transform them into a synthesis. This includes nurturing attitudes, beliefs, and behaviors/practices that include all the contradictory, conflicting, and paradoxical dynamics inherent in the human condition. Truly, there is a time for every experience under the sun— which allows us to face unlived aspects of our nature (Ecclesiastes 3).

Jung defined the psyche or soul of persons as a union of the conscious and unconscious minds. The psyche or soul is where this union may take place and where the miracle of conscious and unconscious minds overlaps. In addition, the psyche must cooperate via the will with the truth before any healing and wholeness can ever take place. The truth must be embraced by the psyche through consciously combining paradoxes inherent in external and internal life. Another way to define truth is that it is integration by the psyche or soul through (1) understanding the principles inherent in creation, and then (2) adapting to them via the choices we make. Thus, wisdom and holiness/wholeness must occur together.

Wholeness and wisdom arise in the context the archetypal pairs of opposites. Heraclitus, an ancient Greek philosopher, recognized that the world is made up of opposites and is in constant flux or change. At the heart of the physical universe, there are positive and negative energies, matter and antimatter, protons and electrons, positive and negative electric charges, etc. Jung postulated that our psyche or soul is similar to matter and energy; it too exists out of the tension between positive and negative energies. Matter and energy are interchangeable and cannot be destroyed. Since psyche is energy, I believe, therefore, our soul is sustained by this clash between its positive and negative natures, and it too cannot be destroyed. Experience bombards us with the need to change through the dynamics of opposites that exist within our psyche. Rationalism, religion, the sciences, and modern philosophy have often become bogged down in one-sided thinking. Logic, traditions, and semantics have thus denied the reality of psyche and her activity. Regardless of our beliefs concerning the psyche, she continues to produce her healing and disease—whether we acknowledge her or not.

To get some overall perspective on the dynamics of truth, we need to turn to history with the help of other disciplines including psychology, philosophy, anthropology, archeology, ethnology, and mythology. My presupposition is we can glean from all the fields of knowledge truths about how we evolved and look for clues about human nature and the human condition; that is what is whole, holy, and healthy and what is not.

Psychoanalytic psychology has studied the contents of the unconscious and recovered from dreams and mythology the mysterious and enigmatic world of archetypal opposites. Two seemingly opposite propensities can be brought into a balance only after a titanic inner struggle of the ego and the will. The ego is the center of consciousness but in a healthy individual, not of the entire personality. The psyche is the center of the personality, and it is that which balances the pairs of opposites. All the pairs of opposites inherent in the archetypes contain a latent, unlived aspect of life that, at certain junctures of our lives, insist to be actualized and lived out. All archetypes are basic structures within the psyche, which have morphed into patterns of behavior with emotions that have been lived and experienced by someone at sometime in our human history; they are channeled by individuals and passed down to each new generation like our DNA and other biological traits unique to each species.

There are primary developmental archetypes that must be grappled with by everyone before their uniqueness can be fully actualized. If you want to be just like everyone else, ignore the life of the opposites that dwell within you. However, if you chose to nurture your inner life, you will be compensated through your dreams and external circumstances by the unconscious into landscapes rich with buried treasures for only within the soul or psyche does truth dwell. Our uniqueness is buried in the treasure trove of that which lies within the mystery of the unconscious, which acts as a guide and messenger. The unconscious mind houses our mysterious center from within where imagination and various energies are pleading to become conscious and seek to ferry us to wholeness and enlightenment.

As I said, the archetypes are universal and primordial pairs of opposites that need to be integrated. If this is accomplished with some competence, we are then prepared to encounter the more unique archetypes specific to our nature and purpose. We will be exploring many archetypal pairs of opposites throughout this work, including the primary ones all are required to integrate if the uniqueness inherent in each personality can ever be actualized. In addition, each archetypal pair of opposites have positive and negative energy that needs to be integrated before we are then capable of completely moving on to the next archetypal pair of opposites. This process of integrating the opposites moves us toward wholeness and away from a life of compartmentalization, separation, and disease. It is the unique combinations of archetypes in each of us with their varying degrees of strength or energy that make everyone different. Another word to describe the union of opposites is termed *dialectic* ("is based on the principle that an idea or event [thesis] generates its opposite [antithesis] leading to a reconciliation of opposites [synthesis]," New World Dictionary of the American Language).

Every personality is unique and therefore not conditioned to wrestle with all the pairs of opposites within the human condition nor with the similar intensities within each archetypes except for those that are universal to our basic development as humans. The developmental tasks differ in the first and second halves of our lives. The first section of this book is *generally* focused on the archetypes, which must be integrated in the first half of life and attempt to describe the basic human condition. The second section generally focuses on the second half of life and offers some of the paths to what is often termed enlightenment and wholeness. However, these sections and the archetypes they contain inevitably overlap. When dealing with something as mysterious as the psyche, our human desire for strict categories and elaborate systems invariably elude and fail us. What I want to emphasize is this, that *all the pairs of opposites/archetypes that we each come across in the course of our existence are unlived aspect of* our life *that the unconscious wants us to learn how to actualize and live out in some practical and specific way.* The soul can forge a synthesis out of the thesis and antithesis in each archetypal pair of opposites. Let me pause and give a brief example. We all need to learn to be independent and assertive. This dynamic includes being stern and gentle simultaneously, which can be brought about only with much inner struggle and practice. At the same time, we need to learn how to be dependent and connected to others in the healthy sense of the word and to surrender our selfish wants at times. And to carry this paradox further, we need to house all of these traits within our psyche and display the proper poise and response at the right time and place.

As we succeed in embracing the true lessons of experience by concentrating on the substance and depths within our psyche, we will participate in the mystery, horror, wonder, suffering, and beauty intrinsic in the human condition. We can choose to stop maturing if we succumb to the fears of life and death, or we can choose to grow throughout our time on earth. We will all fail to differing degrees to actualize our complete potential. However, if we learn to endure our weaknesses and mistakes by being trained by them, subsequently, all our errors become transformed into strengths. Therefore, the only true mistakes are the ones we choose not to be educated by. If we fashion truth through healthy or holistic choices, we will be set free.

Like the snake sheds its skin, we need to dispense with the notion that experiences are inherently positive or negative. Though they have positive and negative aspects and energies attached to them, they are all potentially valuable if we can assemble the proper attitude toward them. This involves a thousand deaths because our ego-consciousness often has an agenda that does not include letting go of illusions and all the distractions they engender. All experiences include positive and negative qualities, yet the "reality of experience" is that "it is" and therefore can always provide opportunities for growth and change. Alas, most cling to the illusion that positive experiences can provide fulfillment to our yearnings and longings. We therefore wish to ignore the so-called negative experiences, which consist of some forms of suffering and pain and, by so doing, ignore the treasures hidden within these experiences. "If I could just win the lottery or possess the mate of my dreams, I will be happy." Meanwhile, we eschew the experiences that evoke suffering with a variety of anodynes. Life is full of vicissitudes and variations, which give life its rich and sundry hues.

But why seek truth when it exposes us to mental anguish and a bevy of sufferings? No wonder little is said these days about the truth with all its intrinsic sacrifices, sufferings, and complexities. I believe suffering is not an end in itself, but a means by which our flimsy foundations and temporal aims are destroyed, thereby creating opportunities to grow in truth. One of the few true paths to inner peace and joy, love and mercy, is through suffering because it seems to be the only reality that rouses us out of indolence, mediocrity, and complacency and creates an inner environment where these fruits can grow. I will attempt to trace some of the experiences of Job, Odysseus, and Jesus of Nazareth as they were ultimately able to experience the inner freedoms born of personal sufferings.

We each have tendencies and temptations to gravitate to one side of any pair of opposites. The reason for this is it temporarily dissipates the tensions and paradoxes inherent in the archetypal pairs of opposites. For example, some of us tend to be more independently focused, while others are more dependent upon relationships and intimacy with others. A balanced life requires us to exercise both independence and relatedness/intimacy with others. Most of us have met someone who, by and large, only expresses the independent side of their natures. He/She appears on the surface to be confident, arrogant, self-contained, and even at times charismatic. But they also often lack the humility, ability to share deeply, care sincerely, or maintain intimacy with others. A perfect example of this type of personality is House on the TV series *House*. On the other hand, if an individual tends toward dependency, he/she is most comfortable surrounded by friends and lovers who will assume a dominant role; he/she is unable and/or unwilling to take responsibility for self in career, relationships, or domestic affairs and has an uncanny knack for sliding these responsibilities off onto others. Wholeness in this dynamic is to both be intimate and related to others while maintaining independence with its appropriate responsibilities and personal boundaries. This is one of the primary developmental archetypal pairs of opposites.

While knowledge is exponentially expanding at an alarming rate and the accumulation of facts bombards us, the individual must struggle to create wholeness and synthesize this bevy of unrelated facts. Without a movement toward wholeness and wisdom, we shall forever remain dumbfounded by human motivations toward evil in all its manifestations: selfishness and greed, displays of petty squabbles and arrogance, violence and war, resentments, etc. In the meantime, each culture wastes vast potentials and possibilities in individuals with our communally superficial preoccupations with temporal aims while wisdom is squandered like those pennies strewn all over our streets and parking lots. Not only do injustices occur daily, but the politics of power, spite, malice, and mendacity filter through our bureaucracy like pollution in our rivers and streams. Sadly, we are far from being rational and reasonable creatures. John Sanford put it this way: "Human behavior is not reasonable, and mankind acts for the entire world as though it was possessed" (John A. Sanford, *Dreams and Healing*, p. 7). In the meantime, neurosis breeds like rabbits, and the vast potentials and possibilities latent and hidden within the human spirit have been left behind in our society's superficial preoccupations with temporal aims, facts, and its enthrallment at the world of "ten thousand things." While many are afraid of the future or stuck in past failures, the present goes unheeded with all its vast opportunities. Now is the time for transformation, love, justice, relationships, and peace. Life can only be experienced in the present. In the present, we occasionally need to revisit the past for the purpose of cleaning up unresolved issues, but not dwell therein. In the present, we occasionally need to entertain future possibilities, but not get stuck in fear and attempting to predict or control it.

If there is one thing we have learned from history, it's that human nature is complex and capable of incredible acts of courage and cowardice. We deceive ourselves with rationalizations that can be so subtle, we never can be sure of our motives or how accurate our beliefs, attitudes, and behaviors really are. I do believe we have come a long way in understanding some of the "dynamics of truth," begotten in the inner life, just as we have done so with truth in the external world of our five senses. There remains a lack of synthesis of all the competing specializations due in part to the wars of words and world views, fragile egos, and its needs for recognition. This animosity makes it difficult to create an atmosphere where a tapestry can be weaved where all the disciplines find their proper contribution to our understanding of truth. I am making an attempt to do so with no illusions that this will do anything more than add my own synthesis to others who have already made the attempt. In addition, it is important to understand that my synthesis overlaps with many others. It is not my desire to take credit for all the ideas in this work; rather, I have drawn from my experience and those of many others whose experience seems to match my own. If I neglect to give credit where credit is due, forgive me. My only desire is that what is presented here will be helpful for you, my reader, in your own journey through this life. My own thoughts will never be able to overcome the tyranny of egomania to ever create a place where a true synthesis of all the disciplines will ever gain universal acceptance in this world. When we scan the world of ten billion egos, many ideas threaten the traditions and those in power that are under the delusion that their ideas must be the defended at all costs. Most egos are fragile for why else are we constantly building monuments to them? I am reminded of the story of the Tower of Babel where people attempted to "make a name for ourselves" (Genesis 11:4). Each intellectual discipline seeks to make a name for itself, and a tower of babble results! I wish to acknowledge each discipline its special place and purpose in the great search for truth. Truth will stand upon its own merits, whether any of us recognize her or not, and the many fictions we produce through our self-deceptions will in the end fall by the wayside of truth. It takes those sensitive and sincere to unlock her mystery and wisdom.

The first section of this book introduces us to the primary and developmental archetypal clashes of opposites as they operate in the human condition/perennial philosophy. We will examine dysfunction, which expresses itself when we have failed to integrate/synthesize these, leading to certain strains of neurosis, psychosis, and addiction. As well, we will begin to explore the journey to wholeness through healthy acceptance and adaptations to these truths.

The second section will explore the second half of life and the process of synthesizing these pairs of opposites through the experiences of suffering. I offer my own interpretations of the book of Job and *The Odyssey*. We will explore the nature of evil, and then, in my final chapter on enlightenment, we explore a unique personality who seems to demonstrate wholeness in action, Jesus of Nazareth. I believe not only are these figures quintessential sufferers, but they personify a movement toward wholeness and become ideals of mental health. They experienced and responded to their suffering in unique ways worthy of the extensive commentaries you will find herein. We will also follow Job and Odysseus though their subsequent transformations to holistic alternative responses to the neurosis of Western peoples in the present age. The book of Job and *The Odyssey* and the four Gospels offers us an inside glimpse at three individuals who were willing to surrender their egos as the sole director of his beliefs, attitudes, and choices to truth while wrestling with the complexities of life and sufferings in all its ambiguities and pain. These three journeys provide us with terrifying and beautiful illustrations of the descent into the abyss of suffering and out again into enlightenment. By following the rocky path of truth, we will be compensated by a sense of wonder and mystery and by the many secret treasures of wisdom, inner peace and joy, and powers concealed within us. I also offer two appendixes that explore community and the unique struggles of blue-collar laborers.

I began with what I believe are truths of the human condition and then fixed music to each chapter. It could just as easily have been the other way around! This work is a synthesis of my experiences and the interpretations of my experiences. Since adolescence, I have contemplated my experiences and read voraciously. I believe the works and music to which I have been exposed to have been synchronistic, selected with my specific experiences and needs in mind. I always contemplated the ideas herein and have come to embrace these truths. I have always tried to discern truth—no matter the cost.

The genesis of this book came to me on my four-month trip overseas to Israel, Greece, and western Europe in 1979. As I have grown in self-knowledge, so has this work. The journey has been long and full of unbelievable twists and turns. I suffer, struggle, fail, wonder, and often contradict myself. I fail to live up to the truths I have identified; no one fully human can completely demonstrate truth, though this has not deterred me from striving for truth and perfection. Herein lies my opus, born of brokenness, nurtured by perseverance, completed by grace. Join me then, you lovers of soul, in the search for truth and illusion.

> Or is this a part of man's evolution,
> To be torn between truth and illusion.
>
> —The Band, "Forbidden Fruit"

> Lover of soul, lover of mind
> Heart and soul, body and mind
> Meet me on the river of time.
>
> —Van Morrison,
> "River of Time"

Section One

Truths of the Human Condition

Showed me the pictures in the gallery,
Showed me novels on the shelf,
Put my hands across the table,
Gave me knowledge of myself
Showed me visions, showed me nightmares,
Gave me dreams that never end,
Showed me light out of the tunnel,
When there was darkness all around instead . . .

Showed me different shapes and colors,
Showed me many different roads,
Gave me very clear instructions,
When I was in the dark night of the soul . . .

—Van Morrison,
"Tore Down a la Rimbaud"

Historical Antecedents

There's a time line
Something like vertical, like perpendicular . . .

Through to some essence common to us, to original man . . .

Where it intersects the space at hand
The shaman with the hoops stands
Aligned like living magnet nee-
dle between deep past and
Looming future . . .

He's the earth He's the egg He's
the eagle always circling
Always turning-always comes back to the center.

—Bruce Cockburn,
"Hoop Dancer"

Before venturing into a more direct description of the human condition, I would like to take a brief look at historical antecedents that
assemble hints together and will allow us an overview of the human
condition.

Approximately13.7 billion years ago, out of an unknown and
mysterious singularity and with mathematical precision, cosmologists
tell us the known universe burst forth with a bang as the fabric of

space-time, matter, and antimatter emerged and began expanding. From a great surge of energy, everything that is began its violent expansion, evolving into more and more complex combinations until matter evolved into life approximately 3.5 billion years ago when the first microorganisms appeared in the oceans on this planet called Earth. With the most recent discoveries, the initial bipeds burgeoned approximately 7 million years ago. At an unknown juncture in life's evolution, consciousness began to thrive, marking the greatest leap in evolution's elaborate complexity. This evolution of consciousness continues to expand into greater and greater complexity, at least in some and is referred to in the perennial philosophy as psyche and/or spirit.

The earliest *Homo sapiens* make their appearance approximately two hundred thousand years ago and, like *Home erectus* and the Neanderthals, labored to survive by hunting/killing, gathering, and having sex. The out-of-Africa hypothesis, the Recent African Origin (RAO), has gained stronger support from conflicting ones due to recent genetic and archeological findings. This theory purports that all present humans can trace their lineage back to one particular group of *Homo sapiens* that originated out of Africa.

From the beginning, our species has been plagued by a plethora of fears, weaknesses, and vulnerabilities in a world full of mystery, wonder, pain, and death. We are also laden with a myriad of biological and psychological longings and urges. Men are predominately imbued with the hormone testosterone while women predominately with oxytocin, predisposing each sex with complementary primordial urges that foster the survival of the species—women's inclination to nurture and men's to kill while each endowed with appetites for sex. The Stone Age or Paleolithic era continued with modifications until approximately ten thousand years ago. This era was by far the longest and most influential in our psychic evolution with patterns of behavior primarily bent on survival. All our primordial and sometimes infantile instincts to survive remain entrenched and imbedded within the economy of our psyche. Humankind also trafficked with primitive beliefs and fears and were predisposed to unconscious reactions fraught with emotions, all bent on survival.

By harnessing fire and killing other animals to eat meat, the table was set for humankind to make some major transformations. The brain continued to grow, and with it, abstract thinking and unconscious symbolic action developed. In addition to our basic survival instincts, we began to grasp and attempt to cope with the mystery and incomprehensibility of life. This was directed largely via the unconscious mind through a growing amount of archetypal strategies, which were shaped gradually as the brain developed. These emotionally charged primordial patterns of coping developed over time and formed the original and enduring archetypes. Externally, the environment contained constant threats to survival, while internally, the psyche adapted to these threats with countless fears and anxieties. These fears contended with an array of impulses and desires, which remained largely unconscious. Our earliest human ancestors subsisted in nomadic tribal units of approximately forty members where hunting and the nurturing of their young was coordinated. Leadership was a natural development, and there has been some debate as to whether these primitive tribal institutions were aristocratic or democratic in nature—and it seems reasonable to assume that they were a combination of the two. Regardless, it's probable our earliest ancestors lacked self-consciousness and the ability for self-reflection while ethical principles and taboos gradually developed for the purpose of group harmony. The primordial enduring archetypal strategies for survival include killing and violence, acting out sexuality, tribal affinities and bias, unconscious fears of the unknown and change, superstition, and the pressure to conform to the group ethos—all of which were to find their roots in the unconsciousness of our earliest ancestors. These are the oldest and most primitive of archetypes and continue to pressure our present consciousness. They also at times dominate the consciousness of far too many individuals to this day.

The study of primitive cultures has provided clues into how our early Stone Age or Paleolithic ancestors believed and functioned. Our primordial ancestors seemed primarily unconscious of their motives, projecting everything from their unconscious minds onto the objects and into the world around them. They were unable to separate their individuality from these objects, and objects took on numinous energy,[2] which held considerable sway on their beliefs, attitudes, and behaviors. The unconscious began producing symbols that were expressed in rituals and myths. Therefore, to understand the early condition of our species, it's imperative we take into account man's early mythologies and rituals. Exactly when the mind began producing symbols remains a mystery, but we do know the earliest myths centered around two categories of beliefs about supernatural beings, which, though distinct, overlapped (*The Larousse Encyclopedia of Mythology*, Barnes & Noble Books, New York, 1994, G. H. Luquet, p.1). Luquet goes on to describe these two categories of supernatural beings as (1) dead ancestors and (2) supernatural divinities (ibid., p.1). We do know from the wall drawings approximately seventeen thousand to ten thousand years ago of the Magdalenians discovered in caves in France that symbolic thinking had developed into the earliest forms of art at least by this time. In addition, they had some form of mythology (ibid., p.1).

In addition, primitive thought was framed by rituals and mythologies that reflected the need to cooperate and expressed a perceived unity that exists between man and nature (see Henry Bamford Parkes's *Gods and Men*, Vintage Books, First Vintage Edition, 1965, p.39). Our primitive ancestors viewed themselves as objects and sought a unity with every other object in the environment; therefore, animals, stones, etc., took on magical properties. In addition, these early beliefs met enormous emotional needs for security, providing meaning, structure, and the illusion of predictability to life. The individual ego as a separate object seems to have been a late addition and adaptation to the psychic economy. These earliest myths and rituals reflect atavistic and primordial dilemmas of our species and our earliest motivations to cope with them.

---

2.   The term numinous was coined by Rudolf Otto and described states of consciousness, which included fascination, mystery, fear and trembling, awe, and wonder due to the direct experiences with the holy/divine. My present point of emphasis on the numinous is not on the nature of the holy/divine, but rather endeavors to depict as best we can what were going on within the minds of early Homo sapiens.

To sum it up, primordial or primitive man was concerned with (1) *survival/annihilation* (hunting and gathering, fertility, and death) and (2) *efforts* to gain some control over the circumstances and objects in their world. Therefore, the survival instincts and those instincts bent on gaining a modicum of control over the dangerous environment (magic) are the most ancient and enduring within the psychic economy. This is reflected in the numerous survivalists, sex addicts, warmongers, and magicians that dot our collective landscape right up to the present.

> Listen to the water still . . .
> Primitive and wild . . .
>
> —REM,
> "Welcome to the Occupation"

Civilization and the Neolithic Village

> You are mad and educated
> Primitive and wild
> Welcome to the occupation
>
> Here we stand and here we fight
> All your fallen heroes
> Held and dyed and skinned alive . . .
> Offering the educated
> Primitive and loyal
> Welcome to the occupation . . .
>
> —REM, "Welcome to the Occupation"

An immense shift in our history occurred approximately between 10,000 and 7,500 years ago where the rudiments of civilizations developed concurrently in the Neolithic or early Bronze Age in the fertile crescent of Mesopotamia, Egypt, and China. This was marked by the first small villages forming around agriculture and by the domestication of animals. The workers of the soil were primarily women while the roaming herdsmen were closer to the earlier hunter-gatherers' lifestyle with its leader of a nomadic clan. The biblical stories of Cain and Able reflect this shift. The story reveals the Hebrews' valuing of the nomadic herdsman and undervaluing tillers of the soil for YHWH accepted Abel's offering of sheep while rejecting Cain's fruit of the ground. Cain then murdered Abel, and the first act of violence/murder was recorded.

These early renditions of civilizations assumed supernatural forces created the miracle world through a number of creation stories and myths. These myths reflect a function that guided the ancient's beliefs and attitudes, providing meaning, direction, and purpose. They were characterized in both masculine and feminine forms/figures/gods/goddesses. However, the great mother-goddess was the most prominent in the earliest stages of civilization and prior to the advent of city-states and empires. Campbell put it thus:

> Now in the Neolithic village stage of this development and dispersal, the focal point of all mythology and worship was the bountiful goddess Earth, as the mother and nourisher of life and receiver of the dead for rebirth. In the earliest period of her cult (perhaps c7500-3500 B. C. in the Levant) such a mother-goddess may have been thought only as a local patroness of fertility, as many anthropologists suppose. However, in the temples even of the first of the higher civilizations (Sumer, c. 3500-2350 B. C.), the Great Goddess of highest concern was certainly much more than that. She was already, as she is now in the Orient, a metaphysical symbol: the arch personification of Space, Time, and Matter, within whose bounds all beings arise and die: the substance of their bodies, configurator of their lives and thoughts, the receiver of their dead. And everything having form or name-including God personified as good or evil, merciful or wrathful-was her child, within her womb. (Campbell, *Occidental Mythology*, p. 7.)

The great goddesses advanced the relationship between the eternal and temporal realms within the soul of each person and offered meaning and purpose in both life and death.

Civilization in the Iron Age / Urbanization and Empire

How many days since I was born
How many days 'til I die . . .

When the baby looks around him
Such a site to see
Shares the simple secret with the wise man
He's a stranger in a strange land . . .

And the baby looks around him
And shares his bed of hay
With the pharaohs in the palace of the kingdom
He's a stranger in a strange land . . .

—Leon Russell, "Stranger in a Strange Land"

Historians approximate that between 3300–2600 BCE, the early Iron Age birthed the first prominent urbanization, which occurred in southern Mesopotamia. With the advent of technology, agriculture shifted to males while irrigation was created from the great rivers, the Tigris and the Euphrates. Surplus goods arose, which led the way to the construction of cities and the belief in redemptive violence, which is good triumphing over evil by violent means.[3]

With enhanced technologies and urbanization came an explanation for the shift from the predominance of feminine goddesses to more masculine ones. Consciousness continued to expand, and in conjunction with the body's neurology and chemistry, the stage was set for an evolutionary split between the unconscious and conscious minds. Alongside the shifting of the political landscapes, a gradual evolutionary thirst and quest for understanding increased, birthing the arts, self-consciousness, and enhanced technologies. Without this split, selective thinking would be unattainable. Though it is impossible to trace the exact point at which this monumental split occurred, we have a remarkable story depicted in the Hebrew Bible's story of the fall of Adam and Eve from innocence in the Garden of Eden, where they gained the knowledge of good and evil. This story marks a *titanic* shift where the unconscious and conscious minds separated and, with it, humankind's shift from predominate reliance upon the unconscious mind. With this modification, the individual's ego became the center of self-consciousness. It appears this shift occurred sometime between the Neolithic/Bronze and the Iron Age. We thus became self-conscious enough to experience shame as knowledge of good and evil arose.

Going further into the biblical text, we come across the sons of Adam and Eve, Cain and Abel. When Cain's offerings of the soil were rejected, he murdered his brother Abel while Cain's son Enoch built the first city. We can observe examples of these monuments built to the egos of kings in sandstone and clay tablets called stela strewn throughout the ancient world that have been dug up by archeologists, which depict victory and power over the kings vanquished enemies.

---

3. See Wes Howard-Brook's work Come Out, My People. In contrast, the creation and Cain and Abel stories in Genesis proclaim YHWH word/will is the sole reason for creation while murder/violence city/ empire building is eschewed. Howard-Brook goes on to say surplus agricultural products spawned cities and the eventual birth of empires with its oppression and violence, kings, priests, and bureaucracy. Nomadic herdsmen and people of the soil both coexisted during this shift from villages to empires.

This urban culture was fashioned by what archeologists call the Sumerians, and they are given credit to the founding of modern human civilization. The Sumerians are credited with a plethora of innovations such as writing, using the wheel for transportation, laws, and the arts. The Sumerians' agricultural wealth was created by vast irrigation networks on the Euphrates and Tigris rivers and prompted trade and the earliest city-states. The city-states were ruled by kings, a growing bureaucracy, and priests. These developments established social classes, and the stages were set for social and economic inequalities, wars, and the first city-state, Uruk in Sumer. History books and TV documentaries are littered with their spotlights on the succession of empires and kings. This discloses the emphasis by a majority of historians to ignore the complex dynamics within the human condition while propagating this rendering of history, which glorifies power and the monuments built to the human ego. This bias consciously or unconsciously discounts and neglects the horrors of war, poverty, arrogance, and injustices reeked upon the poor, the outcast, and the common laborers and people. More recently, there has been a shift in some historical circles toward a new emphasis placed on how the lower classes functioned within the framework of civilization as a whole and exploring their lifestyles with its array of struggles, sufferings, and subjugation to those in power. The histories of the democracy in Athens, the Minoans of Crete, and certain periods in the history of the Hebrews and the early Christian Church seemed to exhibit attempts to fashion a world that promoted a modicum of equality and justice. However, slaves and inner city-state wars were an essential aspect of Athenian life while the Torah, the prophets, and the Christian Bible attest to the struggles the Hebrews and early Christians had in creating and maintaining justice. These early civilizations assumed supernatural forces created the miracle world through a number of creation stories and myths, which justify the "religions of empire." Mesopotamian primordial myths justify redemptive violence and establish humans as servants to the gods.

The fact remains that since the advent of the Iron Age, the masculine deities usurped the earlier feminine fertility goddesses, and that has shaped Western man's psyche to the present to such an extent that only within the last few hundred years has feminine elements within the human psyche reemerged in collective consciousness. The warrior king and his array of priests legitimized redemptive violence from the perspective of a "religion of empire." The warrior king was the God's representative on earth and, therefore, was claimant of divine favor. Everyone who acquired power did so with the help of the gods and violence, and the religion of empire prevailed in the collective psyche. Successful and subsequent revolutions were violent, and this redemptive violence put the new righteous warrior king as God's new representative. This cycle of justified violence recurs throughout history up into the present with our pathetic veneration of the military in the United States. Patriarchal trends began usurping a balance of feminine and masculine archetypal myths during the early Iron Age and to this day prevail, attempting to divorce itself from the dark wisdom of the feminine. Ironically, materialism has been fashioned from patriarchal rationalism and science and finds itself bound to her like a child unwilling to grow beyond the safety of the mother, clinging to a reduced worldview that ignores the traditional wisdom of the soul or psyche. The dark wisdom of the soul expressed herself in the archetypal Great Mother/fertility goddesses that predominated the Neolithic era when she displayed nurturing and devouring facets through her positive and negative characteristics in the Great and Terrible Mother (see Eric Neumann's brilliant work, *The Great Mother: An Analysis of the Archetype*). The psyche or soul is feminine. As we shall explore, healthy aspects of the feminine archetype allow her transformative character to bud into a balanced masculine and feminine will and consciousness. It is imperative to remember that in Western culture, patriarchal as we are in our Judeo-Christian and Greek ethos, was built and altered from the feminine archetypes.

Though by and large, we still live in a patriarchal age, the unconscious mind has all along been at work compensating for this by working to establish a more balanced and integrated consciousness of feminine archetypal energy. Thankfully, her influence never completely waned for we have evidence for her in Jewish texts for the wisdom of God, Hohkma, which was translated into Sophia in the Greek as the goddess of wisdom, and the plethora of other female goddesses (Hera, Aphrodite, Diana, and Circe, to name a few), which continued to flourish in Greece throughout the Iron Age and beyond reflects. Modern examples of the feminine archetype that continue to put pressure on consciousness can be found in the outlook and teachings of the Kabala (Jewish mysticism) and the advent of Mary's ascent in Catholicism. We can also see this in the present with the women's movements, pagan cultic practices bent on saluting the feminine archetypes, and many other forms of women's studies that have begun to compensate for the many years of patriarchal misogynist beliefs and practices. In response to this recent acceptance of the place feminine archetypal energy has upon the human psyche, the men's movement has attempted to make conscious healthy masculine energies, which are equally needed in the healthy functioning of the psyche and the rearing of our youth.

The masculine emphasis in Greek and Judeo-Christian traditions, beliefs, and practices has distorted the feminine archetypal power. *She heals and transforms in the context of our mortality.* I will be discussing a balance of masculine and feminine qualities throughout the second section of this work, and it is worth noting that men and women potentially accommodate both archetypal characteristics within them while the *aim* is to develop a balance within our personalities.

The Greek myths are full of goddesses who come to aid in human development, and I will trace their transformative character in the life of Odysseus in my commentary on *The Odyssey*. I will focus primarily by analyzing the role of Circe in his development. I will also be discussing the book of Job from the Hebrew Bible, and though written with a bias toward the masculine archetypal father, we shall trace feminine healing and transformative archetypal characteristics in the sufferings of Job. It is the feminine within us that bestows on us the capacity to suffer and have compassion. Jesus's life, teachings, and practices contain a balance of masculine and feminine energy, which created a revolution for women. The early church had women and men in leadership roles, and this Jesus movement eventually transformed the Roman Empire. However, the church repressed these early female leaders approximately forty years into the Jesus movement, and with this repression, the church reverted back to a patriarchal one-sidedness that has distorted Jesus parables, practices, and teachings ever since to the degree that the Western church still displays for the most part the same misogynist tendencies you find in traditional Judaism and Islam. Let us not adopt euphemism in the name of political correctness; Western religions have been and are principally misogynist institutions that advocate a glorification of the warrior hero and state and a denial of the soul and everything of the body (primarily sex and death). The female apostles in the early church have long been silenced while Greek myths are consigned to fantasy. Though Western religions have gradually been embracing women in roles of leadership, it has failed to embrace the inner life of the soul, which is a primary reflection of feminine energy. Meanwhile, the top echelon of leadership remains male and fraudulent in its compromises with materialistic science, rationalism, and nationalism/empire. Any honest study of the history of institutionalized Islam, Judaism, and Christianity cannot help but uncover myriad examples full of intolerance, hubris, judgmental attitudes, and unjust, murderous, dominative, oppressive, and repressive behaviors.

When we acquired the knowledge of good and evil and became self-conscious, it fashioned a mixed bag of blessings and curses. The blessings are *freedom and personal responsibility*—the potential of autonomy and uniqueness where self-reflection, choice, and knowledge unite with compassion. On the other hand, the curses include personalities where selfishness, dishonesty, laziness, and/or arrogance come into play with malevolent conscious intent. The problem of good and evil has now been transferred from the unconscious mind to a paradoxical psyche where consciousness and unconsciousness overlap—within ego-consciousness. Out of paradise and east of Eden, we now toil and are afforded the opportunity to become like Cain or Jesus, Stalin or Gandhi, Hitler or Mother Teresa. On the surface, the majority of us do not develop into either of these extremes in sordidness or holiness but fall somewhere in the middle of the continuum (i.e., we are lukewarm). Nevertheless, the freedom and responsibility of choice creates the potential to move in one direction or the other. The jaded and the tawdry circulate with the beautiful and the graceful. Wisdom mixed with the heart of servant commerce with fear, violence, and oppression, and the sun shines on each.

Give me absolute control
Over every living soul
And lie beside me baby,
That's an order!

—Leonard Cohen,
"The Future"

East and West

The antecedents for both Western and Eastern cultures began as we have discussed in the cradle of civilization—Mesopotamia. Generally speaking, the Eastern traditions of the Orient generally emphasize accepting fate and to seek identity with being through experience, which is forever beyond any categories of thought. By contrast, in the Western or Occidental culture of Judeo-Christian-Greek origins, two paradoxical beliefs combine: the first with a Greek and European emphasis where observation of natural law and standing upon human reason to judge/ assert oneself is contrasted with the second, the religions of the Levant (Judaism, Christianity, Zoroastrianism, and Islam) where the emphasis is on an individual's surrender to the will of God (see J. Campbell's series The Masks of God).

Since I am a product of the West, I will confine the remainder of my discussion to the paradox inherent within the Western psyche. The antecedents for the war between science and religion lie here in the apparent paradoxes that lie within the Western psyche. I argue both inclinations are of equal *value*; there seem to be times when we must nurture audacity and pursue change/ wisdom and other times humility and acceptance, holding both attitudes simultaneously within our ever-warring psyche so that when the moment arises and a situation calls forth for one or the other of the possibilities, we are prepared to act upon that side of our nature that best fits the dynamics within the circumstances.

Following the clash of Greek, Hebrew, and Islamic cultures, the Middle Ages evolved, with its emphasis on surrendering to God's will. This predominated without its opposite and partner rational thought, leading to the horrors of religious intolerance, persecution, the Inquisition and holy wars. At this juncture in history, the West undervalued our rational capabilities. History demonstrates an endless array of incomprehensible actions, which are/were justified by the often impotent and thoughtless claim that it is "God's will." Religious intolerance and a fear of the truth that our rational mind could have provided were shunned by the Catholic Church. This period is marked by the desire to return to Eden where the authority of the church replaced God's command to not eat of the fruit of the tree of knowledge. Wherever the appeal to authority dominates, the quest is to regress to the garden where unconsciousness seeks supremacy over consciousness. Fortunately, Islam saved many ancient Greek texts where the Greek spirit of inquest and outspokenness was kept alive, and ironically enough, it was during the Crusades that the West was reacquainted with these texts.

Then a major shift back toward rationalism in our Occidental outlook took place with the advent of the Reformation and the subsequent Renaissance, Enlightenment, and the Age of Science. These developments eventually usurped the absolute authority of the church. The emphasis on rationalism evidenced in humanism and science has led to an overvaluing of our rational capabilities. This in turn has led to bureaucracy, technology, and the industrial revolution. With this one-sided emphasis on rationalism, a lack of substance and meaning in life has supplanted the mindless acceptance of God's will under the guise of the church's authority. The rationalists and humanists believe that we humans are the measure of all things. Meanwhile, religion has lost its pathos and often become wedded to creeds, dogma, and morphed rationalism. Each belief system often tries to exclude the other. When both rationality and spirituality are valued, a balanced perspective ensues where the wisdom of a surrendered but strong and *thoughtful* ego-consciousness is enlisted in the fight against ignorance and tyranny. When applied by individuals seeking wholeness and enlightenment, all experiences and the understanding they engender need be valued equally within our ever-expanding consciousness. However, Western culture has neglected the depths of the inner life and the sufferings it includes since the advent of the so-called enlightenment in the eighteenth century, when rationalism gained hold and eventually usurped religion. In the vain and desperate quest for certainty, science is focused primarily on the nature of matter. This has value when we seek facts about the physical world but has no bearing on any other aspect of being. As the perennially philosophy asserts, reality incorporates a balance of spirit, psyche or soul, will, mind, emotions, and body. However, rationality and science have become bogged down in semantics or has bought into an almost complete preoccupation with matter. The world of matter has become the principal preoccupation and predominant value by our Western culture. In conjunction with these developments, our innate self-centeredness has been nurtured, legitimized, and unleashed. This has come about due to the thistles of materialism. Just a few minutes of TV commercials should be enough to convince us that we have lost our equilibrium. They reflect attitudes and beliefs that the "world of ten thousand things" provides some sort of compensation for our existential needs for worth and meaning. Some aspects of religion have bought into this rationalistic and materialistic worldview by emphasizing dogma and creeds while other strains within fundamentalism religions eschew rationality altogether and justify all sorts of atrocities in the name of God.

With these developments, the wisdom of the "inner life" has been hushed and silenced by an unwillingness to stretch the boundaries of what is "rational." Presently, within some circles of the scientific community, there is a lack of openness to endeavors that are situated outside rational experience. This leaves the realms of intuition and imagination discarded like yesterday's newspapers. It seems to me, healthy skepticism remains humble and open to possibilities beyond our present experiences and belief systems. An imbalance has ensued and taken its toll upon our souls. The medical community's efficacious and much lauded treatment of symptoms fails miserably at healing the wounds of the psyche caused by our increasingly superficial and materialistic culture. Carl Jung recognized that the individual psyche, or soul, seeks wholeness and mending from the numerous injuries triggered by existence. This is achieved through a union of the conscious and unconscious minds. It is through this union that truth is unveiled.

To realistically expect healing, we must venture into the inner realms of truth where consciousness encounters the mystery of the unconscious. To experience health, we need to make truth a companion through our life's journey. We are desperate for some depth within ourselves, which can sustain us and our relationships, but rather are left with only phantoms of true being. Drugs, alcohol, money/political power, and romance seem to be the values that the Age of Science and reason have procured. Mood-altering substances and money/power and romance distract us from the realities of our mortality, and our denial plunges us headlong into oblivion. If we are to begin to trace an outline that can take us out of our present delusions and self-deceptions, we must, with Bruce Springsteen, "mark truth or consequences on our map."

We are now in a position to calibrate these historical antecedents further in the upcoming chapters. We have identified the primordial inner conflicts that exist within man's psyche, *which is understandably concerned with the problems of life and death*. Paul Radin, the imminent anthropologist, recognized our struggle to "come to terms with our adaptation from the ape and that becoming conscious of this fact has been met with a craving to forget this painful truth" (Paul Radin, *The World of Primitive Man*, New York, E. P. Dutton & Co., Inc., 1971, p. 3). We are self-conscious animals that die, and we delude ourselves through a variety of strategies. Much of what is identified as culture is little more than the collective strategies that our denial of death has consummated.

> We took the highway until
> the road went black
> We'd marked, Truth or
> Consequences on our map.
>
> —Bruce Springsteen, "Last to Die"

Birth to Ego-Consciousness

I am a child in these hills.
I am awake.
I am alone . . .

And looking for water,
And looking for life.
Who will show me the river?
And ask me my name?
Is there nobody here that will do that?
Well, I have come to these hills.
I will come to the river.
As I choose to be gone,
From the house of my fathers.

—Jackson Browne, "A Child in These Hills"

Introduction to Pairs of Opposites

I will begin each ensuing chapter in this first section by identifying the archetypal pair(s) of opposites we will be encountering. This chapter includes those pairs of opposites required for a fundamental discussion on consciousness and the human condition: strength/weakness, collective/individuality, necessity/possibility, sensing/intuition, and finally thinking/feeling. Chapter 4 will present the opposite of consciousness, the unconscious. As with all opposites, a union or synthesis/balance is fashioned out of an inner conflict between the pairs. Wholeness is defined by the union of the conscious and unconscious minds. Consciousness without the complementary and compensatory unconscious is subject to arrogance, self-deception, and serious loss of depth to our psyche or soul. Unconsciousness without consciousness is subject to psychosis, extremes in neurosis, superstition, and self-deception.

Out of a primordial mystery, the infant lingers in total unconsciousness. She identifies completely with her mother. This state consists of unity, harmony, and safety. Bathed in unconsciousness and their caregivers' being, the infant lingers in a state of nonawareness. Prior to the advent of self-consciousness, *we are mother* or our caregiver. There is no awareness of the body until consciousness takes hold. As I discussed earlier, this state is not unlike our earliest ancestors who lacked self-awareness. Like the primitive, the infant cannot differentiate self from others, and all objects melt into one.

With the evolution of consciousness, the birth of consciousness is primarily a process where we differentiate self from others, things from things, etc. Everything is a miracle in the budding consciousness; "he is a stranger in a strange land." Historically and collectively; within each individual child, the pattern repeats itself, and the ego gradually develops and becomes the center of consciousness. The child is full of himself, and he believes he can manipulate the environment with his every whim; all he has to do is cry, and magically, his mother appears to soothe every ache and attends to every want. Humankind's birth to consciousness is in reality a birth to ego-consciousness from which we experience the inner and outer worlds. With the birth of ego-consciousness, the child's consciousness revolves around the ego; therefore, we can call this our ego-consciousness. Our ego-consciousness is set up to be self-centered and body-centered. There is me, and then there is everyone and everything else. Ego-consciousness is defined as the "I" whereby as we grow, we perceive ourselves in our uniqueness with such and such interests, abilities, strengths, and weaknesses as opposed to others. Whatever is in orbit surrounding the ego will become prominent in our minds and hearts. Somewhere in early to mid-adolescence, the mind becomes capable of *abstract, symbolic, and imaginative thinking*, which is still dependent upon ego-consciousness. We all develop an inner dialogue with ourselves, which continues throughout life. Our consciousness symbolizes both the inner and outer worlds. We never directly experience the outer world for our ego-consciousness, and five senses *filters* everything.

Ego-consciousness includes the abilities inherent in memory, imagination/images, reasoning, intuition, self-awareness, and thoughts and of all the other aspects of being (body, emotions, values, will, etc.) Ego-consciousness will always remain at the epicenter of our personalities. In its natural and original state, ego-consciousness is fearful of death, selfish, dishonest, arrogant, and lazy. Narcissism seems built into the fabric of ego-consciousness. A portion of all of us wants to survive, be in control, and exist is a state of equilibrium. This self-absorption radiates from the instincts through the ego to the entire personality. The ego has a need to defend itself with defenses against painful truths like weaknesses, death, inadequacies, and fears. All the defenses of our ego-consciousness can be summed up as variations of denial. The ego is fragile and yet full of itself. We all have to struggle with these impulses toward self-aggrandizement, denial, and control. These are all illusory compensations for the ego's puny and fragile nature. On the other hand, we need a strong ego-consciousness to endure and wrestle with life's responsibilities, disappointments, absurdities, and pain. We need a strong ego-consciousness, yet we are weak and must die. We will be exploring what ego-consciousness relies upon for supports throughout this first section. This paradox of strength and weaknesses runs through most of what we do and say, whether consciously or unconsciously.

The Four Functions of Consciousness

Humankind's birth to consciousness is in reality a birth to ego-consciousness from which Jung identified the four conscious functions. He identified them existing in two pairs of opposites: (1) sensing/intuition (perception functions) and (2) thinking/feeling (conclusion functions). The sensing function perceives external reality, tells us something is there; while intuition is our ability to perceive the inner world and peer around the bend as it were with our imagination, monitoring what is, where it comes from, where it is, and where it is headed. The thinking function uses our capacity for rationality and tells us what it is and examines the legitimacy of our thoughts, and the feeling function tells us what its value is. In addition, we are born with one superior function from which we usually build a career. The opposite of our superior function is our inferior function. For instance, if your superior function is sense, your inferior one would be intuition. Further, Jung observed we first integrate the auxiliary functions (the pair of opposites that do not contain our superior or inferior ones), and if we succeed, the possibility exists that we may bring our fourth and inferior function into actuality. In section 2, we will be witnesses to Job's integration of his fourth function. The fourth function is a maze of perplexity, embarrassment, uncertainty, awkwardness, inadequacy, failure, and suffering few ever are willing or able to integrate into their psyche's economy. However, this is the precinct from which we are able to experience wholeness and enlightenment.

I can't recall where I came across the reference to the original four central Star Trek characters as representing the four conscious functions. Regardless, I think they illustrate these succinctly and extremes in such a way that it makes it easy to not only identify the superior functions in action and how the four functions/characters need each other and form a unity. Captain Kirk represents intuition; Spock, the thinking function; Dr. McCoy, the feeling function; and finally Scotty, the sensing function. It seems to me for the series, Captain Kirk, as the main character or personality, represents intuition as the superior function of ego-consciousness as a whole, and it is he that attempts to integrate all four functions while the other three characters seem to exhibit one-sided thinking in their consciousness functions. Kirk's ability to work with the other three characters symbolizes his integration of all four functions within his personality. When watching the show, we can always count on the responses of Spock to be using logic to characterize the thinking function, McCoy portraying feeling values, and Scotty expressing the realm of the senses. However, there are episodes when the other three characters are confronted by their one-sided functions in and of themselves. However, it is always Captain Kirk who symbolizes the integration of all four functions.

The Uniqueness/Collective Dialectic

Our birth to consciousness is limited and structured in many ways from the outset. As humans, we have collective or universal patterns that are existent in every one of us. Our nature and the common human condition is the same for all of us. In each of us, our birth to consciousness is *built upon the foundation* of all that has gone before; as our bodies inherit qualities of being human, so we also inherit instincts, thoughts, emotions, attitudes, and behaviors (archetypes). Of the archetypes, I will go into detail in the next chapter.

We also have unique personalities with its plethora of strengths and weaknesses, which seem innate (a priori; that is, existing prior to experience). Children begin exhibiting certain characteristics very early. The good news is we can change and pass down healthier patterns to each new generation, opening up new possibilities for maturity and growth. The difficulty is there are limits to what each of us can be, despite the nonsense and dribble of successful people telling the rest of us we can be whatever we want to be. I could never have been a mathematician, nor would I want to, and to attempt such an absurdity would be squandering the few abilities I do have. Part of the process of growing up is inducing what we are good at *and* using it for the benefit of others. We can never be more than we are created to be, but we can certainly be less. Rather than being equal, we are all dealt certain limitations in temperament and ability. These differences need to be appreciated for what they are. We all need to be treated equally with the same compassion and appreciation and respect, but to say we *are* equal in the sense we have equal abilities is absurd.

The ethos of a particular culture contains the prevailing values and beliefs that are dominate within that culture. We all have to agree on certain aspects of reality to even be capable of communication with each other. History has shown that the collective consciousness of each culture has inherent strengths and weaknesses within its belief systems and attitudes and, in addition, exerts pressure on the individual to conform.

The collective/individuality dialectic is developed early in healthy consciousness. We all share the collective nature of consciousness, yet it is uniquely expressed in each individual. If an individual is one-sided in emphasizing their particular uniqueness or individuality, they become arrogant and lack compassion for common human limitations and struggles. They often become rugged individualists and take unusual pride in their nonconformity and antisocial behavior. Extreme examples are individuals with character disorders who become narcissistic in the extreme. If, on the other hand, someone is one-sided in the collective or universal aspects of our human condition, they tend to get stuck in convention and follow the masses without the critical reflection needed to integrate their uniqueness and individual responsibility.

The German people during Hitler's rise to power is a classic and extreme example of individuals and the government at a societal level succumbing to the collective, where fear of being unique held most of the German people in line. Any collective attitude and belief system runs the risk of its adherents abdicating personal responsibility with the added temptation to hide in the masses. If anyone tries to stand outside of the national/collective frenzy, they are ostracized and, in Nazi Germany, done away with. Playing it safe creates a prison where the individual fails to accomplish autonomy and independence. This failure to detach from our parents was transferred to the society as a whole in Hitler's Germany. The need to feel safe and secure within a group led to total abdication of personal responsibility and the heinous acts few thought possible. For those willing to learn from history, gone forever is the naiveté of a worldly utopia by becoming cogs in a giant rationalistic and/or nationalistic machine. We have to recognize our need to fit in and feel secure while maintaining our independence and personal integrity. It is easy to see from the extreme example of Nazi Germany that a balanced attitude is needed where we are capable of living out our collective and individual natures simultaneously are required for wholeness, where compassion, individual responsibility, aloneness, relatedness all coexist with an individual. *We need to develop a synthesis* of our collective and unique aspects of our nature where both are emphasized simultaneously. This personality is capable of autonomy and intimacy, taking individual responsibility and having compassion for others.

The Necessity/Possibility Dialectic

Along with the universal/unique dialectic, the necessity/possibility dialectic is one that must be balanced during the first half of life and before one can approach the unconscious with a certain degree of stability. We need to be grounded in the world of necessity where we accept limitations imposed on us by reality (i.e., gravity, needing air, water, food for survival, paying taxes and bills, dying, etc.). Being grounded in necessity, we perform daily tasks and duties because they are there, and we will suffer in some way if we don't. At the same time, we also need the freedom of possibility to avoid getting bogged down in necessity. What could be must be entertained by possibilities; anything creative must first go through this lens before we make the necessary choices to create actuality, what is. Grounded in reality, yet open to change when the situation in our psyche requires it, we move forward one step at a time. Like all opposites and dialectics, there are no universal prescriptions that can be applied to every internal or external circumstance that will fit in every situation. We need to be faithful to life's possibilities while accepting the limitations necessity demands.

The Miracle of Consciousness/Self-Knowledge

I know what I like
And I like what I know . . .

—Genesis,
"I Know What I Like (In Your Wardrobe)"

The word *conscious* is derived from the Latin word *conscire*, which means " to know with" (M. Scott Peck, *The Road Less Traveled and Beyond*, Touchtone, New York, 1997, p. 89). The question is to know with what? Peck speculates that knowing is "with God." We will be exploring spirituality in section 2, but for now I'd like to offer an additional possibility. "To know with" means to know with self-knowledge; in other words, to be conscious or aware of our consciousness. We move along in life and are conscious of things, people, our inner thoughts, etc. Consciousness of our consciousness is where we pause and become aware of thoughts and become aware of our thoughts as they cross our consciousness. I become aware that I am aware. This is the *beginning* of what I think Socrates was after when he proposed the essence of humanness was to know thyself. Self-knowledge is invaluable as conscious awareness is the initial step in freeing us from being bound and imprisoned by our limitations, desires, and self-deceptions. Being unconscious is to be unaware. For self-knowledge to take root, we must learn to reflect upon all aspects of our lives: our motives, inclinations, interests, abilities, defects and weaknesses, feelings, desires, thoughts, actions, etc. Among other things, self-knowledge provides the moral compass by which we create direction for our lives. This all begins in consciousness; self-awareness is the ability to know what makes us tick and thereby begin the process of growth and change. We need to know that we know, like what we know, and know what we like. We also need to translate this into *action and lifestyle and values*, which reflect this self-knowledge. It seems to me then that the miracle of consciousness has evolved to a higher level with self-knowledge, but not the highest levels. These higher levels will be explored in section 2.

From the big bang to conscious creatures! The inner life is full of mystery, wonder, horror, and many questions like who am I? Why am I here? What purpose does my life serve, if any? Why am I equally capable of doing good or evil in the world? We all have deep inner lives we must explore—memories, dreams, desires, fears, interests, limitations, possibilities, weaknesses, strengths, intuitions, values, emotions, and ideas running through consciousness at different cadences, intensities, stages, and levels. If we fail to do so, we will find ourselves doing much more evil that good. Therefore, consciousness is the pinnacle of the evolutionary process, and self-knowledge takes us to higher levels of consciousness. We all know that to know with self-knowledge does not mean automatically we are endowed with the ability to transform this self-knowledge into reality; quite the contrary, we often find ourselves aware of our inability to establish self-knowledge into change and, therefore, aware of our weaknesses, contradictions, and hypocrisy. We are unable to demonstrate the full extent of our self-knowledge *in life*, yet without it, we have no place to start and not a chance at success.

> I'm holding out my only candle, though
> it's so little light to find my way
> Now my story's been laid beneath my candle
> And it's shorter every hour as it
> reaches for the day . . .

> —Jackson Browne, Song for Adam

Light is a universal symbol of consciousness. The candle in this song symbolizes consciousness. Self- knowledge and insight, that is sight of what's within, are crucial to a consciousness, which has any hope of fulfilling its potential. We all are responsible to participate in the creation of our own story. We are responsible to fashion our consciousness and life values/attitudes/behaviors while our candle still burns. It's a dim but an extraordinary light. We are all pilgrims and sojourners as this life is but a temporary journey. What occurs following death is cause for speculation and full of mystery. We play our songs, metaphorically speaking, as our journey continues day by day and as the body gradually breaks down and decays. Every day bring us one day closer to death. We have this great gift of consciousness, and we need to develop this along with all the other gifts granted to us both collectively and individually. Those that are around children know of the wonder and amazement they exhibit at everything new. What a tragedy when, for the majority of us, this sense of wonder and awe is lost in adulthood. This does not have to be so, and I know it is possible to experience simultaneously both the suffering inherent in life with a sense of its wonder and adventure.

We all have our earliest memories of consciousness. My first memory was at age three when I recall being in a playpen in our living room. I had a vague memory of enjoying the time by myself and being annoyed by my two older siblings. Later, my mom confirmed this, and the pattern continues to this day. I like being alone so I can gather my thoughts like a poker player his cards, searching for the significant ones while discarding those I no longer need. I also remember losing my toy car and grieving it for a long time. This loss seemed to foreshadow my lifelong overreactions to loss and grief. It seems I have been destined to lose many things in my life and have chosen or had to start over many times.

As a child, I also dreamt of becoming a professional baseball player. What a miracle those early experiences of consciousness are and the disappointment at many falling by the wayside because they were not meant to be. I have long elicited my clients' first memories and early recollections of their initial steps into ego-consciousness. *I have come to believe they say something quite unique about the nature of an individual's assumptions from which they experience the world.* Is the external world safe or threatening? Can they trust experience and people or not? How did they initially react to disappointments, rejection, and love? Their first memories often tell me a lot about the issues still haunting my clients because that's what stands out when they review their earliest memories. We all remember what we do for a reason; these early recollections reflect the inner landscapes of our being. It is in the very experience of inner tensions and conflict that provides opportunities for consciousness to expand. It seems nothing of value is ever created that does not involve some kind of struggle and strife. I have had the honor to weep with those that weep and rejoice with those that rejoice.

With consciousness comes the ability to experience life. From experience come opportunities to grow more and more by expanding consciousness. The unconscious is conspiring to create all sorts of difficult conflicts from which we can grow. There, like the freshwater springs that lie beneath a lake, are myriads of hidden streams and treasures that underlies the selfishness, arrogance, failures, and dishonesty of our ego-consciousness.

We will move to the unconscious mind in chapter 4 after first taking some time to discuss what science has to say about truth.

The Truth of Science

Time's too big to fit in the brain
Nothing's too big to fit in my heart.
Space-time strings bend
World without end
God's too big to fit in a book
Nothing's too big to fit in my heart.

—Bruce Cockburn, To Fit in My Heart"

All science has one aim, namely, to find a theory of nature.

—Ralph Waldo Emerson, *Essays and Lectures*

At the beginning of the last century, science went through some revolutionary revisions in our understanding of nature and the cosmos and, therefore, in our quest in understanding truth. The world of science was turned upside down by Einstein's theory of relativity of space and time and quantum physics views on the nature of matter/light. Einstein proved that in the macro world, time and space are relative; while in the micro world of quantum physics, the mechanical understanding of the universe was shattered. Fewer and fewer believe that there are laws in the universe where everything is determined, predictable, and ultimately knowable. This revolution has yet to be incorporated by many in the scientific community or by ordinary individuals. Quantum physics has traced disparate and paradoxical rules and principles that exist in the intricate workings of subatomic matter in the context of the observer, that is to say us. These rules or principles continue to befuddle, fascinate, and defy mechanical notions of reality. We don't even know how mass accumulated from the subatomic particles and, therefore, why any matter holds together as a solid. The quantum world has again validated man's consciousness and imagination, which common sense has always recognized, while the notions of a mechanical universe have been invalidated. I presently want to trace what I believe are the most essential of these insights, all of which are interrelated.

First, according to the insights from the micro world of quantum physics, the stuff of the universe, matter, exists only as possibility until it is observed by consciousness as quantum waves. Only then does matter "appear." At times, electrons appear as a cloud of wave possibilities that exceed the speed of light and, at other times, as a particle. The choice we make regarding what to measure determines what is experienced; therefore, consciousness and our selective attention make possible the realities we experience. Whatever the nature of matter, it is inexorably, intrinsically, and ineffably linked to consciousness. There is no way getting around the fact the observer's consciousness impacts the world that is experienced and perceived. By looking at things practically, everything that we create begins in possibility in our imaginations and only later becomes actuality after we have fashioned it with our choices. The principle of complementarily says that the matter in the physical universe is impossible to detect independent of an observer's choice. There are two possibilities to choose from in what to examine. Matter acts like a wave one moment and like a particle the next, and it is the observer who decides! We cannot see the universe both as a particle and wave at the same time, and therefore, we can only experience reality as a duality.

Wolf puts it this way: "By choosing to see the world one way, complementary ways of experiencing the world become hidden or inaccessible" (Fred Allan Wolf, *Book of Big Ideas*, 33). Everything inside and outside our consciousness are forever impacted just in the very act of observation.

Therefore, we will never know what "out there" is exactly because in the act of observing matter, it transforms from a unity of possibility to become an actuality—an actuality that is dualistic in nature.

Likewise, what we choose for an attitude is how we will see the world. This opens up the realm of subjective experiences; subjective experience is truth in that how or what we chose to observe or believe impacts how we see the world. If we believe the universe is merely physical, then that's all we will detect. Our experiences are limited by our beliefs and attitudes! In other words, there is nothing that we really know without our perceptions of "it"—everything we observe is filtered through our five senses and our beliefs and attitudes. The medical establishment has taken many years to acknowledge the connection between conscious attitudes and the body in both psychosomatic illness and the healing process. This has turned around, however, and most physicians have expanded their theoretical base founded upon the medical model and include conscious beliefs and attitudes and the role they play in the health and illness of their patients.

This leads us to the second of the insights gleaned from quantum physics, which is inexorably linked to the first; that is, uncertainty seems to be the order of the day. We can only measure outcomes by means of probability. When experimenting with matter, there is no way to predict exactly what will actually occur. When studying these microparticles and waves, the leap from possibility to actuality remains forever uncertain. These insights are perfectly consistent with the practical and obvious insights of psychology; that is, we may have some control over our effort or focus, but never the outcomes. Uncertainties dominate the micro world of tiny particles and waves and the macro world of everyday experiences. Life is filled with necessities and possibilities! Whenever we make any choice, outcomes forever remain out of our power to manage or control. Therefore, uncertainty is necessary for any real freedom of will; freedoms of choice rip open and rupture actuality out of the mystery, incomprehensibility, wonder, and terror of uncertain possibility. With every turning of the wheel (of our attention), life becomes an adventure where the observer's consciousness transforms, distorts, and alters whatever is observed. Out of the mystery of the unknown, conscious perception transforms whatever was into what is and will be. The common denominator is uncertainty, which creates freedom. However, freedom comes with a price and cost; it just as easily breeds fear as faith, truth as delusion. Many have been seduced by insecurity and arrogance into believing they can capture and control reality. They also delude themselves by attempting to box, package, and confine truth within their finite, limited, and changing minds. Some take their restricted beliefs and try to thrust it down everyone else's throats, occasionally at the end of military hardware. If there are universal truths, they are certainly not like a child's Play-Doh, or to be used as weaponry, nor tossed at each other in the form of bombs, intolerance, self-righteousness, and false pride. The illusions of certainty loiter about in our minds, attitudes, and beliefs; within the fastidious strains of every academic discipline; science, philosophy, religion and world institutions; limiting our choices, offering excuses for our failures, and engendering injustices and mayhem in every imaginable disguise.

The Greeks were on to something when they emphasized fate in their myths and philosophies. Many fear the reality of uncertainty, yet we could not act in the universe without it. Uncertainty guards possibility and free will. Our attitudes and beliefs go a long way in determining our behavior and destiny. The choices we make create the truths we live by and the people we become. At the same time, there are many basic limitations that our existence imposes upon us. Our body reeks of determinism while our consciousness entertains possibilities and free will. We are not completely controlled by outside forces, unless our attitudes permit it. There always exist choices within all circumstances. There often exist limited choices to be sure. In a concentration camp where the body is used as a tool of torture, one can still make choices on what attitudes, beliefs, and behaviors one embraces. Attitudes, beliefs, motivations, and behaviors exist within the landscape of our inner life and can change. We are capable of differentiating between fate and choice, accepting that which we cannot control and taking responsibility for that which lies within our will's orbit. You will also notice I talk about attitudes, beliefs, and behaviors/practices in conjunction with each other. This is due to my belief that the essence and depths of our conscious being and its hope for transformation lie herein.

Thirdly, the baffling world of quantum physics also proposes that an inexplicable underlining unity may pervade the universe. All that is seems inexorably linked to everything else, like a great web. It seems memory itself is inherent in nature herself; all animals pass on intricate nuances of collective memory through cells to each new generation. All the cells for each species are alive with energy! Many scientists who discovered new insights into the workings of reality tell us as they wrestled with conundrums that fascinated them, they often describe experiences where a new insight dawned on them as serendipitous or mystical. Einstein and other prominent physicists believe humans are a part of the whole and believe experiencing the universe as separate is delusional. These earth-shaking insights gleaned from the new science sounds a lot like the realm traditionally set aside for philosophy and spirituality.

Listen to a quote from one of the preeminent cosmologists, George Smoot:

> It seems the more we learn, the more we see how it seems to fit together-how there is an underlying unity to the sea of matter and stars and galaxies that surround us. Likewise, as we study the universe as a whole, we realize that the "microcosm" and the "macrocosm" are, increasingly, the same subject. By unifying them, we are learning that nature is as it is not because of chance consequence of a random series of meaningless events; quite the opposite. More and more the universe appears to be as it is because it must be that way; its evolution was written in its beginnings-in the cosmic DNA, if you will. There is a clear order to the evolution of the universe, moving from simplicity and symmetry to greater complexity and structure. As time passes, simple components coalesce into more sophisticated building blocks spawning a richer and more diverse environment . . . In cosmology there is a confluence of physics, metaphysics, and philosophy-when inquiry approaches the ultimate questions of our existence, the lines between them become inevitably blurred. (George Smoot and

Keay Davidson, *Wrinkles in Time*, Avon Books, 1993, p. 296)

These insights have born themselves out in the macro world of our everyday experience in nature as in the micro world of quantum physics; every change within the ecosystem or environment impacts all in the region surrounding it in a great web of being while subatomic particles themselves seem to know what other subatomic particles are doing. With each new variable that is introduced in the environment, the whole is now relatively transformed into something more complex.

This leads us to a fourth major insight from cosmologists; that is the evolutionary process has exhibited a movement from lower levels of sophistication to the more complex. Starting with the big bang, cosmologists have determined that everything that is began then; energy, space and time, and matter, all were created as we know it. All matter/energy began and continues to expand and combine and change into more and more complexity. Science has determined that matter mysteriously emerged into life and life into consciousness. Science as a whole continues to grapple with the implications and dynamics of the micro world of quantum physics and how energy, matter, and consciousness overlap and interact. To what degree consciousness varies and how many levels it may exist on and are possible has yet to be completely determined, yet dreams and certain states of meditation and contemplation have suggested some remarkable possibilities. In addition, the unconscious mind seems to operate outside the parameters of normal time and space and, as we shall explore in greater detail, to include particular wisdom about the attitudes and fate of the individual dreamers. In addition, the mind seems to hold a considerable sway over matter during certain meditative conscious states. The evolutionary process has taken giant leaps, transcending yet including what came before it. The levels of consciousness continue to evolve into greater and greater depth and complexity. Each higher level transcends and includes the lower levels. Each level continues to evolve, and therefore, we do not live in a static universe, but one that is developing into more and more depth and substance. As we live truth, we serve as important engines in this evolution! This evolution of consciousness is often referred to as psyche or spirit. Evolution and the incredible creative leaps remain unexplained by chance and natural selection. It appears from the infinitesimal particles/waves to the complex psyche, everything craves experience and choices in an endless quest for more and more complexity and depth.

Ken Wilber puts it thus:

> The standard, glib, neo-Darwinian explanation of natural selection—absolutely nobody believes that anymore. Evolution clearly operates in part by Darwinian natural selection, but this process simply selects those transformations that have already occurred by mechanisms that absolutely nobody understands . . . The wing will work only if these hundred mutations happen all at once, in one animal—and also these same mutations must occur simultaneously in another animal of the opposite sex, then they have to somehow find each other, have dinner, a few drinks, mate, and have offspring with real functional wings. (Ken Wilber, *A Brief History of Everything*, Shambhala Publications, Inc. 1996, p. 22–23)

Wilber goes on to make the case for what Arthur Koestler termed *holons*—entities that are themselves wholes and simultaneously a part of a greater whole.

Wilber goes on to explain:

> For instance, a whole atom is part of a whole molecule, and the whole molecule is part of a whole cell, and a whole cell is part of a whole organism, and so on. Each of these entities is neither a whole nor a part, but a whole/part, a holon . . . No matter how far we go down, we find holons resting on holons. Even subatomic particles disappear into virtual clouds of bubbles within bubbles, holons within holons, in infinity of probability waves. Holons all the way down. (ibid., p. 20)

He adds, "So the first tenet of reality is composed . . . neither wholes nor parts, but whole/parts-all the way up, all the way down" (ibid., 21).

Wilber goes on to describe the nature of twenty tenets of how holons operate. The most significant for me are that (1) we can get stuck into thinking a particular holon is all of reality and thereby become arrogant, (2) that our rational mind can never know the complete whole, and (3) we can either be a participant in the creative evolutionary process or get stuck in one holon and/or regress backward. It seems to me an individual is by and large either growing or regressing, though it becomes impossible to judge another due to all the complex histories and missing pieces at our disposal. As I will argue throughout this work, we can, however, make some judgments upon what is further advanced along evolutionary process and what is not. It is important to note that there is an equal inclination for de-evolution; that is for regression of the evolutionary process at any point in its evolution.

In addition, consciousness studies, previously referred to as parapsychology, were recognized by the American Advancement of Science more than forty years ago. Psychic events include the study of telepathy, precognition, psychokinesis, and clairvoyance. More recently, studies in the areas of the death sense, dream interpretation, NDEs (near-death experience), out-of-body experiences, reincarnation, apparitions, and synchronicity have captured the interest of certain segments of science. The philosopher Immanuel Kant attempted to wed the world of empiricism and consciousness by proposing that both sense impressions and a prior constructs of the mind, which include concepts such as space and time, are equally relevant and coexist to create our perceptions of the world (a priori meaning that which exists prior to and independent of experience). In other words, we experience the world via sense impressions and the constructs and concepts inherent and inherited through consciousness. Both are to be valued and are mediated by our senses and mind; therefore, we never actually experience anything directly. Both the a priori concepts of the mind and our sense impressions are recognized in their own right as modes of perception and therefore avenues in the discovery of truth. It also seems memory is inherent in nature herself—all animals pass on intricate nuances of collective memory through cells to each new generation. The nature and contents of this energy remains a mystery.

Also, the immortality of consciousness also seems alluded to in the dreams of many dying individuals. These phenomenon seem to imply consciousness is mediated by the brain, but may not reside there. The brain may be a kind of satellite dish that picks up signals from elsewhere. The notion that some experiences may temporarily suspend space and time limitations opens up a can of worms many scientists are too myopic to look into as their reputations may take a hit if they embrace ideas outside the empirical model. However, significant scientific discovery has always been advanced by radical scientists investigating new ideas that the majority of their colleagues initially ridicule and denounce. It is also interesting to note that the word *radical* has its root in the Latin *radix*, which means "to get to the root of things" (Peck, *The Road Less Traveled and Beyond*, p. 55). It seems only those willing to go beyond the limits of convention while investigating ideas that stem from their imaginations get to the root of things and turn out to be the ones who develop and discover unknown landscapes of truth. Those blessed radicals!

An obvious issue arises: is matter or consciousness primary or precede the other when experiencing reality? Each position believes the one is primary and the other is secondary or an epiphenomenon of the other. Newtonian physics continues to appear to be valid when studying the macro world of large objects. However, there are areas where the macro and micro worlds overlap. There are many new technologies that are based on quantum physic: medical devices, computers, transistors, lasers, digital equipment, quantum teleportation, quantum cryptography, and superconductors, while quantum computation is either made or being researched and developed. These technologies work. In addition, since our brain is a quantum brain, reality is founded upon the quantum or micro level. Is this quantum level of reality primarily consciousness or matter? I side with those who believe consciousness proceeds all matter.

Undertaking an encounter with reality/truth will inevitably engender complications, obstacles, and controversies. There will never be any universal consensus or method by which reality/truth can be defined. There is one branch of philosophy, epistemology, which purports to grapple with this problem head-on (as defined in the dictionary, "the theory or science of the method or grounds of knowledge," the Compact Edition of the OED, volume 1, Oxford English Press, twenty-third printing in the US, 1984).

Philosophy is conspicuously missing from this definition though it was originally posed by philosophy and one which philosophy is ultimately concerned. Dictionaries belie a nineteenth-century prejudice that the scientific method could succeed where philosophy had become superfluous and/or failed. Regardless, the fact is we don't know how we know what we know. Except for a few external facts, we also can't be sure what we know is correct, and indeed, we'll never know the whole completely. Limitation and uncertainty are built into every equation purported in the quest for truth. I will be asserting that universal truths, principles, realities, and values exist, and it is of momentous import we adapt to these truths. However, there is no way science, philosophy, rationalism, religion, or any other intellectual discipline can prove it. While accepting limitations and uncertainties as part and parcel of life, we are nevertheless required to take leaps of faith into beliefs and values that perpetually engender personal commitments. For each created and unique individual human being, our freedom and the imperative to choose, albeit limited, makes life possible. This work is dedicated to synthesizing accumulated knowledge about the history of the human condition as it has evolved in experiences, the psyche, belief systems, myths, behaviors, attitudes, perceptions, motives, etc. To paraphrase my Emerson quote earlier, truth will become known to common sense if it is capable of explaining the phenomenon.

Chance or Purpose

This begs a fundamental question that has intrigued humankind's imagination for eons: has everything unfolded by some teleological or spiritual force or energy or by chance? In the beginning was the word? Regardless of how each may answer this most fundamental question, we are confronted with an imperative to think for ourselves and make up our own mind. Meanwhile, with each and every breath, we ebb closer to our death. Either way, you come to answer this most important of existential questions; each belief system is a leap of faith. We are all philosophers whether we like it or not, and each of us is left with an imperative and responsibility to make our own choices regarding what we believe. Quantum physics is clear that whatever view we have of reality has major implications on how we perceive and therefore experience the world.

I'd like to end my discussion on science with an extensive quote from Jeffrey Satanove and his work *Quantum Brain*," who is I think one of the most balanced, thoughtful, and intelligent thinkers in the areas of quantum theory, psychiatry, and spirituality,

> It is a matter of preference—faith, if you wish—
> as to how you explain the quantum foundational
> basis of the universe, its concentration in life, and
> its amplification by the brain: either its absolute
> chance or absolute will. Opposite as they sound
> at first, between the two sciences can point to no
> distinction and the universe, it seems will offer no
> evidence. Both are equally mysterious as explana-
> tions go. Indeed, they are hardly even that: They
> are merely terms for something beyond our ken.
> You might call it the Toa or Ralph. In the words of
> theoretical chemist Michael Kellman, "In a word
> where 'choices' appear to be constantly being made
> between different outcomes, the idea of divine
> intervention may not seem quite so absurd- or at
> least not so much more absurd than the bizarre
> things we already know about the world" . . . The
> one thing you do have to reckon with, however—
> or should admit that you have to—is that there is
> something going on, everywhere, that creates the
> particular world in which we live, a creation that

occurs not just once, at the beginning, for a time, but always, just as moment to moment it sustains who we actually are in the world. To my mind, it is as big a misreading to claim that science tells us something cannot be God as to assert that science tells us it must be. The world may be pregnant with hope and meaning and propose beyond our belief . . . But one thing it is not: mechanical. If one wants to, one might say that the only essence we have knowledge of God is his seemingly infinite capacity to choose—selecting from quantum alternatives the ones that shall be. If the human brain is designed so as best to capture, distill, and concentrate that essence—at least from a very small region of the universe—perhaps our will is in some sense a miniature portion of his. Or perhaps our will is nothing more than an unusually dense distillation of randomness. In any event, it is no less free than the universe itself and possibly considerably more. Beyond that, science won't say because it can't. (*The Quantum Brain*, John Wiley & Sons, 2001, p. 217–18)

And so science has its limits like everything is life. How could it be otherwise? To live with the notion that everything contains some mystery leaves the mind open to wonder, cringe, and marvel at the creative and horrific nature of the human condition.

It's just a thought
But I've noticed somethin' strange,
Gettin' harder to explain;
All the years are passin' by and by,
Still I'd don't know what makes it go;

Who said to wait and see?
It's just a thought

—Creedence Clearwater Revival,
"It's Just a Thought"

Let us get on with a discussion of consciousnesses opposite, the unconscious mind.

The Conscientious Unconscious: Part 1

All our memories, dreams, and reflections
They keep haunting me
Well it's down the road I go . . .

—Van Morrison, Down the Road

Introduction

The dynamics of the unconscious mind are vast and full of mystery. It is not only the opposite of consciousness but the foundation of all conscious thoughts. My concern is some may struggle with the following concepts. However, there will be many examples using myths in this and the upcoming chapters to assist you in gaining an enhanced grasp of the unconscious mind. You should be prepared to return to this chapter for reference; these concepts will continue to surface throughout the remainder of this book.

The Unconscious Mind

The following is founded upon the work of Dr. Carl Jung.

The unconscious mind is both mysterious and fascinating. What we know is a fraction of its contents. What we know is significant, however, and I want to talk about some of the general insights that will set the stage for later discussions on specific aspects of the unconscious.

I'd like to say a few words before I proceed with a discussion of the unconscious mind. In the following chapters, we will be delving into the dynamics of the human condition in depth. We all wrestle with the same struggles inherent within the human condition, and these I propose are universal to all of us. Whether you understand or agree with the concepts of the unconscious mind will not hinder you in the following chapters for the dynamics of the human condition will be something you will be able to relate regardless on your views on the unconscious mind. The most difficult aspect of the unconscious mind to get a hold of is that of the collective unconscious. It is also the hardest for some to accept. If you find the concept and reality of the collective unconscious too esoteric or difficult to accept, move on to the next chapter. However, I want the reader to know the collective unconscious, though difficult to understand at times, is crucial to my philosophy of the human condition, and I ask the reader for patience and open-mindedness while reading this and part II of the unconscious mind later in the book. We have never been in such a good position to peer into the wealth that exists within the unconscious mind. Most of us are scared of the unconscious, and with some good reason, for its contents has literally taken over the personalities of psychotics. However, when approached with openness, the unconscious is very accommodating to consciousness. However, most of us are totally pre-occupied with the external world or rational though with a sort of frenzy while the apparatus of the unconscious is belittled, denied, and for the most part, ignored. We have come to understand some of the intricate workings of matter and the cosmos while our newspapers are filled with daily horror stories that reflect how little we know about the inner life of the psyche. It is of utmost worth that we gain self-knowledge and a greater understanding of the entire psyche, without which the power to change is impossible. Let us now delve into more detail concerning what has been made conscious in our understanding of the contents of the unconscious.

First for a definition, the unconscious mind is made up of a combination of the personal unconscious and the collective unconscious. The personal unconscious is all experiences unique to each individual that have been forgotten and incorporated into our unconscious. The collective unconscious is universal materials or archetypes that create and use symbolic images in our imaginations to communicate to the conscious mind through the language of myths, music, poetry, dreams, and rituals. The unconscious mind also manifests itself in memories, projections, psychosis, moods, positive and negative emotions, anxiety, depression, inflation, and alienation. The contents of the collective unconscious are made up of our instincts and the archetypes. Archetypes are *patterns of behavior latent with feelings* that are *universal coping mechanisms*, which go back into our primordial past and have accumulated through the collective experience of human kind. They are inherited structures or predispositions and precursors to ideas with emotional affects that have accrued and developed over the collective histories of humankind in order to cope with the inner and outer worlds of experience. Primordial instincts and archetypes are the most ancient and least differentiated. That is they remain general and are the most resistant to change. But as the archetypes and psyche have developed, the archetypes became more differentiated. An example of one these primordial archetypes is the Great Mother, and this archetype has evolved over time into all that is feminine within the psyche of men and women. All of the primordial archetypes have developed and differentiated over time; that is, they have morphed into more and more complex behavior patterns and coping mechanisms within the human psyche.

There are many contradictory desires and patterns of behavior/coping with life that vie with the physical instincts for supremacy within our minds, motives, and behaviors. We are imprinted with a far greater complexity of potential behaviors, attitudes, and motives than we can imagine. This greater complexity is due to the archetypes of the collective unconscious. The collective unconscious is the deepest layer of the unconscious and is the matrix of all the instincts and archetypes. We begin in childhood unconscious of the archetypes and instincts within us, and yet they influence our motives and behavior whether we understand and integrate them or not. The goal is to make the archetypes conscious so as to not be controlled by them. The collective unconscious is the true foundation for each individual psyche and all of what we know of our ego-consciousness through self-knowledge. We are, in effect, seized by archetypes, and it is they along with our instincts that drive our passions, motives, emotions, interests, beliefs, attitudes, abilities, and values—in a word, our unique personalities. The collective unconscious is the true foundation for each individual psyche.

Specifically, we are able to *recognize* the workings of the unconscious mind by the following data: in the states of dreaming, by studying mythology, by studying psychosis, by examining the roots of words (i.e., by studying their etymology), when we do and say things that are contrary to our conscious intentions, and by using active imagination. I want to briefly describe each in turn.

First, while in the state of sleep or hypnosis, our conscious mind is passive, and yet the psyche goes on operating. Our mind is animated by the unconscious (to learn how to interpret your dreams, see Robert Johnson's *Inner Works*, Harper, San Francisco, 1986). Dreams divulge the agenda and inclinations of the unconscious mind. We will be looking at some dreams to offer examples. In hypnotic states, the individual surrenders his or her will to the hypnotist, and the unconscious mind is accessed directly.

Secondly, we can study the collective myths that captivate a particular civilization as they are windows into the collective unconscious, which have made their way into collective consciousness. Worldwide myths and individual dreams contain symbols that are created by the collective unconscious to communicate to conscious. We will be exploring many myths throughout this book.

Thirdly, psychoses are examples where the unconscious mind strangles and overwhelms ego-consciousness to the degree where we can observe the unconscious mind's autonomous structures and ideas along with its destructive tendencies. When we listen and dialogue with a psychotic during a psychotic episode, it is often possible to identify the archetype speaking directly through them. For some people, what makes conversing eerie with psychotics is an absence of the ego and the direct and sheer archetypal energy confronting the listener. Nevertheless, the unconscious speaks through the psychotic to those who are trained and able to garner its ruminations.

Fourthly, another example is etymology, which studies the original and historicity of a word, most importantly the roots in their original language. The roots of words contain unswerving correlations to the unconscious, conveying original meanings that have sometimes been forgotten as the word has evolved. The roots of words rest closer to the unconscious mind. An example is psychology where the root of the word means study of the psyche, yet some in the field don't even acknowledge a psyche! The study of etymology or the roots of words is an incredible treasure trove of wisdom that arrives directly from the unconscious. I have and will continue to use etymology as a means to get to the roots of words, which contain these insights from the unconscious intended for consciousness.

Fifthly, in our waking conscious state, the unconscious intrudes upon our consciousness in what is known as slips of the tongue (when we say something that our conscious mind did not intend to say, but it comes blurting out to our dismay). We have all found ourselves sticking our foot in our mouths and, with some reflection, become conscious that what we said laid bare deeper and more honest beliefs and attitudes.

Finally, we can identify the workings of the unconscious by participating in active imagination. The second half of Robert Johnson's *Inner Work* explores this avenue, and I again refer the reader to this monumental book. A quick note: When I first encountered Jung's belief that all these archetypes were autonomous, I found it esoteric while intriguing. It was not until I began interpreting my dreams and using active imagination for myself that I have come to believe these archetypes are real and autonomous, and they want to develop a relationship with our ego-consciousness for the purpose of leading us to enlightenment and wholeness.

With the birth of consciousness, the unconscious and conscious minds became separated. This separation has caused a great deal of growth in consciousness, the zenith of the evolutionary process. However, with this separation has come a split between our two minds. The problems of the psyche are due to this split, where our two minds often war and clash. This clash takes place in the form of opposites and in competing desires. This clash also includes negative and positive energy attached to each pair of opposite. The goal is a reconciliation of sorts between both minds where both are valued and given their rightful place within the economy of our psyche. In fact, the conscious mind is restricted in many ways, including most significantly, the inability to think of more than one thought at a time. The truth is our *entire consciousness is built upon the unconscious mind.* There is nothing you think that is not originated in the unconscious mind! We have traced in our brief look at history the evolutionary development of our psyche; the unconscious mind preceded the conscious one.

Furthermore, the unconscious mind provides compensatory and complementary functions to the conscious mind. This compensatory function is an attempt by the unconscious to balance conscious attitudes and beliefs, which are deficient and biased. It seems the unconscious mind is anxious to achieve wholeness by compensating for the conscious mind's one-sided thinking by laying pressure on consciousness with an opposing attitude, belief, or behavior presently entrenched in consciousness. This leads us to the second function—it complements the conscious mind in that both minds are dependent upon the other for their proper functioning. We know that (1) the unconscious mind desires to communicate with consciousness and uses symbolic images to accomplish its mission—this is owed to the fact that symbolic images are comprehended by both the conscious and unconscious minds, and (2) the conscious mind seeks depth and meaning by companying and trafficking with the unconscious mind.

The Symbols of the Unconscious

Symbols are "an image or representation which points to something essentially unknown, a mystery (Edward Edinger, *Ego and Archetype*, Pelican Books, 1973, p. 109).

The unconscious mind communicates to the conscious mind by way of symbols. The contents of the collective unconsciousness are made up of the archetypes, which use images/symbols as the language to communicate to consciousness. As I discussed briefly in the introduction, symbols carry the dialectical pairs of opposites in unified forms. However, what makes symbols so difficult to interpret is they carry mysteries and many different levels of meaning. It takes time to place any symbolic representation or image in its proper context; that is within the specific unique psyche by those interpreting them. At the same time, this difficulty in interpreting symbols does not preclude our ability to unpack these symbols and experience their transformative and healing powers as long as we maintain faithfulness to the context from which these symbols arise.

Both dreams and myths use symbols to stimulate consciousness with powerful emotional effects associated with their motifs and conundrums in order to entice consciousness out of its indolence and reliance on the physical instincts and the selective attention ego-conscious uses as the primary directives of our attitudes, beliefs, and behaviors.

Again Edinger says, "Symbols are carriers of psychic energy. They provoke and provide meaning and harmonize our psyche's conflicting urges and desires. That is why it is proper to consider them as something alive. They transmit to the ego, either consciously or unconsciously, life energy which supports, guides, and motivates the individual" (ibid., p. 110).

The transfer of energy occurs when we recognize the importance of symbols and attempt to interpret their meanings through meditation and concentration upon the images they produce. We have no other way of interpreting the meanings of the collective unconscious mind. Consciousness seeks the depths of the unconscious, while the unconscious seeks the light of consciousness.

Myths incorporate universal symbolic images while dreams comprise both individual and universal symbols. The reason symbols are efficacious is they contain the power and energy needed for transformation and change. The symbols produced by the unconscious mind are accessible to ego-consciousness and contain power that can be seen by our fascination with symbols throughout our history. For instance, in many American Indian cultures, each individual has a totem animal. This animal is a specific symbol that reflects their particular personality's purpose and meanings. The initiate goes out on a vision quest to meet their totem animal. This is an animal that is met in various states of consciousness and conversed with. The totem animal is with the individual throughout their life, helping guide and strengthen the initiate toward their life purpose.

Symbols are contained in all religions and exhibit a rich history, providing meaning to the life of the initiate. For those whom religion has no or little significance, symbols created in dreams and the imagination offer other opportunities to communicate with one's inner life and depths to find meaning, direction, guidance, and purpose in their lives. If we become alienated from symbols and, therefore, the power they contain, we become neurotic, and this is just what has happened in our Western culture. Generally speaking, I believe institutional religion in the West has failed to faithfully transmit living and captivating symbols for our youth. I have much more to say about this in chapter 8.

The next question is how do symbols behave in our collective consciousness? Regarding unhealthy ways, they are lived but not perceived. This occurs by evoking savage rites and rituals or neurotic symptoms and/or perversions. If the symbol is projected and therefore unconscious, we become fascinated with an object or activity. The instincts become congested with energy, and it evokes compulsiveness and/or negative moods. Inflation also occurs when an individual identifies with symbols created by the unconscious, and we observe arrogance in an individual. Alienation occurs when the symbol is stripped of its power by ego-consciousness as it reduces and degrades these symbols by constructing them into simple signs.

How then do we discover the hidden images in these symbols and make them conscious for constructive purposes? Let's start by studying the etymology of the word *symbol*. The word *symbol* comes from the Greek word *symbolon*. This contains two roots, first *sym*, which means together, and *bolon*, which is that which is thrown; therefore, the word *symbol* etymologically means that which has been thrown together. Reality is split into two/opposites, and symbols bring them back together to form a union. This is yet another example of wholeness's requirement to integrate the pairs of opposites. The individual ego becomes alienated from the sources of the unconscious energies during the developmental stages of childhood and young adulthood. The budding ego-consciousness must develop some independence and the ability to survive attacks upon its central role in the workings of consciousness. However, we need to take this strong and independent ego-consciousness and reconnect to the ground of its functioning, the unconscious. We begin to do this by identifying central symbols that tickle our fancy, so to speak, as these symbols carry the wisdom of the unconscious to consciousness. We then need to begin living a symbolic life by integrating rituals that have personal meanings where we bring together that which has been split or separated. Living a symbolic life is where we create personal rituals that are pregnant with meaning and bring about the unions of opposites. An example is some people face east when they pray, and this is a way to live symbolically because east is a symbol of spirituality, enlightenment, and the contemplative life.

The Personal Unconscious

The personal unconscious contains our personal histories, not currently conscious. This includes all that is not presently the focus of consciousness. In addition, the personal unconscious includes all the repressed experiences with their corresponding feelings that we have chosen to avoid. The contents of our personal unconscious contain memories not conscious at the present time. It also contains what once was referred as our complexes. This term *complex* is used to designate all the unresolved issues that have been consciously repressed and contain intense and unresolved emotional baggage. When we are overreacting emotionally in some way, this is a clue that our complexes have become activated. Association tests and everyday topics of conversations are useful in identifying these unresolved issues and problems. Hesitations, emotional outbursts, and the words we choose give away these underlying unsettled quandaries. For instance, if someone begins discussing their mother and they hesitate or overreact, chances are you have unresolved issues with your mom. The personal unconscious is a repository for all the conscious experiences you have ever had. Our consciousness can recollect these past experiences via the capacities of memory and self-reflection. If there are repressed contents that we resist facing, the unconscious will repeatedly construct situations that evoke them until they are made conscious and resolved. Circumstances will recur until we confront our consciousness with these repressed and unresolved contents. The personal unconscious requires we revisit our past periodically; however, the purpose is never to live there.

The Collective Unconscious/ The Archetypes

The collective unconscious is made up of the instincts and the archetypes. Basically, the archetypes are patterns of behavior with strong emotional contents that have built up throughout human history to cope with the human condition. The archetypes are autonomous structures that exert strong influences upon our desires and longings and in which we are "moved" to act and behave. The archetypes use dreams and mythological motifs/symbolic images for the purpose of communicating with consciousness. The symbolic images attract the attention of consciousness for the purpose of stimulating particular modifications in our attitudes, beliefs, and behaviors. Specific archetypes determine each unique personality by exerting its will with tendencies, desires, interests, motivations, and passions. Mythological motifs also fascinate consciousness, and in fact, the whole of mythology could be taken as a sort of projection of the collective unconscious and the archetypes.

For instance, we observe this clearly if we look at the heavenly constellations and the Zodiac, "where the originally chaotic forms were organized through the projection of images . . . just as the constellations were projected into the heavens, similar figures were projected into legends and fairy tales or upon historical figures Carl Jung ("The Portable Jung" from *The Structure of the Psyche*, Viking Penguin Inc., 1971, p.39).

Certain myths and symbolic images fascinate each of us in unique ways, and whatever fascinates us says a lot about what specific archetypes are currently pressing on consciousness for our recognition and which archetypes are central to each unique person. All consciousness is built upon our instincts and the collective archetypes of the unconscious. *These are basic structures that develop into forms from specific inherited patterns of coping with experience.*

Again I quote Dr. Jung, "The deposit of mankind's whole ancestral experience—so rich in emotional imagery—of father, mother, child, husband, wife, of the magic personality, of dangers to body and soul, has exalted this group of archetypes into supreme regulating principles of religious and even of political life in unconscious recognition of their tremendous psychic power" (ibid., p. 43).

The archetypes are active reactions and aptitudes that are hidden and situated behind the scenes, guiding and directing an individual's life. In my case, the archetype of the knight of faith is extremely prevalent and has shown up repeatedly in my reactions and capacities in the situations I have encountered in my life. This pattern of behavior is not something I ever sought or created; it resurfaces whenever I am in situations that activate the archetype. My work as a chemical dependency counselor and this book are, in part, products of this archetypal energy as it has driven me onward to fulfill obligations inherent in my personality. My psycho/physical makeup has engineered some significant obstacles, and yet passion of "the knight of faith" has been a primary motif and motive, which assist and inexorably direct me toward particular endeavors. I first experienced the passion to write this book at age twenty-three when I was traveling in Israel, Greece, and Western Europe. This calling or task was settled after spending about a week living with a philosophy professor in Munich, and where, incidentally,

I bought my first work of Jung. This inner force is relayed in a variety of terms—chi, the unconscious, libido, the Toa, God, etc. It has authored definite archetypal energies and abilities within me. I did not choose this mode of being; it surfaced after I discontinued use of drugs and alcohol at age twenty. When I began my abstinence, the latent archetypal energy of the knight of faith was liberated. I have found this is always the case when working with successful recovering addicts; some archetypal passions and interests surface, which replace the drug use as far as the guiding principles/motivations in their lives.

It makes it more difficult to get a hold of specific symbolic images and myths because they expand and change over time. Each archetype has opposites within it, and they always correspond and complement each other. The pairs of opposites inherent in the developing archetypes have separated over time as well. Like the parables of Jesus, the archetypes are more than one-dimensional and hold a variety of subtle and multifarious meanings. Archetypes are collective in the sense they are universal and passed down to everyone. In contrast, the collective conscious is our social ethos; that is, social rules and regulations that a particular culture accepts as binding, whether they are healthy or not. Like the physical instincts, which are passed on from generation to generation via the body, the archetypes are passed on from generation to generation via the psyche or soul. Archetypes are basic formations from which patterns of emotion and behavior exist within us and from which we draw on to cope with life. I'm not sure if it was Jung or someone else who termed these archetypes spiritual instincts; this is due to the fact universal principles or laws find their power in the archetypes. Again, these are basic structures that develop into forms from which inborn patterns of coping expand with repeated experiences in life. When searching the myths, we always trace principles that permeate life. Another example is the myth of the impetuous adolescent Icarus. In his insolence, ignorance and inflation, he failed to follow the counsel of his father and flew too close to the sun, and because the wax on his wings melted, he drowned; the principle is adolescents lack in life experiences and therefore are often arrogant, naïve, and impetuous without respect toward life's limitations and dangers.

We need to recognize the intensity of these archetypes and how they influence our ego-consciousness. The goal is to integrate these archetypal energies into consciousness, thereby divesting them of their apparent autonomous energy. The autonomous nature of the archetypes is induced by how they seize us through desires and thoughts, which often control and fascinate us. These desires and thoughts have their own energy and are highly charged with emotions. They seize our desires and feelings and extract urges, which, at times, we seem possessed. When we say, "What's gotten into him?" we are acknowledging the autonomous nature of the archetypes. If we fail to integrate these autonomous energies into our total personality, this energy continues to amass and imposes its pressure on our will. We also can recognize their autonomous nature when we act contrary to our conscious intent. Jung's stated goal is to integrate these contents consciously in such a way that they no longer are autonomous. Autonomous and unconscious, they overwhelm our will and can dominate our ego-consciousness to such a degree they overtake the entire personality with obsessions or psychosis. Archetypes are meant to be integrated and are not to control or take over neither our will nor personality. One frequent archetype perceived in psychotics is the savior archetype. This archetype captures the personality of the psychotic. The individual psychotic believes they are the savior, special messenger, saint, hero, etc. These archetypes frequent each mythology the world over. In contrast to the psychotic, the real heroes traffic with the gods (who represent an archetype) in a way that integrate their positive qualities and overcome their negative ones and then bring back a boon for the rest of humanity in some form.

We are all seized by specific archetypes in different chapters in our lives. These manifestations occur spontaneously and frequently as compensation to the attitudes and tendencies of particular one-sided conscious attitudes. As we integrate archetypes, new ones appear. There are groups of individuals from different cultures who seem to simultaneously be captivated by a new and developing archetype, which bursts upon history for collective purposes. I might remind you they have manifested themselves in positive or negative ways. Human consciousness seems to evolve and erupt in historical sequences. These evolving patterns of behavior encompass a much larger scope of possibilities in adapting to the life of consciousness. I have talked earlier of unlived aspects of our lives, and it is both spontaneous and compensatory archetypal manifestations that provide opportunities for expanding our life's experiences. When a particular archetype begins to assert its influence, they pose queries through difficult experiences that will require different adaptations or changes in our conscious attitudes, beliefs, and/or behaviors. *We do not create them or our consciousness.* Many are under the illusion that they create inner experiences. How naïve and inflated it is to believe that our ego-consciousness authors our thoughts, impulses, longings, abilities, etc. Life happens, both from within and without us, and the best we can do is act upon what we experience. Our creativity is fashioned as we participate with the archetypes present within us and evoked by experience.

The goal is to uncover and identify the intent of the unconscious archetypes through their symbolic images. What is this new experience that is going on within me? Let what is just be and proceed with caution. The intense emotions of the archetypes often lead to snap judgments and reactions, which are distorted and end up harming rather than resolving anything. Like Chicken Little, we often over react and formulate impetuous judgments, which are also archetypal in nature. I am as guilty of this as anyone. However, by letting whatever is just be for a period of time, we are able to get a better handle on what these symbolic images have to say to us, and therefore, we are able to integrate these archetypes in such a way that they do not control our will, personality, and choices, but rather, expand our consciousness. Only then do we need to make subjective judgments about whether these new experiences are good or bad, right or wrong, etc. Let there be no mistake, it is imperative we make subjective judgments as the moral universe of our collective unconscious demands it. But this is to occur only after we have identified what is going on inside us.

The numbers of archetypes are equal to the sum of all coping patterns we have accumulated throughout our species' existence. Again, we do not choose these urges or desires; they choose us. At the same time, there are a number of archetypes that must be integrated before a door is unfastened, and archetypes specifically geared to our uniqueness will seek consciousness. It is all the unique groupings of archetypes present in an individual that makes all of us different. It is also worth repeating that if we fail to integrate unconscious archetypal contents into our consciousness, these archetypes will grip us in ways that restrict and nullify our freedom to choose. We will become obsessed by the contents of the unconscious. What begins as an urge becomes an obsession. We all go through some problems or urges, which seem to appear out of nowhere and ensnare us by surprise. We are taken over by some desire or another. We are all potentially saints and sinners, capable of the most sublime or hideous of behaviors. The point is not to feel guilty, frightened, alienated, or inflated by these desires, but rather to accept these legacies from our psyche and then work to integrate or adapt them into our overall ego-conscious personalities. Some patterns we will want to nurture and others reject. However, initially, all archetypes that seek the light of consciousness have potential life-expanding qualities and need to be accepted. Subjective judgments are critical for morality and maturity, yet in the initial stages, we need to accept their presence. They are what they are; what is, is! *Every form of denial leads to compulsive behaviors and dysfunction eventually.*

There are those who stretch their consciousness to such creative degrees that they are adding to the collective archetypes. This usually occurs in mature individuals who have not avoided their inner and external experiences but rather have embraced each new experience as an opportunity to grow. As an individual's consciousness adapts to life, new and more constructive responses are acquired and shaped within the archetypes. If these more adaptive and constructive archetypal patterns are integrated by enough people, they will naturally be repeated until they become archetypes themselves. These unique individuals also take the time to contemplate and meditate on these experiences. It is then when sudden and new ideas, attitudes, and behaviors seem to pop into their consciousness. All impulses, thoughts, interests, etc., are either inherited or being created in combinations that occur within us or in the daily circumstances we experience. These new and more adaptive archetypes (motives, attitudes, beliefs, and behavior) will exist potentially in each new child. There are very few men and women in the world and history who are able to adapt to new realities by gradually cooperating with archetypal energies, thus creating new patterns of behavior (archetypes). These individuals have made great strides in integrating the given archetypes and thereby are capable of creating new archetypal behaviors and attitudes. These types are what Jung called manna personalities.

All the coping patterns that have been exhibited from the matrix of experience conspire to drive us back into less constructive adaptations. We shall ever be influenced by the more archaic and infantile urges no matter how many new and healthier coping patterns evolve. All coping patterns or primordial archetypes were at one time adaptive. An example might be polygamy. Having sex with as many partners as possible ensured the survival of the species, but with the population stabilized, there is no longer a survival need for this type of behavior. This primordial urge is no longer adaptive, in my opinion, and the archetype has since been differentiated and developed into more mature form where monogamy and the feelings and needs of our partners are essential within the context of our sexuality. Since more primitive archetypal patterns are also passed down to each new generation, both within our particular families as well as the greater human family, they will also always have to be dealt with in particular families and cultures. Specific patterns become so ingrained in families or cultures that patterns repeat themselves in each subsequent generation. It seems the cells in our bodies and with the psyche itself, memories and dynamics of our ancestors are passed on until they are broken by an individual or group of individuals in a subsequent generation. The sins and health of our parents are truly visited upon the children and children's children and continue to be passed down until particular individuals break these patterns during their life journeys. We all seem to struggle with what our parents struggled with, whether they talked about it and whether we like it or not. If we reflect a while, those burdens and archetypal issues that our ancestors were unable to overcome flourish in our behavior as well. Some families seem to struggle with responsibility, others addictions, others sexuality, others specific dynamics in marriage, still others with arrogance and inflation. This also includes certain innate abilities and strengths.

Many are able to overcome these barriers in their lifetimes and so pass on those healthier patterns to their decedents. I have been privileged to work with many clients who have broken very destructive patterns, replacing them with healthier and more adaptive coping patterns. It is important to recognize that there are innate variations built into a person from birth. The archetypes each person struggles with and calls for integration during the course of his or her life are somewhat predetermined. However, each archetype as it appears needs to be integrated, or trouble brews below the surface. Each person living is responsible to integrate these human motives or patterns of behaviors into their own psyche or soul, and I suspect the ones we failed to overcome will have to be wrestled with not only by our decedents but by ourselves after death. Some never integrate infantile survival instincts in mature ways and so go on acting in ways that were once adaptive but now have become archaic and maladaptive. Another example is those who continue to pursue violence and wars, which plague the human race to this day. In my view, violence is an outdated and archaic archetype. I have chosen nonviolence no matter the circumstances as a more adaptive coping mechanism and trust the outcomes to providence.

Emotions/Feelings/Pathos

No one ever talks about their feelings anyway
Without dressing them in dreams and laughter
I guess it's just too painful otherwise.

—Jackson Browne, "The Late Show"

Many are the wounds we accumulate over the course of a lifetime, with sadness, grief, loneliness, rejection, hurt, disappointment, failure, and weakness being our bedfellows.

All emotional reactions and feelings are evoked by experience and associated with the unconscious mind and housed in the archetypes or instincts. There is never an emotion that we unearth that is not associated with some dynamics within the archetypes or instincts and therefore the human condition. Archetypes and instincts are motivations, impulses, desires, inclinations, or behavioral tendencies where emotions are attached. Emotions are full of extraordinary energy and intricately connected to the energy within the archetypes (i.e., within the human psyche or soul). Emotions contain that which drives us this way or that. Our emotions are intricately linked to our thinking function and must never be severed from it. The core emotions are anger, sadness, guilt, fear, loneliness, hurt, joy, and inadequacy. We must all learn to channel our emotions positively. When someone pushes our buttons, what is happening is that a given situation has stirred complexes or archetypes, which are activated within us. These have yet to be integrated. Nobody can push our buttons if we don't have any buttons to push, but when we find ourselves in this position, we can use our overreactions to stop, reflect, and attempt to identify the activated complexes or archetypes at work and what aspects of these we have yet to incorporate. Almost all our feelings and the situations that evoke them are universal, that is others have gone through what we are going through. For instance, hurt, shame, and angry feelings are universal emotional responses to being rejected or belittled. Being rejected by others and specifically by fathers and mothers is an archetypal dynamic that is primordial in nature and contains potent emotions in our young. Pathos is suffering with deep emotional affects. As we grow, our emotions become more appropriately differentiated, and thus, less overwhelming. We can separate pain into their various states like hurt, loneliness, guilt, etc., and with this identification, the ability to work through these specific feelings occurs to the degree we learn to experience them without being overwhelmed by them. This is not an easy process, however, and takes time and effort.

The fact is we all experience deep emotional pain at different junctures in our lives, and these can leave lasting traumas within us. We will be exploring the problem of pain and suffering in the second section as we delve into Job and his archetypal sufferings. For the time being, I wish to emphasize the fact that the degree to which we all experience pain is contingent upon life experience and our willingness to feel the emotions associated with living out the archetypes. This takes a great deal of courage to endure our feeling as they surface and company with them as long as they linger in our psyche. Feelings come and go if we are willing to feel them honestly and entirely, but will not do so if we repress and deny them.

To use the above example of how emotions relate to the archetypes, let me take the primordial archetype of the father. We all have fathers who are imperfect. If we have been brought up in the West with religion, we often associate God only as a father figure without the balance of proper feminine energies. We may have a negative father complex as well as a positive one, meaning one either needs the father's love and blessings and/or one hates the father—all masculine energies get contaminated with the father archetype, and these contaminations are wrought with strong emotional reactions. The emotional reactions can be hatred, fear, rejection, loneliness, emptiness, guilt, or self-worth, pride, love etc., all associated with a negative or positive image of the father. Regardless of our reactions, the archetypal father image is influenced by our biological fathers. We inevitably project onto any concept of God as Father the emotional baggage left over from our biological fathers. Our image may or may not be accurate, but as we have discussed earlier, we do know each archetype has positive and negative aspects or energy. The negative father archetypal symbolic image is the ogre—a greedy, intolerant, cranky, judgmental jerk of a man, while the positive one is visible in the myths surrounding King Arthur—the king who is kind, courageous, just, and who initiates the great quest for the grail, which brings with it healing and wholeness and abundance and joy for everyone. Because humans have experienced negative and positive fathers, the archetype itself has taken on these characteristics. This leads us to the next major topic, projection.

Projection

Looking hard into your eyes
There was nobody I'd ever known
Such an empty surprise

Too feel so alone . . .

I don't know what you loved in me
Maybe the picture of somebody you were hoping I might be.

—Jackson Browne, "Late for the Sky"

Whatever resides within us is projected outwardly into the world around us. This is a normal process. The external world is filtered through all our beliefs, desires, attitudes, experiences, and behaviors. This includes our creativity in works of art, which are projections of that which lies within us. If we care about ourselves, we will project care and concern for others. If we hate ourselves, we will project hate and negativity into the world as well. What enlightens or defiles us begins from within us; perceptions and desires, beliefs and attitudes, which are then projected into the world. Every time we look into the night sky and recognize a constellation, our memory of the ancient's knowledge is an understanding of what our ancestors projected onto the stars. The external world exists but is never experienced objectively as we discussed in the introduction. It is experienced subjectively in that it is wrought through the filters of our inner perceptions and then projected back into the external world. We will never eliminate these projections, and in fact, they are a natural process that offers us opportunities to mature in understanding of both the inner and outer worlds. The real work is whether we are conscious of our projections or not, and are we willing and able to properly withdraw these, that is recognize what lies *within us* as opposed to what is external.

Projections begin as an unconscious content, whether it is something from our personal past (personal unconscious) or as an archetype (collective unconscious). Then it becomes attached to something external or out there. Unconscious projection is a primary function of the psyche where we presume what is inside us is out there. Projections can be positive or negative in that we subjectively assign value to external objects or circumstance. Projecting positive qualities can be individualistic or cultural; where we see positive qualities in, say, a celebrity or famous political or religious leader, like JFK or MLK. This person then can contain our own underdeveloped characteristics or values. What occurs is we look up to a person or set of circumstances for support and strength to fulfill our inner needs. Projection is also negative as natural defense mechanisms shield ego-consciousness from disagreeable desires and urges, which reside within us, and therefore, we attribute or project them onto others. An example of negative projection would be in a present relationship we project past rejection and abandonment we experienced onto the new partner. These unresolved issues from the past are initially unconscious. A new partner may not return a call right away, and we then project onto our new partner that he or she is abandoning us.

One of the most common forms of negative projection is where we project unconscious unwanted personality characteristics onto another. The stronger the reaction of dislike we have initially for a person we meet, the more the other person probably reflects our own unwelcome personality characteristics. We are destined to repeat these projections and view them as external to ourselves as long as they remain unconscious. These personal projections will remain unresolved and destructive as long as we fail to take ownership of them by making them conscious and adjusting to the truth about ourselves.

The most common form of projection is what is called transference where we project positive or negative qualities onto others that are projected patterns of our relationships to our parents. These patterns are primordial as the father and mother archetypes are two of the oldest archetypes as reflected in the historical experience of ancestor worship. Today, this dependency upon the parents is most often reflected in the adult, continuing to hold onto the parental bond to the detriment of their individuality and autonomy. Our needs to be taken care of and our desires for independence are wrapped up in the dynamics associated with our parents and are the most common archetypal dynamics found in therapy.

In both positive and negative projection, there is a lack of differentiation between subject and object, for the conscious mind is unaware of the difference when a projection occurs. The task at hand is to withdraw our projections (whether they stem from the personal or collective unconscious or both) by identifying consciously what is going on inside us and thereby beginning to take ownership and responsibility. Problems arise only when we are unconscious of our projections. The task at hand in withdrawing projections is determining what the unconscious is saying and trying to teach us about what resides within. In other words, what does the unconscious want us to be conscious of, and what inner conscious adaptations are required to resolve these projections. Taking an example from our discussion, it would be making conscious the fears of abandonment and facing the feelings and possibility of being alone and rejected/abandoned while remaining willing and open to grow in intimacy with our new partner. This kind of independence and interdependence is a dialectic and paradox whereby these opposites are held together in a tension, which induces anxiety and serenity with the willingness to be *intimate and alone* within a mature personality. I have much more to say about this process of change in the coming chapters.

All projections are destructive as long as they remain unconscious. All the repressed aspects of our nature that we deem negative are what Jung called the shadow archetype. The shadow gets projected whenever we hate, blame, or dislike others. This can occur with individuals or entire groups. We project our inner negative qualities (shadow) onto the opposite sex, another race, an individual, etc. The hated other now houses the repressed contents of our personality. Fears are often projected onto others for the purpose of overcoming the fear. Historically and on the collective or archetypal levels, men have long projected their repressed sexuality and femininity onto women. Women are, in fact, the objects of lust from within a man, but the projection is that women are seductive. The witch trials and their subsequent burnings at the stake murdered innocent women but kept repressed those unlived aspects of these men's natures that related to their sexuality and their own undeveloped feminine qualities. Women were murdered because of some men's unwillingness to accept their own sexuality and feminine qualities. This dynamic also played out in the early Christian Church, which initially accepted women in leadership roles as reflected by authentic Pauline letters. It was only later that male Christian leaders who wrote letters in Paul's name marginalized and then eliminated women leaders within the early church. Women leaders had obviously become a threat, or these male leaders would not have to write such retractions and additions to Paul's letters or epistles. This myopia and narrow-mindedness toward women and sexuality still exists in the Catholic Church today, where only supposed celibates males can become priests. Unfortunately, how many are pedophiles and/or really celibate? The choice to become celibate is an honorable one, and I have a close friend who has taken the vows of celibacy, charity, and poverty. He seems to have integrated his sexuality within his broad personality without the need to act it out physically.

Psychologically speaking, we develop broader awareness and healthier attitudes by making the unconscious conscious. We are then able to accept what is going on within us and take responsibility for it. Once we muster the courage to become self-aware of motives, issues, etc., then we are able to make the difficult choices to change and resolve these issues and develop latent archetypes into our entire personality. Externals are never the main problem, whether circumstances or other people, jobs, etc. *The problems are within us.* The arena where all depth lies is within our inner life, heart, psyche, or soul. One must root out the evil within oneself before we can see clearly and see the evil around us to be then capable of confronting it with the good that is within us. If we want to know how to identify our projections, all we have to do is observe our overreactions. Our feelings are always the easiest path to determining what projections and issues are in need of immediate attention. Whenever I overreact emotionally, I can be sure a repressed unconscious content is present and seeking the light of consciousness.

What's the Matter with Matter?
The Flesh/Instincts: A Birth to
Ego-Body-Consciousness

We each occupy the same space/time
Matter, antimatter, tangled like vines . . .

And the embers of Eden burn
You can even see it from space.

—Bruce Cockburn, "The Embers of Eden"

Introduction to Pairs of Opposites

Traditionally, matter and spirit are opposites, and I will be discussing the material world in this chapter. I will be exploring spirit in the second section of this book. What I have observed where matter predominates or is believed to be all that exists produces an antiseptic world devoid of meaning, passion, love, possibility, and hope. On the other hand, spirit devoid of matter is difficult to conceive as one without form, actuality, common sense, and an ability to appreciate the miracle world of the five senses. The second pair of opposites that proceeds from the conflict of spirit and matter is life/death. I will be delving into death in this section. Death without life is incomprehensible and life without death is one set up for megalomania, addiction, neurosis, stagnation, evil, convention, and boredom.

The Natural World

We are spirits in the material world.

—The Police, "Spirits in the Material World"

The natural world is the one science is concerned with and which our five senses register. In the present age, there is an obsession with matter and materialism related to the body and external objects. Ironically enough, in addition, there is a regrettable modern disposition where the natural world is largely invisible due to our addictions to electronics. It often takes a natural disaster to strike before many of us record the world around them, and then our TV stations cover the devastation with a sensationalistic fervor. In the meantime, a holistic approach is lacking as science cuts and slices everything into small bits for the purpose of measuring and studying its mechanisms. We need to value the natural world without being obsessed by it.

The natural world has been a source of mystery from our primordial past to the present. The natural world fills the imagination with wonder and terror precisely because we as *Homo sapiens not only have evolved from the natural world, but we are as much a segment of the natural world as anything else. Our bodies are made up of stardust.* Our ego-consciousness evolved out of the natural world. No amount of reductionism can eliminate the mystery and wonder of the natural world. Whatever theories that are proposed to understand the natural world have to take into account the perceptions/projections of the psyche; it is our consciousness that makes an effort to organize and theorize about the natural world.

Science recognizes a delicate balance exists within the ecosystem in which all the diversity in matter is interdependent. The natural world contains a unity in its diversity as everything impacts everything else in a great web of being. The seeds and sun and water feed the plants, which feeds the animals, which feeds other animals; on and on each intricate circulation nourishes and maintains the system that we call life or the natural world. The natural world is also shaped by the cleverness of humans fashioning objects into new creations both useful and destructive. For me, watching a carpenter work is akin to listening to a sublime symphony.

Few are able to appreciate the beauty and wonder of the natural world. Meanwhile, the natural world inspires and stirs us with images and metaphors that fill our imaginations with beauty, which has birthed the visual and literary arts. She inspires virtue and awe and wonder.

Let me quote Emerson for I could never express his metaphor of the natural world as a moral law any better:

> It has already been illustrated, that every natural process is a version of a moral sentence. The moral law lies at the center of nature and radiates to the circumference. It is that pith and marrow of every substance, every relation, and every process. All things with which we deal, preach to us. What is a farm but a mute gospel? The chaff and the wheat, weeds and plants, blight, rain, insects, sun—it is a sacred emblem from the first furrow of spring to the last stack of which snow of winter overtakes the fields. But the sailor, the shepherd, the miner, the merchant, in their several resorts, have each an experience precisely parallel, and leading to the same conclusions: because all organizations are radically alike. Nor can it be doubted that this moral sentiment which thus scents the air, grows in the grain, and impregnates the waters of the world, is caught by man and sinks into his soul. The moral influence of nature upon every individual is that amount of truth which it illustrates to him. (Ralph Waldo Emerson, *Essays and Lectures*, The Library of America, pp. 21–23, 29)

The natural world was close at hand until the industrial age commenced. We are in need of new metaphors to relate the world to our youth, yet there is a change at work as more and more people have again put time into experiencing the beauty and wonder of the natural world. Sitting in silence by a river, lake, or mountain can thrill the heart and stimulate the five senses and our imaginations.

The Flesh

I learned as a child not to trust in my body
I've carried that burden through my life
But there's a day when we all
have to be pried loose . . .

—Bruce Cockburn,
"Last Night of the World"

How come all my body parts so nicely fit together?
All my organs doing their jobs, no help from me!

—Crash Test Dummies,
"How Does a Duck Know?"

The human body is of intricate complexity as it regulates itself for the purpose of homeostasis, seeking a balance and consistency. The chemical makeup of our brain and body are miraculous, to say the least, and any of us who is not amazed at the miracle that is the body has lost touch with reality in its wonder and mystery. Our ego-consciousness is inexorably fixed to an awareness of the body. Ego-consciousness cannot be complete without the informed understanding of the body; therefore, a more accurate designation of our being would be to declare we have an ego-body-consciousness. I will be using the terminology of the ego, ego-consciousness, and ego-body-consciousness interchangeably throughout the remainder of this work. We learn to understand, abhor, trust, mistrust, and are enthralled by our bodies. *The body is where the five senses operate and link us to the physical world.* Consciousness has evolved with the body and brain. The basic aspects of physical and mental/psychological health are interrelated, and the fundamental principles include healthy nutrition and exercise. Our bodies have various needs for proteins and healthy doses of carbohydrates, minerals, and various vitamins as well as aerobic and muscle resistance exercises.

In America, the large consumptions of processed sugars have become a major obstacle in our physical and psychological health. Physical and psychological health cannot be separated. We know the complexity of the cerebral cortex could never have evolved without incredible amounts of protein extracted from meat. As we discussed in chapter 1, our earliest ancestors, the hunting societies, adapted to the environment by killing and eating meat. The consumption of meat extends back and predates *Homo sapiens'* appearance on earth. Therefore, the killing of animals for fresh meat was essential for the evolution of our species. In addition, though cells in the brain do not regenerate themselves, the numbers of brain cells is staggering, and new pathways of neurons are created with each new experience or interaction with the environment. The evolution of the body with its complex brain in *Homo sapiens* is an astounding development, and one which evokes awe and wonder in anyone who gives this much thought.

Matter's most developed and evolved forms that we are aware of is that of the human body, especially and most significantly the human brain. There is no doubt the most sophisticated level of the brain is the neocortex, where all the higher brain functions subsist, including intuition and imagination. These higher levels of functioning can prevail over the lower levels of the brain where conscious thought can impact the emotional centers of the limbic system or midbrain and the vegetative level where involuntary functions operate. The part of the brain that is connected to our instincts is the portion just above our spinal cord and is called the mesencephalm or midbrain. These core or deeper structures of the brains or limbic systems go through development like the rest of the brain and adapts in the first few years of life. This core functioning of the brain later becomes the least adaptive portion of our brains and where the instincts reside. Early childhood experiences affect this portion of the brain more than any other. If our mother is stressed during pregnancy and/or during breastfeeding, hormones infiltrate through the umbilical cord and milk and alter our ability to adapt in new ways to stress; it is imprinted in the midbrain. In addition, if we experience trauma early in life, these traumatic experiences are imprinted in these deeper structures of the brain, including the hypothalamus where aggression and feelings are centered. Again, they are more rigid than other portions of the brain, and they do not adapt well to new experiences. Shame, fear, and love are primary examples of the impact of early childhood experiences on these deeper portions of the brain and tend to become autonomic functions whereby they impact the entire central nervous system and inhibit later abilities to change and adapt to life. All early experiences affect the child's brains and therefore their ego-body- consciousness. It is said the first five years of life determine most of what makes up a person's personality.

At the same time, the body reeks of limitations, necessities, determinism, and death. To different degrees, we are all ashamed of our bodies functioning with its excrement, numerous odors, and gradual decay. Anyone perusing TV cannot help but observe the almost complete preoccupation of society with our five senses, looking younger and staving off the inevitable decline of the body. Materialism and its plethora of tributaries dominate our Western culture and is paraded in the TV programming and commercials, which expose an almost frenzied preoccupation with youth and virility. Men's channels are superficially focused for the most part on a materialism saturated with sex, control, money/power, and youth. As I look over TV stations dedicated to women, I notice they are inundated in superficiality, which prorogates the myths of romance and physical beauty. I am aware that in India, cable TV also is ubiquitous in the poverty-stricken areas, and the cable guy is one of the most powerful persons in the community. I would classify this as a neurosis due to the fact TV is used around the world as a means to avoid the anxiety and realities of both the complexity of life and reality of death.

The Body and the Instincts

Jung defined instincts as "uniform and regularly recurring modes of action and reaction." Instincts are impulses to act without conscious thought. They are also compulsive by nature and originate in the unconscious. The instincts are the primal motivating factor to our behavior during infancy and, for some, remain primary motivations throughout life. The instincts put pressure upon our budding ego-body–consciousness to act according to her wishes. Our basic instincts predominate at the archaic levels of human desires; they are automatic and mirror the animal kingdom, of which we are a part. We have inherited from our cousins, the monkeys and apes, our biological functioning, which is oriented toward survival. We eat, breath, drink, and copulate with impulses to live and survive and have our being. Yet we are animals imbued with consciousness. Our animal nature mirrors other primates. The alpha (first) male rules the group, and their status is primary; they rule and lead. These basic instincts are selfish and aggressive and seem to be bent on power and control. This is how we have survived as a species. The male has penchants to kill and have sex. His instincts are created primarily from the hormone testosterone. The female's basic instincts are toward nurturing and sex. Her predominate instinctual hormone is estrogen. Without both of these primal instincts, you and I would not exist in our present forms and probably not at all. It's vital to understand that each sex has some hormones and genes from the opposite sex. On the societal level, instincts for power and control have not changed from the primordial past. Our modern civilization has science, materialism, governments, and technology, which now rule our complex society. Therefore, money has become the tool for the alpha members. At present, we have the rich; they are our alpha males/females. They dominate those who have bought into a materialist world; economics has replaced the spear and the bow. It is important to recognize that this dominance only occurs in those who share these values and rules for power, dominance, and control.

All the instincts are bent on survival. We also have come to recognize that the body is the center of the erogenous zones and all physical instincts. Sexuality drives us, as does the other instincts, for water and food with the goal of survival. We have evolved out of nature and therefore a part of nature! The body is of the earth. Adam is taken from the Hebrew *adamah*, which means ground. In addition, at about fourteen or fifteen, we become capable of abstract thought and, with it, consciousness of death. The body stinks; it exudes fate. Sex traffics with the body to set up shame. Shame is associated with the body because of all limitations and the smells and noises that are exuded, which hint at our finitude. Sex, eating, and drinking are the quintessential biological functions. Psychologically, humans have craved for life after death, and when in the sexual act, it is interesting many invoke the name of God during orgasms. Most of is also want to feel we are loved as whole persons, not just sexual objects. We want to be viewed as whole; an ego-body- consciousnesses with an individuality, purpose, and uniqueness all our own.

Anger and Violence

With, without
And who'll deny it's what the fighting's all about.

—Pink Floyd, "Us and Them"

Anger and violence seem to have evolved to assure our species survival. Fight or flight. I'd like to add compliance as another survival instinct. Become aggressive, withdraw, or comply. Fear and anger are primeval instincts bent on survival. Survival of the species no longer is dependent upon the kind and degree of aggressive and/or fear responses as in our primordial past. The obvious problem is each of us has been imbued with instincts toward anger and violence. Fortunately, our brain has evolved with the cerebral cortex, which allows for the ability to go beyond the instincts as the primary motivating factors of behavior. We are capable of wide ranges of responses to conflicts. The problem lies in the individual as some are unwilling or unable to integrate their anger and violent urges within their overall personalities in such a way that alternative coping mechanisms are used to dispense with the anger and instinct toward violence appropriately. The daily news reflects the fact that mostly men have failed to use and summon the contents of their cerebral cortex adequately; anger and violence are still used to resolve conflicts. Too often, our anger turns to violence and becomes ineffectual and destructive. However, anger is also constructive when turned toward confronting injustices within ourselves and others and expressed in nonviolent ways. There are also many other roots of anger than instinctual ones bent on survival. We also get angry when people-pleasing others and when we fail to accept our needs as legitimate, when we've become spoiled and have not learned to let go of our wants and to tolerate legitimate suffering, when we use anger as a defense against pain, and when we project our anger onto others. Understanding the roots of anger is essential in our ability to accept and express it in constructive ways. We will also be exploring how anger and violence is a defense against shame and a reaction to our needs for security and worth.

Mental Health/Illness

The lunatic is in my head
The lunatic is in my head
You raise the blade, you make the change
You rearrange me 'til I'm sane.

—Pink Floyd, "Brain Damage"

Recent study of the brain has brought the question of what comes first, physical biochemistry or psychological factors in the understanding and causes of mental illness. Are we depressed, anxious, or psychotic because of physical brain chemistry or psychological factors? I believe the answer lies somewhere in between. When physically sick, it impacts our moods and perceptions. We also know psychological stress mixed with dysfunctional coping techniques cause physical and somatic symptoms. Likewise, some families have inherited biochemical problems, which make those members predisposed to certain physical and psychological problems. In addition, the way in which individuals face problems impacts brain chemistry. We do know that medication has mixed results, at times doing wonders with the mental health issues for individuals, and at other times making matters worse. There are so many different medications out there, and we know many people react differently to different medications and doses. It is a crap shoot when the medical profession makes specific medication prescriptions. Each individual is responsible to participate in their own healing and be open when trying these medications or alternative and more homeo-pathic modes of therapy to treat their mental health issues. There are also the most obvious modes of treatment, which include diet and exercise. I have seen medication do wonders for some while becoming a nightmare for others. Like any complex problem, there are no simple solutions or road maps that can guide each individual upon their path to understanding all of the causes and resolution of their personal trib-ulations and sufferings.

I do know the more we avoid truths about ourselves and live out lies, the more depressed or anxious we become, and the more vulnera-ble we are to all forms of mental illness. We need to learn to pay atten-tion to our bodies and how we perceive reality. We need to delve into the roots of our dysfunctional ailments and/or sufferings in the hopes we can take our sufferings and make use of it for constructive purposes. All illnesses are trials of one sort or another and opportunities to grow. They also offer us opportunities to learn to endure and by so doing build character. We can choose to use these illnesses to sort out truth from falsehood. The line between biochemistry and psychology is often muddled, and you are sure to hear all kinds of possibilities and advice along the way. Some of these problems seem never to be solved, while others take enormous amounts of time before diagnosis is coupled with proper treatment modalities to effect healing and health. Regardless of the cause, the suffering drones on, with temptations to give up the quest for healing. Perseverance is a virtue that is required by the very suffering we experience. The attitudes we take when struggling with mental and physical ailments begins with first identifying the symptoms, accepting the present state of affairs, and then learning to adapt as best we can. By adapting to what we know, we begin the process of transforming our illnesses. It is never easy to differentiate illnesses, which we are to surrender to our fate and persevere in a search for healing or seek immediate healing. Where are we to draw the line between them? For the seriously ill, we often struggle to understand if we should try to fight our illnesses and live or accept death. Our unconscious mind holds the key to how we are to approach illness, sickness, and healing. When facing mental health issues, we have to sort it out the best we can, and hopefully, with patience and faith, allow fate to steer us in healthy directions. I have found the most difficult of the alternatives is usually what's required for my own development. In working with others, it seems those that naturally surrender and want to give up are usually required to fight on and with great effort seek healing, while those who innately battle tribulations are often mandated or forced to surrender and accept their illnesses.

In addition, all habits, attachments, and addictions alter brain chemistry to the degree it becomes difficult to change because the chemical reactions of our neurotransmitters and neuroreceptors become dependent upon these behaviors for normal functioning. When any behaviors are altered, the brain must also alter its chemistry to accommodate these changes. It is the interim period of stress that makes changes tricky and problematic. The point is that change is complicated and problematic, but with time and patience, it does happen.

The mind-body problem has long been a primary focus of philosophy. Is there a duality, or is the mind/body essentially a unity? If they are united, is one a precursor to the other? And what is the connection, if any? It seems behind experiences of duality there is a unity, but what that nature is seems to me to be pure speculation. For our purposes, what is crucial is both valued and accepted responsibly. Our health is impacted by our thinking, and our thinking is impacted by our health. Each is tied to the other in some form of dialectic, and beyond this, I don't think we can say with any assurances.

Ego-Body-Consciousness

I, I, I, oh here I stand before me
But something's out of place here
My mind's eye is missing from my body
Well I know it's there but I can' see where.

—Crash Test Dummies, "Here I Stand Before Me"

We have arrived at the reality that we have an ego-body-consciousness that must interact with the external world of experience. We have a body, and our bodies with their instincts are part and parcel of our conscious awareness. We need to allow for our body and its instincts without allowing them to be our sole motivation. Prior to developing more depth to consciousness, the body and its instincts must be accepted and integrated. In addition, our collective birth to consciousness forever cut us off from the automatic nature of the instincts in regard to our motivations and behaviors. We are conscious and capable of making choices—using our will regarding our beliefs, attitudes, and behavior. The fact remains we are driven by many disparate and conflicting urges; some of which are constructive and healthy and others destructive and unjust.

Death

I don't know what happens when people die
Can't seem to grasp it as hard as I try
It's like a song I can hear playing right in my ear
But I can't sing
I can't help listening.

—Jackson Browne, "For a Dancer"

Death visits us all, and not by appointment. I once worked with a dying client who relapsed prior to obtaining a liver transplant, destroying any lingering hope of his living much longer. His treatment centered on accepting his impending death; courage and acceptance were crucial for him to remain sober. He seems to have made the choice to leave this world with dignity. I heard he had died sometime later and do not know if he died abstinent or not—I suspect he did judging from the effort he put forth in treatment. The therapeutic process necessitated he face his death without any denial; so prevalent is our society that he seemed to do without flinching. He modeled for me an acceptance of death I hope to emulate when my time comes to lay my body down one last time. I tried to work with all my clients on facing their death and using this to help them crystallize the meaning of their lives. The denial of death is probably the most universal and destructive deception and problem posed for us in the West. *The fact is, we will all die and need to face and integrate this into our philosophy of life.*

What's that you say?
You're bound for the graveyard?
Oh I wish you well . . .

You know I'm going to miss you when you're gone . . .

See you soon
Maybe tomorrow
You never can tell . . .

Wish I could hide away.

—Creedence Clearwater Revival,
"(Wish I Could) Hideaway"

We have briefly explored consciousness as it is separated from the unconscious and body. Let's look into this separation and its consequences.

Separation at Dawn

Riders on the storm
Riders on the storm
Into this house we're born
Into this world we're thrown
Like a dog without a bone
An actor out alone
Riders on the storm

—The Doors, "Riders on the Storm"

Introduction

The pair of opposites discussed in this chapter is separation/union. Union is taken up throughout the second section. When separation is overvalued, loneliness, antisocial behavior, and compartmentalizing persist. When union is overvalued, the real world of suffering, personal responsibility, and abstract thinking is devalued, and life assumes unrealistic hues.

Separation, Aloneness, and Abandonment

I'm a half a world away here
And I had sworn to go it alone . . .

Oh, this lonely deeps and holy way.

—REM, "Half a World Away"

Along with the separation of consciousness from the unconscious, we become aware of our separation from other objects (i.e., each other). We are alone in our ego-body-consciousness. In normal development, we come to recognize our physical bodies as separate from Mommy. We are separated from others, both externally through the body and the inner worlds of others. We become aware and discern we are alone and trapped within the confines of our ego-body- consciousness. A disharmony develops, which consists of being separated from others and is marked by the experience of dualism; where there was one, now there is two. Without separation, there is no differentiation; without differentiation, there is no consciousness. Our ego-body-consciousness has an irrevocable split from within and without; we are separated from parts of *ourselves* (consciousness and unconsciousness) and *other objects* in the environment.

With this prevalence of separation come the inevitable experiences of loneliness and abandonment. It seems everyone is consigned to go through these most difficult of emotions, no matter how caring and loving the parents are, because the fact remains we are left to ourselves and alone in our ego-body consciousness. Nobody can hold our hand throughout our childhood and life as we each wake up alone with our thoughts, passions, and longings, whether there is someone next to us or not. These feeling of abandonment vary, of course, depending upon the dynamics of family life and our genetic heritages. It is my opinion that these experiences of abandonment and loneliness are two of the most painful and difficult feelings to negotiate throughout our lives and what drives our personalities, especially in our early years.

Our separation, with its contingent consciousness, comes with it both blessings and curses. The blessings include the freedom of choice or free will and insight (i.e., we can peer to see what is within us). These blessings also include the gifts of experiences and the recognition that wonder, mystery, horror, and complexity are inherent in the human condition. The curses include disparate longings, yearnings, loneliness, unfulfilled desires, failures, impotence, and death. We navigate through our lives facing or denying these truths. I made the decision in my early twenties to attempt to not run and hide from reality. Reality and truth are painful. On the other side of our separateness, with its appendages of fear and pain, reside joy, peace, and the power to change and become whole. There are few that can testify to this because so few venture into loneliness and face the reality of our innate separateness. Alas, I have met very few who are willing to endure the truth of our separateness long enough to set the stage for true inner freedom.

There is no getting around our experiences of separation and the conscious experience of feeling abandoned. We are alone in our bodies. It can be awfully quiet or noisy in there! Sex and breastfeeding are the closest we can come to another physically. Emotional and physical distances can be extremely painful, which is why some of us cannot stand to be alone and/or may cling to others like a drowning person to their rescuer. We can seek intimacy with others, which is an innermost ingredient in maturation, but that does not guarantee its realization. Ironically, we can feel lonely around others and be alone and feel intimate while being alone.

Who has not experienced separation? Most everyone wrestles with this issue one way or another. Most are forced separations, like when we are young our parents go off to work or someone moves away, a parent dies, or a romantic relationship ends against our will. Going it alone is difficult, and few are willing to venture into this unknown out of their own free will. Life is full of ten thousand deaths. Unfortunately, it usually takes a crisis before we are usually willing to let go, act, and/or change. We all need to be separate to the degree we find meaning by listening to our still and quiet inner voice. Accepting separation is difficult as many losses/deaths are accumulated along the way. Every one-year-old goes through this stage, and some never get past it. My children all have gone through that stage where my legs and their arms become one appendage. "Don't go, Daddy" with an orchestra of tears.

It does not end in childhood. The losses of friends, objects, and the illusion of being in control all need to be accepted before any realistic stage of maturity can be accomplished. The loss and end of relationships is always painful due in part to fears and experiences of being abandoned and separated. The fact is many more relationships fail, and we lose many more friends than we maintain. The primary separation that is required by the psyche is from the comfort and security of our parents.

I have worked with many individuals stuck in clinging to parents for financial or emotional support when the fact is this support is, bit by bit, draining their sense of worth and psyche of much-needed independence. There are times when this situation is complicated by maliciousness on the part of the parents. Regardless, each of us must learn to become responsible, separate, and alone within ourselves. This brings us full circle by winding us back around to the historical antecedents and our primordial struggle to forget we are cousins with the apes for this actuality reminds us we are mortal and, essentially, alone within the confines of our ego-body-consciousness.

We have now come across the uniqueness/dependency dialectic. Can you be at peace with solitude and separateness? Are you comfortable with your needing others? This seems to depend upon our ability to befriend and follow our own path wherever and/or whenever it leads and accept that you need others to survive. If we can become our own friends and heed the small still voice within, aloneness and separateness is a joy. The healthy aspect of our separateness or individuation is that I am responsible for myself, and therefore, no one else is responsible *for* me and vice versa. The beauty and genius of this belief and attitude is there is nobody to blame for my circumstances, failures, defects, etc., but myself, *and* I am also not responsible for others' failures, mistakes, etc. I cannot fix anyone, and nobody can fix me. Under normal circumstances, no other human being has any power over me, excluding that which I willingly surrender. I never presume or wish any longer to take responsibility for another adult who is capable of taking responsibility for themselves. I know when others are dependent upon us, we lose respect for that person. I respect the autonomy and separateness of each person and try to guard this whenever I can; others need to make their own choices. No matter which way the dependency travels, it is destructive and degrading. My separateness is therefore, in this instance, a blessing. However, this does not preclude us from being responsible *to* others. There is a great abyss situated between appropriating responsibility *to* and *for* self and others. Responsibility to someone else is being honest, trustworthy, respectful, caring, thoughtful, etc. Responsibility for someone else is attempting to take care of them and doing for them what they can do for themselves. Intimacy, on the other hand, grows in the soil of those psyches, which are autonomous and fully developing their own capacities and capabilities.

What do I do when I'm alone? Who am I apart from my family, friends, and lovers? How am I similar to others, and how am I distinctive? These questions will hunt us down until we find some answers, and the answers change as we grow and mature.

I've said too much,
I haven't said enough.

—REM, "Losing My Religion"

I have worked with many clients where the necessity is to accept their inherent aloneness and create an authentic friendship with themselves. Many therapists mistakenly rush in and assume their clients need others, and it turns out to be counterproductive. In those instances, the person has limited themselves and their choices to an extreme degree while becoming dependent on others. They have confined their freedom and become prisoners in their need for others and been converted into nonassertive individuals. They are bogged down in the collective and have yet to solidify their uniqueness within the context of their autonomy. Only when one has acquired some autonomy is one ready for intimacy and have something of substance to add and bring to relationships. There are times when the need is not to make friends, but rather to become friends with ourselves. These times often come after a relationship ends, and we are left with our separateness and aloneness. However, there are also many opportunities to face our separateness and aloneness within the context of relationships. We have to recognize our loneliness and separation, and aloneness is not due to lacks in our relationships, but to our unwillingness to accept our inherent separateness and become at ease with being alone with ourselves. Many pursue extramarital affairs, cutting themselves off from learning this valuable lesson and causing no end to pain and suffering with their mates.

On the other hand, there is the one-sidedness of being too separate from others that is equally destructive. That is, some are stuck in their uniqueness and independence. Though fewer in number, they overvalue independence and become disconnected to others and the world around them. They emphasize their uniqueness at the expense of connecting with others; that is they fail to understand or accept their health dependency on others. They become arrogant and selfish while they emphasize how they are different. This one-sidedness leads to a lack of compassion for others; they discard the common human condition, which binds us together, including vulnerability and suffering. They need more understanding and more relatedness to the pain and suffering common to the human condition. A solid connection with suffering inherent in the human condition and within the hearts of their neighbors tends to coerce arrogance out of its brooding enclaves. Those one-sided on independence need more social contacts and familiarity with how their experience of suffering is common with the rest of humanity.

> Everything to share,
> Everything to hide . . .

> —REM, "Radio Song"

The reality of our existential separation causes anxiety. I want to move now into the realms of the pervasive experiences of anxiety.

Do You Dread Dread?

Every nerve in my body
Is so naked and numb
I can't even remember
What it was I came here to get away from . . .

—Bob Dylan "Not Dark Yet"

Introduction

The pair of opposites we will be wrestling with is anxiety/serenity. Serenity will be discussed in the second section. Serenity without anxiety is superficial and counterfeit, while anxiety without serenity is nihilistic and immobilizing.

Fear and Anxiety

Racing alone in his fright.
Tell me why. Tell me why.

Is it hard to make arrangements
With yourself
When you're ole enough to repay
But young enough to sell?

—Neil Young, "Tell Me Why"

Anxiety is the afterbirth of our newborn ego-body-consciousness. We have separate bodies and minds. We are separated from others within the confines of ego-body- consciousness. We become aware of disparate and enigmatic longings and yearnings, which often percolate in the human heart but remain unfulfilled. From possibility to actuality, there exists a chasm of uncertainty where anxiety finds its residence. With consciousness and abstract thought comes the capability of understanding that possibilities exist wherein anything can and does happen! "Shit happens." Anxiety is a healthy response to facing the truth of our condition in the world. The fight, flight, or compliant response to threat is part and parcel of our instincts to survive. Our body's biochemistry reacts to uncertainty and real threats because they both exist within the confines of our experience. In addition, our ego-body-consciousness is now capable of grasping painful truths; that is we can lose anything and everything. We can't control possibilities. Life happens to us and is full of mystery and terror, wonder and horror.

Failure, loss, and the temporal nature of our life rings in reflective minds like fire alarms. In effect, we are capable of recognizing that an abyss exists between what may be and what is. We are all anxious of possibilities with its inherent uncertainties; we are afraid of what happens or could happen. These truths author anxiety. The more in touch we are with reality, the more we will experience this existential anxiety.

There are anxiety disorders of all kinds, including phobias, panic attacks, OCD, (obsessive-compulsive disorder), anorexia, hypochondria, sleeping problems, and mood and adjustment disorders. Anxiety's focus is fear of and on the future. We want to know and control this future, yet anxiety communicates the impossibility of our control over outcomes. There is always some new conspiracy or apocalyptic scenario giving form to our anxieties and fears. For those sensitive souls who recognize the insecurity-anxiety authors, it often inhibits the ability to attend to the needs of today, especially those of the poor, the outcast, the orphan, the widow, and the incarcerated. Prominent is the anxiety and fears of rejection, abandonment, death, and failure. At the bottom appears to be the fear of death. I have completed a number of continuing education courses on anxiety disorders, and not once was death discussed! The denial of death within our culture is pervasive and neurotic. This most obvious of all the causes of fear and anxiety is the one least understood, faced, or talked about. Death is the ultimate venture into the unknown where we have absolutely no control.

There are times when anxiety seems to be a state that is free-floating or general in nature. I disagree with this surface perception and believe there are specific uncertainties and reasons for our angst. I believe we have just not taken the time to identify them. All anxiety ultimately stems from our impotence in the face of the mystery and horror of creation with its endless possibilities. We are so weak and powerless that we cannot keep our heart beating. There are many involuntary muscles of which we have no control. We are dependent upon so many things for our very life. The body is so intricate, and yet something can go wrong at any moment. We have truly been cast from the Garden of Eden and the tree of life, separated and alone in our ego-body- consciousness. We are now capable of wrestling with our separateness and aloneness. There is no superhero who can save us from ourselves and our eventual separation from our bodies. We are impotent in the face of creation. We are anxious because we are powerless and weak in the face of so many possibilities. The natural inclination is to deny these truths. My goal is not to inspire fear for I believe we must fight it like the plague, but to deny it is to give it more power. What is, is, so to speak, and we must face reality before we can effectively hope to deal with it.

Unfortunately, many of us choose to avoid our fears and anxieties and the self-knowledge they could engender. The sleepless nights have crept up and pounced on all of us as the inner turmoil and dialogue can't be turned off. Lying in bed, our mind seems to take on a life of its own as we struggle to turn it off. We go over and over the issues in our head, which need to be faced. We are afraid of the responsibilities. The night haunts us as we stare at the ceiling; the night slips away. I will be tired tomorrow, can this problem be fixed, what's going to happen? What ifs reverberate off the walls and ceilings of our bedrooms.

Projection of Anxiety and Fear

The forms that we use to deny these basic truths take on horrific proportions. Some project all their anxiety onto others. Hence, we have prejudice and hatred, wars, and genocide. If I can find something outside myself to focus and blame my anxiety and fears, I never have to look too close within myself and find lurking all sorts of fears and weaknesses I don't want to accept. *Hatred is born of fear!* Because of anxiety we avoid, we act these out in neurotic and self-destructive patterns. We can go on denying our weaknesses, anxieties, and mortality, but at what cost? I am in accordance with Earnest Becker's thesis that much of human evil is caused by our denial of death, weaknesses, and our ultimate powerlessness in the face of creation. Our history is littered with examples of fundamentalists of all kinds, especially in religions—projecting fears of their ultimate death, sexuality, differences, uncertainty, and weaknesses onto others. Fear is evil. These anxieties create an "us against them" mentality. This also includes all "-isms," where barriers are set up between us and the other. We must remove evil within ourselves prior to confronting it in others or institutions. That means removing fear from our hearts and minds. Rather than blame others, the true prophets wrestle with their own anxieties and pain and fear while *their messages are aimed at themselves as well as others.*

The Quest for Self-Knowledge: Ignorance Is Not Bliss

There's a skeleton in everybody's closet
I can think of one or two in my own room
But I would like to introduce them both to you

116

And shake their bony hands and so dispel the gloom
And the things I fear just wouldn't seem so near.

—Crash Test Dummies, "The Ghosts That Haunt Me"

For many of us it seems we would rather avoid our anxieties and fears than face them. The self-knowledge this would engender in facing these truths would be earth shattering and transforming. Thus, many of us chose to remain unconscious and ignorant of the roots of our fears and anxieties. However, the unconscious mind seeks the light of consciousness and will extract a price if consciousness does not accommodate. We become bound by the chains of our dread and denial. Life asks much from us. We all have our crosses to bear. Like the police at a speed trap, the unconscious pursues the offender until they pull over and face the charges. Our unconscious initially speaks to us with a still, quiet, but insistent voice by reminding us of our issues. She does so by setting us up with the same problems over and over again until we begin to pay attention to them. If we fail to heed her hints and truths, she will become more and more persistent until a consequence mounts, and some crisis or another is visited upon us. We need to face our current dilemmas, or we cannot "pass go and collect two hundred dollars." The unconscious will nudge, gently insist at first, and then if not heeded, finally take on the face of the enemy. The unconscious creates some complications and consequences from which we may or may not recover. It all depends on us and our willingness to hear and respond to the truths she delivers. If we do so and face our issues and fears, we will indeed dispel the gloom because when we face ourselves and overcome fears, there is a natural lifting of negative energy.

Death and the Unknown

My days are numbered . . .

Won't you come to my funeral when my days are done
Life's not long so I hope when I am finally dead and gone

117

You gather around
When I am lowered into the ground
When my coffin is sealed
And I'm safely six feet under . . .

—Crash Test Dummies, "At My Funeral"

As I have said repeatedly, death is the ultimate fear or anxiety because it discloses our finitude, inadequacies, and inherent weaknesses and the ultimate end to our ego-body-consciousness. Death is the great unknown where we have no control whatsoever. For this reason, we deceive ourselves and avoid dealing with our mortality and integrating death's reality in our philosophies of life. The reality of our mortality will continue to crop up throughout our lives through the inevitable workings of fate until hopefully, we come to terms with our own death. Acceptance is a better pill to swallow, but very sweet to the stomach. This process is unique to each of us and needs to be nurtured in the quietness and silence of the heart.

Nobody knows the existential dread
Of the things that go on inside
Someone else's head . . .

—Van Morrison, "Meaning of Loneliness"

We now turn to the will to choice and how it relates to our discussion of the basic human condition.

Will, Will Power, and the Will to Power

But all I'm thinkin' is
I'm the same old story same same old act
One step up and two steps back . . .

Another battle in our dirty little war
When I look at myself I don't see
The man I wanted to be
Somewhere along the line I slipped off track
I'm caught movin' one step up and two steps back

—Bruce Springsteen, "One Step Up"

Introduction

The archetypal pairs of opposites discussed herein are free will/determinism and intricately related certainty/uncertainty. Determinism is the opposite of free will and believes *everything* is predetermined with a cause, which can be ascertained if studied long enough. The execution of our will without some determinism is a prescription for megalomania, and utter delusion and determinism without free will lays the groundwork for living the role of victim.

The Will to Choose

You are locked into your suffering and your pleasures are the seal.

—Leonard Cohen, "Stories of the Street"

As we have already discussed, the birth of consciousness separates us from the original unity of the infant's unconscious harmony. We gradually become conscious and capable of making choices *with our will* regarding our beliefs, attitudes, and behaviors. While instincts exert not an inconsiderable sway, they are not the only basis for our actions. Animals adapt to the environment with little consciousness and therefore without much choice. Nature has seen fit to produce human "beings," which are complex and able to adapt to a far greater number of possibilities than other creatures on the earth. We become conscious of ourselves, and we choose. Our will is that which steers our path in one direction or another. Our brains are set up to either attend to a particular stimulus or ignore it. Our will is what decides between these two alternatives. The word *decision* originally meant "to divide" or "cut in two," as our decisions slice life into two (both from F. Huxley, *The Way of the Sacred*, p. 20). Our decisions are creating a certain reality every time we make a choice. It is interesting to note that the same family of words that comes from the word *divide* includes *vision, wisdom, history*, and *idea*. This makes perfect sense because it is our will and its choices that create history, vision, wisdom, and ideas. We make choices, which divide possibilities into actuality. Without separation, there is no differentiation; without differentiation, there is no consciousness; without consciousness, no freedom to choose. Therefore, though separation and division are painful and wrought with anxiety, it seems necessary for choice and growth in consciousness.

We need to value both sides of every pair of opposite or both choices in a given situation. Every choice we make creates a certain "reality of the moment." One day life may insist we choose to share something, and the next, keep it to ourselves. Both choices are to be actualized by an ability to be flexible and make the choice that best serves wholeness/truth within a given context. We need to choose our values and then try to live consistently within these beliefs. I wake up alone with my consciousness every morning, and no matter the outward circumstances present in my life, I need to take responsibility for my choices. The truth reveals itself in each given situation. Are we willing to sacrifice what we want for the truth?

Possibility, Uncertainty, Certainty, and Choices

Well yesiree Bob them there's the breaks
That's how it is my friend don't make no mistakes

Man has to take some action all of the time . . .

Man has to create karma that's the way it is
Man has to keep going way beyond his will . . .

—Van Morrison, "Man Has To Struggle"

By the very nature of the human condition, we are thrust into a plethora of possibilities and choices. While animals do not recognize the uncertainty in a given situation because they lack the complex conscious awareness we humans do, individuals are capable of such differentiations and therefore can become aware that anything can happen (uncertainty). History has exposed humankind's desire for certainty in our futile and endless attempts to control objects and events. Human propensities toward superstitions, conspiracies, oppression, authority, torture, mental health dysfunction, etc., all testify to our desires to be in control and our inability to secure control. We strive for security and control wherever we think we can find it, however pathetic and fraudulent it is. The subterfuges we create are limitless, and it would take forever to make some sort to comprehensive list. We hide behind everything imaginable, lie to ourselves about it, and believe our own lies (self-deception). Ambiguity and uncertainty have become anathemas while self-deception the counterfeit panacea in an endless array of fabrications, fictions, distractions, and addictions. I plan to explore these themes in the next few chapters.

The fact of the matter is life happens to us! Despite our desire to have certainty and therefore security, life explodes into our consciousness both from within and without. Outwardly, "shit happens" as the slogan bears witness, and we can only, at least initially, choose to attend to these external circumstances or ignore them. Shit happens regardless of our desires. Inwardly, we also have inner reactions, thoughts, impulses, feelings, desires, passions, certain attitudes and beliefs, etc., which interact with the external environment and our ability to make choices. If complete certainty existed, there would be no choice because everything would already have been determined. The need to make choices guarantees a certain amount of freedom. The degree and quality of our choices and, therefore, our true freedom depends upon the degree in which we accept uncertainty and the anxiety it engenders. At the same time, a definite degree of certainty does exist within universal laws that dot the landscape of the known universe. For example, it is certain that if I jump off my roof, I will fall downward due to the physical law of gravity. There are many laws in the universe that we are bound by and through which we are capable of learning the hard lessons of life. However, the choice remains whether I adapt to these laws or not. As I adapt, the laws of uncertainty continues to rock our world. We can try to prepare for the unknown through seeking equanimity of spirit, but this does not control outcomes in any way.

When we make any choice, the opposite choice remains in the realm of possibility. The complementary choice or alternative is hidden and remains an unreality until conjured up by choice. The courageous response then is to consciously make choices and take responsibility for the choices while remaining open to choosing the opposite alternative. The inner tension created by such an open attitude is enormous. We naturally seek a state of homeostasis with security and stability. However, the opposites naturally contain a great deal of tension. These tensions cry out from our nature for quick and easy solutions and decisions. However, it usually takes patience and a cautious attitude to allow for an inner struggle between possibilities to play itself out before a decision is prudent. So many times I have come across a truth and applied it at the wrong time, in the wrong circumstances, with the wrong people. We need much maturity and poise to be capable of choosing whatever is required by life at a particular moment in time. The *true choice for us* needs to overshadow by what is convenient.

No manner of intellectual masturbation will resolve these inner struggles. Resolution of these tensions takes time and a willingness to be patient and act cautiously upon either possibility. None of us will always make the right choices, so mistakes must be taken into account as we struggle with possibility and the multiple choices that bang upon our doors daily. The only mistakes are those we don't learn from. We need to remember only those engaged passionately in life will inevitably make mistakes. This is part and parcel of living and will always be so. Nevertheless, the truth will require one or the other responses to act. Fortunately, we also have the gift of reflection and self-awareness, and therefore, when we make a wrong choice, we will know soon enough by the negative consequences and/or lack of inner peace the decision generates. We are then capable of changing our choices and correcting them. If we take time to reflect upon our choices and notice the inner and outer ripples established by our decisions, we will find our answers from that quiet and still inner voice, which demands our attention. Peace will eventually come when we have made the right choices and/or acknowledged the mistakes so the situation can eventually be corrected and resolved. We need to keep in mind that the opposite choice is always possible and may be require at any time. This seems to me to differentiate those individuals who are really moving forward from those who remain stuck. Are you willing to live with the inner tensions and/or willing to loosen your grip or let go of some delusions and wants altogether, *choosing rather the truth and therefore whatever life seems to require?* We have now entered some difficult territory as this inner tension requires emotional, intellectual, and physical suffering during and after which the decision-making process is made because all choices confront our desires for security and certainty. I need to know myself. To know myself, I must be capable of self-reflection and be willing to make difficult decisions based on the truth that self-reflection discloses. Choices always have consequences, and we need to keep on keeping on and repair the damages as we go. Freedom comes with a heavy cost, and that cost is responsibility.

The Will's Limits

You're fathers gone a hunting
For the beast he'll never bind.

—Leonard Cohen, "Hunter's Lullaby"

Although we have choices, these are often limited. These limitations include external and/or internal ones. Our choices are over certain alternatives and rarely over the alternatives themselves. As discussed earlier, our brains are set up either to attend to a stimulus or ignore it. This process goes on; we choose what to attend to, and this opens up new choices. We do not create the alternatives themselves, but rather life does.

The will bends our ego-body-consciousness in precise directions, and the process of what we become is on. We are all in the process of becoming, and our choices are what dictate what we become. We are a conglomeration of all the choices we make.

Our ego-body-consciousness is unable to summon truth by itself. Our will, like our mind, operates more like a channel. The mind and will's power have limits. It seems to me, we use our mind to seek understanding and our will to choose what directions our understandings take. Our will has a limited amount of energy designated to its function. We all have experienced a will to change something in our lives, only to fail. This limitation of our will power demonstrates the fallacy that "where there is a will, there is a way." That is due to the fact that will power is limited in what it can accomplish on its own. We struggle to become what we want to be; one step forward, two steps back, or hopefully, two steps forward and one back. We are left with the necessity to choose. Yet we struggle to bring our minds, bodies, and will together and forge some kind of harmony. Our mind reaches to the stars, but our will seems bogged down, and we are often unable to bring them together into some form of peaceful coexistence. Self-knowledge is crucial, but not enough to make changes. It seems we have two wills and two minds where conflicting desires vie for supremacy. We therefore find lurking within us a divided psyche.

The Divided Soul or Psyche

I fought with my twin
That enemy within
Till both of us fell by the way.

—Bob Dylan, "Where Are You Tonight?
(Journey through Dark Heat)"

We now move me into the topic of the divided psyche, an inner war that we all have to battle. The soul is at war with itself as competing desires contend with each other, and the battle extends into the precincts of our will. Part of us wants one thing, and another part of us wants the opposite; we often find ourselves ambivalent or torn. Both pairs of choices/opposites are theoretically valid, but we make choices that convert possibility into actuality. These inner conflicts produce a great deal of suffering in the forms of guilt, shame, pain, mental anguish, confusion, and ambivalence. It seems often we have two conflicted wills, desires, and minds vying for supremacy. In addition, there are always consequences for the choices we make.

The goal of the process is to overcome these inner battles so as to experience a subsequent unity and inner peace within ourselves by making a right choice within a given situation. We are of two minds very often, and the imperative to decide and then choosing of one mind over the other. We recognize these battles and inner conflicts cause a great deal of suffering because we are literally split in two; one mind wants to set off this way and another the opposite direction. It is easy to be a witness to these inner wars for the addict as a part of the inner self wants to indulge the addiction and another to be set free from it. What most fail to realize is we all are attached and addicted to one thing or another. If you doubt me, try pursing solitude and silence for an extended period of time while turning off that electronic device—TV, music, computer, or cell phone and take note of your inner turmoil. Whatever your creature comforts, let them go for a period of time and observe your reactions. You will find yourself at war as one mind will cry out for your technology, and another will try to hold the line and just be in your solitude. We have become seduced by our creature comforts and jaded in our constant gratification of our attachments to these temporal aims.

Probably the two most universal inner wars are (1) whether to share a particular experience or keep it to oneself and (2) whether to face a particular difficulty or run away from it. The more we run away, the less conflicted we may *feel*. That doesn't mean we are not divide within, but rather we are in denial to the degree that all the inner turmoil is reduced as we simply avoid the difficulty. Once we decide to face a difficulty, many more inner divisions will surface.

The goal is to overcome and resolve these inner wars where we will experience some inner peace with a decision that lies on one end of a particular pair of opposites. We also must keep in mind what is one situation or time in one's life calls for one decision, while at another time, its opposite will need to be fought with and sometimes chosen.

To resolve these inner wars, first we need to entertain both options as honestly as possible. Addicts are encouraged to accept their addictions for life because it's an acknowledgment that the inner war will continue in one form or another throughout their life (often the addict will simply switch addictions; for instance, from drugs to gambling or work).

Resolution of a particular difficulty/inner war can come quickly or happen over a long period of time. In addition, the inner peace that comes from accepting an inner division may elude us our entire life. The resolution may come through altered feelings or powers of action/interests, intellectual insights, or God's power manifested in mystical experiences. Inner peace may also come from facing both of these opposing wills or the irruption by some new passion or interest. Overcoming the inner battle too quickly is no solution, especially if we seek a false unity by denying the conflicts altogether. Again, these inner tensions and conflicting motivations are not forged out of our will or conscious mind but seem to be authored out of the conflicts between our conscious and unconscious minds. We need always to be honest about the inner tensions as long as they linger and/or bind us. Many feel abandoned and lost during this process, and the need to endure and wait is crucial to resolving any inner or outer conflict.

Further complications develop because there are no interpretations or interpretations of interpretations of laws, which are universal in *every situation*. Our uniqueness and the specific needs of each person cannot possibly be set in stone and applied to every person in every situation. Human history is littered with attempts to interpret laws justly and apply them in every given situation. Alas, our desire for strict regulations that cover every possible setting author many Kafkaesque rules and regulations, which baffle the mind and end up doing more harm than good. Rather, we need an attitude that is open and honest while recognizing that we are not all the same, and what is required of one person may simply be wrong for another. It takes much self-reflection to tease apart our divided motives, identify their sources, and begin the process of attaining a resolution. The entire endeavor requires the willingness to assume responsibility and remaining open to new variables or circumstances, which may demand that we start this process all over again. The process of resolution comes in many distinct forms, and we have no way of knowing ahead of time how it will come out in the end. This is where the attitudes of endurance, faith, and patience come in. If we are sincere and willing to go the extra mile, the resolutions will eventually come. Some may come even after death. The vast majority of us are only partially aware of the chasm that exists between what we want to be, what we are, and what the real truth is. The point is there is no human that can be the ultimate judge of another's motives, and when we try to do so, we end up making matters worse while becoming judgmental.

Even when we take time in self-reflection and recognize a need to change, our will cannot conjure up the change automatically. Our will is only capable of steering us in the right direction. Most of us intellectually accept we are limited in what we can do by our will alone. The fact is there are no codified laws that create simple and quick solutions both to what the right answer is or how to achieve it. Some work themselves out in their own time with anguish and persistence. Our responsibility is to be honest and recognize these are moral dilemmas that we must face and endure and trust the inner struggle has a purpose and will eventually resolve itself. The point is to bear the inner tension of the divided self without deception and, if we are sincere, trust that the outcome will be made known to us in due course. We also need the courage to make the right choices when they present themselves to our mind. Our will is often split and also in need of extra energy to fulfill its end of the bargain. In these situations, part of us wants to be faithful to the truth and another part to what is expedient, and even when we are of one mind in the matter, our will may fail us.

We all also experience two archetypal divergent urges, one toward life and the other toward death. The former urge pushes us onward to more and more experiences. We are driven by desires, not only to live but to expand our world, experiencing what we can. We thirst after life because it is in our blood. This life force has different names in each cultural milieu: the toa, chi, spirit, libido, etc., with diverse beliefs about where it originates, in matter, psyche, or spirit. On the other hand, everyone has an urge toward death and some form of rest or homeostasis. To be or not to be—that is the question.

The Will to Power

Give me absolute control
Over ever living soul . . .

—Leonard Cohen, "The Future"

Among others, great minds like Nietzsche, Schopenhauer, Machiavelli, and Adler all believed the primary bend of our will is toward power; that is the will to power is a basic motivation that must be addressed one way or another. I believe the will to power is a compensation for our unconscious weaknesses and inadequacies surrounding our mortality. This primal urge is noticed in children without much subterfuge. The alpha male among the primates and humans is another obvious example of a will to power making its appearance in the economy of our motivations. The shape and degree this exists within human beings assumes grotesque, comical, and horrific proportions as history is littered with individuals and groups who digest, destroy, maim, betray, manipulate, murder, and oppress others with their will to power. All individuals in power are bombarded with temptations toward inflation and aspirations to increase, maintain, and utilize power to their own advantage. It is also vital to be aware that this primal urge is not the supreme urge in everyone, just as Freud was wrong by labeling all urges as primarily and ultimately sexual. I believe many motives are potentially dominant in a given individual, and what is decisive is hidden within each unique personality and the choices that person executes throughout their lives. However, whenever we land upon a new motive or rather an old one in the latest guise, it is a significant truth to integrate into our psyche. Whether this is the dominate motive for us or not, *we all have the will to power in our psyche and are responsible to integrate this motive in such a way that we do not become inflated and prone toward manipulating and harming others through power and control.* We all house a self who is selfish and seeks power over one thing or another. The dynamics of this basic motive is where we now turn.

We are now prepared to discuss the *two most significant* of all psychological motivations.

Mirror, Mirror, on the Wall

Introduction

So many miles, so many doors
Some need patience, some need
Force
All fall open in their own due
Course
To allow us this time.

—Bruce Cockburn, "Look How Far"

We now delve into our search and need for meaning in our lives and how this plays itself out within the human condition. The pairs of opposites are security/insecurity and worth/worthlessness.

The Two Primary Motives in Human Nature: Security and Self-Worth

There are two primary motives that emerge out of our primordial experiences of separation, anxiety and our will. First, our ego-body-consciousness seeks a sense of *security* in a world where anything can happen. Second, our consciousness hunts for meanings and purpose that will proffer some of measure of *self-worth*. Want of security, worth, meaning, and purpose are the primary motivations within the human condition. These two fundamental and universal archetypes must be worked through before we can move on into deeper levels of development and motivations like true love and sacrifice. However, these motives are often hidden from view in the unconscious. All motives hidden from awareness are converted into narrow and compulsive beliefs, attitudes, and behaviors. Many of us act without the slightest awareness of why we do what we do; we become lost souls forever, making the same old mistakes. Without consciousness of our motives, especially these two, we cannot change. We become imprisoned and bound by these motives. The prison takes on the configuration of an array of compulsive and self-destructive patterns of behavior.

Security Comes First

Person in the street shrugs—"Security comes first"
But the trouble with normal is it always gets worse.

—Bruce Cockburn, "The Trouble with Normal"

Human cravings for security seem self-evident and are built into our physiology and psyche, from prosaic creature comforts to addictions. We often pursue an illusory and distorted security in all the wrong places. What level of security can realistically be achieved when existence is temporal? Mortality is the ultimate example of how weak we really are as we cannot even keep our heart beating. The fact is we have so little control, and our mortality is the axis of all our insecurities. We've truly been thrust out of Eden. Since we are normally unwilling to contemplate our mortality, fears and insecurities are displaced into neurotic symptoms and dynamics wherein all our relationships, attitudes, beliefs, living situations, actions, jobs, and finances are all infected with absurd trivialities, superficialities, and pettiness—or outright evil.

We often seek security in settings where it doesn't exist, which is in temporal aims. The necessity for security coerces us toward self-deceptions. Lying about reality is the easiest technique to acquire albeit a false sense of security. If one finds security in money, then its acquisition is all that matters. From the child who clings to his parents, through adolescence with its almost pathological attachment to friends, into adulthood where anxieties plague us with financial, employment, our living situation, and/or relationships, and on into old age where regrets and death tracks us down with each *tick tock, tick tock, tick tock* of the quartz clock, security motivates our daily struggle. Nation states are built upon the war machine, capital, power, law, etc., for national security. Individuals seek safe living space, capital, tenure, guaranteed contracts, guns, automobiles, boats, and toys of every conceivable shape and size, all for at least the illusion of security. We have become addicted to things and objects and ideologies for they bring us the illusion of security.

We need structure to create order in our lives; order affords a modicum of security so we can act. A lack of order degenerates into chaos, irresponsibility, neurosis, and psychosis. Life becomes muddled without structure and order. However, a few problems have arisen from this legitimate need: none of the structures we create can ever eliminate insecurity since one day these structures will give way and crumble like castles made of sand. Our attachments to structure and order often generate modes of denial while restricting the personality. People become rigid, judgmental, and intolerant of differences while others fritter away in prisons of their own designs. Having structure and being responsible and organized is essential to being productive. However, insecurity is by no means eliminated by being organized and creating structure in our lives; ironically, the experience of insecurity is an honest and healthy response to the human predicament.

Ortega put it thus:

> The man with the clear head is the man who frees himself from those fantastic "ideas" and looks life in the face, realizes that everything in it is problematic, and feels himself lost. And this is the simple truth—that to live is to feel oneself lost—he who accepts it has already begun to find himself, to be on firm ground. Instinctively, as do the shipwrecked,

he will look round for something to which to cling, and that tragic, ruthless glance, absolutely sincere, because it is a question of his salvation, will cause him to bring order into the chaos of his life. These are the only genuine ideas; the idea of the ship-wrecked. All the rest is rhetoric, posturing, farce. He who does not really feel himself lost, is without remission; that is to say, he never finds himself, never comes up against his own reality. (Reprinted from *The Denial of Death* by E. Becker, p.89)

We are all shipwrecked and lost on some existential levels. If we do not face our insecurities, we will experience neurosis and addictions in one form or another. The fact is we all have some forms of neurosis and addictions, which are attempts to run away from the reality of our insecurities. The houses of cards we create are blown apart by the slightest gusts of wind. The fact is most of us experience losses of employment, financial difficulties, finding adequate housing, etc., at some point in our lives. When threatened by the storms of experience, we usually have a crack at recreating these edifices or crafting more constructive designs from the debris left behind. The specifics of how we attempt to recover our security are the topic of the next chapter and the second section. These attempts vary from culture to culture, from the comic, to the heroic, to the tragic.

Self-Worth

I've proven who I am so many times,
The magnetic strips worn thin . . .

It's as if the thing were written
In the constitution of the age
Sooner or later you'll be wind up
Pacing the cage.

—Bruce Cockburn, "Pacing the Cage"

We all need to leave a signature of our worth somewhere. Everybody needs to feel their lives matter to others, ourselves, and often to some form of higher power, and that our lives are somehow worthwhile. Along with security, self-worth is also a primary motive; few actions are not motivated by these quests for both security and worth. We become acquainted with this motive in countless behaviors (i.e., when we are on the lookout for recognition, respect, power, authority honor, and love). When others recognize our achievements or accomplishments, this provides a sense of being worthwhile. Our culture gives out all sorts of rewards where trophies and badges of honor litter our houses, museums, history books, and junkyards. Being recognized, appreciated, and loved offers something concrete from which to be able to hang our hat on and proclaim to the world, "I am significant, and therefore, my life is justified." I believe this need for self-worth is a primary and universal archetype. Another way of saying this is we have a need for meaning and purpose. Each civilization agrees to a playing field from which the masses are required to extract a sense of worth. For the vast majority, one becomes dependent on others for their sense of worth. Most of us seek security and our worth from others and, therefore, in the collective or social arena. What society and others say and agree upon seems to carry the most weight for the vast majority as they construct lives in such a way that will convey a sense of security and worth. Nevertheless, becoming a part of the mass breeds a false sense of security and worth. Seeking safety in numbers, the masses, and noise keeps us from being alone to confront truths about ourselves and the human condition. While the need is valid and innate, the vast majority seek security and worth in dependency upon others. This mode of acquiring these twin motives is often destructive and cowardly since no human being or institution can ultimately provide such personal value; instead, it must come from within.

We are driven by a need to feel we count, we matter, and existence has meaning and purpose. These needs for worth or meaning are natural and normal. They only become a problem when (1) we are not conscious of them, and/or (2) we gain our meaning and sense of worth from that which cannot provide it (i.e., temporal aims). Being unaware of these motives sets us up for all kinds of unconscious behaviors where we end up using some form of subterfuge to extract worth from the world around us. When unconscious, these motives will control the individual as their radar will be constantly searching for approval and strokes from others. Attempting to find our worth in the wrong places is dangerous and is a setup for excessive grief. We often seek self-worth from precincts too constricting, and therefore, we become our own captives.

I often shared with my clients that what you live for is where you extract your worth, and then, does what you live for open you up to the complexities, sufferings, and wonder of life or not? This seems to me to be the criteria to estimate whether the truth someone is living for is well grounded or a temporal aim.

I have also observed that the place where individuals find their security and worth often changes over time. What may have been nothing but open spaces in one stage in our lives becomes a detention center in the next. We grow into and out of things. All endings are new beginnings, and all new beginnings are endings. I believe most of what we live for is superficial and illusory. We create illusions to avoid the complicated dynamics of the human condition. Most seek temporal aims, which, by their very nature, wilt and pass away like summer flowers. Let us not be anesthetized by the inconsequential.

Another way of describing these needs for worth and security are the opposite urges to be independent and dependent. To authentically resolve these needs for security and worth for independence and dependency, we all need to find the balance between our uniqueness as individuals and our connectedness to others. These interdependent motives or urges are paradoxical because the tensions that exist between them, we are drawn in both directions at once. Ernst Becker sums this up as follows:

> The paradox takes the form of two motives or urges that seem to be part of creative consciousness and that point in two opposite directions. On the one hand, the creature is impelled by a powerful desire to identify with the cosmic process, to merge himself with the rest of nature. On the other hand, he

wants to be unique, and stand out as something different and apart. (Becker, Ernest, *The Denial of Death*, p. 151–152)

We want to be separate and unique but also feel safe, certain, and secure in our connection and dependency with others. To put it constructively, we strive for intimacy and separateness. To put it pejoratively, either one believes we don't need others, or we can't live without them. If we overvalue our uniqueness, we become subject to arrogance, rigidity, and close-mindedness. If we err on the side of dependency, we sacrifice who we are to fit into the environment, becoming people pleasers. These interdependent motives or urges are paradoxical because in the tension between them, we are drawn in both directions at once.

Creative types extract meaning and worth in their creativity and their natural intelligence and ability to produce images and works of art. I am using art in the broadest possible sense. This includes careers. There is a pattern where creative types often struggle with mania, addictions, and madness. This is due to their propensity to rely on themselves and the richness of their inner worlds without recognizing they are channels of the unconscious, *and* they have a responsibility to adapt to the creations of their unconscious. They are not the authors of the unconscious symbols and images any more than they are of their lives, yet the temptation toward inflation are often too great for many creative types. Those that are willing to adapt to the creative forces of the unconscious become the true prophets of their age and are thrust against their will by greater forces that reside within them. They recognize they are driven by a higher power to speak truths that are universal in nature, and their egos are not significant in the grand scheme. These few prophets are able to remain grounded and humble and live relatively balanced lives. I believe the four main musicians I focus on are just such prophets as they seem to have been willing to practice what they preach, so to speak, and recognize they are channels of the truths they encounter and not the authors of them.

There is another prominent category of individuals who obtain their worth by caretaking others. They focus their energy on others to avoid facing their own issues and problems. If one focuses on and caretakes others, then one doesn't have to face one's own problems.

Unwilling to face the human predicament and taking responsibility for their anxiety and fears, they try to fix everything and become martyr personalities. Martyrs become experts in manipulating others by making others dependent upon them.

Finitude

However we experience our security and worth, resolving our needs for meaning and security must take into account our mortality and finitude. We will continue to come back to this reality because it is the central truth of the human condition we must come to grips with. The fact we die and are yanked from this temporal abode needs to awaken an honest appraisal of what we are living for and how honest and courageous our lives are. Again, the primary litmus test I use to gauge the truth of an individual's philosophy is whether what they are living for opens them up to life and death in all its complexity, suffering, ambiguity, and beauty or not.

Such is our common fate. We are alone and imprisoned in our vulnerable and mortal bodies. Like Pandora, when she opened her box, the human condition is exposed to every imaginable woe and suffering. Together with all of the woes from Pandora's box, hope was also released. There is hope in our common human predicament, but like a dog looking for the bone, we'll have to dig for it.

It amazes me that when someone dies, we all make statements like "It came so unexpected." Death never comes by appointment, and therefore, it *is* to be expected at anytime. The way we live our lives should have this reality integrated. Regrettably, most are lost in illusions and unconscious of them. The tragedies of loss and grief can become an opportunity to break the spells of our illusions and start living life with an openness to life and death and all its complexity. Joseph Campbell said somewhere that tragedies are the renting or our attachments to the temporal.

Now I am going to set forth some examples on how our quest for security and worth impacts the four stages of life: childhood, adolescence, adulthood, and old age.

Children

Everyone's wearing a disguise
To hide what they've got left behind their
Eyes.
But me, I can't cover what I am
Wherever the children go I'll follow them.

—Bob Dylan, "Abandoned Love"

When we appraise children and adolescents, there is no subterfuge or camouflaging their motivations. By adulthood, most of us hide our motives from ourselves and others with a variety of defense mechanisms. But in young children, parents are witnesses to the daily clamor for attention and praise. Simultaneously, they seek reassurance and safety. By their failure to succeed in being recognized or safe, their subsequent insecurities and feeling of worthlessness become painfully apparent. These children are bound for trouble since everyone will seek attention, whether negative or positive. All parents have experienced their children clamoring for their attention in incessant attempts to garner a sense of security and worth. If we as parents are otherwise occupied and fail to respond to our children's needs and tears, they will well up faster that a New York minute. Often, we accept this in younger children, but get to a point when they are older, we become intolerant and rejecting. As adults, we are often uncomfortable with naked displays of these needs for worth and security since they remind us of our own more-shrouded impulses for the same. We don't recognize the same fears and insecurities because we hide them from ourselves. The degree of our repression is exposed by the quantity and quality of our intolerance and overreactions. The child above all searches for their sense of worth and security in their primary caregivers, usually the parents. The caregiver walks a fine line between providing safety and opportunities for our little ones to mature in their own way. In the right circumstances, a child trusts their caregivers with faith undaunted by cynicism and fear.

Adolescents

Why should I care
If I have to cut my hair.
I've got to move with the fashions
Or be outcast.

—The Who, "Cut My Hair"

What about adolescents? I heard a quote from Mortimer J. Adler a while back but have been unable to locate it, and it went something like this: "Adolescence is a lamentable disease." While he may be accurate, most adults display little understanding or compassion when confronted with an adolescent's inner conflicts and ambiguous natures. The adolescent find themselves in toxic situations with all forms and fashions of hormones and needs for acceptance while they are on the journey of self-discovery and gaining a personal identity. Most adolescents seem to exhibit borderline personality characteristics as they try to negotiate relationships with themselves, their parents, and the all-important social networks of friendships. One minute they are enthralled with themselves or someone else in seething bordering on idolatry, and the next they seem full of self-hate or disdain that contaminates everything in their path. There constellates within them vicissitudes of moods, which astonish even the most veteran of folks effective at working with them. Sadly, adults all too often respond with intolerance and impatience since we fail to identify the underlying motives and dynamics within ourselves that adolescents reflect. We react emotionally to their motives and end up projecting our discomfort back onto them. They mirror our true motives. Because the adolescent is so impetuous and emotional, it makes it easier for the adult to repress any similarities with their adolescent's plight. The adolescent is ill-equipped as they have fewer defenses and coping skills learned from experience at their disposal. Like many adults, they often lack understanding of their unconscious needs or how they are going about trying to fulfill them. They exhibit extremes in their emotions with outbursts and demands with the added accessories of tears and shrieks. When we as adults fail to recognize and resolve our own inner conflicts related to the needs for security and worth, we become reactive and rejecting of adolescents. Rather than drama and overreactions, many adults develop anxiety disorders, drug problems, depression, phobias, etc. If adults could identify, understand, and empathize with the adolescent struggles while integrating our own needs for security and worth in healthy ways, our relations with adolescents would improve dramatically.

Adolescents and children intuitively sense a lack of understanding from those adults who have yet to resolve these motives in an open and conscious way. They also observe compromises adults make to the social rules and regulations, relationships, employment, etc. They also observe a lack of independence in some adults that they themselves are struggling with. They are often a lot smarter and more intuitive than we give them credit for. The adolescent turns off any adult whom they judge as superficial, full of compromises to ideals, dependent, and uncaring. Ironically, adults who are immature and often act like adolescents are more likely to gain their trust, a classic case of the blind leading the blind.

Adolescents seek their identity and therefore their worth and security through their social group. The adolescent's groups are often gangs, cliques, and sports. Antisocial behavior is often a reaction to the hypocrisy of adults and a cry for help. They are trying to make sense of all the inner conflicts and tensions. The adolescent is crying out for substance and answers, which are commensurate with their inner desires, feelings, and motives for a personal identity. In addition, hormones are raging, and this is one more inner conflict that is present during this most difficult of times.

An adolescent will respond to an adult whom they perceive as having wrestled with the same issues for worth/security. The problem is there are so few true mentors around; many adolescents are led astray by the "cult of personality," which they find in leader types like gang leaders and other charismatic people who appear confident and secure. These figures mask their insecurities by attachments to the superficial styles and forms (fads) presently perceived as hip or cool. Fads are sad commentaries on the herd instinct and disclose the fact too few adults are truly unique and possess some real depth to their character.

Adults

And take off your thirsty boots
And stay awhile
Your feet are hot and weary
From a dusty mile
And maybe I can make you laugh
And maybe I can try
Just looking for the evening
And the morning in your eye.

—Bob Dylan, "Thirsty Boots"

For adults, security and worth are primarily garnered through employment, financial security, and romantic relationships. The mere threat of losing jobs or relationships universally unleashes an entire panorama of self-doubt, anxiety, insecurity, and feelings of failure. Careers and relationships are planted in gardens where we try to harvest our worth and security. We feel insecure if our finances are threatened and worthless if our competence comes into question. Conflicts with our lovers and supervisors breed a multitude of fear and loathing. The actual loss of relationships and jobs can call into question one's entire sense of worth and security. For those under the illusion of being in control, these losses and uncertainties challenge not only security and worth, but possibly sanity as well. When the stock market crashed in 1929, suicide became a reasonable alternative to numerous individuals. After this period of transition subsides, we usually look back and recognize how we have a more expansive perspective, and the experience itself changed us in some ways. We become stronger and able to accept this transition as being a positive one. This is especially so when we know we are much more than what we do—or what particular set of circumstances we find ourselves in. The fact of the matter is self-worth and security must come from within! The adult find themselves in the situations where they must learn to endure life's complexities with patience and poise while expanding their philosophy of life.

Old Age

The memories of a man in his old age
Are the deeds of a man in his prime.

—Pink Floyd, "Free Four"

It is sad and deplorable that in our present era, the vast majority of our elderly are underappreciated and ignored. They no longer serve the materialist function and therefore have become the expendables. The fetish of the present age is on youth, vitality, and success. You don't look young or can't get it up, well, you better get a face lift, boob job, or a prescription for Viagra. The old are mostly forgotten except by their children and grandchildren. This plight of the elderly is compounded by the elderly themselves. After they lose their status and worth with retirement, they often become ogres or go into a corner to die. Many have bought into the American dream and are now crusty old codgers living the nightmares this illusion nourished. Most of the aged have lived life only as a duty, a duty to families and employers, rarely piercing below convention to query about their uniqueness and obtain self-knowledge while striving to ascertain their soul's purpose and destiny. They never grew past the first half of life's tasks and, because of this, grow to be ogres and witches populating homes, apartments, and nursing homes. Having bought into the cultural hero system, they believe they are no longer useful because they are no longer productive by society's superficial standards. How ironic to have bought into a culture selling false dreams and then be rejected by the very cultural ethos they endorsed. Meaning and purpose lies hidden in the wealth of experiences that they have lived through and survived. I see a story behind every pair of eyes, tales and narratives just waiting for the light of day. Every person I have ever worked with has a story that fascinates, cautions, forewarns, troubles, and admonishes me in some way or another.

We therefore have a double tragedy, the waste of potential wisdom and instruction that some of our elderly can provide. Our youth complain that the old have nothing of value to offer, and the old complain of a lack of respect the younger generations demonstrate. With mendacity, the elderly who are rich lord it over the young, hanging on to their last bits of power and dragging us into wars and other catastrophes before it all ends for them. They wish to sacrifice others with them, not unlike the kings in history who killed off their servants and slaves so they could be buried with them and attend to them in the afterlife.

Example

Though among the regrets I can't get by
There are just one or two
Unkind things I said to you . . .
I don't know why it was so hard to talk to you.
I guess my anger pulled me through . . .
Living your own life day after day,
Soon all your plans and changes
Either fail or fade away
Leaving so much still left to say . . .

—Jackson Browne, "Daddy's Tune"

My father was a brilliant and accomplished physician with a great sense of humor. Like most doctors of his generation, he valued life while lamenting death as failure rather than valuing its reality. He accumulated a number of warranted trophies and awards, which he attached to his ego, and he supplemented his self-worth with hard work, excellence, and at times a rigid and conservative arrogance. He smoked cigars while providing no ventilation without the slightest common sense of how this impacted his children. We all suffered, and I acquired asthma is the process. Children were ornaments like trophy wives that he showed off if they met his standards of merit. He had a bit of the genius about him, yet he seemed to lack common sense with regard to healthiness and wholeness. Following his retirement, he worked part-time as long as he could until he had a stroke and circumstances stripped him of the dignity and self-worth "befitting a man in his position." Losing his practice altogether, his world began to crumble; within a few years, he deteriorated to the degree Mom had to put him in a nursing home. His depression was palpable; his sense of security and worth dissipated like those victims of the atomic bomb in Japan. Physicians can't heal themselves; he was unable to break on through to the other side of his depression. In terms of his new lifestyle, he went from the penthouse to the outhouse. No doubt, he had put little thought into fate's ironies, where the first is last and the last first. What was remarkable was as he lived on in quiet desperation, he was without any discernible self-pity. He also took ownership of neglecting his family, especially my mother. He did not say at the end, "I wish I had spent more time building monuments to my ego and securing more money and acclaim for the afterlife." No, he was able to confess his poverty and thus become rich in an ironic sort of way. He had forsaken authentic relationships and self-knowledge for the vain glory of society's tributes and accolades. Fortunately for us both, we were able to share with each other a few tears together prior to his death. Though this tête-à-tête did not appreciably change the dynamics between us during his last months, we were able to at least make peace.

He grew in those last years, broken and humbled by his fate. My dad suffered and eventually died with the dignity of accepting much of what he spent his life avoiding and denying. I miss him sometimes.

Silent as a day can be
Far off sounds of others on their chosen run
As they do all the things they feel give life some meaning . . .

—Genesis "Heat Haze"

We now turn in more detail to the dynamics of how we endeavor to attain self-worth and security in a world where these are not predetermined nor conferred by fate.

The Cords That Bind

We will stand in time
To face the ties that bind
The ties that bind
Now you can't break the ties that bind
You can't forsake the ties that bind

—Bruce Springsteen, "The Ties That Bind"

Introduction

The opposites we now delve into are attachment/detachment. Attachment without detachment is a humiliating dependency while detachment without attachment lacks compassion, intimacy, and love.

Ego Attachments

Built to last till lightness fades,
And darkness falls on all.
Built to last 'till years roll back
Our couch perched in the sky . . .

146

Three blue stars set o'er the hill.
Call them back; you never will.
All these trials, soon be dead.
We all need something built to last.

—Grateful Dead, "Built To Last"

We create and carry many illusory extensions to our ego, which, in the end, amount to nothing. Attachments to temporal objects or ideas are where we extend our ego-body-consciousness boundaries to include *things and ideas* external to our inner selves. By extension, our worth and security become tied up in these attachment. Our house, families, and careers are potentially extensions of our ego. These attachments to our ego become defenses that repress our underlying anxieties and fears. Our sense of worth, identity, and security are often projected onto our cars, jobs, significant others, etc. When we lose something dear to us, we often use phrases like "a part of me is gone, I'll never be the same." By temporal, I mean the attachments are to something that is temporary and that which fades, rusts, or can be stolen. This also includes *ideas* or *beliefs* that do not stand the test of time and are flat-out untrue. Cars, houses, foods, clothing, drugs, sports, money, self-deceptions, falsehoods, and our physical looks are examples of temporal objects and beliefs. Beauty and all material things fade with time. We often become bound and gagged by our temporal attachments. Our ego attaches worth and security to external and temporal objects or beliefs. The ego identifies and hides behind these particular externals, which are in fact symbolic extension of our ego-self. We project our longings for security onto these objects or beliefs for security and worth. Our ego can become so enmeshed in these objects or beliefs—whether a house, job, religion, team, car, hobby, etc.—that it can be almost impossible to figure out where the person and their attachments begin and end.

For an example, a sports fanatic wears the paraphernalia of their team, and when the team loses, a part of his ego suffers a loss of worth. He is overidentifying his ego with the team as the team and his ego become almost one. The fan gains a sense of worth or worthlessness through his identification with the team's success or failure. Someone

147

dies, and they are buried in the uniform of the team. Others are buried with booze, cigars, etc. We often laugh at these displays of affection, but not only can the dead not take these things with them, they likely used these attachments to avoid opportunities in their life for growth. It's easy to accept our attachments without thinking and processing our true motives and values. Kierkegaard said somewhere that most of us are tranquilized by the trivial.

Social Illusions

I've given up the game, I've got to leave,
The pot of gold is only make-believe.
The treasure can't be found by men who search
Whose gods are dead and whose queens are in the church.

—Bob Dylan, "Abandoned Love"

The vast majority seek security and worth in the collective or social arena. The cultural norms and mores of our cultures or subcultures carry the most weight for the majority of folks when it comes to attaining their worth and security. What society and others say and agree upon seems to carry the most weight when constructing these attachments. Becoming a part of the mass breeds a false sense of security and worth. Worldly attitudes and beliefs litter our Western landscape with attachments to convention, superficial styles and fads, and the search for eternal youth in the temporal realm. The lengths we often go to gain acceptance is both comical and tragic when we step back and view the ethos of what is cool at the moment. Better to be safe in the masses than alone to confront the human condition in all its ambiguity and uncertainty. We then become deluded in our dependency on others and the fashions of the day for our sense of security and worth. Many want to be respected and thought of as in or cool. Sadly, this externalizing is illusionary. Additional examples in our Western culture of these superficial externals include money, status and power, careers, mood-altering substances, sports, materialism/shopping, and the cult of personality where many become enthralled by celebrities.

Throughout history, each culture has a hero system or common playing field in which individuals compete and achieve status or worth. Every culture is shaped and sustained by creating a value system that is accepted by the majority. Each culture distinguishes between the winners and losers by affording rewards and punishments to individuals belonging to said culture. Whatever a particular culture values, it offers its badges of honor from which members garner their worth. The losers often withdraw and/or give up in self-pity. These folks usually end up rotting away in obscurity in a prison or some such institution. They then abdicate personal responsibilities, become resentful, or attempt to find alternative hero systems to gain recognition they feel they deserve.

Within a cultural heroic there also develops a dependency on charismatic leaders to the point a cult of personality emerges. Since many of America's charismatic individuals are dead, tracing any connection with that person initiates automatic credibility and therefore a modicum of self-worth. There is, however, plenty of "celebrities" ready to take on the mantle of hero given half the chance. The emptiness and numerous tragedies of most celebrities' lives should be a clue as to futility and falsehood of such hero worship. Each of us must stand alone within ourselves and learn to shake off the crowd with its addiction to superficialities, its clamor, and hand-clapping.

When the cultural or collective hero system no longer carries a believable ethos and mythos, revolutions and apocalyptic fears increase before the old hero system dies out and a new one replaces it. For instance, this is what happened during the first century. The Jews and others were anticipating that divine intervention would overthrow the Roman social order, and God would establish a new order and social-political system. Jesus came but disappointed most of the populace because his kingdom failed to materialize with their apocalyptic expectations. His kingdom was present in his actions and parables, a kingdom that was to come from within the person first before it would impact the external social system. His kingdom came with healing and fellowship around meals to the lowest classes in both Judaism and gradually extended to the entire Mediterranean value and social systems through individuals carrying the kingdom within them. He shattered the walls of class, sex, and race to those who had ears to hear. It is much easier to embrace the tangible rather than one that centers on a different kind of revolution where the inner life is transformed before the external one is manifested. The external Roman Empire did crash and burn, only to be replaced by similar dynamics in different attire, the Roman Catholic Church.

In the present age, it is my opinion that our Western cultural/institutional religion fails to provide meaning and purpose for the majority of people. Cultural values have been lost by those in religious power who twist the true messages of true prophets like Moses, Jesus, the Buddha, and Mohammed. Real revolution can only be achieved by inner transformations, and this has been exchanged by institutions built on superficial materialism advanced by science and rationalism or fanatical fundamentalism. Science, materialism, and rationalism have failed to generate the depth our conscious mind craves while Western religion in particular has become so compromised, it has lost its passion, dynamism, and credibility to the degree it no longer captures the imagination of the human heart. The reality is our youth are rejecting the existing materialism and phony religion and have been turning to drugs, sex/romance, and music (the new trinity) since the sixties. This new trinity provides a faint echo of spiritual experiences by distracting us from mundane materialistic myopic values. Drugs, music, and romantic relationships/sex provide a temporary high, which ultimately ends in superficial and existential nausea.

Other scenarios include subcultural hero systems hiding behind every corner dictating politically correct terminology and behavior. Each seeks authenticity from the majority and to be recognized for their "unique" hero system and thus legitimizing their worth. In psychological terms, we have failed to listen to the depth of the unconscious mind where some real answers to the body politic can be located. As a culture and in spiritual terms, we have generally neglected to pursue the depths of the unconscious mind.

Each new hero system/culture rises from the scrap heap of the old one while offering new illusions. In my opinion, the closest any cultural hero system came to contributing truth in a social context was the early Hebrews and Christian Church in the first century and ancient Athens during the classical period fifth century BC. However, each has longed since silenced its true prophets by killing Socrates, Jesus, etc., and silencing women leaders and the risen Christ with male hierarchy, doctrines, and creeds. Athens entered into war with the rest of Greece, only to be brought down by Sparta. It seems movements that begin with authentic spirituality deteriorate over time into corrupted institutions, which eventually promote the darker sides of human nature.

Eros Love/ Relationship Attachments

Well, you know that I love to live with you
But you make me forget so very much
I forget to pray for the angels
And then the angels forget to pray for us.

—Leonard Cohen, "So long Marianne"

Our culture has elevated romantic love to the level of a religion. Yet physical beauty fades, and romantic relationships are temporal. Our longings, insecurities, and chronic dissatisfaction will linger, and the violence of emotion they elicit will continue ad infinitum if we continue to locate our security and sense of worth in someone else. Our longings and the excitement of romantic love preoccupies many of us, and we easily forget to pray for the angels and attend to our personal journeys and other passions. It is easy to see why, as materialism has gained the ascendancy; romance or eros love at least offers something that takes us out of preoccupations with self. Romantic relationships do provide a sense of belonging and a place where our needs for others can find a modicum of authentic expression. We all feel incomplete within the boundaries of our ego-body-selves, and eros does stretch these boundaries and at least contains within her some semblance of selflessness. The emotions of eros act upon our ego-consciousness with a force that is greater than the ego. However, romantic love lasts for a short period before the need to grow in a love that transcends eros itself. When eros disappears from relationships, it tosses too many individuals into the arms of another relationship where eros is rekindled. Our identity has been attached to this person for our sense of worth and security, and we find it hard to live without romantic love. It is with attachments to temporal objects, in this case another mortal creature, that we have located a primary archetypal pattern of coping with our collective human predicament.

Addictions

I fought against the bottle,
But I had to do it drunk—

How come you called me here tonight?
How come you bother with my heart at all?
You raise me up in grace,
Then your put me in a place,
Where I must fall.

—Leonard Cohen, "That Don't Make It Junk"

By examining our archetypal needs for security and worth, we have happened upon the psychological dynamics of addiction. How do attachments become addictions? The answer to this question offers the key to the dynamics of psychological addictions. The dynamics of addictions are well documented as the addict loses control over their behavior with emotional pain, denial, self-hate, preoccupation, increase in tolerance, changes in social life, attempts to control that fail, etc. All addictions are related to the need to avoid pain and reality while self-worth and security is bound to the addicted object or idea. This is measured by the degree the addict feels insecure and worthless without the object or idea of their addiction. The level of discomfort an addict feels when deprived of their addiction is an indication of the degree the addiction has progressed. Addicts are like musicians playing everything in the same key. Preoccupied and driven, the ability to respond and cope with the complexities of life is reduced incrementally until it attains such constricted dimensions that the addict lives an extremely restricted existence. I once heard a family member say the addict was "boring."

Addicts are afraid of facing the reality of their addiction and how it is controlling their lives and the existential issues revolving around the meaning of their lives and the certainty that they will die. Addictions are a crutch to avoid all painful realities. This raises an issue: isn't everyone addicted to something? I would say yes to greater and lesser degrees. Every activity, object, or idea is a potential addiction. As we have discussed, the present age has its own culturally conditioned addictions: sports, money, gambling, nicotine, shopping, material goods, drugs and alcohol, computers, pornography and/or sex, food, relationships, status, TV, cell phones, work, video games, or ideologists in politics, science, and religion. Where legitimate interests end and addictions begin is often hard to measure. The question whether an interest is an addiction can be summed up by asking, do these activities open us up to creativity and the complexities of life and death or not? The issue is not that we have interests, but will we delve below the general interest and peer into our motives in any given stage of life as to why are we active in these interests and what type of behaviors are we engaged in? Are we using our attachments to whatever objects or ideas to lie to ourselves about some truth about ourselves or the human condition?

Letting go of addictions becomes a Herculean task. We cling to our addictions for security and worth. The addict's life becomes constricted to frightening degrees as everything revolves around these addictions. To go a day without shopping, TV, our smart phones, the game, casino, the hit music, the buzz, etc., propels us into a frenzy of anxiety and disorientation. The addict has been so used to gratifying all these attachments that the slightest hint or threat of losing access to them drives the addict toward intimidation, hiding, lying, stealth, and every form of specious behavior. Our habits and personal rituals have become so ingrained it is hard to tell the difference between these and addictions. We become aware of anxiety when something impedes the acting out of these rituals. Try fasting or abstaining from any of these attachments, addictions, rituals, superstitions, or habits, and you will soon experience the anxiety of which I speak. When they are interrupted or gone, we become preoccupied with our habits or addictions and the anxieties and fears they occasion.

By our denial, these attachments and/or addictions are like cords that bind and imprison us. Jung used the term *participation mystique* for addictions. The thrill of the ten thousand things captures our emotions and our attention. These are projections of inner archetypal realities that captivate our attention and emotions in an effort to make themselves known. They take on a magical quality only when we, the subject, and it, the object, merge. To break the spell, we need to separate our inner consciousness from external objects. Jung called this withdrawing our projections. This occurs when we detach from the external object or distorted idea. The reality is the problems lies within us rather than with the object. The difficulty is we are left with responsibilities to overcome our anxieties, insecurities, feelings, and whatever we uncover that is in there, which surfaces when we let go of our addictions. Letting go of our addictions is painful, yet there are inner experiences of freedom that await us when we do detach. As much as I know these truths and principles, I continue to struggle to integrate them into my being.

Sadly, the lengths we go to shield ourselves from these self-evident truths and hang on to our attachments and addictions is so dysfunctional that treatment centers, psychiatric units, homeless shelters, and many other social programs are brimful with these casualties. The depth of what resides within each individual psyche seems overwhelming. The more we understand, the more we are responsible for. We are called to meet head-on our being that is born in freedom and destiny, in choice and fate.

Jung describes the individual without addictions thusly:

> This is the case when life has been lived so exhaustively, and with such devotedness, that no more unfulfilled obligations to life exist, when, therefore no desires that cannot be sacrificed unhesitatingly stand in the way of inner detachment from the world. It is futile to lie to ourselves about this. Whenever we are attached, we are still possessed;

and when one is possessed, it means the existence of something stronger than oneself. (Carl Jung, *The Secret of the Golden Flower*, p. 114)

The Inner Connection between Attachments, Addictions, Security, and Worth

Let's now examine how attachments and addictions relate simultaneously to our personal sense of worth and security. Most of the addicts that I've worked with, including myself, switch addictions, whether to their careers, motherhood, gambling, etc. I have worked with countless men who, when their chemicals use threatens a job, quit using and become dependent upon their occupation, working ridiculous hours to the point nothing else seems to matter. Inevitably, they will get bored and begin using again, usually when they have finally dug themselves out of the hole that chemicals put them in the first place. Careers and jobs provide us with a sense of worth in that we gain recognition. Our employment also provides for financial security and, therefore, for the illusion of security as well. No wonder our employment and careers are such a major player in our struggle to experience a meaningful and authentic sense of worth and security. It seems that when jobs are threatened, most people will make cowardly compromises to maintain these jobs, whether they are fulfilling or whether they are being asked to compromise their values or not. Many drug addicts are awakened to the reality of their drug addiction when their jobs are threatened. It is also equally the case when anything of value like romances, driver's licenses, and relationships with children are threatened and etc., many addicts will stop and reevaluate the importance of their addictive behavior. Switching addictions seems inevitable when we define addictions from this perspective. This is due to the difficulty in surrendering all our illusions and opening up to experiencing the terror, pain, and disorientation that occurs when our sense of worth or security is threatened. There are no simple solutions to the predicaments of the human condition. It's hard to swallow that even faith and uncertainty are bedfellows. Faith is not striving to deny reality or stuffing God into a box. Freedom from addictions occurs only when we are able to find our worth and security are ways that open us up to life and the reality of uncertainty, insecurity, worthlessness, and mortality.

You're born with nothing,
And better off that way . . .

When we found the things we loved,
They were crushed and dying in the dirt.
We tried to pick up the pieces,
And get away without getting hurt . . .

And us running burned and blind,
Chasing something in the night.

—Bruce Springsteen,
"Something In The Night"

We turn now to the dynamics of the self-deception within the context of the human condition. These various responses to the human predicament, whether individual or collective in nature, which fail to address the fundamental problems of our human condition, let alone provide authentic answers to the riddles of life and death. We will examine what I believe some healthy and mature responses in section 2.

Defenses, Denial, Self-Deception, and the Nature of Illusion

And all you see is an illusion . . .

And one peculiar point I see
Of one of the many wrongs of me
As truth is gathered I rearrange
Inside out, outside in everyday.

—Yes, "Perpetual Change"

The pairs of opposites that lies herein: truth/falsehood and good/evil. While I accept both as instrumentally valuable, I do not believe synthesizing these opposites is neither possible nor healthy; only truth and goodness are of intrinsic value. Evil can be transformed, however, as we will explore in section 2 where I tackle these pairs of opposites in detail.

Desperation laid her bare . . .

She told herself a story
That flat out wasn't true.

—Bruce Cockburn, "Different When It Comes to You"

Defenses, Denial, and Self-Deception

The opposite of truth is falsehood. Our various attachments/addictions are in fact defenses or lies, which deny painful realities. They are but diverse strategies/defenses used to run away and avoid reality and the pain associated with reality. All our defenses have one main goal, which is to *deny reality*. In fact, all the defenses are different forms of denial, and denial is the form in which falsehood is couched.

Self-deception is simply that we believe in our lies and falsehoods. We believe these lies and act as if they were true. We become attached to our self-deceptions. We and those unfortunates who are in our lives pay a price for such distortions and dishonesty. The need to hide behind external illusions is so powerful that everyone seems to periodically struggle with attachments and the self-deceptions they engender. The collective capacity to lie to ourselves and believe these fabrications is what is referred to as self-deception. We all are our own worst enemies when we believe our own lies. They all have one thing in common: they are variations on the theme "to run away from truth." Defenses are constructed to avoid painful truths of whatever origin and content. We defend ourselves because there are real threats in the environment, and we think we have something to lose. The point is to be aware of our defenses and use them consciously and without deceptions. More often than not, our defenses are unconscious and therefore become walls erected to protect ourselves from painful truths. Denial is the major defense used to avoid painful truths—the primary dynamic behind self-deception. Sadly, the truth is often forsaken and discarded like yesterday's garbage.

The forms of our self-deceptions are varied. Regardless, they are all forms of denial. Here are some examples, to name a few: justifying, making excuses, minimizing, blaming, projecting, and intellectualizing. We as humans have convinced ourselves that to kill, hate, judge, gossip, forsake, displace, control, condemn, and betray others is justified provided our delusions cross certain thresholds. The more fears, guilt, and/or insecurities we house, the greater the motivations for self-deception. By contrast, the more fears and guilt we overcome, the more we will be capable of taking a stand on truth. However, the fact is that the majority of us choose to distract ourselves in all sorts of superficial endeavors to avoid taking an honest account of ourselves. It takes emotional and mental courage to reflect upon our motives and behaviors. The world is complicated, and we have little control over outcomes. We are all full of contradictions, and these set us up for self-deceptions. The way of truth is painful beyond description. It is easy to give in to self-pity, throw up our hands and give up. I have often found myself using these defenses for periods of time. We all fail and fall short. We must identify our self-deceptions and then tell ourselves the truth. Those of us who choose to seek truth *will* have compassion on others, for how can one who traffics with truths about themselves judge their neighbor?

The fact is self-deceptions are so subtle we often miss them. One of the functions of our mind is to rationalize, give reasons for the way something is. This is secondary to the initial experience. Initial experiences are raw, and without giving them some form and context, we are lost. However, this process of rationalizing is intrinsically flawed in that our mental conceptions can never match the original experience, nor can this ability to reason be assumed to be accurate. In fact, our mind plays tricks with the truth spontaneously as unconscious defenses scurry into the mode of self-protection. Our history is littered with horrors enacted in the name of religion, politics, etc., which is built upon self-deceptions. Today, fundamentalism, liberalism, and most "-isms" continue to distort, delete, and generalize the truth to catastrophic heights. Truth is painful and shit happens. The truth liberates the psyche from its ills. This can only occur when our ego takes a backseat. This includes an ability and willingness to grow in self-knowledge, uncovering all the dark aspects of our individual and collective nature. Only then can one take these bitter seeds and watch them yield fruits in their season. Following self-knowledge is the adaptations to truth. This is a Herculean task. Because of the pain and responsibility required, we take refuge in all forms of denial—making excuses, justifying our motives and behavior, blaming others, hiding in the crowd of public opinion or some system like political parties, corporations, or institutions, which develop a value system of their own. We can measure the degree of self-deceptions by their manifestations. Self-deception grows exponentially. The fruits of self-deceptions are churned out like factory parts and include the abuses of power and ills of the soul we have already discussed.

Self-worth is tied up in large part to our self-image or concept. If you wish to really face your self-deception and therefore your shadow, just talk to those who know you best. You will more than likely find yourself hearing about some painful truth about yourself that you have heard before but no doubt minimized as your loved ones have been sharing these shadowy characteristics with you for years! Self-knowledge takes tremendous courage because we have to face truths, which initially impair and possibly destroy our self-image that is tied to a persona, that is a social mask that we present to the world. This is often phony and concerned with a superficial image. We all play roles in society, and the persona is the mask we use to play these roles. Western culture has been inundated with image consultants, PR departments, advertisers, and lawyers spinning (which is a euphemism for lying), buying into image and rejecting content and substance. On an institutional scale, there have been so many cover-ups by our military and government that either we don't care or can't trust anything they say. All large institutions develop a collective persona and shadow; that is what they present to the society as a whole as an image and the lies that are believed and perpetuated by each member who chooses to remain in that system.

Most self-deception is easily remedied by learning to attend to our inner voice, which in sensitive individuals is an immense guide to the truth. Some of us become completely phony and live behind the social mask, becoming what are called hypocrites. However, most of us are not this blazingly dishonest and phony—yet we all hide some urges, feelings, thoughts, and motives that contradict the image we have of ourselves and/or the image we want others to have of us. Many aspects of our shadow are those thoughts, impulses, and feelings that we were taught in childhood that are bad or dirty. Everyone carries variations of these social taboos within us. We are human and share a common inner life in which we discover a great variety of desires, longings, fears, etc. We all have to filter our inner motives and desires that cross our minds. I am not disgusted by much—except by evil, those motives and actions that attempt to desecrate and fabricate the truth. Self-deception does not fall into this category *unless we willfully choose to remain in our self-deceptions.* Our shadow contains a wide variety of truths about ourselves we are not inclined to be honest about. When we repress truths about ourselves, the shadow is animated with infantile desires. We need to learn to identify what is going on within us and accept what is prior to making subjective judgments about what to do with what is within us.

Like I have discussed, the consequences of all this self-deception is that our health-care facilities and prisons are littered with all manner of neurosis, psychosis, character disorders, anger management programs, drugs, alcohol, gambling, sex, programs, etc., to deal with these bevies of dysfunction.

> How can I be?
> What I want to be?
> When all I want to do is strip away
> These stilled constraints
> And crush this charade
> Shred this sad masquerade.
>
> —REM, "Walk Unafraid"

As a chemical dependency counselor, I wrestle with self-deception in my clients daily.

Addicts are almost always the last to know they are addicted. Their lives are in shambles, and their emotions are charged with an inordinate amount of pain and anger. However, many maintain fictions it's someone else's fault, and they minimize their use and its consequences to absurd proportions. The addict is in denial, avoiding the truth that they need to surrender their addictive behavior while maintaining fictions that they can continue using. When addicts abstain, they will be hurled back to face their self-deceptions regarding the addiction itself and their needs for security and self-worth. This is where a good addiction specialist will explore routes that will ferry clients to purposes that fulfill their destiny and, in effect, replace the addiction.

Are you schooling yourself in self-deception? If you are honest, the answer is oftentimes yes. I suggest you begin the process of accepting the truth about yourself by asking those you care about the most to give you honest input about your self-deceptions. Secondly, set regular time aside for self-reflection. By the way, our growing awareness will be bitter to the tongue but sweet to the stomach.

> Did I hear someone tell a lie?
> Did I hear someone's distant cry?
>
> —Bob Dylan, "Love Sick"

> I can hear the turning of the key
> I've been deceived by the clown inside of me.
> I thought he was righteous but he's vain
> Oh, something's a-telling me I wear the ball
> And chain.
>
> —Bob Dylan, "Abandoned Love"

The Shame of Weakness, Inadequacy, Failure, Cowardice, and the Fear of Death

I asked my Father, I said Father change my name,
The one I'm using now
It's covered up with fear and filth, and cowardice, and shame
Yes and lover, lover, lover, lover, lover, lover,
lover come back to me . . .

—L. Cohen, "Lover, Lover, Lover"

Ring the bells that still can ring.
Forget your perfect offering.
There is a crack in everything.
That's how the light gets in.

—Leonard Cohen, "Anthem"

Introduction

Powerlessness and weakness is the opposite of strength. Weakness without strength is feeble, while strength without weakness is delusional. We should be able to draw consolation from the fact we share all these archetypal experiences.

Weaknesses and Inadequacy

Yes, you must leave everything
That you cannot control;
It begins with your family,
But soon comes around to your soul.

—Leonard Cohen, "Sisters of Mercy"

Most of us have to lose our physical strength before we come to grips with the intrinsic weaknesses and inadequacy inherent within the human condition and within our own souls. It takes a lot of courage and strength to confront ourselves about our weaknesses and inadequacies—some we're born with, others we create, others are part and parcel of our destiny, others coupled with the human condition, others we die with. In point of fact, it is the strong that recognize and wrestle with their weaknesses, *simply because they are honest* about the suffering provoked by the intrinsic truth that we are all weak and inadequate and dying. Those who face inadequacy and impotence are strong in their weaknesses and are not paralyzed by them. We are not equal and never will be. We are not equal in every sphere, discipline, or ability. We all are weak, not only in particular skills and abilities, but in experience and wisdom and in our inability to control life. We are constricted by nature, the human condition itself, lack of experiences, self-deceptions, and fears. From our basic personalities, to the experiences we are afforded, to everything that is outside our control, life is what happens to us, and how we decipher these riddles becomes the measure by what we become.

Existential Guilt

We all struggle with existential guilt (i.e., that is guilt that is intrinsic to the human condition. This guilt is born of (1) inner oppositions and divisions, and (2) our inherent powerlessness over creation. Regarding the former, we are split between opposing desires and, in particular, the urges and desires toward good and evil with an imperative to choose. We are born with these inner divisions, and our guilt is normal due to the fact we are required to grow in consciousness through these inner tensions of opposites. The unwillingness to face life by wrestling with the opposites is one of our main weaknesses. Regarding the latter, we are fragile beings tethered to life by a few heartbeats and the workings of fate. Can you make all your own food, clothing, shelter? Is your will power enough to change all that you want to change? Change is impossible until we first face our predicament honestly, admitting the truth of our mutual interdependence and inherent weaknesses. This guilt relates to being puny and weak in the face of creation. We have consciousness that can imagine unlimited possibilities while simultaneously a body, which fastens us to limitations. As E. Becker said, "we are gods that shit." Such inherent contradiction stings where we are most vulnerable.

Failure and Disappointment

We all fail at resolutions, projects, and relationships; anything we pursue is potentially a failure. Only those engaged in life risk failure, and this takes great courage. Disappointments haunt us as many possibilities, dreams, and plans have been pilfered, lost, or rotted on the vine. Many of these dreams were never meant to be. We also fail and disappoint others and ourselves. We are disappointed in those we love. We harbor disparate feelings toward those who once held prominent roles in our lives and, for one reason or another, have been bumped from the scenes. The burdens of past failures can drown the idealists and any of us in self-pity, self-hate, resentments, and sadness. Each reacts differently to failures and disappointments, and what seem inconsequential to one can destroy another. Regrets burden and haunt scores of souls wrestling with the past to the extent they get ensnared and struggle to reside in the present.

Saving Face/Shame

The social mask (persona) does not allow for any honest show of weakness. The irony is, as we shall see with Job, all our weaknesses set the stages for significant transformations. Each culture has its own set of values, which sets us up to repress the weaker sides of our nature. I have often heard a client share how inadequate they feel, and I reply, "Right, you are inadequate, so why don't you just join the rest of us?" Shame has subjugated mid-Eastern ethos where if one loses face, they become dead to the group. Shame is attached to our shadowy underside like stink to a monkey. We are shamed by our weaknesses from the get-go, and we inherently hid these from ourselves and others.

A friend of mine, Kevin O'Grady, put shame this way in making a distinction from depression: "Depression says a problem can't be fixed while shame says I can't be fixed." Shame internalizes weaknesses and inadequacies and believes we are bad, inadequate, inferior, or wrong. The reality is our attitudes, beliefs, motives, and behaviors are not perfect. A problem arises when shame and guilt are not differentiated, and mistakes are converted and internalized into feelings that we are constitutionally inferior. Shame is also a form of self-protection in that if we find fault in ourselves, we don't have to wrestle with existential guilt while we mine for sympathy from others. Much of shame is self-hatred that gets fossilized as a defense against the truth. We need to pry shame, guilt, and weaknesses apart so we can face the truth and adapt to it without becoming its hostages. The nature of our shame necessitates unique differentiations and the ability to detach from internalizing our weaknesses and mistakes.

I talked about our inferior function in chapter 3. I said this inferior conscious function contains large deposits of weaknesses and shame. Believe it. When and if you get to a place where you are confronted with these weaknesses, hang on, and remember, all your developed and competent functions will collapse for a season. Hold out; you will see from the narratives of Job and Odysseus, winter inexorably flows to spring and summer for those who patiently wait and endure.

Legitimate Guilt

Well, I've been where you're hanging
I think I can see how you're pinned.
When you're not feeling holy
Your loneliness says that you've sinned.

—Leonard Cohen, "Sisters of Mercy"

We make multitudes of mistakes and fail to hit the mark (the literal definition of sin). As we discussed in chapter 8, our will has a limited amount of energy, and we inevitably fall short and miss the mark. We are incapable of perfection, and our missing the mark can haunt us with restless nights. Missing the mark is when we fail to live according to spiritual principles or laws that appear to be as fundamental to creation as the physical laws. These principles are varied, and this entire book is concerned with these principles and truths. We will cart around the same mistakes until we make them conscious. When we miss the mark, we need to gather valuable self-knowledge in order to be capable of adapting to new truths/insights. It takes humility to admit when we are wrong and unable to hit the mark. Asking for help is a sure sign of humility.

Legitimate guilt is that inner understanding that we have broken one of these principles or laws. For instance, when we lie to someone, we know by our inner experience of guilt that we have committed a wrong. The Ten Commandments are specific examples in which these laws take shape. There are different kind of laws—physical, psychological, spiritual, universal—which, when broken, cause guilt or some kind of pain and suffering. Guilt is a positive experience due to the fact it offers us opportunities to turn around, change, and mature. We need guilt feelings to help us gauge our attitudes, beliefs, and behaviors—for the purpose of making proper corrections. We need to sincerely acknowledge our guilt, admit when we are wrong, identify our motives and weaknesses (which set us up for miss the mark), and make proper reparations when necessary, with the intention to not continue making these same mistakes. Living in a state of sin is when we know something is wrong, and yet continue to consciously live the lie while propagating the behavior. When we feel guilty, we are then capable of adapting and changing in such a way as to overcome it. None will ever hit the mark entirely every time, but we need to aim well with passions to hit the center of the target.

Change is impossible until we first face our predicament honestly, admitting the truth. To begin the healing process, we need to empty self while accepting what is. Constructing moral conclusions take time and power that stands outside our limited ego-body-consciousness. The drowning man must be rendered helpless before a rescue can commence. We shall witness Job's and Odysseus's spiritual awakening in this very context in section 2. In all our grandeur and sordidness, we are part of the human experience. Guilt is as much a part of our human experience as our abilities and strengths. The person who knows their weaknesses are stronger than those who don't. Every strategist knows it at our points of weakness that the enemy strikes, not at our strong points. We will go on in our delusions and muddle along until the bubble bursts and we fall. Then we must pick ourselves up by facing the truth that lies within us.

> You raise me up in grace,
> Then you put me in a place,
> Where I must fall.
>
> —Leonard Cohen, "That Don't Make It Junk"

Cowardice

Cowardice is when we run away from ourselves and the truth, give in to our fears, or just give up because it's just too damn hard. Self-pity and fear are the antecedents of cowardice as we just give in and give up. It is ordinary to be a coward for the avoidance of reality and truth is effortless and easy. On the other hand, it takes courage to face reality and the pain it entails. When we allow fear and self-pity to control us, we become depressed and neurotic, and the pain and nuisance we cause others who are present in our orbit are boundless. So many decisions we make are unconsciously driven by self-pity and fear, they are too many to describe here. That is why it is so important we cultivate the attitude of self-reflection and self-knowledge so we can delve into our motives and ferret out these poisons and begin the process of overcoming them. The process of overcoming will be discussed in depth is section 2. But make no mistake, overcoming self-pity and fear are essential to growth into real wholeness and enlightenment!

Futility and the Absurd

Creation seems to have deposited a certain measure of futility and absurdity upon beings that intermingle with matter. Incomprehensible catastrophes visit the human condition with the absurd—famines and earthquakes, birth defects, Alzheimer's disease, floods, tsunamis, accidents, pestilence and diseases of unimaginable dreadfulness, hurricanes and tornadoes, along with all the manipulations, guilt trips, abuse, evil, and violence we heap on each other as if we were all garbage dumps. We all have our motives misconstrued, and the accusations fly in all sorts of absurd directions. We are smitten with so much we can't control, and events seem to hurl us in into a futility of powerlessness and weariness. Our grasping at solutions often makes matters worse. We often apply the right principles to the wrong situations; we share the right things at the wrong times. It seems our powerlessness and mistakes track us down until it seems all that is left is weariness and futility. Obstacles weigh us down with a heaviness that often leaves hope in its wake. The futility inherent in creation stretches archetypal coping strategies beyond their capacity to counter with even a modicum of proficiency. There are so many problems that lie within and without, and it seems we can do so little about it all, and the little we can do sometimes seems so fruitless. The absurd visits us all at one time or another, and futility will track you down like a well-trained hound dog. Be of good courage—this is part and parcel of the human condition, and it too shall pass. To alleviate these distressing experiences, I often read Kafka, and

I usually am able to find some latent humor in the incompressibility of it all.

Death

And the sword outwears it sheath,
And the soul outwears its breast . . .

—Leonard Cohen, "Go No More A-Roving"

Disease is often camouflaged within our body, and death comes without appointment. Death exposes us to futility, weakness, guilt, shame, failure, and inadequacy. Death uncovers our ultimate weaknesses and futility at the heart of a world where we are limited in how long we live. Death is so uncomfortable because it reveals how fragile and weak we really are while housing the unknown, the unmanageable, and the incomprehensible. One minute we are a breathing vital being, and the next an inert and silent body fit only for the grave or some form of disposal before our decaying flesh becomes too revolting to witness.

I've had cause to experience the anguish of futility, weakness, inadequacy, guilt, powerlessness, etc., on many occasions. My being trembles as failures and weaknesses leave me dumbfounded. I sense in myself endless rays of disappointments compounded by inadequacies. Sometime no one seems at fault, but creation itself seems conspired against my ailing faculties. It seems creation is hard-wired for futility, primordial style. I am suffocated by a growing sense of how much suffering and futility exists in this created world. I long to assuage the suffering I see round me and yet feel so frail and powerless to do anything about it. What can a fragile and mortal man do to overcome pollution, corruption, poverty, suffering, injustice, ignorance, fear, hatred, abuse/violence/torture/murder, and war? When my internalized shame is activated, I find myself paralyzed in a self-loathing and drenched in the conviction that I am fundamentally inferior, resolutely deficient. I am unlovable and worthy of all rejection and contempt. My shame is contaminated with the blues, alchemy of putrid puss and stench from infections where no cure seems possible. Depression and anguish hover about like the little birds around a hawk that has glided too close to their nests. A futility sometimes permeates my every thought and memory, every emotion, every possible activity of will, every synapse and muscle, and my every desire and need is tainted by this relentless mood. It feels like nothing can be done to change anything, nothing will change, so what's the point of trying? Temptation's fire swirls about my desires in an attempt to get me to regress into every past neurosis— in a doomed quest for temporary anodynes and reprieves.

This process of accepting futility, death, guilt, inadequacy, and weaknesses is difficult. Maintaining faith and hope that things have an ultimate purpose and will get better is often hard to hold on to. I've felt like I have fallen into a void where darkness was my only mate. Admittedly, I've felt plundered and fleeced of all redemption. I felt incapable of being enlightening from such dread. Hope has all but disappeared for a season. This has been referred to as the dark night of the soul and a wilderness experience.

My heart's like a blister
From doing what I do . . .

Now the deal has been dirty
Since dirty began
I'm not asking for mercy
Not from the man
You just don't ask for mercy
While you're still on the stand . . .
It wasn't for nothing
That they put me away
I fell with my angel
Down the chain of command.
There's a Law, there's an Arm, there's a Hand . . .

—Leonard Cohen, "The Law"

In the time of my confession, in the hour of my deepest need
When the pool of tears beneath my feet flood every new born seed
There's a dyin' voice within me reaching out somewhere,

Toiling in the danger and it in morals of despair . . .

Like Cain, I now behold this chain of events I must break . . .

Oh the flowerers of indulgence and the weeds of yesteryear,
Like criminals, they have choked the breath
of conscience and good cheer.
The sun beats down upon the steps of time to light the way
To ease the pain of idleness and the memory of decay.

I gaze into the doorway of temptations angry flame
And every time I pass that way I always hear my name . . .

I hear the ancient footsteps like the motion of the sea
Sometimes I turn, there's someone there, other times it's only me.
I am hanging in the balance of the reality of man
Like every sparrow fallen, like every grain of sand.

—Bob Dylan, "Every Grain of Sand"

A Study in Contrast:
Inflation and Alienation

Well the walls of pride
Are high and wide
You can't see over
To the other side

—Bob Dylan, "Cold Irons Bound"

Introduction

The obvious pair of opposites is inflation/alienation. This is discussed in great detail below. First, I will explore the experience of arrogance or inflation. Secondly, the opposite experience of alienation. Both conscious experiences are tethered to the same archetypal dynamic.

Inflation or Arrogance

As we approach the sources of creative truth hidden in the archetypes, we readily fall into a trap by identifying with the energy of its emanations. This is the state called inflation. The problem is our ego identifies with this influx of positive energy (truths) the archetypes birth in our consciousness. Other terms include arrogance, egotism, superiority, and conceit. There are temptations to believe we are the source of the archetypes, that our egos authors truth. A good example in my field of chemical dependency is after the client gains valuable self-knowledge and begins adapting to the truths of their addictions, they inevitably identify their ego with the positive energy that the archetypes have facilitated. I hear statements like "I got it now" or "I'll never use again." The clients set themselves up for relapses and slips as they lose the humility that went into gaining the initial insights and positive energy to begin with! They feel great while integrating an archetype, and the influx of energy becomes identified with their ego-consciousness. Pride comes before a fall. I believe we all can recall a time when we were enlightened by a new insight that changed our life and we felt on top of the world. Everything comes together; we succeeded at something we had failed at repeatedly, and life seems peachy. Then a subtle process takes place as we gain energy and new responsibilities and power as a result of integrating an archetype. We become full of ourselves. The fall occurs when a subtle arrogance seeps into our ego-body-conscious-ness. Lost is the conscious awareness of our inherent weaknesses and gratitude for our newfound growth. We begin to believe we can handle whatever comes our way. This is but one example, but I think you get the idea. The crux of the matter is we will and do repeatedly and subtly lose humility, which makes integrating the archetypes possible in the first place. Our ego did not create these new competencies and changes, nor are we the source of the archetypal truths. *We do not create the truth.* We can only channel it through our ego-body-consciousness. We've become too big for our britches or full of hot air. It's not that we can't be thrilled by successful changes and transformations that have occurred within us. However, the measure of health is we *never lose our gratitude* for the assistance our ego received, which made our successes and changes possible. We must not forget where we have been, where our neighbor might be right now, and that we will inevitably fall into this trap again. When we are gripped by the archetypes, the positive energy is so powerful and the temptations so great to identify with them. Reality is we have tapped into something bigger than ourselves, yet all our weaknesses have not disappeared! The truth has the *power* to liberate the most confined prisoner. When we integrate truth, we become enlightened with its positive energy, and we become capable of channeling this energy. As we integrate new archetypal energies, we must accept we are channels whose responsibility it is to keep the channel free from the obstructions of our inflation and egocentric attitudes. When we forget that we are not the source but only channels of the truth, we will inescapably fall into alienation.

Alienation

When seduced by inflation, we eventually are flung like cannonballs into alienation. We feel worthless, full of shame, disconnected to the world, and depressed. Our unconscious mind responds to inflation by compensating with its opposite, alienation. We are either too close (inflation) or too far (alienation) from the source of all positive energy, the archetypes. Inflation only can last for a short time before we are flung downward toward reality, thus experiencing alienation. The ego takes a needed hit, and we fall from grace. We will remain in this state of alienation until we recognize the dynamics of our inflation and begin to adapt to the proper attitudes of humility and gratitude toward the power and energies of the archetypes, which extend well beyond our limited ego-consciousness and wills. This is one psychological aspect of depression; the other is where we allow our fears to control us.

Balance

We will always experience this ping-pong dialectic, back and forth, to and fro, as we sway and dangle between these extremes of inflation and alienation. This is a natural and normal progression; everyone vacillates between these two until a healthy balance is attained. Mood disorders are mental disorders that are examples that reflect this vacillation between arrogance and alienation. These disorders may have biochemical or psychological causes, but the dynamics are the same. We need to acknowledge these extreme moods, which vacillate between inflation and alienation and wrestle with our inner life to achieve balance. Our ability to achieve any such balance is beyond the control of our ego-consciousness alone. The source where we can access our potential for wholeness has many names—some call God, others call the archetypes of the unconscious mind, chi, the great spirit, the toa, etc. The toa means the middle way with the goal of balance and wholeness whereby our moods are neither hurled too far in either direction. It matters not what term is used, but only that the ego is no longer identified with this positive source/energy. In all the twelve-step programs, it's called the higher power. The goal is to become one with the source without identifying with it. We will shuffle back and forth in this cosmic dance throughout our life as we swirl and carom toward and away for this source of power and energy delineated by these various terminologies. We did not create ourselves and we will die, yet most of us intuit we are part and parcel of a cosmic, mysterious something that resides within, besides, and beyond us. *Again, we are only capable of being channels of the truth, not the truth itself.* We all swing on the pendulum of inflation and alienation. Alienation transports us into depression while inflation ferries us into delusions of grandeur. The many addicts I work with take this ride on the pendulum from one day to the next. "All is well, I got it now," says Joe while shortly thereafter, a relapse occurs or some other humbling experiences send Joe to the brinks of despair, and he exclaims, "I'll never make it." Neither extreme belief is true.

> Whole lot of people seeing double tonight
> From the disease of conceit,
> Give ya delusions of grandeur
> And a evil eye
> Give you idea that
> You're too good to die,
> Then they bury you from your head to your feet
> From the disease of conceit.

> —Bob Dylan, "Disease of Conceit"

Attitudes of the Heart and Their Ripple Effects and Behavior

If my heart could do my thinking
And my head begin to feel
I would look upon the world anew
And know what's truly real.

—Van Morrison, "I Forgot Love Existed"

Introduction

The pairs of opposites we delve into now are positive and negative attitudes. While everything comes in pairs of opposites as one of the pairs without the other makes each meaningless, I work toward the positive ones while accepting the negative ones within myself and use them as opportunities for growth. As we have learned from quantum physics, everything has an impact on everything it comes in contact with—ripples of karma, so to speak.

Attitudes of the Heart

There is another prominent aspect of the consciousness we have yet to qualify or discuss in any depth. We carry with us throughout the journey of life *attitudes* like we do our beliefs. Attitudes are often less conscious than our beliefs, though each may have been acquired without much forethought, choice (brain development), or serious thinking (most form in childhood and many acquired from our parents). Like all energy, attitudes are gifts wrapped in both positive and negative forms.

Here is a list of the primary attitudes I have wrestled with. I call them attitudes of the heart. These are attitudes that we adopt throughout our journey through this life. They are in no particular order:

humility/false pride   gratitude/ingratitude

compassion/hatred   open-mindedness/
close-mindedness

forgiveness/resentments   modesty/vanity

justice/injustice   trust/distrust

courage/cowardice   patience/impatience

benevolence/malevolence   grace/shame

kindness/cruelty   love/fear

mercy/merciless   phoniness/sincerity

detachment/enmeshment

I call these attitudes of the heart as they measure the depths of one's character, and they reflect the levels and depths in the ones who embody them. Attitudes are archetypes as well. In fact, attitudes are as significant as our beliefs for we are bathed in both. An entire book could be written to describe and discuss these attitudes in great detail, and I do not wish to do so here. The main point I'd like to stress is we house these attitudes in our soul or psyche, and we are responsible for the attitudes we nurture. Most spiritual teachers emphasize the attitudes of a person are the authors of behavior along with our beliefs.

There is little doubt the most important of these are *truth/dishonesty, compassion/hatred,* or *mercy/judgment, humility/false pride,* and *courage/cowardice.* These five I have prioritized and recognize as paramount in the fleshing out of my own moral destiny. What I wish to stress is our attitudes contain a level of import and consequence to the overall economy of our psyche or soul we had better not forget. The moral aspect of our being is of the utmost significance and meaning to our lives. When my attitude is positive, possibilities are vast, and hope springs from despair.

I had a dream in my midforties, which fits in nicely here and will also offer an example of dream analysis. Here is the situation and my conscious attitude: I was a senior counselor at a treatment program in the Twin Cities. I was supervising a counselor whom I thought was not particularly competent.

The dream: In my dream, I began using mood-altering chemicals again, and I was assigned to his group to receive treatment.

Interpretation: As I discussed in chapter 3, the unconscious mind often takes a compensatory position to our conscious attitudes and beliefs. The dream did this by reversing the circumstances between the counselor and myself; now I was in a position beneath him while he was above me—the exact opposite of our positions in reality. Therefore, the dream was informing me that my attitude was the opposite of what it should be, and I had underestimated him.

I recognized this and adjusted my attitude toward this person. I began to exhibit more appreciation and to treat him with more respect. He had obviously picked up my condescending attitude, and after I made the proper adjustments to my attitude, he reversed his attitude toward me, responding in kind with a change of his own—by letting me in on his life. I realized not only had I underestimated his counseling abilities, I had no idea he had the large degree of depth and mystical experiences, which were of specific interest to me. We became friends for the rest of our time together, and when I left to begin writing this book, he cried with me during a staff gathering to wish me well. As a footnote, I have been a supervisor to many counselors, and while I have questioned the competence of more than a few, I never was confronted by my unconscious in any other case. In addition, when I questioned the competence of other particular counselors, I never wished them ill, never tried to judge them as people, or never tried to go beyond the limits set by my job description when working with them.

Behavior

Broken hands on broken ploughs'
Broken treaties, broken vows,
Broken pipes, broken tools,
People bending broken rules . . .

—Bob Dylan, "Everything Is Broken"

Behavior is external and, therefore, the easiest to identify and recognize when change is needed. Our behavior poses the query, "Why did I do that?" Understanding behavior is crucial; I have had countless clients whine about lovers' actions—after I have warned them they both better dig deeper and discover some understanding as to what the problems/ motives were, or it would inevitably repeat itself. If they fail to grasp the dynamics behind their or their lover's behaviors, they are destined to find it repeated. I have heard too many examples of infidelity and sit in wonderment when my client forgives these betrayals without getting an ounce of insight from their partner into why they acted out in this manner. In addition, there are thousands of examples of where couples fail to sort out their actions and reactions with each other and leave a problem without resolving it and then begin complaining to me about their partner and the unresolved behavior patterns. Self-pity oozes and puts stains on the relationship and everyone within earshot until they make conscious the dynamics and take responsibility to change it.

My heart is broken whenever I really give some newspaper articles some serious thought and reflection. The things we do to each other, the incredible acts of ignorance and violence we humans have committed on the world, are beyond imagination. The human suffering we inflict on each other is so indescribable. However, behavior is more understandable the more we delve into the secret places of the heart, and when in conjunction, we come to grasp our motives.

> Terrible deeds done in the name
> Of tunnel vision and the fear of change
> Surely are expressions of
> a soul that's turned its back on love

—Bruce Cockburn, "Put It in Your Heart"

Ripples Effects

> Like a stone on the surface of a still
> River
> Driving the ripples on forever
> Redemption rips through the surface of
> Time
> In the cry of a tiny babe . . .

—Bruce Cockburn, "Cry of a Tiny Babe"

All our attitudes, beliefs, and behaviors affect the world around us like ripples in the water. All that we are and do and think radiates outward to the circumference (toward everyone around us). Other people and all living things are impacted by our attitudes, behaviors, and beliefs. Positive or negative energy branches out from the center of our soul. Attitudes and beliefs are part of our inner consciousness and author our every action. We have all felt negative and positive energy in our every-day experience. When politics are present, therefore power, whether at work or wherever, everyone's intuition picks up the vibes. When people are carrying energy above certain thresholds and enter a room, their energy is palpable. We often know when we are in unsafe or safe places and with compassionate or egocentric people. Our influence on the environment and others around us goes far beyond what we register with our five senses!

Although we have been discussing many of these universal principles all along, it seems appropriate to spend some time on the dynamics and content of these universal principles. We know that natural laws have consequences if not respected and adapted to. Touch fire, and your skin will burn. We can intuit from experience and natural laws that moral laws exist—and if we flaunt and abuse them, dire consequences will occur.

The wise thus intuit moral laws gleaned from nature and temper their ego's assaults upon the moral universe. These laws are reflected in positive and negative energies. Whether these energies are separate intelligences or are built entirely from within our psyche is a matter of dispute. At any rate, the wise expand consciousness as these universal principles are valued and adapted to. Adapting to these principles or truths provides the psyche guidance to ward off potential inner or outer disasters.

From the sordid to the sublime, we project what is inside us out into the world at large. The ripples we each create spread like wildfires. If we could only see with spiritual eyes the impact we have on one another, it would cause us to pause and contemplate on how we act toward those around us. Many of the things we say and do are powerful tools by which we affect the world. We each pick up from others much more than behaviors alone for many of us are capable of sensing attitudes much easier than behaviors. As an intuitive, whenever I am around others, impressions flood my consciousness. While I take life seriously, there are times when laughter need accompany love for these ripples transport healing to a wounded world. Despite the many ills in the world, I have witnessed much love and healing in my day, and I will always hang on to my faith and hope that a better world is possible.

> There's a parasite feeding
> Everybody's bag of rage
> What goes out returns again
> To smite the mouth and burn the page
> Under the rain of all our dark tomorrows . . .
>
> —Bruce Cockburn, "All Our Dark Tomorrows"

Beliefs and Faith

I need someone to believe in, someone to trust
I need someone to believe in, someone to trust.

I'd rather trust a countryman than a townman,
You can judge by his eyes, take a look if you can,
He'll smile through his guard,
Survival trains hard . . .

But down here,
I'm so alone with my fear,
With everything that I hear.
And every single door, that I've walked through
Brings me back here again
I've got to find my own way.

—Genesis, "The Chamber of Doors"

The pairs of opposites henceforth are belief/unbelief and faith/faithlessness. Belief and faith without skepticism is naïve and subject to all forms of distortions, deletions, and generalizations and fanaticism; unbelief without belief is nihilism taken to the outer reaches where purpose, direction, and meaning no longer exist.

Belief and Faith

Beliefs are what we hold to be true. Beliefs and our attitudes are inextricably linked; they both precede all behaviors and many of our emotions. These include our values, priorities, ideas about the dynamics of how things operate, etc. Our beliefs birth our vision concerning the world and our place within it. False beliefs hinder our ability to love and keep us stuck in delusion and self-deception. This is often due to repression. We all have beliefs that are assumptions from which we perceive the world. We cling firmly and hold most of them dear because as we explored earlier, most people attach differing degrees of worth and security to their beliefs. Everything we do stem from some belief and attitude or another. This entire work is about what I hold to be truth and is full of my assumptions and beliefs.

However, it's essential to remember some beliefs will change over the course of time as we experience more and more of life. Hopefully, we will be making adaptations to truth, and if so, it will have a major impact on what we believe. As I said earlier, no one has a monopoly on truth, and therefore, we need to be humble and open-minded about what we believe. This does not imply we are to be wishy-washy or that we need to fail to make commitments to our beliefs. On the contrary, we need to be thoughtful about what we believe and then make commitments to the implications our beliefs engender. What we don't need, however, is shoving our beliefs down the throats of others or to become rigid and self-righteous about them. As the song from the Genesis epitaph implies, we need to be cautious and thoughtful about what we believe.

Beliefs and faith overlap *but are not the same.* Basically, faith is belief plus trust. Faith confers various levels of intimacy and meaning and therefore furnishes legs for our beliefs. We all have faith in something, whether it be combinations of science, other people, our tribe or nation, God, nature, whatever. Faith is stretching a belief to the point of trusting it with portions or all of our life. The stronger the faith, the more we are willing to trust and sacrifice. Faith is in that which cannot be registered by our five senses. Faith requires a leap into the unknown and unseen. Faith is an experience of the soul.

If we believe without thinking adequately and we make commitments to these beliefs, they will fail to stand the test of experience. If we think through our beliefs and fail to make any commitments to them, we exhibit our fear of living in the real world and become detached to the degree we fail to lay it all on the line. Do you reflect upon what you believe and only then make commitments of faith that reflect your beliefs? Some are too quick to commit without thinking through the ramifications, and others stand on the fence too long and leave behind opportunities to grow in wisdom and wholeness/holiness.

We're playing those mind games
Together
Pushing the barrier, planting seeds . . .

Some call it magic, the search for the grail,
Love is the answer, and you know that for sure,
Love is the flower; you got to let it,
You got to let grow,

So keep on playing those mind games together
Faith in the future outta the now

Yeah we're playing those mind games forever
Projecting our images in space and in time
Yes is the answer and you know that for sure
Yes is to surrender, you got to let it,
You got to let it go

Putting the soul power to the Karmic wheel . . .
Raising the spirit of peace and love . . .

—John Lennon, "Mind Games"

I encourage anyone who will listen to be open-minded. Beliefs that are true encompass broad spectrums and complexities and seem contradictory while simultaneously appearing simple. It seems truth is clothed in symbol and paradox, which is why it is frequently expressed in parables, hyperbole, myths, and stories. The other side of complexity is simplicity. An example would be that love is the most important truth we can know and live. The fact is that love is complex in its many dimensions and subtleties, yet the truth that love is the answer is simple and can appear so when spoken without the advantages of the depths of experience. Two individuals can bring the same message, yet most know instinctively whether it is shared in platitudes or real wisdom. I believe most of us have had the experience where something you've known all along is suddenly seen in a new light. We may say, "Ah, now I get it. I didn't realize it from that angle before" or "I've heard that a thousand times before but never heard it explained that way, wow."

> The priest and the magician,
> Singing all the chants that they ever heard;
> They're all calling out my name,
> Even academics, searching printed word.
>
> My father to the left of me,
> My mother to the right
> Like everyone else they're pointing
> But nowhere feels quite right . . .
> I'd rather trust a man who doesn't shout what he's found,
> There's no need to sell if you're homeward bound.
> If I choose a side,
> He won't take me for a ride.
>
> Back inside,
> This chamber of so many doors;
> I've nowhere to hide . . .
>
> —Genesis, "The Chamber of 32 Doors"

Summarizing the Summary

There's roads and there's roads
And they call, can't you hear it?
Roads of the earth
And roads of the spirit
The best roads of all
Are the ones that aren't certain
One of those is where you'll find me
Till they drop the big curtain . . .

Little round planet
In a big universe
Sometimes it looks blessed
Sometimes it looks cursed
Depends on what you look at obviously
But even more it depends on the way
That you see

—Bruce Cockburn, "Child of the Wind"

Let us examine where section 1 has brought us. Our collective history and the birth of ego-body-consciousness have evoked an awareness of our separation from the original unity of the unconsciousness. Naked, alone, and dying, our separation from others and mortality causes anxiety. Anxiety has birthed a need to feel secure and worthwhile in a world where neither is provided and where we have the freedom and responsibility of choice. Most of us respond by attaching our security and worth to temporal aims. We create these deceptions to give us the illusion of being in control. We need our illusions because truth is often too painful to face. Behind our illusions stands weakness—individuals whose body stinks and are powerless over possibility and often actuality as well. Humans respond by becoming inflated and/or alienated; it just depends upon what portion of the pendulum we happen to be suspended. We are truly sojourners and exiles in the earthly life. In addition, we are gripped by archetypal forces beyond our control. These archetypes come in pairs of opposites; they create almost unbearable inner tensions. We can choose to face the human condition and the nature of the archetypes or not. Out of the matrix of these myriad facts and fictions, we struggle on in a world where the archetypes have birthed a bevy of laws and principles, which demand our assimilations and accommodations. Our attitudes, beliefs, and behaviors gradually grow and mature out of the matrix of the human condition. We impact others and the world around us via our attitudes, beliefs, and behavior like ripples on a pond after a stone has been cast. Our attitudes, beliefs, and behaviors are set in motion by the degree to which we are willing to adapt to the universal principles and laws that the universe houses. In other words, we need to adapt to the truths inherent in the universal principles that lie within us via our ego-body-consciousness or suffer the inevitable consequences. *The truth lies within*. We are required by life itself to create a union out of the clash of opposites as we move toward wholeness.

I have now outlined what I believe are the basic truths of the human condition. In section 2, I wish to discuss the dynamics of how suffering ferries us to the truth and wholeness and describe what a whole person might look like.

> Running into the darkness
> Some hurt bad some really dying
> At night sometimes it seemed
> You could hear the whole damn city crying
> Blame it on the lies that killed us
> Blame it on the truth that ran us down . . .

> —Bruce Springsteen, "Backstreets"

The blizzard of the world
Has crossed the threshold
And it's overturned
The order of the soul.

—Leonard Cohen, "The Future"

Section 2

Show me the place
Where the word became a man
Show me the place
Where the suffering began.

—Leonard Cohen, "Show Me the Place"

Tried and tested
By the cries of birds
By the lies I've heard
By my own loose talk
By the way I walk
By the claws of beasts
By the laws of priests
By the glutton's feast
By the word police

By the planet's arc
By the falling dark
By the state of the art
By the beat of my heart
By the poverty trance
By the dark finance
By the marketing dance
By the fateful glance . . .

By the spurs of desire
By "what does love require'
By what I waited for
By what showed up at the door . . .

By the nation wide
By the tears I've cried
By the lure of false pride
By the need to take sides
By the weight of the choice
By the still small voice
By the things I forgot
By what I haven't met yet . . .

—Bruce Cockburn, "Tried and Tested"

Introduction

And Jesus was a sailor when he walked upon the water,
And he spent a long time watching from his lonely wooden tower
And when he knew for certain only drowning man could see him,
He said, all men will be sailors then until the sea shall free them;
But he himself was broken long before the sky would open-
Forsaken, almost human,
He sank beneath your wisdom like a stone.

—L. Cohen, "Suzanne"

We are now going to embark on what is termed the baptism of fire. Human beings have been plagued by suffering and pain since the birth of consciousness. All human suffering brings with it opportunities to become less judgmental and more compassionate. It also fills us with anxiety and confusion and feelings sometimes beyond our capacities to cope. There are no easy answers to the problem of suffering and pain.

Hinted at in section 1, we will now be embarking on a specifically spiritual quest for the sacred in attempting to make some sense of suffering within the human condition. Spiritual experiences are demonstrated by a plethora of spiritual traditions and individuals who have ventured into the varieties of religious experiences. I encourage the reader to familiarize themselves with William James's *The Varieties of Religious Experience*, a seminal work that describes the psychological nature of religious experience by offering examples of a wide range of spiritual experiences of ordinary men and women. James offers us a glimpse into the depth of human experiences with the divine and our common struggle to capture a vision using language to describe what I believe are authentic spiritual experiences. He seems to have canvassed the spiritual landscape with a realistic and skeptical approach yet, at the same time remaining open to what individuals have conveyed through their personal experiences. We need to differentiate between religious and spiritual experience because of the confusion these two terms have engendered. To use a metaphor, religion is the husk and spirituality the seed. Spirituality is situated in the imagination where symbols meet consciousness and where vision meets inspiration. Religions are the forms spirituality take. James was really describing the varieties of spiritual experience based on my definitions.

However we slice it, authentic spirituality is impossible without taking into account the problem of suffering. I will be tracing the experiences of suffering in three heroes from the patriarchal age, but which all reflect common elements of both the masculine and feminine archetypal energies. Odysseus and Job are precursors to Jesus of Nazareth in the unfolding of wholeness and enlightenment for Western consciousness and life. Out of the matrix and womb of sufferings, Odysseus and Job were both historically planted in the period of transition between the Bronze and Iron Ages. Odysseus was the classic Greek conquering hero of the Iron Age, yet it was a female goddess Circe who tempted, chastised, nurtured, and eventually unlocked wisdom and wholeness within his soul. It was therefore a transformation from his attachment to the hero as warrior, reflecting the Greek patriarchal tradition of externalizing and projecting toward inner experiences, which liberated Odysseus from his suffering and fate and led to his enlightenment. Joseph Campbell identified this transition period (middle second millennium BCE) where a struggle occurred between the masculine and feminine elements within our Western psyche. The repressed elements of the feminine goddesses ferried Odysseus beyond his one-sided masculine warrior hero archetype and led him to a more balanced psychic equilibrium, which I believe is the hidden message behind *The Odyssey*.

Job's story can be traced to Mesopotamia and also to that same period of transition between Bronze and Iron Ages. The patriarchy of the Levant traditions includes Islam along with Judaism and Christianity, which, as we spoke of earlier, emphasize surrender to God's will but generally from within a misogynist schema. Job was a tormented and lonely hero, far from the conquering Odysseus, for he was abandoned, rejected, and whose attachments were sundered by a personal baptism of fire. Job's story encompasses clearly masculine archetypal energies but, as we shall discover, represent a transformation in man's understanding of God, which sets the stage for Jesus of Nazareth, a man who epitomized as close to an androgynous being as ever lived in the annals of history. Odysseus and Job are antecedents and set the stage for Jesus of Nazareth, who is the culmination of the suffering hero who modeled wholeness and enlightenment within his entire personality. Nobody could have created the personality of Jesus of Nazareth that comes through the Christian Bible, and we will be exploring that personality in some depth to achieve an enhanced glimpse of what enlightenment is and looks like.

Suffering and Pain

Man tries to keep things but they're taken away
Man has to struggle all the livelong day
Man has to sweat and toil his life filled with trouble
Man got to step and fetches it on the double
Man has to work so hard to make it all pay
Man has to struggle all the livelong day . . .
Man has to create karma that's the way that it is

Man has to keep on going way beyond his will
Man has to keep being 'cos there's nothing else . . .

Take all the gurus when they meditate
Transcend the mundane into some altered state
You just might just get there, but you'll have to pay
Man's got to struggle all the live long day . . .

Man has to watch the weather and the food that he eats
Man has to keep fit 'else he's prone to disease
No matter what he does there's stress every which way.

—Van Morrison, "Man Has to Struggle"

Here comes the blind commissioner
They've got him in a trance . . .

And the riot squad they're restless
They need somewhere to go

As lady and I look out tonight
From Desolation Row . . .

And the only sound that's left
After the ambulances go
Is Cinderella sweeping up
On Desolation Row . . .

And the Good Samaritan, He's dressing for the show
He's going to the carnival tonight
On Desolation Row

Now Ophelia, she's 'neath the window
For her I feel so afraid
On her twenty-second
She already is an old maid . . .
Her sin is here lifelessness
And though her eyes are fixed upon
Noah's great rainbow
She spends her time peeking
Into Desolation Row . . .

Dr. Filth, he keeps his word . . .
Now his nurse . . .
And she also keeps the cards that read
"Have Mercy on His Soul"
They all play on penny whistles
You can hear them blow
If you lean your head out far enough
From Desolation Row . . .

They're spoon-feeding Casanova
To get him to feel more assured
Then they'll kill him
With self-confidence
After poisoning him with
And the Phantom's shouting
To skinny girls

"Get outta here if you don't know"
Casanova is just being punished
For going
To Desolation Row

Now at midnight all the agents
And the superhuman crew
Come out and round up everyone
That know more than they do
Then they bring them to the factory
Where the heart- attach machine
Is strapped across their shoulders
And then the kerosene
Is brought by insurance men who go
Check to see that nobody is escaping
To Desolation Row

Praise be to Nero's Neptune
The Titanic sails at dawn
And everybody's shouting
"What side are you on" . . .
Between the windows of the sea
Where lovely mermaids flow
And nobody has to think too much
About Desolation Row

Yes, I received your letter yesterday . . .
Right now I can't read to good
Don't send me letters no
Not unless you mail them
From Desolation Row

—Bob Dylan, "Desolation Row"

Introduction

For hundreds of thousands of years, humans have been suffering and struggling in direct proportion to the evolution of our brains. There is a vast difference between experiencing suffering and making intellectual formulations of these experiences. The concepts we create cannot be faithful to our true experiences. Language is incapable of capturing the essence of any experience, let alone suffering. Nevertheless, we remain obligated to make stabs at it for understanding truths of experience results in wisdom and become the first leg on our journey to wholeness.

The human condition and predicament are laced with myriads of sufferings, and whatever the rational explanations are offered, the effects remain full of anguish with complications hard to decipher. When facing the suffering within the human condition, we have to take into account the problem of evil if any authentic view of suffering can hope to be complete. Evil and the suffering it entails will never be completely comprehensible, and what follows has taken my lifetime to formulate. Sufferings can never be completely illuminated by our limited and finite conscious minds. I hope what follows will be helpful with this caveat: *there are no systematic or theological arguments that could ever unlock all the doors of the mysterious, ineffable, and painful experiences of sufferings humankind has had to endure through the ages.* We need to take the truths of life and death seriously and, therefore, delve below the surface and attempt to excavate some kind of understanding of suffering and evil. The way in which we formulate an understanding of suffering and evil will impact the way we live our lives. Therefore, whether we like it or not, our beliefs about suffering and evil impact our attitudes and behaviors. If our philosophy has any wisdom or validity, it needs to tackle such thorny realities and experiences. Such is the situation we find ourselves in; life is full of incomprehensibility, cataclysmic suffering, mystery, and uncertainty. The fact we and those we love experience and prorogate suffering and evil demands we take responsibility and face up to suffering with some formulations that make some sense. And since humans have been suffering from primordial times to the present, it is essential we learn how to suffer with courage if it can be said that wisdom inhabits man's consciousness—a consciousness peering out from Desolation Row. For only those who live within the metaphoric boundaries of Desolation Row know the anguish and suffering intrinsic to the human condition. Only in those alleys, streets, and rooms is one able to cast aside all the distractions and self-deceptions that prevent one from experiencing the suffering inherent in the human condition. Becoming aware of the anguish that suffering produces obligates honest people to adapt to these painful truths, which require self-discipline and obedience to those truths that reside within each of us. Few are the Good Samaritans of this world who listen and act upon the still and quiet voice within, which reveals truths of compassion they will need to guide them through their unique life journeys and on to the other side. Only they are able to suffer for others with true empathy, compassion, and love and as well bring the healing touch so desperately needed in our world today. The problem of suffering has haunted our species for eons, yet few venture and endure within her womb long enough to extract the joy and serenity only she can induce. Suffering seems one of the primary archetypal experiences. As I have said and shall say again, few embrace the realities by living with her as a friend and faithful companion; nevertheless, only she can guide one into an authentic and whole life. This means living in Desolation Row. This entire work is not intended for the shallow and phony ones who distract themselves and others from experiencing the truth of suffering via all the sordid, trivial, and superficial byways that keep them from dodging and avoiding Desolation Row.

Perhaps the question could be posed another way, that is, why have there been experiences of joy, peace, and love over the course of human history? In the evolutionary process, it has taken billions of years of struggle, strife, and death to produce consciousness. Where have the positive emotions and inner experiences come from? Also, what makes any of us so special that we should not have to suffer the anguish and horror nature has forever used to shape life upon this planet? Why shouldn't I suffer? Why is there any true love, compassion, wisdom, unity, kindness, and humility in this creation of carnage, terror, horror, and death? Where do positive attitudes and beliefs originate anyway? Let us delve further into these mysteries.

Suffering and Evil

Suffering and evil cannot be separated. Why do we suffer, and why is there evil in the world? How do these two relate? I will begin by undertaking a general definition before exploring theories that purport to explain why these two truths exist, then I will go into more detail concerning how they specifically manifest themselves, and finally I will draw some tentative conclusions. I have decided to put off my own conclusions regarding evil toward the end of the book. I believe my perspective will shed light on the nature of evil, suffering, and wholeness and how they are interconnected.

By suffering, I mean the bearing of pain, whether physical, emotional, or mental. The essence of suffering is to struggle. The essence of struggle is suffering. The position anguish, torment, horror, loneliness, fear, anxiety, depression, hatred, dishonesty, guilt, etc., has had on suffering is both incomprehensible and ineffable. As I said earlier, words are inadequate to describe such vast and far-reaching experiences. I hope some of my examples in the first section were able to elucidate some of its emotional nature. Suffering demands our attention. Like the news, it haunts us in our familiar enclaves. If we ignore its declarations, we do so at our own peril. Inevitably, the truth of inner conflicts and sufferings will rise from our denial and seize its pound of flesh. For those willing to take notice, we need to transform our suffering and pain into endurance, understandings, compassion, and action. The casualties of our collective and individual unwillingness to engage the truths of suffering are cited in every daily newspaper the world over.

All theories of suffering boil down to two basic categories: either human suffering is ultimately meaningless or it has some purpose.

I.   Meaninglessness of Suffering

Materialism. This theory begins by assuming that life evolves and devolves in a random fashion with no discernable purpose beyond the survival of the species. In this theory, there is no purpose beyond the general rule that evolution has haphazardly created a world where the fight for survival and death are the only known qualities. The individual life-form of whatever type only exists for the survival of the species. There is no purpose beyond this, and therefore, nature has set it up where the most hardy and strong are to survive for a while to spread their seed while the weak live a shorter duration and whose genes are less likely to survive and be passed on. The individual is of no particular importance beyond species survival. Suffering is part and parcel of the instinct, which drives us to survive at the expense of everything else. For some to live, others must die. Philosophically, our duty is to propagate the species and adapt as best we can. Suffering is part and parcel of the struggle of life. This is set up by biology. As I discussed in section 1 on the instincts, it seems males are to be driven by instincts/hormones to have sex and kill while females seem to be driven instinctually/hormonally to have sex and nurture. Some studies suggest that our biology has developed in such a way as females attempt to choose a mate with the best genes and ability to support their young, while males on the instinctual level will engage in sex with whomever they find attractive. Our culture has a fetish for everything material, including the flesh as objects, while most of what we call religion and faith has become a hostage of and a prostitute to materialism.

This belief system sets up three possible responses to suffering. These are nihilism, hedonism, and humanism.

1.   Nihilism is the belief that nothing really matters for there are no values or purpose for life of the individual. Nothing

is of import; therefore, there is no ultimate meaning to life. Nothing you do matters or makes any difference.

2.   Hedonism is the pleasure principle taken to be a virtue, where one takes this lack of purpose and makes the decision to act selfishly to satisfy our basic desires and drives. The pleasure principle is supreme. Nothing matters; therefore, I might as well seek as much pleasure as possible and as long as I can. To sum up, suffering is intrinsic to the human condition because instincts exist, and nature has evolved where the strong survive. Whatever it takes to survive is the aim—if it is my best interest to cooperate, then I will cooperate; if not, I won't. Enlightened self-interest is the motivating factor of such a belief system. The fact that some believers in materialism but don't appear to act this way on a consistent basis is evidence they are good at hiding their motives, or they are not in fact hedonists.

3.   Humanism picks up where the others leave off. We create our own values system. Humanism, in effect, attempts to minimize suffering as much as possible. This underlying value seems to resonate from within a humanist—even though there is no philosophical foundation to support it. There is one humanist in particular that I have an incredible respect for, and if I had not taken the leap of faith, I would subscribe to his philosophy; that is Albert Camus. He held that while there is no rational explanation for the cause of suffering, its reality is the most important truth within the human condition. He became an agnostic existentialist (briefly, existentialists believe that facing the problems of existence as honestly as possible is of the greatest importance rather than believing in detached philosophical thought, which doesn't face the issues and problems of daily existence). There are atheist and religious or spiritual existentialists who agree with Camus that we must face life as it is with the greatest courage but differ on whether or not God exists. Camus, as an agnostic, stated he could not believe in God due to the extent of suffering in the universe, but he welcomed those

who do to embrace his primary value of minimizing suffering as much as possible. He knew eradicating suffering is doomed to fail because there is no way to end suffering. He believed it takes courage to fight a losing war, yet there are no other realistic alternatives.

II.   Meaningfulness

Spiritual beliefs house another belief system, which is in stark contrast with materialism. It declares that suffering has some purpose, though it may or may not be comprehensible to our rational mind. This view takes into account faith; one is asked to take a leap of trust in some type of higher power. The book of Job and *The Odyssey* have so much to offer, it would be absurd to enter discussions on faith based beliefs presently. However, I feel it is imperative that I introduce some theories on suffering, which will serve as an introduction to my commentaries on Odysseus, Job, and Jesus of Nazareth.

Categories of Suffering and Evil

I.   Legitimate Suffering

First, let us start with legitimate suffering. Suffering is necessary for our growth. Without physical pain, we would not have survived as a species. Jung believed all neurosis is due to an individual's unwillingness to suffer legitimately. Without emotional suffering, we would remain complacent, infantile, and self-satisfied. Neurosis is an avoidance of reality and the emotional and mental anguish it engenders. Neuroses are really various forms of denial. Common examples of why we typically avoid suffering are the following: when our will is blocked; when we don't get our way; we disobey a law of nature; we disobey a moral law; experience guilt; and experiences of losses. It seems to boil down to this: if we are to be healthy, we need to accept the truth that suffering is beneficial. No amount of whining, complaining, or self-pity will stave off the inevitable needs to grow up and endure the basic problems of human existence and all the suffering it entails. The problems are not in someone or something else, but within us—in our beliefs and attitudes!

II.   Self-Inflicted Suffering

There are two categories of self-inflicted suffering: through ascetic practices and masochism, which are those that harm themselves. Asceticism can convert into masochism in a twinkling of an eye, and where one draws the line is tricky to differentiate. Self-discipline has an essential place in the economy of suffering as long as it doesn't become masochistic. Self-discipline had a long history of adherents where one chooses to abstain from certain activities or pursue others, which the adherent deems beneficial, and yet they cause conflicting forms of suffering. Masochism is where someone takes pleasure in harming oneself. I subscribe to the theory that masochism is behavior bent on attempting to exert control over the body by punishing oneself as an expiation for sins and weaknesses. All forms of control are reactions and denial of mortality and the body. Anything that reaches extremes turns out to be caustic to the spirit.

Self-discipline strengthens the ability to endure and accept hardship and pain. The practice of self-discipline also nurtures all the positive character traits such as humility, patience, self-control, kindness, gentleness, etc. Many men and women in history have been models of self-discipline, pursuing ascetic practices, and by accepting suffering in its many forms (emotional, persecution, martyrdom, torture, etc.). It seems the confidence of faith is capable of providing strength to endure sufferings and death with integrity and dignity. There are no lasting transformations of a personality that emerge without some form of suffering. If we want to grow up and become men and women of courage, we need to learn how to live without the creature comforts/ attachments that hold us in thrall and bondage and accept legitimate suffering as a faithful friend and companion on life's journey.

III.   Natural Disasters and Calamities

When I'm sampling from your bosom
Sometimes I suffer from distractions like
Why does God cause things like tornadoes and train wrecks?

—Crash Test Dummies,
"Swimming in Your Ocean"

A third category of suffering is what we call natural disasters or calamities, including famines, earthquakes, car accidents, tornadoes, etc. Much more difficult to understand and make sense of, natural disasters push rational explanations to their limits and beyond. What design or purpose could account for the scale of the suffering we experience in natural disasters? It is at this point the problem of evil and its relation to suffering enters the equation. The question arises: if God exists, what kind of loving purpose can there be in allowing or willing such suffering? When talking about children, the problems of suffering and evil surface with deadly force. I am not referring to sentimentality, that despicable facade that substitutes for genuine suffering in our society. No, the real horror of what nature visits on the human condition, especially that of children who are orphaned, maimed, killed, and so damaged emotionally, that PTSD haunts them to death unless somehow, healing takes place. This suffering has driven some to desperate inner states of mind and acts of suicide, along with insane and destructive behavior toward themselves and others. Natural disasters are the main category or type of suffering, which convinces some to swear off beliefs in a loving God. This is a challenge to people of faith, far more so than many are willing to accept without platitudes being hurled about. Anyone willing to deal with truth must confront truth in all its manifestations. What are we to do with this crisis of meaning? Are there rational explanations for the magnitude of such sufferings? How can anyone trust God, or anything for that matter, if we are unsure of being safe, understood, accepted, forgiven, guided, and secure in God's love? We will be going in-depth to the problem of evil later, so I ask the reader for some patience as I tackle the relationship between evil and suffering.

Briefly, Buddhism proclaims that all suffering is a result of desires, and if we eliminate our desires, our suffering can be overcome. Hinduism believes human suffering is the result of karma and our birth, and whatever caste we are born into is the result of our past attitudes and behaviors. Christianity, Islam, and Judaism believe God uses suffering in those with faith to direct them toward wholeness and enlightenment. Christianity in particular teaches that in some mystical sense, humans who follow Jesus enter into his suffering as some kind of imitation and reproduction of his sacrifice.

I will be addressing this mystery in one way or another throughout the remainder of this book. Nevertheless, let me be straight from the start—there are no simple solutions. Simple solutions can never be applied to complex problems without causing additional sufferings. Many have made an effort to make sense of these most anguish-filled subjective experiences. Regardless of how we respond to life's sufferings, the problems of evil and suffering are here to haunt us—at least until the day we die.

IV.   Human Evil and Suffering

Let there be no doubts, *the majority of suffering in the world must be laid at our own feet.* What of our inhumanity to other creatures and nature herself? Gazing at the front page in every newspaper, the dreadfulness outlined horrifies, repulses, and disgusts us. Children are neglected, rejected, abandoned, maimed, tortured, raped, murdered, enslaved and/or forced into prostitution by adults—daily. There seems to be no limit to the horrors humans inflict upon children and each other. No other species can be said to be close to the brutalizing and neglect we wreak upon our children. I'm much more inclined to accept suffering in adults with more straightforwardness than children because adults choose to evade truth, visit pollution on Mother Earth, gossip, and in one way or another, torment each other with a variety of psychological games and manipulations.

Rather than face difficult truths within, humans project their fears and weaknesses onto others—women, blacks, Jews, whatever. We are afraid of the inner work truth demands; therefore, we project onto others all the evil and suffering within the human condition. As we have and shall continue to explore, men project all sorts of their inner fears, needs, and portions of themselves onto the women in their lives. Our neurosis projects itself onto others, taking on many manifestations, such as blaming others for our mistakes and inadequacies, laying guilt trips on the doorsteps of our neighbors, and manipulating others to get our way. Let's face it; we are naturally selfish and dishonest with fragile self-images. It's human nature to be afraid of identifying our faults because it damages the fragile ego. We need a strong ego-body-consciousness to survive, but in reality, a strong and healthy ego is forged when integrating painful truths. Projections may offer the ego a momentary respite, yet it ends up causing more suffering. Since I have been focused on the individual up to this point, I want to discuss systemic evil. Those interested in a psychological study of evil, I refer you to W. S. Peck's *People of the Lie* and Earnest Becker's *Escape from Evil.*

V.   Systemic Evil

> We live in a political world
> Love don't have any place
> We're living in times
> Where man commit crimes
> And crimes don't have any face.

> —Bob Dylan, "Political World"

Systemic evil is the evil fueled by institutions and group dynamics and is studied by sociology and psychology. The immoral and impetuous mob mentality certainly can take its share of responsibility for heaps of suffering perpetrated upon the world. Experience has shown individuals in a group will commit injustices that they would not commit individually. This includes not just mob behavior, but institutional dynamics as well. There is pressure to conform to the ideals of any group or system—for good and ill. When groups or systems take on dysfunction, it exhibits the ugly side of human nature. All of us go through the stages of what I call infantile morality, based on social constraints rather than internal values.

I believe it is institutions that propagates the greatest social injustices, and therefore the greatest amount of suffering upon humanity. Herein lays the seeds of wars and power politics of every variation and category. Most of us buy into the social heroic that is the values and mores of a given society. In America, status and power is equated with military power and wealth. This value system lives in stark contrast to egalitarianism, where everyone is valued equally as each has something to contribute and where doing good unto others is of supreme value.

We discussed earlier the dynamics of systemic evil, and now's the time to discuss its impact. The rich and powerful hoard most of the material benefits of human labor. Each culture has an elite class; historically, it was the priestly, gentry, educated, kings and royals, and aristocracy. In Western cultures, the rich are more highly valued because wealth = power. The elite in America follow the so-called American dream. The American dream is built on building monuments to the individual ego. This translates to becoming one of the rich rather than the poor and therefore becoming one of the *predators rather than victims.* The freedom in America is not the problem, but the inevitable abuse of power is. Power is always translated into material blessings and certain privileges/status, which inevitably is foisted upon the backs of the common man or women.

A prime example is our so-called justice system where the rich are offered endless advantages while the poor rot in jail. Our economic system allocates all the advantages to the rich via interest on the lending of money and investments with interest, which increases wealth for the rich while they fail to contribute anything of real value to the needs of others. Riches aggregate on the backs of laborers who produce the goods and services. In addition, various prison systems are abusive as they offers little medical care or mercy to those so confined. The American military is a system where mistakes are covered up to save face, and veterans are given the runaround and neglected. Our government wastes money and offers contracts to the rich corporations without looking for quality of service and economic affordability. Most of us know all this! However, we tolerate it while raving flags and thereby avoiding the truth that the system needs to change. The health-care systems are wrought with corruption while insurance agents often stonewall, lie, rebuff, and deny services to almost anyone unwilling to pressure them with a plethora of phoned calls and appeals. The rich and famous get the best care. All CEOs perpetuate injustice by accepting outrageous salaries. I can go on and on.

The system itself is evil, as rich become richer and gain more power and privilege while the poor and the outcasts are ignored and marginalized. The middle class does most of the work, and the poor suffer the consequences if they fail to achieve middle-class status. This is not to say the poor are without responsibility. Regardless, the upper classes are the chosen ones in this world; they reap the benefits of a system where they consume most of the goods produced. I just saw a brief snippet on TV about the businesses that cater to the rich. The jaded nature of what I saw nauseated me. These businesses effectively pander to the status of the egocentric needs of the rich consumer. However, there is only so much to go around. For example, it has been estimated that in the first century of the Roman period, the rich, a mere 1% of the population, had 90% of the land. They controlled the goods produced by the peasants. There was no middle class in the Roman period. The present era is moving in that direction as the middle class is being systematically pinched and squeezed. Most who work in these systems know what is happening, yet we rarely hear a peep out of them. Codes of silence propagate systemic evil. The media calls the few who confront evil in institutions and corporations whistle-blowers, further disparaging their heroic acts.

Each culture offers medals and trophies, which confers status and rank. This dynamic is most effective as it panders to our egocentric natures. The systemic evil and the suffering it manufactures, if added up with moral calculators, significantly surpasses the suffering propagated by individuals. We must keep in mind that with systemic evil, it is still individuals at the top who command underlings and influence them to do their biddings. The code of silence accepted by the majority of working men and women is astronomical. If the working men and women would not comply and buy into the injustices inherent within these systems, these systemic evils would eventually cease because nobody would be there to follow orders. Without many German people following Hitler, there would have been no Hitleresque nightmare. Hitler did not seize power in a vacuum; he was endemic of the German collective psyche as a whole. The German people needed a deception to compensate for losing World War I. Insecure, economically and psychologically weak, and humiliated, Hitler provided compensation with horrific consequences. At the same time, evil is *always* perpetrated by lost souls who are gripped by fear and have forgotten how to love.

My name was Richard Nixon only now I'm a girl
You wouldn't know it but I used to be king of the world . . .

I was the boss the last time around
I lived by cunning and ambition unbound
The sucker said they'd stand by me right or wrong
As if they thought that hubris was the mark of the strong
I was an arrogant man . . .

I'm back here learning what it is to be poor
To have no power but the strength to endure . . .

Now you have to call me Rose

—Bruce Cockburn, "Call Me Rose"

The Unconscious Mind: Part 2

I dreamed I saw St. Augustine . . .

Searching for the very souls
Whom already have been sold.

—Bob Dylan, "I Dreamed I Saw St. Augustine"

Introduction

I will now tackle the primary archetypes in sequential fashion. You may want to review the chapter on the unconscious in section 1 before proceeding. Briefly, Jung believed the psyche or soul is the combination of both the conscious and unconscious minds. The soul also has male and female components. We have looked at consciousness and are now in a position to plummet into the primary archetypes of the unconscious mind. I'm going to attempt to offer you a brief, lucid, and concrete summary of what we know of the unconscious mind and how it relates to our ego-consciousness.

But before I proceed, I want to share two personal anecdotes that will offer the reader a glimpse of the dynamics by which the archetypes manifest themselves in the destiny of an individual.

Anecdotes

I believe these anecdotes will give you an idea of how we experience the archetypes and how they manifest themselves both internally via dreams and externally through synchronistic experiences.

I will start with a dream. A few years prior to beginning this book, I was reading from Carl Jung's collected works and struggling to understand him. He is not the most lucid writer. I was thinking about giving up and moving onto something else less enigmatic when I had the following dream: I had a book of Jung's, and when I first opened it, all the pages were blank. Suddenly, little marks or blots began to appear on a page, and gradually, vague outlines of a face began to form. I knew intuitively these blots were God's features taking shape on the page. Although I did not get a detailed graphic, the face that I was able to perceive was the most beautiful, awesome, and mysterious I had ever seen. The face filled me with a sense of awe and wonder as well as fear and trembling for I knew I was experiencing something numinous and mysterious. When I woke up, the dream's message was clear and irrefutable. I had better continue delving into Jung's work's if I wanted to experience a greater comprehension of God. This book would never have been written without this dream. This dream image is still vivid and continues to stir and inspire me.

The second was an external synchronistic experience. Though I have had many of these types of experiences throughout my life, this one in particular is worth noting here because of its timing and content. I had just taken the risk of quitting my job in 1996 to decompress and begin writing. I was sitting outside on my deck daydreaming when a red-tailed hawk flew and perched on my deck, no more than ten feet from me. The hawk and I just stared at each other for about a minute, which seemed to me like an eternity. Initially, my mind was incredulous as I was in a condition of bewilderment. My mind was racing as I was astonished that such an occurrence could transpire right in front of my eyes. As we continued to stare at one another, I knew this was a type of communication while wondering to myself if anyone would believe my experience. The beautiful hawk eventually flew away, and I was left thunderstruck. I can still see him in my mind's eye. The next winter, my family was walking around the property by the river when we came upon a dead red-tailed hawk lying in the snow at the end of our property, which we call the point, where I go often to be alone and meditate and where I had constructed a personal Mandela. The dead hawk had no observable causes of death as it was in perfect condition lying inert in the snow. I initially interpreted the experience that I had been given a special sight and insight by the hawk, and the hawk was my personal connection to Native American spirits on the property. I also knew I must finish this work. The dead hawk in the snow confirmed this to me along with the notion that the hawk's gift of sight was a sacrifice. I knew at that time that the American Indians had offered their gratitude toward the buffalo, for they believed the buffalo sacrificed themselves willingly to provide food and clothing for the common good. I later read Ted Andrews's book *Animal Speak* about how animals and birds are symbols and totems and realized the hawk is my totem. I have a place on the property where I dance around my Mandela in ways reminiscent of American Indians. I know that the land I live on is not mine; I am only a steward and that American Indians that have lived on this land and gone before me linger somehow. I know these type of interactions are available to one and all who are open to them, offering opportunities to link up with their destiny.

These experiences were not random coincidences but consequential and meaningful (Jung's definition of synchronicity is "meaningful coincidences"). They both transpired with uncanny timing; they were epiphanies that marked crucial junctures in my psyche, where the narrowing of my purpose, destiny, and development were inexplicably and intimately linked.

Psyche or Soul

This section on soul derives from my own beliefs, while much of what I have to say is identical with John Sanford's lucid discussion on the soul in *The Kingdom Within: The Inner Meaning of Jesus's Sayings*. He seems to bring much of what I have read and believe into a lucid synthesis. I strongly recommend that you read Sanford's work.

The psyche is the Greek word used in the Christian Bible to designate soul. The word *psyche* also means butterfly in Hebrew. The soul, like the butterfly, is hard to pin down, and to do so kills her. In Greek mythology, Psyche was a woman who had a relationship with Eros, the son of Aphrodite, the God of romantic love. The psyche or soul is made up of a conjunction of the conscious and unconscious minds and our will. Depth psychology deals with soul or psyche as it penetrates to the depths of the unconscious and attempts to bring it to consciousness. Psychology means the "study of the soul." Unfortunately, most of the religion, philosophy, and psychology have been seduced by science while neglecting the soul altogether. I am not disparaging these disciplines as they have lead to a great deal of knowledge and understanding. Yet I rarely hear within psychology or the church anything about the connection of the soul to God. I don't think I've ever heard anyone use the term *soul* in all the psychology classes I took in college. Rather than honor the depths that the inner world the soul represents, our ego-consciousness seeks to control and attain personal honor and power, leaving all the intricate workings of the soul repressed and devalued, stifled, and forgotten. Her values have been rejected, and her revenge is evident in the plethora of categories of mental illness, which have swept through the West like an unchecked virus. She communicates to us via dreams, myths, religious symbolism, and mental illness (especially depression and anxiety)—always with her emphasis on *emotional energy*, making demands for our attention.

It is important to note that the anima is not the soul, but is the soul-image. We can't contain the soul or psyche in language; therefore, we can only talk about her with the use of symbolic images. Everything we talked about in my discussion on symbols stands within the total economy of our psyche or soul. The soul reveals herself symbolically as a woman or bird in our dreams. My wife Trina and I named our first daughter Ava, which means birdlike, and therefore purposely linked her name with soul. I'd like to quote from John Stanford to help delineate what we mean by soul or psyche:

> The soul is subjective. She experiences. She suffers and rejoices. The soul reflects. As Cohen goes on to say, the soul both receive psychic impressions and creates them, both gives birth to and takes in psychic life. Fantasy, image, imagination, and a "religious concern for values and meaning"—these are the province of soul. Soul longs to be loved, and longs to love; soul brings the food of life to us, but also herself hungers. (The Kingdom Within, p121)

I want to add she also is responsible for inspirations and the precinct where potentially the body and spirit join in a union. In addition, pathos is our ability to suffer with compassion and is ability to care deeply and relate to suffering intimately, and these are allied with soul and spirit.

The psyche or soul is responsible for bringing consciousness and the unconscious minds together. She is concerned with the relationship between ego-consciousness and the depths of the inner world, the unconscious. She relates instincts and meanings, ideas and sex, matter and spirit. She is always concerned about relationships, and her present state is intimately tied up with the level or depth of our ego-consciousness. Psyche, as Sanford puts it, "is what binds together, unites, synthesizes, and heals . . . it gives us the capacity to love, is also the ground of faith" The psyche includes our will and the total conjunction of the conscious and unconscious minds. Our psyche or soul is what relates to our body and the instincts—and the archetypes of the unconscious. The soul is therefore the link or nexus to both our physicality and spirituality. Religious traditions have always placed the soul between instinctual and spiritual desires. The psyche both is involved in our transformations and is the object of these transformations. Jung recognized the importance of mercury in the alchemist's quest to transform physical matter into spiritual matter, and therefore Mercury or Hermes, the messenger of the gods, was associated with soul. Our soul or psyche is in part what transforms and is that which is transformed. Jung viewed the soul as feminine, and Greek mythology agrees as Psyche was a woman. She offers us abilities to relate to the outer and inner world; she is the bridge over which we walk between the flesh and spirit.

If men can develop a healthy relationship with the psyche of which the anima is the image, she will bring forth secret wisdom and lead men to the archetypes that are unique to wholeness. Jung believed the anima archetype is representative of men's entire psyche or soul. For women, it is the animus. I refer the reader to R. A. Johnson's work *She* and Sanford's *The Invisible Partners* for a complete picture of how the animus operates in women.

A quick note: When I first encountered Jung's belief that all the following archetypes were autonomous, I not only thought it nonsense, I found it esoteric. At the same time, I was intrigued. It was not until I began interpreting my dreams and using active imagination for myself that I came to believe these archetypes are real and autonomous, and they want to develop a relationship with our ego-consciousness for the purpose of leading us to enlightenment and wholeness.

The Persona

The initial aspect of personality we all form is the persona. The word literally means mask; persona is the mask worn in presenting ourselves to the world. Like in a Greek play, the mask reflects a role played, and the persona is the role we play in society. This mask is false in the context of our true identity. We do need defenses to survive, and the persona is the primary defense we present to society. We use the persona in establishing our careers and use it to establish the primary task for the first half of life—independence and autonomy. The major problem related to the persona is if we identify with it, we become phony and superficial. Another problem arises when some identify with the role they play in society, like a government official. Examples of this are judges, politicians, police, and pastors. People can become so identified with these roles; they believe they are the literally the persona that they identify with as consummate to their particular role. We all have a hidden side or skeletons in our closet, which leads us to the shadow.

The Shadow

Conquistador in search of gold . . .

The Midas shadow that's so hard to please and
Follows wherever you go . . .

But still the shadow that the night won't free just
Follows wherever you go.

—Al Stewart, "Midas Shadow"

Much of what appears here was taken from my experience and John Sanford's *Evil: The Shadow Side of Reality*.

The following archetypes are the foundations of all mature personalities. The initial archetype that needs to be integrated beginning in midlife is the shadow. This is the parts of our souls that we reject and are afraid to admit to ourselves. These are qualities we perceive as negative, and therefore, we repress them due to our ego's need for self-worth and self-protection. These are aspects of ourselves we don't like and which accumulate during childhood and young adulthood. These discarded qualities are typically linked with society's values. The Ten Commandments are an example. These prohibitions would not exist if we were not capable and engaged in these behaviors; therefore, many of these behaviors become repressed and lodged in the shadow. The shadow also contains all those unlived aspects of our lives. The term *alter ego* refers to the shadow. For instance, the lusts for uninhibited sex and power, our dishonesty, and anger are often contents of the shadow because most of us fail to accept these unwanted aspects of ourselves. Making the shadow conscious is crucial in overcoming its negative aspects. The negative aspects of the shadow are lived out by gang members; they have identified their ego with the shadow, and by so doing, its autonomous nature becomes manifested directly in their personalities.

The shadow is integrated by the painful process of accepting all those unwanted portions of our nature. The normal reaction to being confronted with our shadow is denial, for to acknowledge these facets of ourselves, our fragile ego will need to take an incredible hit. When the ego is weakened, the ability to cope and adapt to the world deteriorates. It takes immense courage for ego-consciousness to remain solvent while facing the dark truths about ourselves. These shadow truths induce shame, self-hate, embarrassment, hurt, and guilt. These emotions can overwhelm our fragile ego to the degree we deny them in the first place! Acceptance is easier said than done; the humble pie consumed is indeed bitter. Most people project their shadow defects onto others. All the repressed aspects of the personality are spotted in other people. This is the reason we have initial reactions of dislike toward others; we observe in others our own character defects and flaws. This is the primary reason for the propagation of hatred and violence in the world, and it will carry on ad infinitum until each takes ownership of their shadow.

As an example of the shadow taking over an entire people, we have Nazi Germany. Identifying Nazi Germany's collective shadow is easier to accept than America's collective injustices—where ego gratification, greed, and power are highly valued to the detriment of our outcasts, the poor and underprivileged. Most bureaucratic institutions promote a culture where no one assumes responsibility for the decisions and where lies, dishonesty, greed, and deceit are cultivated like bacteria in the laboratory. There has been a moral crisis in American business practices for some time where speciousness has often become the norm. Most Americans want to ignore the fact that the leaders in our government, corporations, the military, and the justice system have been built upon deceit. This is the main reason conspiracy theorists populate every nook and cranny on the Internet. Conspiracy theories abound, and our government, many cooperate businesses, and the military only have themselves to blame. Government contracts are not dispensed fairly, and our politicians will continue to be in the pockets of big business until real campaign finance reform is instituted. This is unlikely to happen unless there is a public outcry because politicians in charge of changing the laws are unwilling to surrender the perks and privileges of the present system. What ever happened to integrity? Little is said or done, which registers our outrage! There are plenty of honest and morally responsible Americans; however, the silent majority is too often silent. Our government officials attempt to cover themselves with the flag and yet are, in reality, attempting to hide behind it. America will destroy itself and gag on its injustices unless we completely change the present system. America's collective shadow needs to be faced.

The shadow also contains many positive aspects of us. For instance, if we integrate our shadow, it bears the gifts of energy and constructive anger, which can confront evil within others and ourselves. The shadow also can enhance our sexuality and help us to overcome our naiveté within the context of what the world is like: "Be yea wise as serpents and innocent as doves" (Matthew 10:16). I think contact with the shadow also enhances our sense of humor. Facing the shadow also helps us forgive others for when we see ourselves as we really are, we know grace is that which supports our own foundation.

The only way to overcome the darker aspects of ourselves and integrate our shadow is first to accept we have this dark and destructive side to our personalities. Only then can we later find healthy and constructive ways to express our dark side without it controlling us or harming others. Both positive and negative aspects of our nature must be accepted before we can begin the long struggle to integrate them into our entire personality. *Even though it is impossible in practice to integrate any archetype completely*, it remains worthy of our effort. We will never be done integrating our shadow or other aspects of our personalities. Nevertheless, we push on and wrestle away until, like all the archetypes, we face the truth of the opposites and feelings associated while attempting to develop a realistic and honest attitude toward them. Secondly, we then make adaptations based on this, and they will eventually bring forth their fruit. Thirdly, we learn to endure the tension created by these opposites. And finally, we muster enough faith that the unconscious itself will come to our aid if we continue to respect its agendas. We can gauge our progress when the destructive aspects become less compulsive and the positive ones manifest themselves in our lives. The inner struggles with our dual natures themselves increase our consciousness, and the pain it occasions forces us out to engage in many of the unlived aspects of our lives.

It is important to note, the shadow is not equated with evil but contains those aspects of ourselves that we have identified as unacceptable by the standards of ego-body-consciousness. However, the shadow is connected to the archetype of evil, which we will explore later.

The smart money is on Harlem
And the moon is in the street
And the shadow boys are breaking all the laws.

—Tom Waits, "Rain Dogs"

Masculine and Feminine Potentials

Before I move on to the next archetype, the anima, I need to pause and discuss masculine and feminine qualities to facilitate grasping the role the anima plays in the psychology of men and women. I'm about to quote John A. Sanford. He says,

> The development of both the feminine and masculine potentials in a person is also important to wholeness. The masculine aspect of personality may be variously described as logos or outgoing reason, active creativity, controlled aggressiveness, psychological firmness, the causticity to strive for goals and overcome obstacles in route. The feminine aspect of personality comprises Eros, or the capacity for relationships, understanding, awareness of others, creativity through receptiveness, and indirect way of attaining goals, patience, compassion, the valuing and nourishing of life. Everyone, man or woman, contains possibilities for both masculine and feminine development, no one can approach wholeness without some development in both areas. A person who is only developed in the masculine area will be brutal rather than aggressive and will be intellectual in a sterile, academic way. The undeveloped feminine side will show itself as

moodiness, pettiness, and irritability. A person who is developed only in the feminine area will be weak rather than receptive, oversensitive, rather than capable of deep relationships; the undifferentiated masculine side will show up as stubbornness rather than firmness, opinionated rather than reason. (The Kingdom Within, p. 21–2)

The Anima

I'm looking for a girl, who has no face,
She has no name,
Or number.
And so I search within this lonely place . . .

But I can't stop this feeling deep inside of me,
Ruling my mind . . .

I'm a part of it,
It's part of me . . .

—Traffic, "No Face, No Name, No Number"

I have taken most of my discussion of the anima from John Sanford's *The Invisible Partners* (Paulist Press, New York/Ramsey, 1980). If you wish to gain a full understanding of both archetypes (anima and animus) and how they work in men and women, read this work; you won't be disappointed. Since I am male, I have decided to restrict myself to the role the anima plays in the psychology of men.

We now enter a discussion on the next archetype that sequentially is manifested as the shadow is being integrated; that is the anima. The anima is the most elusive, developed, and difficult of archetypes to describe, and it is as if she protests when men and women attempt to describe her. She is also the most developed representative of the transforming aspects of the feminine archetype as a whole. She remains elusive and cunning, yet is the link for men and women to gain access to their unconscious. I thought this was just so much nonsense until I engaged in active imagination and experienced her for myself. The anima is the image by which the soul is manifested; she represents the feminine aspects in men's and women's psyche. Men and women have both male and female genes and hormones and, likewise, have both aspects represented in their souls. The anima is the link to the depths of the inner life or spirit of humankind.

Since I am a male, I have chosen to explore the journey a male hero takes to encounter his anima and the wise old man archetypes in *The Odyssey*. Like all the archetypes, the anima has destructive and constructive aspects. Her destructive aspects manifest themselves when she possesses the consciousness of men through dark moods and compulsive sexual fantasies and/or behaviors. Men often are engulfed in these moods where one mythological figure, Medusa, personifies men's inability to be related to their own feminine nature or to women of flesh and blood as she turns men into stone. To be turned to stone is to be without compassion and the ability to relate and be intimate. Men enter in withdraw mode when they are in the web of anima possession. If the withdrawal is inappropriate, men are passive-aggressive as their moods permeate a negative atmosphere. Men also become prejudiced and full of many forms of negative bias while logic and rationality seems to disappear for a period of time. She brings with her compulsiveness, depression, and on occasion, suicidal ideation. She is discontented and wants what every real woman wants: to be in a relationship. When I neglected my wife, she became negative and resentful in the precise mode as my anima's mood engulfed me for she is feminine. The negative anima also creates mountains out of molehills. Her negative aspects reflect not the truth at all but create falsehoods by the second. Her negative features reflect an inexorable fate with a lack of hope for good measure.

If related to properly, she leads a man to the inner reservoirs of creativity, energy, and wisdom. She is geared to life and pushes men to expand their consciousness through engaging in new experiences and ideas. She bears gifts of guidance, direction, and relatedness. Sanford puts it this way when he refers to the feminine aspects of personality, to which the anima leads:

> The feminine aspect of personality comprises Eros, or the capacity for relationships, understanding, awareness of others, creativity through receptiveness, an indirect way of attaining goals, patience, compassion, the valuing and nourishing of life. (*The Kingdom Within*, p. 21)

She arouses men out of slumber to relate to others in relationship. She is the bridge between the conscious and unconscious minds. She is neither good nor evil—she just is. She brings with her many archetypal images that enlighten men. She also evokes four archetypal dynamics in men: the sexual (Aphrodite), romantic love (Eros), love of the spiritual (Mary, the mother of Jesus), and wisdom (Sophia). These aspects need to be integrated and unified. She inspires and directs us to these aspects of ourselves when we are ready to integrate them. These four aspects of the feminine are within each man and are represented by these symbolic figures. I want to take a closer look at each.

Sexual Love (Aphrodite)

I showed my heart to the doctor.
He said I'd just have to quit.
Then he wrote himself a prescription:
your name was mentioned in it.
Then he locked himself in a library shelf
with the details of our honeymoon,
and I hear from the nurse that
he's gotten much worse and his practice is all in ruin.

I heard of a saint who had loved you.
I studied all night in his school.
He taught that the duty of lovers
is to tarnish the Golden Rule.
And just when I was sure that his teaching
was pure he drowned himself in the pool.

His body is gone but back here on the lawn
his spirit continues to drool.

An Eskimo showed me a movie he'd recently taken of you.
The poor man could hardly stop shiver-
ing; his lips and fingers were blue.
I suppose that he froze when the wind tore off your clothes
and I guess he just never got warm,
but you stand there so nice in your blizzard of ice—
Oh please let me come into the storm.

—Leonard Cohen, "One of Us Cannot Be Wrong"

Aphrodite was the goddess of love. She was unfaithful to her husband and inspires sexuality. I will be looking at the psychological aspects of our sexuality. I delved into physiological aspects in chapter 2 of the first section. What seems completely physical is only a superficial depiction. Our longings for sexual union are metaphors for desires toward wholeness. All archetypes and instincts lead to wholeness, and it is no different with our sexual instinct. Men and women surrender to each other in a sacrifice during the sexual act. Both sexes have to work at orgasm. For developed and mature individuals, there needs to be trust before offering themselves sexually. Sacrifice and trust are psychological dynamics that are inexorably linked to the sexual desire as our yearning to be intimate with one another. To be sexual with a partner, we become vulnerable in our sexual desires and longings. Sex evolved as one of the first components of relationships between men and women. If we repress our sexual desires in the context of vulnerability in relationship, it is not only this instinct that suffers. By avoiding vulnerability in sexuality, it will find a way to confound our ego-consciousness. Freud's sexual theory was born during the age when sexuality was repressed. When he looked into the mystery of the unconscious, he found sexual pathology precisely because this aspect of human nature was devalued by the culture he was born into. In my opinion, he projected onto each patient the sexual problem. When all you see is Aphrodite, sexuality will be the basic motive of all human behavior. He used the myth of Oedipus to validate his findings, which was insightful related to this archetype, but sadly, he failed to value the constellations of the many other archetypes.

We therefore need to look more closely into sexual fantasy. It is important to note, as I work my way into pornography and masturbation, sexual fantasies contain these longings for wholeness. Sexuality is a means to achieve wholeness. The fact that we all entertain sexual fantasies should tell us something about the nature and power sex has in the total psychic economy in the human condition. It is crucial to identify what the anima is driving at, whether toward or away from something when she arouses sexual fantasy. Sexual longings and fantasies though grounded in lust also have hidden urges toward wholeness, which I will examine in much more detail in my discussion of *The Iliad*. Suffice it to say, I ask the reader to keep this in mind during my next discussion of pornography and masturbation.

Pornography

A ghost climbs on the table
In a bridal negligee
She said my body is the light
She says my body is the way
I raise my arm against it all
And I catch the bride's bouquet
So where, where is my gypsy wife tonight?

—Leonard Cohen, "The Gypsy Wife"

There needs to be more honest discussions of pornography as it has become a much bigger problem since the advent of the Internet. Pornography is now available with much more anonymity. I have worked with many men who are intimidated by their own feminine nature and/or by real women; this usually goes back to experiences with their mothers. Therefore, I believe pornography is experienced by some men as a safer approach to their feminine side and sexuality in general (i.e., relationships with real woman). Pornography is therefore pushing these men toward the desire for real and intimate relationships. Many men find relationships with women threatening to their masculine ego and find in pornography an outlet to approach their sexuality and women without having to be vulnerable. Whenever this occurs in men, you can be sure some erotic fantasy is being fashioned by the anima to push men beyond themselves and into some form of relationship with real women. The more a male avoids relationships with his own anima and real women, the more compulsive will any particular sexual fantasy take, including and most often pornography. Most men addicted to pornography are lonely, and no wonder! For many men, therefore, viewing pornography is therefore an ill-fated attempt toward *independence*. Much of the view of women as a threat goes back to the relationship of the male child to his mother and whether he experienced her as safe or not. Many men avoid women's anger because they project their unhappy experiences with their mothers into relationships with women. They have failed to confront this fear by standing up to their mothers. Inevitably, these men feel responsible for mothers' or women's feelings, believing it is their fault. This repression of men's anger is a normal response; if, however, it is not dealt with directly, it will express itself indirectly in sexual fantasy and/or violence. Repression of all feelings including anger builds until it explodes and often becomes abusive. Men already have violent tendencies procured from nature in the hormone testosterone. Some men involved in pornography also carry shame, knowing regularly viewing of pornographic material is not healthy. Those able to work toward intimacy will experience a change in their desires for pornography. However, it is noteworthy that this is only one aspect of men's sexual dynamics. I believe men's sexuality is generally based on visual stimulation, and I do not make the assumption that women's naked bodies are dirty or bad; in fact, I believe just the opposite. Sexuality is a great mystery, and I do not want to reduce all pornography to the animas urge toward relationship. This does not account for female interest in pornography nor healthy curiosity toward the naked body. In any event, there *is* a difference between compulsive and recreational behavior of whatever kind.

Masturbation

His ships are all on fire . . .

She's eaten with desire . . .

And she will learn to touch herself so well
As all the sails burn down like paper . . .

But let's then leave these lovers wondering
Why they cannot have each other.
And let's sing another song, boys
This one has grown old and bitter.

—Leonard Cohen, "Sing Another Song, Boys"

I also want to touch upon masturbation because this is one of those areas where many partake and few are willing to talk about. All orgasms release stresses in the body, whether sexual or otherwise. Sex is a great stress reducer and helps with depression as it releases serotonin and endorphins in the brain. Each of us also seems to have different levels of the sex drive related to the levels of testosterone in ones system. Testosterone is responsible for both men and women's sexual desire. The degrees of sexual desire also vary with age. Women who are given a boost in their testosterone for whatever reason generally report an increase in the sex drive, some to the degree that it becomes a problem. The levels in the male are usually quite high during adolescents and are one way nature has assured the propagation of the species!

Certainly, society's beliefs about masturbation have been and are all over the map. My purpose is not to make any value judgments; these are reserved for the individual. My intent is to explore the psychological aspects of our collective sexuality and our inclinations to masturbate in particular. Like pornography, masturbation can be an attempt to avoid relationships, and it can also become compulsive and therefore fall under the category like any other addiction. Since orgasm feels good, we can surmise that people do it to medicate emotions as well. Some believe it can be an expression of self-love while others believe it's a result of a lack of self-control or discipline. The latter usually does associate sexuality in general as bad or a necessary evil, and I wonder if this isn't a defense against strong impulses to engage in such activities. Masturbation seems to be a universal behavior these days for the majority of people that to categorize it as inherently bad or destructive seems myopic to me. As I have said before, repression of any aspects of the human condition including instincts will trigger a negative reaction by the unconscious mind.

Our soul longs for acceptance for who we are, and our longing for acceptance from the opposite sex reflects this in most men's sexual fantasy—hunger for love with a healthy sexual relationship and component where each partner can explore the other with an openness to fantasy and desire unfettered by social constraints and "proper" sex. The fantasy contains a desire that your partner is opens to sexual fantasy—both their own and yours. If a partner is thus open, it is translated as a confirmation that we are accepted as whole persons, sexuality and all. An ideal partner is someone who really values and wants you, intellectually and sexually. These romantic and sexual elements, it seems to me, include a desire for healthy connectedness, mutual respect, communication, and uninhibited sex. However, the projection of sexual fantasy onto a real partner should be taken symbolically as well; that is recognizing in sexual fantasies a quest for wholeness with acceptance and self-love. This can only be developed from within oneself by integrating the opposite (masculine, yang or animus for women, and anima or yin or feminine for men). Individuation and wholeness imply an inner marriage where all the disparate aspects of being are bound together in a unity. This experience of wholeness produces an inner serenity and equanimity in the face of storms that rage within soul. When one does not have a partner who accepts them in their totality, sexuality and all, sexual fantasy—which includes masturbation—seems to be a natural inclination.

I do believe men and women can achieve some sexual intimacy in the context of sexual fantasies, but this takes a convergence of factors normally outside their control (i.e., luck, fate etc.). When we fall in love, it is impossible to know the degree of sexual desires and fantasies your partner has and is open to. Ultimately, men's sexual desires can be integrated into a healthy relationship with a real woman only when men can extricate themselves from projecting the anima onto a flesh-and-blood woman. It is only here where men are able to develop any kind of substantive intimacy with women because they have first done so from within. Men who have never felt safe with women (due to dynamics of never feeling safe with their mother or their own feminine nature or both) will inevitably approach women and sexuality from a distance, or approach sexuality where women are sexual objects only. Along with pornography, this distance also takes the forms of masturbation, one-night stands, and soliciting prostitution. These are ways men experience sex anonymously; therefore, they approach their sexual fantasies without making themselves vulnerable with a women—where intimacy can develop. They attempt to approach women from a safe distance. To be sexually and emotionally vulnerable with real women, men need to feel safe and integrate their anima. If this is achieved, the urge to masturbate does not disappear, but the fantasies associated with them does. As with all behavior, we must always look behind and delve within to find the motives for the behavior, and when we do, we find many variables and conflicting dynamics that any simple explanations always fall short of the mark.

Romantic Love (Eros)

I need to see you naked
In your body and your thought
I got you like a habit
And I'll never get enough
There's no cure for love . . .

All the rocket ships are climbing through the skies
The holy books are open wide
The doctors working day and night
But they'll never ever find that cure for love
Ain't no drink, no drug
Nothing pure enough to be a cure for love . . .

I don't need to be forgiven for loving you so much
Its written in the scriptures
It's written in blood
I even heard the angels declare it from above
There ain't no cure for love.

—Leonard Cohen, "Ain't No Cure for Love"

Eros/Cupid was the son of Aphrodite and became associated with romantic desires. Eros is a male God of romantic love, and wherever his arrows struck, romance was sure to follow. He discloses the need for sex to be associated with relationship. Relationships are crucial for people as it seems our fear of intimacy holds considerable sway despite our intellectual and rational inclinations. The scientific and analytic spirit of our age likes to analyze and break down reality into parts so we can get a better handle on what is going on. Eros was a male; therefore, men are innately capable of relationships just as much as women are capable of breaking down reality and analyzing it. The psyche needs the anima to inspire our needs for the feminine and relatedness, experiencing wholeness where there are only unrelated facts. The anima or soul image awakens romantic feelings and longings through Eros. The anima is concerned primarily with relationships, no matter how complex and sticky this gets for either sex. Erotic fantasies grip men when they are in need of more intimacy in relationships. Men's fantasies often combine romance with sexual longings regardless of who the longings are attached too. Here we find one of the many complications the anima contrives to get men to seek relationships. Men can befriend their anima and so seek a relationship with her directly and thereby break the spell cast by the anima for compulsive erotic fantasies and behavior.

All healthy relationships hinge first upon the one we have with ourselves. As we grow in self-knowledge, we become more independent and capable of offering from the depth of our psyche something of substance to any relationship, whether romantic or not. The process then involves letting others gradually in on what is inside us, and the relationship will either grow or die out. The purpose is not to take care of others or to be taken care of, but rather to be intimate. Intimacy involves an organic process where the mutual sharing has the capacity to draw us closer together. As we learn to love, we will be capable of offering input and support while maintaining and respecting the autonomy both individuals need in any healthy relationship.

> Well I loved you all my life
> And that's how I want to end it
> The summers almost gone
> And the winters tuning up
> Ya, the summers almost gone
> But a lot goes on forever
>
> And I can't forget
> I can't forget
> I can't forget
> But I don't remember what.
>
> —Leonard Cohen, "I Can't Forget"

Wisdom (Sophia)

> We live in a political world
> Wisdom is thrown into jail
> It rots in a cell discarded as hell
> With no one to pick up the trail.
>
> —Bob Dylan, "Political World"

The subsequent archetype that the anima leads men toward is Sophia or wisdom. In Greek tradition, Sophia is feminine and was borrowed by Hellenistic tradition in places like Proverbs. She is said to exist from the beginning with God. Why this has not been expanded upon in the Judeo-Christian tradition is lamentable. She has, in some mysterious way, been with God from the beginning and adds another feminine element to the Godhead.

Paralleled with Sophia in the Hellenistic tradition is Athena within Greek mythology, the patron goddess of Athens. She was born in the brain of Zeus; she had no mother. Again, we can see a close link between these traditions and a male/female wholeness pattern that is highly developed. The anima guides men to Sophia or Athena as they become more able to intuit truths from within in conjunction with the rational conscious mind. Insights just seem to come to men and women when they have been guided to wisdom's door. Wisdom is also responsible for all great innovations, insights, creations, and discoveries that men and women have accomplished since time immemorial.

Love of the Spiritual (Mary, the Mother of Jesus) and Circe (in Greek Myth for Odysseus)

I can hear a gentle sweet voice calling
It must be the mother of our Lord

—Bob Dylan, "Duquesne Whistle"

The last feminine archetype the anima guides us toward is love of the spiritual and holy. The veneration of Mary by the Catholic Church was lauded by Jung, though the Immaculate Conception is nowhere in holy writ. Pure feminine love had to balance the male-dominated conceptions of the institutional church as it formulated the dogma of the Trinity. Except for the first thirty years of the Jesus movement, the institutional church has been unable to appreciate the holistic Jesus, who encompassed the feminine in his personality and embodied as balanced a being as ever graced humanity. Jesus referred to himself as a mother hen protecting her chicks (Luke 13:34)! In addition, one of his most powerful disciples was Mary of Magdalene or Mary Magdalene, with whom he first appeared after his resurrection and appears to have been a prominent disciple in the early Jesus movement. Jesus valued children, and his ability to be compassionate belies the fact he was obviously in touch with his own feminine side. I will have much more to say on Jesus of Nazareth merging of the masculine and feminine in my chapter entitled "Enlightenment and Wholeness."

The image and symbolism of the virgin is extensive throughout mythology; these mythological motifs put the focus on other aspects of the feminine, including to a large degree spirituality. Women in general seem more hard-wired to the inner spiritual life as the values of self-sacrifice, acceptance, compassion, humility, and forgiveness appear more natural. Our image of the pure virgin speaks toward holiness/wholeness. The feminine aspects of human nature are essentially healthy in her nurturing of life and natural grief at loss when death calls, with numerous raw and unmitigated emotions are given their proper place in the yearnings and vicarious suffering of soul or psyche.

Circe, though not virginal, symbolizes the anima's guidance toward spirituality as she leads Odysseus to the wise old man, Tiresias, the symbol of spirit (wise old man archetype), which is intricately connected to God's Spirit of Truth. These symbolic themes will be amplified in my commentary on *The Odyssey*; therefore, no further discussion is necessary at this time.

How can men develop a relationship with his anima or soul image?

As we have seen, one of the main problems the anima presents is a compulsive attachment to erotic fantasy and behavior. First, I will start with the dark moods she arouses. Initially, men need to recognize the projected figure of their erotic fantasies and withdraw it. Men withdraw the projection by accepting and taking responsibility for these fantasies and the desires, moods, and the feelings they occasion. Secondly, men need to pose and ask themselves, "What are my feelings, and what are they telling me?" Thirdly, men need to share their feelings with their friends and lovers. Feelings are the language of the anima, and she unleashes negative moods when men fail to share their feelings. This is easier said than done as many men feel shame for having feelings. This is because they evoke vulnerabilities and insecurities, which situate the person outside their comfort zones. I have found the more men accept their feelings while letting women/lovers/friends in on their feelings and lives, the easier it gets. Generally, I encourage men to exclude using their mothers for this work as the mother complex is often too contaminated with the anima. In fact, I encourage men to initially process their feelings with themselves and then with other men to accumulate and accommodate their masculine energy and perspectives; men do not experience feelings exactly like women do and therefore need to *learn* how to do this from older men or their male peers prior to doing so with the women in their lives. Regardless, whether within a woman or man, it takes a strong and courageous ego to accept the vulnerability and confusion these feelings evoke. Men and women display *strength* in their sharing of emotional weaknesses. Therefore, the answer is obvious: develop intimate relationships with the women/ lovers/friends in your life by letting them in on your feelings, desires, fantasies, thoughts, wants, interests, needs, and problems—not for the purpose of being taken care of (women/lover/friends do not want us to be their children), but rather having already taken responsibility for these feelings and issues, let them in and watch this key as it unlocks the doors of intimacy with yourselves and the women/lovers/friends in your lives.

I want to go into two examples from Greek mythology to demonstrate the destructive and constructive aspects of the anima in men. First we explore the destructive in the psyche of Paris and then the constructive in Odysseus.

Paris and Helen of Troy

Prior to examining the positive aspects of how the anima or soul image works in healthy ways through my commentary on *The Odyssey*, I want to take from Homer's first epic *The Iliad*, a story which will provide an example of how a myth examines and reveals the negative experience of the anima as it is related to romantic love. As we have seen, it is the anima that initiates romantic relationships and entanglements.

In *The Iliad*, Paris, a prince of Troy was on a mission to Greece to retrieve the king's sister but instead fell in love with the beautiful Helen. Helen is the projected archetype of the anima for Paris. Because he fails to recognize her as a portion of himself that has yet to be integrated into his entire personality (his inner anima), she becomes the carrier of the negative aspect of this archetype. When we avoid the work necessary to integrate an archetype, it takes on compulsive and infantile aspects. Therefore, Paris becomes enthralled with Helen, and he must have her for his own. This is despite the fact one of his brothers had prophesied that if he acts out his love for a woman from Greece, it would lead to the entire downfall of Troy. He ends up sacrificing his family and the lives of all the people of Troy, only to follow his projection. The beauty he sees in Helen that is not attached to his sexuality resides within Paris himself. There are many latent aspects of our personality we never encounter because we are too afraid to live out those aspects of ourselves in the grim and grit of our everyday lives.

Real females have always been the carriers of men's soul projections. We as men need to develop these feminine qualities in ourselves. Women represent for men relatedness or groundedness with others as well as to the earth and matter. They personify some qualities generally men do not possess by nature: gentle kindness, acceptance, wisdom, strength in weakness, feelings and emotions, receptivity, serenity, and grace, among others. I am not attempting to pigeonhole male or female qualities. I am sharing what women seem to contain within them that men lack. Paris has fallen in love with a woman who has qualities that are unlived or undeveloped aspects of his own nature. He erroneously believes that by possessing her, she would complete him or make him whole. It seems to me Paris's willingness to sacrifice his honor, his family, and people cannot be explained by sexual desire alone. His willingness to give up everything for her can only be explained by the projections of his anima onto Helen. Projections fulfill a vital function as we gain insight to a particular archetypal dynamic. The problem arises only when we fail to withdraw these projections when the unconscious mind demands it. Paris's failure to withdraw his projection cost him and his great city.

Example of the Anima

She was a friend of mine when I needed one

Wasn't for her I don't know what I'd have done
She gave me back something that was missing in me
She could have turned out to be almost anyone
Almost anyone
With the possible exception
Of who I wanted her to be

In the dead of night
She could shine a light
On some places you've never been
In that kind of light
You could lose your sight
And believe there was something to win
You could hold her tight
With all your might
But she'd slip through your arms like the wind
And be back in flight
Back into the night
Where you might never see her again

The longer I thought I could find her
The shorter my vision became . . .

—Jackson Browne, "That Girl Could Sing"

I also want to offer a real and practical example of how the anima labored in me. I fell in love for the first time as a sober and abstinent individual in my twenties. This woman initially pursued me, and it started slowly enough but soon developed into a passion and longing I had never experienced nor felt before. I did not perceive my feelings for her coming from my unidentified anima. We dated, and as I got to know her and later reflected, she embodied all the aspects of my character, which, in an embryonic stage, had yet to be lived, experienced, or developed. She was a perfect fit for my anima projection because she had in her personality that which I did not have in my own. She initially accepted me as I was; she accepted my sexuality (which was repressed at the time like so many young Christians). As we pursued a mutual fulfilling sexuality, she also had a serenity, a firm grounding in what she wanted, and a certain grace and ease with which she interacted with the world. As the relationship developed, I became afraid of losing her. What initially was an experience of wonder and joy with a dash of naiveté thrown in gradually degenerated into a situation where slowly and imperceptibly at first, living without her began to dominate my consciousness. This became inevitable when a flesh-and-blood women became a projection of my anima. As the delusion ripened, I endeavored to acquire the traits that were projected upon her and to capture the flesh-and-blood woman for my own. As long as she stayed with me, I believed on an unconscious level I could secure all the qualities she manifested to my soul. (Paris was unable to withdraw his projection, and therefore, he destroyed everything.)

She seemed to embody everything I wanted in a woman and potential wife. My growing insecurities drove her away. She not only contained my projected anima or soul image, she inadvertently became a new drug while medicating all the unhealed wounds from my past; the pain, inadequacy, abandonment, and insecurities left unresolved from childhood; and my addiction to drugs and alcohol. I'd always had keen radar to the pain in others because of my own unresolved pain. This was all unconscious in me at the time. She had inadvertently become a projection for my anima and all the accumulated pain that had become trapped within my personal unconscious.

One spring afternoon, all my projections were torn apart, and repressed pain surfaced when she told me that me she was ending our relationship. I was devastated and cried a few days later for the first time since my early teens. I felt abandoned and full of shame like I did in childhood; all those corroded contents of my unconscious came surging into consciousness with the force of an explosion. When I was younger, I experienced a number of losses of people with whom I was close. In typical childhood ego-centric fashion, I had unconsciously assumed others left because of a substantial lack or inferiority within myself. Now this woman, who seemed to contain a plethora of gifts that were never developed within myself, had departed. With her rejection imprinted upon my psyche, acceptance of my sexuality and self disappeared like the dusk gives way to darkness. Lost too was my willingness to be vulnerable and weak and the childlike faith I had in God at the time. The love I required for myself also vanished. She opened gaping wounds, which were canopied quickly by my usual defenses. When she left, a task was set before me that took many years to come to grips with. I broke down and went into the pain gradually, making conscious these personal unconscious issues (pain associated with abandonment feelings) and collective unconscious contents (anima projections). What I realized later was I did not miss her as much as I missed what I felt when we were initially together. I had to surrender those feelings and my attachment to her and all that she represented before I was capable of experiencing them again in a transformed and more mature state—one called grace. As I have gotten older, I have gradually grown in self-acceptance and love. Love eventually heals all wounds and opens us up to new and more enriching experiences. It seems to me that by letting go and experiencing the pain of my grief, though scars were created and still remain, these scars remind me of the possibility and hope that all I experience will one day be made whole and complete. The essential truth is we uncover buried treasures within us when we endure and wait long enough in our pain for them to heal and thereby move toward wholeness. I have succeeded in withdrawing these projections, and although the scars remain, the healing process has begun. It seems to me that this is all we can expect while we wait for the final fulfillment or consummation of any painful experience.

In my own experience, all the archetypes are neither good nor evil. They seem to just be there, and the negative or positive qualities come forth simply based on the attitudes consciousness take toward them. The goddess and the witch are both illusions that the anima instigates to get our attention. Both will continue to haunt men's fantasies as long as the anima is not integrated into men's consciousness.

One more footnote. This particular woman has repeatedly resurfaced in my dreams whenever a new archetype has surfaced and accumulated enough energy to attempt a wedding with my consciousness. I learned to interpret dreams in my early thirties and have since used this source to access abundant and valuable insights into myself. Initially, I was angry that my unconscious would not let her go as I have attempted to do consciously. I eventually recognized that her presence in my dreams was symbolic and a demarcation point toward new personal and archetypal stages and transformations. My unconscious mind has obviously parlayed the emotional significance that she had in my conscious experience as a signal that major changes were/are in the offing. When I quit ruing her presence in my dreams, I finally recognized the muse my anima had long used as a disguise. All experiences are potentially positive, and I *strive* to regret nothing in my past or in my present and let new experiences make an approach of their own accord.

> In the chilly hours and minutes of uncertainty
> I want to be in the warm hold of your loving mind
> To feel you all around me and to take your hand along the sand
> Ah but I may as well try to catch the wind . . .

> When rain has hung the leaves with tears
> I want you near to kill my fears
> To help me leave all my blues behind
> Standing in your heart
> Is where I want to be
> I long to be
> Ah but I may as well try to catch the wind.

—Donovon, "Catch the Wind"

> I sat outside the window
> It was just like Romeo
> But it was only a dream.
> Van Morrison, "Only A Dream"

Archetype of the Wise Old Man

> Señor, Señor, do you know where we're headin'?
> Lincoln County Road or Armageddon?
> Seems like I been down this road before.
> Is there any truth in that Señor?

Señor, Señor . . .

I can smell the tail of the dragon,
Can't stand the suspense anymore.
Can you tell me who to contact here Señor? . . .

Señor, Señor, let's disconnect these cables,
Overturn these tables.
This place don't make sense to me no more.
Can you tell me what we're waiting for, Señor?

—Bob Dylan, "Señor (Tales of Yankee Power)"

The anima leads us to the wise old man, symbol of wisdom and the part of our spirit that leads us to wholeness. In the legends of King Arthur and the quest for the Holy Grail, Parsifal, a man originally of lowly status and seen as a fool, was led by his anima figure to a hermit, who guides him to the Grail castle where the Holy Grail resides. This is the place in the spirit that leads the soul to the truth where wholeness and oneness, completeness and enlightenment merge with God. The wise old man represents symbolically our human spirit, which is already connected with God. It is interesting that in the grail myth, the wise old man is a hermit, a solitary wise man who rarely is seen or heard from until that point in development where he is needed. As we will explore in *The Odyssey*, Odysseus is led by Circe, his anima figure, to Tiresias, another mystical wise old man who is a blind prophet and is encountered in the land of the dead. Both these myths represent the soul's contact with the human spirit that resides as hidden treasures within each of us. The spirit lies behind and amid the soul and is meant to counsel the psyche or soul into all wisdom and holiness/wholeness because it most resembles God as spirit and is the part of us that is made in His image. The wise old man is an essential part of ourselves that we are drawn toward because he is the essence of all who we truly are; our true identity and that part of us which is to rule and guide the soul and body. That still and quiet voice within us is the wise old man directing, correcting, and stirring us into all wisdom.

Individuation and the Transcendent Function

> On the road with my
> Sword
> And my shield in my hand . . .
>
> There's a battle for the throne . . .
>
> And it's raging down in
> Your soul
> It says this love will
> Surely last forever
> This love will surely last
> Always
>
> I've been accused
> Of truth and alchemy . . .
>
> Here comes the horseman
> Through the pass
> They cast a cold eye
> On life and death
> There's a battle for the
> Truth
> And it means to thine
> Own self be true.
>
> —Van Morrison, "Here Comes the Knight"

Individuation, simply put, is the *process* of becoming a unique person. It is the questing for our direction, which is both unique to ourselves but simultaneously links us with the rest of the humanity and the cosmos. This is experiencing our true identity and beginning to answer the question of questions: who am I?

The path to individuation begins by becoming independent of our parents and their world. We first begin by becoming autonomous as we parlay a career that reflects our values, interests, abilities, beliefs, and attitudes. Secondly, we need to establish a healthy ego from which to tackle life's problems. The ego-body-consciousness needs to be strong enough to handle disappointment without crumbling in the face of external or inner conflicts. We can achieve a certain amount of independence only by taking responsibility for ourselves. This is usually firmly established around the midpoint in life, the midthirties. If a person has thereby taken responsibility and become autonomous in the best sense of the word, they are ready to begin developing the third stage in the individuation process: developing the transcendent function. This is where the ego learns to die to being the center of the personality. This death means the ego becomes only the center of consciousness and not the center of the entire personality. Instead of being at the center, the ego works to bring together a union of the conscious and unconscious minds. The ego, in effect, becomes a satellite of the truth and the wisdom of the unconscious. This includes all we have talked about with the pairs of opposites that underlie each archetype within the unconscious and the union of matter, body, soul, and spirit. Ego-body-consciousness has the tendency to be one-sided in its thinking; that is to say we grab hold of one of the pair of opposites to the exclusion of the other. This is done for security and worth as we have discussed and is often the mistake of prioritizing our wants over our needs. Like matter in its positive and negative charges, the unconscious and conscious minds complement and compensate each other. Each complements the other like positive and negative poles in a battery; we need both for reliable functioning. The unconscious mind also compensates for one-sided conscious thinking and attitudes by taking up the opposite perspective in its attempt to regulate psychic health in the same manner our body functions, which regulates our body temperature, insulin and sugars, acids and bases, adrenaline, etc. Our psyche and body attempt to maintain homeostasis in its functioning, that is to say a balance functioning for its health. The transcendent function offers up the opposite attitudes, beliefs, and/or behaviors from the unconscious, which attempts to maintain the homeostasis of the psyche. The ego-body-consciousness needs to take the lead by first learning how to bring unconscious contents to the surface of consciousness. The unconscious seeks the light of consciousness, and consciousness seeks the substance and depths that the unconscious produces and provides.

I want to again refer the readers to Robert Johnson's *Inner Work* as a practical guide to bringing up these contents into consciousness as well as the second step in the process of the transcendent function, which is creating an inner dialogue with these contents in the hopes of finding a third position that respects and validates both the conscious and unconscious positions. A third position (synthesis) is the union of the two positions (thesis and antithesis) taken up by both our minds. This is the process of bringing together the union of opposites—of whatever opposites you are wrestling with. This self-regulation of our psychic system fashions wholeness of body, psyche, and spirit.

There are two primary methods to gain insights into the contents of the unconscious. The first we will examine is active imagination. There are inner wars caused by the clash of opposites—within the context of our consciousness and unconscious. Our mind will often struggle with opposing views to the degree we carry on an inner dialogue. One form of active imagination is concentrating on this conflict and writing down the inner dialogue as it pops up in your mind. I considered active imagination strange and confusing until I read Sanford and began practicing active imagination for myself. I have experienced these archetypes as real and autonomous.

It's amazing what thoughts counter your conscious perspective. Our conscious perspective needs to be honest and assertive while maintaining openness about what the unconscious brings to the surface. I have found myself accepting, editing, and rejecting input from this inner dialogue. This inner clash precedes all external wars we create—with our spouses, neighbors, other nations, coworkers, whomever. Generally speaking, these inner wars do not surface until the second half of life. In the first half of life we are busy establishing autonomy, careers, a healthy ego consciousness, and primary relationships. At the midpoint in life we are required by our unconscious to turn our attention more and more inwardly to balancing the inner conflicts within the pairs of opposites hidden within the unconscious mind or soul. The outer life and body gradually declines while the inner life becomes activated with turmoil and meaning hitherto unfamiliar to the ego.

We can also learn to interpret our dreams. I do not intend to go into detail as two books I strongly recommend were written just for the purpose of learning how to engage in dream interpretations and active imagination. The authors do an excellent job of helping the reader to learn the tools they will need to confront the unresolved issues and opposites with the added benefit of doing your own work without spending money on a therapist! See John Sanford's *Dreams and Healing* and Robert A. Johnson's *Inner Work*.

Learning to interpret our dreams greatly enhances our ability to get at what position the unconscious mind is taking. We are strengthened by the symbolic images the archetypes produce in our dreams. Drawing the symbols from our dreams or active imagination is another effective method to begin wrestling with the inner wars and symbols of the unconscious. We do not need to be artists, and the aesthetic quality of our work is not important. What is important is we allow ourselves the freedom to draw what the unconscious has produced so we are able to enter into a dialogue with it. I have had clients draw out these images, and then we discuss them together like one does with a dream in an attempt to get at the symbolism in the context of the present life situation and conflict. The obvious value of this process is your unconscious houses the data needed to identify the personal conflicts and solutions whereby you can form a synthesis through different life choices and attitudes that reflect a balanced perspective within your conscious mind that the unconscious mind is driving at.

We all have an inner voice, which is opposed to our conscious intentions. For instance, all those who were raised in shame know that destructive inner voice: "You idiot, you are worthless and stupid." This is called self-talk and is the basis of different forms of cognitive therapy. We can actually have dialogues with these inner voices by meditation and writing down the dialogue as it progresses; we must stand up to these destructive voices and integrate them into our psyche. The shame that is within me will always be there, but it does not have to take on autonomous power over me if I make reasonable compromises with its perspective. Perhaps an example of this inner dialogue will be helpful. "I am not stupid, but I do make stupid decisions sometimes. I no longer will allow myself to accept your judgments without my conscious participation." The shame is within me; it is mine whether I choose to face it or not. Shame does have a place as it has confronted my arrogance and naïve attitudes and beliefs. By confronting my shame and by allowing it to personify itself in my imagination allows for an inner dialogue from which I can craft a balance position. *Truth or wisdom involves finding a synthesis of understanding and will, knowledge and actions, insight and behavior. Wisdom takes knowledge and integrates it with the cooperation of the will. It is here a healthy balance is achieved where priorities are fashioned and truth is lived and valued. Thought and life must be wedded.* I don't know anyone who has accomplished these ideals; however, this must not deter our quest. Be ye perfect, and yet ye shall never accomplish perfection on earth! *Here is a paradox and dialectic of the first order.*

We need to maintain the tension the opposites occasion while passionately pursuing both sides of these opposites. Dialectics are where both a truth's pair of opposites are valued and experienced. Both the pursuit of perfection and its impossibility in its achievement are simultaneously believed and valued. Because paradox goes beyond the rational, it is often assumed to be irrational. However, the irrational has rational elements hidden within it. It is so because it goes beyond the confines of the rational mind. The great oracle at Delphi had two temples, one to Apollo, the God of the rational, and Dionysus, the God of the irrational. We can, along with the Greeks, celebrate both elements within our psyche that is soul (mind, emotion, will) along with the body and spirit, while also attempting to develop and live them. Our intuition is not always rational yet often turns out to be true and very helpful when we have learned to heed its inclinations and intimations. Out of such balance comes inner peace and love. We all want to be loved and to love, yet we are often immobilized from receiving and giving it due to the lack of wholeness and balance in our lives. This process briefly discussed initiates the inner dialogue between the conscious and unconscious minds; both need to make concessions and adaptations. You will find the unconscious is more than willing.

At the midpoint of life, the unconscious mind conspires to produce an antithesis from some thesis or position our conscious mind has taken. A problem will get amplified as it pushes for a synthesis that is achieved through suffering, mystery, and understanding as we wrestle with a particular pair of opposites. As the tensions build, ego-consciousness needs to hold them together by endurance until a synthesis is constructed or naturally grows out of the conflict. There is no way to cheat the process. We are all impatient and often strive to move the process along by our impatience. The synthesis is not created by our ego but blossoms within those that are open to the work of synthesizing the opposites with the help or counsel of the ego. When unavoidable failures transpire, we have to get up and start over, probing for what we may have missed. The suffering and anguish all these inner conflicts accrue can only be lived out by initially suspending judgments, eschewing quick fixes, and enduring. The pain and inner anguish produced by these conflicts are baptisms of fire. It seems evolution demands we endure these inner conflicts and work toward synthesizes. It's within the psyche where the synthesis of opposites takes shape. The pairs of opposites are all the apparent disparate aspects within us that make up the totality of the personality. Each personality is unique and simultaneously enfolds something universal. A *subtle unity underlies* all the inner conflicts that are carried out daily in our kitchens, bedrooms, meditations, reflections, jobs, relationships, etc. Frequently, periods crop up when changes in attitude, behavior, and/or belief are called for. This requires a willing ego schooled in endurance, patience, and courage. A decision to accept these inner wars within ourselves is required. These inner wars and conflicts differentiate experiences and allow us to expand consciousness and mature in character. We are stretched and pushed out of the confines of which we have been imprisoned. We need to grow and cannot do so without these inner wars creating new experiences and opportunities for development. *The inner tension these wars occasion is made up of conflicting pairs of opposites in our desires, fears, urges, and longings.* The anguish these inner conflicts construct is enormous. The natural response of our fragile ego-consciousness is to construct defenses and distractions to protect ourselves. The fact that I use these defenses and distractions bothers me, but then I came to the realization that this is part of the process in which the conflicts take shape, and no amount of self-deception or self-pity will dismantle the process unless I choose to remain stuck therein.

When we avoid truth, it is taken up by the unconscious, and when the time is right, it is thrust upon our consciousness with enormous force so the human will is often cast aside like junk mail. The unconscious energy is too powerful, and our will is pilfered of its limited energy. Our will is strangled until the unconscious is reckoned with and the ego compromises and adapts to the counterposition of the unconscious. Our will is strangled and rendered impotent until we begin the process of facing ourselves and making these adaptations, whereby the unconscious is merged into consciousness as a peace is forged between them. When this occurs, it is said the individual's consciousness is expanded; that which was unconsciousness is now conscious. This is most often accompanied with surrendering something—behavior, attitude, or idea—and embracing new ones. Every death brings new life.

Here is an example of how the transcendent function and the process of individuation works in therapy. I begin by listening and getting a read on a new client in the second stage of life. Gradually, a one-sided attitude or belief came to the surface as he shared his personal struggles with me. He was a fascinating client who lived primarily in the realm of imagination and intellect (possibility). He rallied against the limitations and necessities of daily life with his wife and children. I never try to discourage the one-sided perspective for we need this in order to bring about a synthesis. I acknowledged his inclination for living with possibility and discussed its place while simultaneously exhorting him to face his daily responsibilities and depicting the advantages of a whole and balanced outlook. He quickly recognized the need and, before long, seemed to have made an adjustment in his attitudes, beliefs, and finally in the behavior in his home life.

Let's take another client whose conscious attitude was too constrictive and conservative. Her need for therapy conveys the conflict in the present situation. Her unconscious was trying to initiate consciousness to take more risks in life and expand her horizons. I have worked with many clients who were stuck in a dead-end job or in some attitude or belief. As her counselor, I took it upon myself to mirror the unconscious attitude while pointing out data from her dreams and life that led both of us to recognize the counterposition of the unconscious, which occupies some imperatives if she was to grow. This can begin only after she acknowledged her one-sided attitude and belief that playing it safe was stifling her and preventing her from staying sober and maturing to the next stage in her life. Often, a client will revert to self-deception and want to deny the unconscious truth, which is attempting to lead them to wholeness. I then become the adversary in these situations. I try compassionately to not let go of the unconscious position. A compromise in attitudes, beliefs, and/or behaviors will need to be created, or long-term change and abstinence is extremely unlikely. The dialogue may have been initiated with me but later takes shape within them on the conscious level. In fact, in general terms, I frequently adopt this state of affairs with my clients. I take the position of the unconscious mind initially, and later, the healthy clients gradually make peace with the opposite position. *A footnote is in order. I also must make concessions to the client's conscious perspective.* Unless the client is open-minded, ready and willing to acknowledge the inner conflict, I try not to push anything. It's only after the clients recognizes the conflict and then begin striving to deny, avoid, distract, or switch the subject do I bring them back to face their inner conflicts. Since I have designed two relapse programs and worked them for many years, I've had opportunities to work with ex-clients. Inevitably, many acknowledged they had not resolved the initial inner conflict and hence relapsed. In many scenarios, the client would specifically want to return to me for they knew the relapse was linked to their unwillingness to face the inner conflicts we had already addressed the first go-around in treatment and were now ready to resolve them satisfactorily. I negotiate with my clients and work with them to find the middle ground—I never force a client into doing anything they were not willing to do. I take the position that a client's resistance is important, and I never assume I know everything that the client needs to do. For without the cooperation of the client, no progress will be made because each individual needs to make their own decisions. None of us is God to others, and if we act in ways that try to subdue the client into accepting our perspective, we could say inflation has overcome the counselors. Timing is everything to our health. I try to discern what the unconscious is saying to the client at a given moment in time and not what I may believe is right or wrong. I have tried to leave alone issues until I believe the unconscious itself is developing the inner tensions. I use the aftercare plan to address issues that are identified but left unresolved in treatment.

Jung talked at length about the need to live from the ground up; that is to say, we need to integrate the physical instincts (teens and twenties) prior and facing life's responsibilities (by age thirty-five), and only then do the more complex archetypes make their initial appearance. The goal is integration; that is the living out of the instincts or archetypes without being controlled by them. To do so, we first identify what the unconscious mind has in mind for us. What needs changing lies in our attitudes, beliefs, and behaviors. Then we are in a spot to adapt with new attitudes, beliefs, and/or behaviors. Changing behavior is a very difficult process as we discussed earlier; our will has only so much energy and power at its disposal. The point is to begin by identifying the truth, for only then we can begin to live these truths out in the concrete arenas of our lives. This is very difficult work as our nature struggles with the opposites and our need to change. We have for too long placed our security and worth in our attitudes and beliefs that are one-sided and narrow. The unconscious can be our friend if we take the attitude that we need to constantly grow and change and that mistakes and faults are part and parcel of our human condition. We are not whole and need to change to bring about this process to becoming whole, and this process will always be painful and seem like death to the ego as we come across new inner frontiers within our psyche.

Well I'm grinding my life out steady and sure
Nothing more wretched than what I must endure . . .

Hear me holler,
Hear me moan,
I pay in blood
But not by own.

—Bob Dylan, "Pay in Blood"

The Mandala: The Symbol for Wholeness

I dreamed of a circle, I dreamed of a circle round. And
In that circle was a maze, a terrible spiral to be lost in.
Blind in my fear, I was escaping just by feel . . .

—10,000 Maniacs, "Circle Dream"

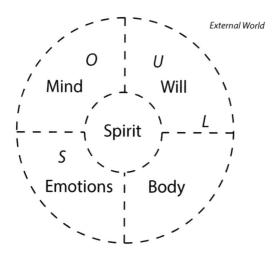

"Strictly speaking, the word 'mandala' means 'circle', although it is a complex piece of drawing and often framed within a squared boarders (taken from *The Penguin Dictionary of Symbols*, published by the Penguin Group, 1996, pp. 632–634. *An Illustrated Encyclopedia of Traditional Symbols* by J. C. Cooper, 1978, Thames and Hudson Ltd, London puts it thus on p. 103).

In Hindu tradition, the mandala represents the symbol of the presence of the godhead at the center of all things. In all the traditions that use the mandala, it is a means of meditation to achieve wholeness and oneness with God or supreme reality. It is believed by many that all symbols themselves contain energy within our imagination where all creativity and wholeness lies within the context of faith, the mandala being the supreme symbol of wholeness. The symbol of the mandala

253

is often associated with the squaring of the circle, which represents wholeness further. The mandala is often used in symbolic ritual where the initiate moves toward the center in an approach via symbolic act of reaching toward wholeness within to join with God.

In my midtwenties, I went to a presentation by my then girl-friend on the "whole persons wheel" and have been gripped by this image ever since. I have transformed it countless times in conjunction with my inner growth. The wheel had no center, and I created a hub (which never moves) and placed spirit there. The cross symbolizes the fact I invited Christ into my spirit/life at age twenty. My mandala is conceived as a spinning wheel where only the hub remains unmoved and the corresponding symbolism is of the process of becoming for the spokes of the wheel and of being for the hub. We all have heard and/or engaged in talk of centering ourselves and finding within a secret and quiet place from which we can experience balance, poise, and inner serenity. The dotted lines represent the fluidity that must occur from both within and without the wheel. Each impacts the others, and the *center* engineers a balance and synthesis. I have constructed a mandala on my lawn and danced around it in a ritual of my own.

As you can see in my mandala, I have the mind, will, body, and emotions circling around the spiritual center. The center represents the spirit while the rest of the mandala represents the soul and body. Everything outside the circle represents the other; that is everyone and everything else that has been created. Since there are dotted lines all around the mandala, there are no complete demarcation points for what is outer and what is inner as everything is interconnected and forms a unity. All things, through different manifestations that appear dualistic and separated, are ultimately one in my philosophy.

All the archetypes lead to the center, which is toward wholeness and its fruits: joy and wholeness and inner peace. Jung believed the center of the personality is represented by the mandala, the sacred cir-cle. He noticed the sacred circle was a universal symbol in all the cul-tures of world history. The center of the personality is full of depths and mysteries unidentified, and no one will reach the center while on earth; but we can approach it through this labyrinth called life. We all feel that at times, we are going nowhere but round and round while making no progress toward the center, like the poor hamster on his wheel in his cage. However, we are evolving like a tapestry, one stitch at a time, one choice or day at a time. And life is like a tapestry in that we will not see the entire product until the end as a tapestry is stitched from the back.

This quest for completeness or wholeness is the living out of all the tensions the pairs of archetypal opposites evoke within us; that is to say we find a place to express or flesh out all the patterns of behavior the archetypal and instinctual pairs of opposites that lie within. The primary ones are the following:

male/female	positive/negative
life/death	necessity/possibility
collective/uniqueness	the temporal/eternal
independence/dependence	

There are countless other archetypes as we have discussed, and others such as the knight, the king, the queen, the fool, the joker or trickster, the hero, and many others that have been written about. Living a one-sided life is one definition of neurosis. Let me take an example: the independent/dependent archetype. We have all run into people who overvalue their independence and are unwilling to connect with others. This is an individual who tries to be self-sufficient and take care of him or herself but lacks the humility to relate and become intimate with others. They often get stuck in some form of false pride, and fate creates circumstances where they become dependent upon others if they don't make some concessions on their own. On the other hand, if an individual becomes too one-sided in dependency, they are unable and unwilling to take responsibility for themselves as they look for others to take care of them in some way or another. The problem is others can never live out the life of another, and eventually, the one depended upon usually recognizes this and eventually opts out of this role. Wholeness in this dynamic is to both be intimate and related to others while maintaining independence with its appropriate responsibilities and personal boundaries. This balance is a product of wholeness, and meditating upon the mandala is one of many paths to this state.

I'd like to make one final note on the archetypes. Archetypes are collective in nature while being expressed uniquely in each of us. There are so many different archetypes that none of us contain all the archetypes or their infinite combinations. Due to the sheer numbers of archetypes that have developed over time and the endless possible combinations, we find a seemingly infinite number of possibilities of human personalities. Hence, the diversity we find in the uniqueness of each individual person. Think of all the people that have lived throughout history and the fact that each had assuredly been unique unto themselves. There will always be room for more unique individuals born into this miracle world. However, time, personality, and death limit the potential or possible archetypes any one person can integrate in a given lifetime. In fact, life/death is one primary archetype to integrate, which is a willingness to embrace both life and death in all their complications, futility, and esoteric mystery. However, we are preprogrammed to live a certain number of these archetypes out in their unique combinations. In other words, we can never create more archetypal growth than our destiny prescribes, but we can scuttle the processes and fail to accomplish our destiny, which the mandala symbolizes.

You can't let go,
And you can't hold on,
You can't go back and
You can't stand still,
If the thunder don't get 'cha,
The lightning will.

The small wheel turns by the fire and the rod,
The big wheel turns by the grace of God,

> Every time that wheel turns around,
> It's bound to cover just a little more ground.

—Jerry Garcia, "The Wheel"

The time has come to examine some myths and stories of the hero's journey, starting with *The Odyssey*.

The hero's journey was studied and mapped out by Carl Jung and Joseph Campbell, and it is not my intent to regurgitate their ideas here as I would refer the reader to their works. However, there will be some inevitable parallels.

Commentary of *The Odyssey*

Introduction

Take a little trip back
With Father Tiresus
Listen to the old one speak
Of all he has live through
I have crossed between the poles
To me there's no mystery
Once a man like the sea I raged
Once a woman like the earth I gave
And there is in fact more earth than sea.

—Genesis, "The Cinema Show, Aisle of Plenty"

The Odyssey was Homer's classic and read by all Greeks during the golden age of Greece in the fifth century BCE. Odysseus himself represents the Greek highly developed rational or thinking function (and therefore his superior function), as he is referred throughout *The Odyssey* as "Odysseus of the nimble wits." Consequently, as we shall see, his inferior function is his feeling values as his personality will disclose in his earliest encounter on his trip back home with the Cirones. The Greeks were influenced by the unconscious as their extravagant and innumerable myths reflect the wide range of archetypes that untimely all originate in our collective unconscious. The ten-year odyssey of Odysseus is where he encounters the unconscious as it works as a compensation for one-sided attitudes and unlived aspects of his rational psyche. In Odysseus's case, like the Greeks in general, he over emphasized rationalism without the counterposition of feeling values. Odysseus is in need of integrating his other three conscious functions as we all who are governed by our superior function.

On the surface, Odysseus is the typical Greek male hero, overcoming every external obstacle with his courage and wit in the playing field of war, fate, monsters, material treasures, women, and death. He eventually makes it *home* to reclaim his kingdom in Ithaca and become one of the greatest heroes in Western history. Home in another metaphor for wholeness, of which the unconscious is guiding us. We will be exploring how these external obstacles are really projections of the inner state of Odysseus and the Greek mind in general. Our real enemies are the ones hidden within ourselves and behind these Greek masculine projections. We will be hunting down Odysseus's inner enemies by catching and isolating his projections and then retrieve them from his archetypal psyche through Poseidon, the God of the sea, who symbolizes the entire unconscious, the Cyclops, Polyphemus (who symbolizes the basic instincts for fight and sex), the female goddess Circe (his anima figure), and Tiresias (the wise old man archetype).

The epic poem *The Odyssey* probably was created during the Mycenaean age in oral poetry shortly after the purported events had taken place (i.e., shortly after the siege of Troy around the thirteenth century BCE. Along with *The Iliad*, which I referred in chapter 2 related to Paris and Helen, Homer put these two epic events down in writing sometime in the eighth century BCE.

The Odyssey is about Odysseus's ten-year struggle and sojourn back to his native lands and to his wife, kingdom, and son following the ten-year Trojan War. The number 10 is significant as it is another symbol of wholeness and completeness. *The Iliad* is the account of the Greeks' ten-year siege at Troy, where the Greeks finally destroyed Troy by the inspiration of Odysseus, who came up with the ruse to build the Trojan horse where he and his comrades hid away to gain entrance into the city and beyond the impregnable walls of Troy. My commentary will be presented in the chronological order of his return home, which Homer doesn't. I have chosen to present it thus because it is easier to follow and mark the archetypal maturation of Odysseus. Odysseus has accomplished the tasks of the first half of life, and he is not only respected as a hero, he is a king, rich, and a man of prestige and privilege. We will run across this similar dynamic with Job. His persona is well established and respected, and therefore, it is easy to be seduced into identifying with it.

In the classical age, Zeus is, in ultimate, patriarchal controller of destiny, and yet the goddess Circe takes center stage and guides Odysseus to his own inner truths. Joseph Campbell identified the period of middle second millennium BCE as "a process of fusion of the two mythologies of the goddess and the gods." From all the focus on the goddess Circe that the female goddess were still a primary focus of worship in the Bronze Age, when *The Odyssey* was originally transmitted orally. It is for his reason I will be focusing on Odysseus's encounters with Circe and Tiresias for my commentary. I have use the Penguin classic *The Odyssey* by Homer, translated by E. V. Rieu, Penguin Books, Baltimore-Maryland, reprinted edition, 1962. I also use *The Dictionary of Symbols*, Penguin Reference, written by Jean Chevalier and Alan Gheerbrant and translated by John Buchanan Brown, 1996.

The Cirones

Following the conquest of Troy, Odysseus and his men set sail from Troy, and the winds carried them to the island of Ismarus, where promptly they conquer the city of the Cirones, killing the men and dividing up their wives and riches. They commenced to butcher the cattle and sheep while engorging themselves with meat and wine and sex. Odysseus, like modern athletes after having completed a great triumph or championship, celebrates with his teammates by partying in a jaded, inflated, and selfish fashion. Odysseus and his men are in a state of inflation where their ego is king. Today, the fellas head to the strip clubs and carouse until many are brought down from their inflation by getting arrested for some transgression or another or by losing all their riches soon after their careers are over. Odysseus and his men were eventually confronted by the Cirones from the hill country and had to pay heavy consequence by the deaths of six of his men from each of his twelve ships. The dynamics are the same; men become inflated after a great triumph and are eventually broken after experiencing a fall from grace. Unless we assume a humble attitude, we will eventually become alienated from the source of all energy. The unconscious is now activated by the shadow personality for Odysseus and his mates as we shall see in his next adventure. Odysseus and his men have become murders, rapists, jaded partiers, and gluttons following their victory at Troy. Odysseus's inferior function is clearly seen as his despicable and deplorable behavior toward the Cirones and his unconscious will begin to confront him through his shadow with his encounter with the Cyclops.

The Cyclops

Zeus sends a gale via the north wind, and Odysseus and his twelve ships are hurled then encased in darkness while having to row for nine days after their sails are shredded. Storms and wind, especially the north wind, is symbolic of the Spirit of God and is an omen of divine activity (i.e., the unconscious has become activated). The fact that Zeus sent the wind is another clue as he was viewed as the king of the gods in Greek mythology. There is little doubt that this is a case of *natural consequences* following the killing of innocent men and the rape of innocent women. Boreas is the personification and symbol of the north wind in Greek mythology. He was unable to woo a nymph he loved, so he took her for his own and therefore becomes symbol of consequences for rape and kidnapping. Odysseus and his men are chastised for their sordid violence, arrogance, and inflation in their dependence upon the thinking function.

The north wind carries them first to the island of the lotus eaters, and there they have to leave before the entire crew is enchanted by eating the lotus flower, which makes them forget their homeland. The initial response to guilt is to want to forget, but Odysseus overcomes this temptation. We will discuss further the dynamics of forgetting when the company ends up on the island of the goddess Circe.

They then are guided by a dark cloud to the land of the Cyclops. The race of Cyclopses are described as lazy, self-centered, uncivilized, and having no laws. The Cyclops is a manifestation of Odysseus's shadow in the area of his infantile physical instincts. He must face his physical instincts, which are uncivilized, self-centered, and having no ethical boundaries or laws as seen from the behavior of him and his men in their dealings with the Cirones. Odysseus and his men are trapped by the Cyclops Polyphemus, son of Poseidon, in his cave. The Cyclops devours some if his men. The shadow does the same with those who deny or identify with him. Odysseus eventually gives the Cyclops some enchanted wine no one can resist that he received from the priest of Apollo whom he had once protected. Apollo is the God of the sun (consciousness and prophesy, inner spiritual/insight). With insight and conscious awareness, Odysseus succeeds in blinding the Cyclops Polyphemus and so insuring their escape. We must escape the darkness of our passions and violent instincts by integrating the shadow and overcoming our symbolic one eye. He blinds the Cyclops and so symbolically becomes himself blind. Blindness to the external world of the five senses is to begin the process of gaining the inner sight or spiritual sight (insight). And so he does, for as the story continues, Odysseus is able to face his dark side and acknowledge his arrogance and foolhardiness in believing he could tame the Cyclops by himself, having done so with the help of Apollo's priest's wine (self-awareness), creating spiritual insight and wisdom. Odysseus becomes known for his wisdom, and facing his shadow is the first major step in becoming wise. His wisdom comes through when he tells the Cyclops his name is Nobody. So when the Cyclops asks for help from his fellows, they believe it was "Nobody's treachery and violence" that blinded him, and therefore they take their leave of him, which ensures Odysseus's escape from the island and therefore symbolically from the destructive aspects of his shadow. Odysseus is therefore recognizing that he is nobody in himself if we take this experience with the Cyclops as a projection. However, Odysseus laughs to himself at his cleverness in his ruse; the shadow does not disappear with one experience of self-knowledge! He also goes on to taunts the Cyclops, which almost destroys his ships, and though his friends grieved the loss of five mates, Odysseus does not in his inflated state.

Whenever we gain insight into ourselves, this insight comes with positive energy. However, this energy when identified with the ego inflates the ego and sets the ego up for further trouble from the unconscious. This is exactly what happens as the story proceeds as Polyphemus prays to his father Poseidon to punish Odysseus. Poseidon (his unconscious) does so in the sense that when Odysseus becomes inflated, he is humbled. Once we have uncovered the uncanny energy of the unconscious archetypes, their destructive and constructive qualities forever attach themselves to those individuals willing to wrestle with them. It is no ordinary task to face the furies from within oneself, which are brought about first by the shadow.

Odysseus has now had his entire unconscious activated. His shadow has surfaced, and this was inevitable as his conscious superior function activated his inferior one. We can recognize the inner struggles of Odysseus because after all, who were the uncivilized ones that killed the peaceful city of the Cirones, or the selfish and lazy ones who became gluttons, lustful, and coveters of their neighbor goods and wives? Odysseus and his crew are already under the influence of the shadow, and that is why they were carried to the island of the Cyclops. The Cyclops also symbolize not only brute force, but lacking in spiritual and moral insight for they only have one eye (symbolic of low levels of understanding while instincts rule, and Apollo was often killing them with insight; that is overcoming the instincts by working with them to make them serve the spiritual). The third eye so prevalent in the marks on the forehead of Hindus is symbolic of the spiritual eye.

After the ships reach safety, Odysseus grieves the losses of his comrades. He is able to grieve after he has come down from his inflation. He is becoming healthy as he realizes sides of himself he does not like and heretofore has been unwilling to make conscious and accept. Conscious awareness/self-knowledge of our shadow is the first step in the transformation of the psyche into wholeness. Grief and lamentations are frequent in *The Odyssey* as in the book of Job and reflect the difficult work of making conscious painful truths about ourselves and the human condition. We cannot forego this grief process, and the *pain can be overwhelming with bouts of depression normal for this stage.* The inner struggles for the truth about ourselves is a very agonizing process full of anguish and confusion. Sometimes all we can do is persevere as we come to consciousness of our defects.

The Floating Island of Aeolia

Odysseus and his crew landed next on the island of Aeolia, where Odysseus received a gift by Aeolus (who, by Zeus's will, was the Warden of the Winds), which was a leather bag of the wind that assured his ships safe passage home. However, Odysseus does not let his crew in on the contents of this mysterious bag of wind, and they believe the bag contains silver and gold that Odysseus is hoarding for himself. Odysseus also trusted no one to handle the rudder as he was filled with anxiety and did not trust anyone else to guide the ship home. Inevitably and eventually, he falls asleep. Odysseus gets stuck in self-sufficiency and not sharing the gifts of the gods. He falls asleep at the wheel; falling asleep is a symbol of unconscious ignorance, self-deception, and laziness for we are unable to remain conscious. Having been held out of the loop, Odyssey's men open the bag out of curiosity, and the wind rushed out and carried them back out to sea. Prior to ending up back where they started, on the island of Aeolia, Odysseus says, "My spirit failed me, and I had half a mind to jump overboard and drown myself" (p.156). We observe a link between his spirit and mind, and when the spirit failed him, he had half a mind. When we give up in self-pity and hopelessness, our mind is halved! He did not do so and was able to overcome half a mind and endure his fate. By not trusting his comrades and not letting them in while attempting to stay awake for ten days to remain in control (self-sufficiency), he ends up where he started. The ego wants to be in control at all times and the center of our personality. We are left to eat humble pie and start over, recognizing that we need to surrender our ego to the powers greater than the ego symbolized by the gift of the bag of wind from Aeolus. Odysseus goes back to

Aeolus for more help but is now rejected. Odysseus will have to learn to surrender his self-sufficiency and learn how to share and trust others with the gifts he is given before he can return home and complete his Odyssey. His shadow personality has and will continue to reveal itself throughout its personal odyssey like it does for us all. Odysseus has yet to face this side of his shadow, and his journey must continue. The voyage inward continues as Odysseus comes in contact with his anima figure.

Circe

There's a woman I long to touch . . .
But she's drifting like a satellite . . .

And a lonesome bell tone in that valley of stone
Where she bathed in a stream of pure heat . . .

There's a babe in the arms of a woman in a rage
And a longtime golden haired stripper on stage
And she winds back the clock and she turns back the page
Of a book no one can write.
Oh, where are you tonight?

The truth was obscure, too profound and too pure, to live
It you have to explode.
In the last hour of need, we entirely agreed, sacrifice was
The code of the road . . .
I couldn't tell her what my private thoughts were but she
Had some way of finding them out . . .

She could feel my despair as I climbed up her hair
And discovered her invisible self . . .

I fought with my twin, that enemy within, 'til both of us fell
By the way . . .
There's a white diamond gloom on the dark side of this

Room and a pathway that leads up to the stars.
If you don't believe there's a price for this sweet paradise,
Remind me to show you the scars.

There's a new day a dawn and I've finally arrived,
If I'm there in the morning baby, you'll know I'm alive,
But without you it's just doesn't seem right.
Oh, where are you tonight?

—B. Dylan, "Where Are You Tonight"
(Journey through Dark Heat)

Odysseus is now chronologically prepared to begin integrating the anima, and sure enough, the Gods direct Odysseus and his men to the island of Aeaea, where the goddess Circe lives. As we shall discuss, she symbolizes the sexual and spiritual aspects of his anima, which ironically are never far apart.

Circe was fathered by the Sun and mothered by the daughter of the Ocean, Perse. She therefore represents, symbolically, the union of conscious and the unconscious contents. She is an anima figure and, as we shall see, represents all of the anima for men—sexual, wisdom, romantic, and the link to the spiritual. Circe's palace was up on a cliff in the center, with forest around and below, while the lower lands were encircled by the sea; in other words a perfect circle with Circe's house built on stone and standing in the middle—a perfect mandala. The stone is a symbol of permanence. We have earlier discussed the mandala and its center. I wish to add the symbol of islands to add to our understanding of the dynamics present in Odysseus's personal journey. Islands are also forms of a mandela. *The Penguin Reference Dictionary of Symbols* puts it thus:

> Modern psychoanalysis has laid particular stress upon one of the essential features of islands-they evoke sanctuaries. One of his basic themes of literature, dreams, and desires is the quest for the desert island, the unknown island, with a wealth of surprises . . . Islands may be sanctuaries where will and consciousness come together to escape the

assaults of the unconscious, as rocks provide a refuge from the ocean waves.

Islands are spiritual places of safety and refuge and, when merged
with isolation and aloneness, become symbolic opportunities to achieve
mystical states of wholeness. This is exactly what we will come across as
we trace Odysseus's encounter with the Circe on her island.

After a brief glimpse of Circe's palace by Odysseus, the crew casts
lots (symbol of seeking God's will) to see who will explore the palace.
The leader Eurylochus stays out of reach, suspicious of a trap, while the
rest of the group hears the beautiful songs of Circe while observing her
weaving at her eternal loom. They can't figure out whether she is a goddess or mortal woman but—enchanted by her song, beautiful luxury,
and domestic weaving—shout to attract her attention. Circe's presence
makes anyone forget their homeland, which is symbolic of choosing to
remain unconscious. These men were obviously unable to differentiate
the inner anima from flesh and blood and were seduced by her songs
(later Odysseus and his men will encounter the Sirens who seduce men
with their songs, which leads most men to their deaths). These women
of beautiful song seem to symbolize the projection of the anima into
sexual urges and into longings for the safety in feminine traits (mother
complex where the woman represents only nurturing and taking care
of men). Circe quickly transforms them into pigs. When men project
their sexual longings and their mother complex onto women, it will
always turn men into pigs The anima is always destructive when she
remains unconscious and where men devalue feminine facets of their
own natures. The flesh-and-blood women we men choose in our lives
are usually full of these projections.

Odysseus is told of his men's transformations by Eurylochus. He
refuses to go with Odysseus to help his men out of fear while Odysseus
goes forth to rescue his men out of his sense of duty. Odysseus is under
the spell of the negative aspects of his own anima as he describes his
journey to "the witch's castle" before Hermes intervenes to save him
from the negative features of his anima. Hermes is the messenger of the
gods, and Jung associated him with Mercury, his Roman name. Jung
recognized within alchemy, Mercury was a projected element, which
symbolized soul or psyche of which the anima represents to men.

Hermes was a messenger of the gods and the underworld. Hermes provides a "drug of real virtue" to Odysseus, which will rob Circe of her enchanted potion. Odysseus is then told to grab his sword as if to kill her, and she will shrink in terror and invite him to her bed. He is then instructed to accept the goddess's sexual invitation if she will act kindly to him and his men. Hermes goes on to tell Odysseus while he is to accept her sexual advances, he is to make her swear a solemn oath by the blessed gods not to attempt any more tricks or, when he is naked, strip him of his courage and manhood. What are we to make of all this?

First, Odysseus needs to differentiate between his own psyche and external women. Women often contain these negative and positive facets of the anima, and by removing all the projections and providing a proper advance to his inner soul, he will be able to develop a healthy relationship with his soul image. His anecdote is a "drug of real of virtue," which provides the proper approach. This drug of real virtue robs her of her black magic and power. This real virtue breaks the spell cast by the negative anima with her poisoning of men's creative capabilities with exaggerated negative moods. His gift from Hermes is *consciousness* of her negative energies, which he recognizes through his projections, that is making men forget (remain unconscious) by offering them domestic (mother complex) and sexual bliss. His ongoing instruction reveals Odysseus will overcome his mother complex as Hermes tells him to use his sword and act as if he will kill Circe. The sword is a symbol of power with positive or negative masculine energy. Here it seems to represent positive masculine energy, which, in this case, destroys ignorance but also can be used to destroy injustice. I think Jesus used this symbolic image to destroy injustice when he said he came not to bring peace, but a sword (Matthew 10:34). Odysseus becomes conscious with the help of Hermes then to use the ruse that he is threatening her life to bring out her positive aspects. The negative anima then disappears, and she invites him to her bed.

We talked earlier of the nexus between sexual fantasies and our urges toward relationships and wholeness, and this sexual scene represents Odysseus's relationship with the inner anima through a projected external sexual act. Viewed inwardly, the sexual behavior between Odysseus and Circe symbolically represent the beginning of a healthy relationship between Odysseus and his anima. That is all the anima is after and is identical with the women in men's lives. I stress the anima is the primary symbolic image, which links men to their souls, yet the soul itself is masculine and feminine. The masculine characteristics needed by Odysseus in facing his anima with Circe are symbolized by the sword and the masculine characteristic of assertiveness. Constructive anger and healthy assertiveness are needed by men and women alike to fight for justice and overcome obstacles. It is also needed when confronting our inner selves and the archetypes. It contains the will to act, and Odysseus must be assertive and stand his ground with the anima if he is to maintain his manhood while approaching the feminine. No female is ultimately attracted to a weak man devoid of courage and self-knowledge. These qualities provide an opportunity for a mature relationship between Circe and Odysseus (i.e., between ego and anima or soul image).

Odysseus heeds all Hermes instructions, and Circe invites him to bed where in love, sleep, and conversation, they learn to trust one another. Only after she has swore the solemn oath and returned his men to their proper form did he and Circe develop an intimacy, which after one year, guided him to the truth that had to continue on his personal odysseys of suffering by facing death. She guides him to Hades and the land of the dead to be instructed by Tiresias, the blind prophet, who has sight from within (insight), "who understanding even death has not impaired."

As we will examine in the next section, Tiresias symbolizes the wise old man archetype. The wise old man is a symbol of spirit. Tiresias was the only human being in Greek mythology that spent time as a woman as well as a man, further emphasizing the symbolic wholeness of *spirit*, which includes *both male and female archetypal energies.* Our spirit personifies wisdom and love and knows all about the numerous psychological and physical death(s) we must experience as we move toward wholeness and union with God. Odysseus's anima now leads him into the major tasks of the second half of life and to the wise old man (i.e., to his own inner spirit). When we develop a relationship with our soul, it will ferry us to our Spirit. It is here we become capable of dying a thousand deaths and accepting them all, including the possibility that physical death not only can come at any moment, but by accepting death without fear because he will have learned from her the secret wisdom of eternity. That wisdom is where wholeness and enlightenment dwells within the psyche (soul) through the Spirit where human and divine intimacy dwell.

Circe sends them favorable winds toward his destination of Hades, and thus Odysseus continues his odyssey. He enters his ship, and Odysseus comments that after putting his gear in order, it was time to sit still. Rest is essential before facing any new task and transition in our journey of rebirth and growth. Waiting and patience seem to be new companions of Odysseus as his character has matured immensely in the company of Circe. We must keep in mind he is following the counsel of her instructions as she guides him to Tiresias, the wise old man, who symbolizes Odysseus's own spirit. They reach the River of Ocean, which is at the borderline between this world and the next (rivers are sometimes symbolic of the boundaries between this world and the beyond). A mist and fog shield the sun and stars from the Cimmerians, who dwell in what's called the City of Perpetual Mist, for dreadful night permeates all who dwell therein. This land symbolizes depression, anxiety, and alienation; all who experience any death and rebirth are required to endure a form of depression and anxiety where no sun can penetrate. The Cimmerians are those who are stuck in depression and do not recognize their depression is sent by their unconscious to inspire them to live those aspects of their lives, which remain unlived and that which is a form of death and rebirth. The sun is a symbol of God's Spirit and the source of all, and it seems withdrawn for a time as depression and anxiety/fear percolate from the unconscious into consciousness and which always seems to precede any rebirth. Odysseus follows Circe's instructions, digs a trench there in the City of Perpetual Mist, *and makes sacrifices to the dead* with honey, milk, water, wine, and sheep while a promising to also sacrifice a heifer for all the dead before making a specific sacrifice of a jet-black sheep to Tiresias when they returned to Ithica. Odysseus is still under the influence of his anima as she guides him toward Tiresias.

We need to pause and look at the symbolism of honey, water, milk, wine, and sheep to get a grasp of what these sacrifices symbolize as Odysseus enters Hades. Hades is the place of the womb: birth, death, and rebirth. I'd like to quote Carol P. Christ from her work *Odyssey with the Goddess: A Spiritual Quest in Crete* (the Continuum Publishing Company, 1995, p.97), where she acted out the same ritual that Odysseus did minus the sacrifice of sheep before he embarked into the land of the dead:

> The ritual began with the offerings of libations: first mild, the nurturing liquid that pours from female breasts, both human and animal; then honey, sweet gift of the bee, reminiscent of the juices that flow from the women's sacred place; followed by water, source of life bubbling up from the rocks; and finally, wine, giver of joy, loosener of limbs and spirits, symbolic of women's blood, the blood of birth and renewal.

Circes instructions differ slightly in the order with milk and honey mixed together, then water, and finally wine. The symbols of water and milk seem to me to be the same; Odysseus is sacrificing the sources and nourishment of life to the dead. This gesture appears to be a ritual symbolizing a sacrifice of *the living to death itself—a surrender and acceptance of death's place in life.* We have to find to an inner peace where we accept our mortality and the death of our ego as the center of our lives and the death that will come to all those we love.

However, Odysseus, as a male and though he offered these same four libations that are quoted from Carol Christ, we need to differentiate the symbolic use of honey and wine sacrificed by a male in contrast to that of a female. Honey is also a symbol of fullness, wealth, and sweetness as pictured in God's promise to Abraham that his decedents would be led to the promised land of milk and honey. Odysseus was sacrificing not only his sexuality to death, but in addition, his wealth, fullness, and the sweetness of life. Odysseus was a rich and powerful king, and this ritual was a sacrifice and symbol of his willingness to let go of his attachments to his privileged life as he prepared to enter the land of the dead. Remember, Circe directed him in this ritual, and it is his feminine soul image that recognizes the need to endure a death prior to rebirth. The fourth and last libation was wine, and it is associated with joy and the later development of the Dionysus cult in Greece and the blood of sacrifice of Christ's blood from the cross, and hence, in both cases, *immortality*. In sacrificing wine, Odysseus is letting go of joy for a time as he enters the land of the dead. There is no death that we go through that is initially joyful. In fact, it generates depression and anxiety. However, it symbolizes *immortality*, and therefore, wine is symbolic of the joy that will be reawakened with any form of rebirth and belief in immortality. Dionysus was the God of wine and joy, and his cult eventually included the belief in immortality. Jesus during the last supper referenced that this was the last time he would drink wine until the banquet at His kingdom's physical inauguration. The fourth libation, the number 4 is symbolic of wholeness in emphasizing immortality. Immortality and wholeness are inexorably linked. The fifth sacrifices are of sheep; they have their throats slit, and the blood is added to the other four elements. Sheep are closely linked to lambs and are symbolic victims—helpless, unintelligent, and followers in need of a shepherd. The blood of lambs and sheep therefore are quintessential victims and sacrificed for the defects and sins of others. Odysseus is also counseled and agrees to sacrifice a jet-black sheep to Tiresias when he returns home; the perennial black sheep is the one who is evil and always doing wrong. This is closely associated to the sacrificial lamb, and later, Christ was viewed as the Lamb of God, sacrificed for the sins of the world. Therefore, the sacrifice of the sheep was symbolic of the repentance, penitence, and humility by Odysseus. Odysseus's ego must become nothing as he must sacrifice its kingship with all its comparison, competitiveness, control, and needs to dominate. We all must be willing to become nothing and empty ourselves of all the refuse that the ego as king has encased over our true selves with its false self. With his sacrifices, Odysseus is doing just that in the symbolic sense.

With Odysseus's conclusion of prayers in conjunction of his five sacrifices, the souls of the dead make their journey from below: the souls of "fresh brides, unmarried youth, old men with life's long suffering behind them, tender young girls still nursing this first anguish in their hearts, and a great throng of warriors killed in battle, their spear-wounds gaping yet and all their amour stained with blood." This litany of suffering souls were full of pain, and their pain evoked fear and anxiety in Odysseus as they do for all who consciously venture toward a voluntary death of one sort or another. In this case, Odysseus faces his anxiety and depression related to the sufferings of the human condition and overcomes it by following through with his appointed tasks despite the temptation to give in to despair that depression and anxiety these litany of suffering souls induce. His anxiety and depression are sent by the unconscious through suffering and pain to inspire further maturation by forcing Odysseus to consciously face unlived facets lying dormant within his psyche. He must suffer with these tormented souls by empathizing with them. However, Circe instructs Odysseus from talking to these tormented souls or allowing them to approach the blood of the sacrifices before Odysseus has had his counsel with Tiresias. These souls cannot enter the precincts of the sacrifices until Odysseus has encountered Tiresias, a symbol of Odysseus's true self and inner spirit. This is due to our need to make contact through our psyche with the spirit, which resides within us, and thereby we can become conscious of our spirit. Authentic sacrifices must be performed by detaching from all that distracts *us from the knowledge of our true inner status as made in God's image.* Our Spirit is the pinnacle of being and the animator of our psyche while intimately being linked to God's Spirit.

Paul put it thus:

> When we cry "Abba! Father!" it is the Spirit himself bearing witness with our spirit that we are children of God, and if children, then heirs, heirs of God and fellow heirs with Christ, provided we suffer with him in order that we many also be glorified with him. (Romans 8:15b–17)

Jesus also said our names are written in the book of life, which is the same need to recognize our status as spirits created by God's Spirit in His image. Since everything created by God is united with and a part of God, we need to recognize our true status as sons and daughters of God. This realization is the beginning of all true contemplation and wholeness. As we explore the chapter on wholeness, we are called to share in the paradox of the suffering and joy of God.

There were two souls Odysseus encountered and had dialogues with prior to meeting Tiresias. His psyche has some important tasks for him to face before encountering his spirit. The first is Elpenor, one of his men who had died due to a falling off a cliff due to drunkenness, and as Odysseus felt much urgency to complete other tasks, he had neglected to bury Elpenor. Odysseus also had used wine as a superficial implement to experience joy without the demands of self-discipline when he partied and killed the Cirones to partake in rape and drunken debauchery. He had agreed to bury his friend as soon as he left the land of the dead. His agreeing to bury his dead companion symbolizes his own need to deal with unfinished business before experiencing a new spiritual awakening and letting go of puerile and infantile sexuality, violence, and drunkenness as a false path toward *joy*. This unfinished business includes grieving the loss of his friend and facing his guilt and shadow behaviors. Moral virtue is demanded of Odysseus as we have discussed earlier in the text as it is for any hero, and that includes not harming or using others in anyway. Love is just the opposite of this and is the measure of all moral virtue. The unconscious mind in general, and especially Odysseus's anima will brook no self-deception nor unfinished business or tasks in his/our development toward wholeness.

The second encounter Odysseus has is with his mother. His mother had committed suicide at the thought her son was dead and in her grief he would never return to her. Odysseus must overcome his mother complex by guarding the trench of his sacrifices even from his mother. This dynamic is repeated by Jesus, who often discounted his mother's influence and power over him throughout his ministry, stating among other things that his true family were all those that did the will of God. We must encounter our spiritual center and so must detach from every distraction and integrate every archetype, which is capable of strangling our ego-consciousness. Odysseus exhibits great courage and wisdom in facing his grief on seeing his deceased mother with compassion through this encounter with her yet without giving into her cravings for his sacrifices. The *anima demands* we overcome our mother complex and learn to deal with our own feminine nature without projection of our need to be taken care of by the mother.

Odysseus's Journey to Hades and Death and His Consultation with Tiresias

Take a little trip back with father Tiresias
Listen to the old one speak . . .
I crossed between the poles, for me there's no mystery.
Once a man, like the sea I raged,
Like a woman, like the earth I gave.

—Genesis, "The Cinema Show"

Only now does Tiresias appear out from the land of the dead with a golden rod and by saluting Odysseus with the quintessential "Odysseus of the nimble wits." He asks why Odysseus has forsaken the sunlight (the realm of ego-consciousness as the sole director of his life) to visit him in the land of dead in this depressing place. Tiresias then asks him to stand aside so he can partake and drink the blood of his sacrifices and thereby prophesy the *truth* to Odysseus. Odysseus does so and has now sacrificed his ego-consciousness to a new center, that secret place within him where his spirit dwells and where all truth and knowledge and wisdom reside. He is now willing to seek the counsel of the Spirit and begin the process of adapting to the inward truths and guidance of his inward spirit through the archetype of the wise old man. The initial counsel Tiresias furnishes is that powers above will not allow him to reach his home by easy means but rather his journey home will be hard and full of suffering and pain. This initial counsel symbolizes that our deepest inner authentic self knows that the journey to wholeness is a hard and painful one, full of suffering, heartache, anguish, and pain.

Specially, Tiresias counsels that because Odysseus blinded the Cyclops, Poseidon's son, therefore he will have to face the ire of Poseidon, the God of the sea, symbolic of the archaic, instinctual, and immature aspects of his/our psyche. This is the warning that the shadow will follow us throughout our journey home (into eternity), and no matter how much we develop and grow, we cannot escape our shadow and the constant and persistent painful truths it will bring to the surface. Before Hermes gave him the key to unlocking his soul image by approaching Circe accurately, Odysseus was naïve, and his ego-consciousness was ruled by his Greek rational mind yet his passions for violence, dominance, and lust ruled him. All who have the thinking function as their superior function are stuck with the feeing function as their inferior one and therefore are subject to infantile feeling values from time to time. The lack of differentiation of feeling values is always awakening our inability to live a life full of feelings and values. We are truly of two minds. We are required to face our shadow, and it often contains the infantile desires of selfishness, self-deception and dishonesty, lust and violence, and indolence.

Tiresias goes on to warn Odysseus that he will reach home if he keeps a tight hand upon himself and his men as he will approach the isle of Sun God Thrinacie, where he is to not harm the sheep and cattle that dwell there. Maintaining a tight hand upon self is a symbol of self-knowledge and self-discipline. Tiresias goes on to prophesy that he will suffer much, and if he and/or his men eat the cattle and sheep, his ship and men will be destroyed. Also, if he does not give in to the temptation to eat the cattle but his comrades do, he will be spared, but he will come home late, in evil plight, upon a foreign ship, with all his comrades dead. He will also find trouble in his house as suitors are wooing his wife in the hopes of marriage and becoming the new king of Ithaca, that he will need to leave his homeland again and offer sacrifices to Poseidon after disposing of the suitors, and Death will come to him out of the sea and at an old age, but in a gentle disguise.

And so it happens thus. Like everyone on the path toward wholeness and enlightenment, Odysseus, like us all, is faced with a destiny specific with a myriad of temptations, sufferings, and death itself. The offering of sacrifices after his return home to Poseidon symbolizes the need of our conscious ego to continually sacrifice and surrender its position as the center of the personality to the truth and harmony that the psyche as a whole contains as we struggle to bring the opposites together. Tiresias as the wise old man knows that life is a school of sorts, and we have much to learn while many of our lessons have to be learned over and over in a cyclical pattern. This is represented in the turning of the mandala wheel at all the points of the circumference and outside the center. The wheel keeps turning in space and in time, and it is our task to live in mindfulness in the moment where its center resides.

We need to pause and discuss the spiritual legacy the Greeks that Odysseus's encounter with Tiresias symbolizes. The following is a summary of what I believe are the essential contributions to spirituality by the Greeks outlined in chapter 15 entitled "The Religion of the Greeks" by Edith Hamilton in her work *The Greek Way* (Avon Books, 1930, First Discus Printing, January, 1973, sixth printing). She argues that Greek religion was developed by the poets, artists, and philosophers. She also argues convincingly that the Greeks emphasized the individual's responsibility to take the leap of faith into the truth of God's love that was not held hostage by priests and dogma like in the rest of the ancient world. This mature leap of faith would come later during the classical age with Socrates and Plato. But we can observe the antecedents in Odysseus as he seeks the truth by listening to his anima, the goddesses Circe, and aspects of his soul as they lead him to the wise old man, that part of himself which is spirit, symbolized by the blind prophet, Tiresias. Nothing was more important to the essence of the Greek way than finding the truth; Socrates personified and proclaimed the quest for the wisdom inherent in truth while Homer exemplified it in his rendering of the two great epics, the *Iliad* and the *Odyssey*.

The example in the *Odyssey* is where Tiresias asks Odysseus what brought him to the land of the dead to *hear the truth* that his prophesies would disclose. Odysseus also had to struggle to adapt to truth through self-discipline—again an emphasis on the individual's responsibility. Though the world was full of dread and horror, the Greek sought to make sense of the miracle world through logos by trying to grasp its universal principles. This brought with it an element of appreciating beauty, harmony, and wholeness while abolishing savage rites and practices that were universal in every other civilization. Hamilton says,

In the very earliest Greek records we have, a high stage had been reached. All things Greek begin for us with Homer, and in the *Iliad* and the *Odyssey* the Greeks have left far behind not only the bestialities of primitive worship, but the terrible and degrading rites the terror- stricken world around them was practicing. In Homer, magic has been abolished . . . The stamp of the Greek genius on his two epics is everywhere . . . in the courage and undaunted spirit which the heroes faced any opponent, human or divine, even Fate herself; in the prevailing atmosphere of reason and good sense.

Hamilton goes on in the following quote to argue that the Greeks began asking for a more just and righteous image of Zeus than the one portrayed in, "The Odyssey."

His gods, however, could not continue long to be adequate to men fired by the desire for the best. They were unable to satisfy people who were thinking soberly of right and wrong, who were using their critical powers to speculate about the universe, who, above all, were trying to find religion, not the doubtful divinities of Olympus, but a solution of life's mystery and a conviction of its purpose and its end. Men began to ask for a loftier Zeus, and one who cared for all, not only, as in the *Iliad*, but for the great and powerful. So in a passage in the *Odyssey* he became the protector of the poor and helpless.

In addition, Greek tragedy recognized the universal nature of suffering, and the human body was a vessel of divine thought and spirit. Unfortunately, when the democracy in Athens put Socrates to death and went on to attempt to dominate the Greek world before Sparta put an end to Athens political agenda and megalomania, the Athenian democracy succumbed to the darker aspects of our nature as it did in

Odysseus's men and as we see so often in human nature in general and in ourselves in specific.

Following his encounter with Tiresias, Persephone, daughter of Zeus and wife to Hades, sent up all the women who had been wives or the daughters of princes. Though they wished to drink the blood of the sacrifice together, Odysseus forbade this and talked to each in turn by allowing each to drink the blood of his sacrifices one by one. Tiresias had earlier explained nobody could converse with him without first drinking of the blood of the sacrifices. There are number of symbolic dynamics we need to explore as we examine Odysseus conversations with these dead women. First, the symbolism of talking to them one at a time is that our ego-consciousness must face unlived aspects of our inner life *consciously* one at a time or consciousness will be over-whelmed by the unconscious forces and psychosis will ensue.

Second, we must examine the symbolism of Persephone; she was the daughter of Zeus and Demeter, the fertility goddess, and husband of death, Hades. She is the symbolic link between life and death, and she initiates a death for those who encounter her for the purpose of being reborn as she lived with Hades in winter and on the earth for the other three seasons. She also was associated with the mystery religions where the initiate lives in Hades to be reborn in heaven. Odysseus's venture into the land of the dead was in winter as Persephone's presence signi-fies. Therefore, it is the women she sends to Odysseus who will rein-force this link between death and rebirth. All the women Persephone sends to him were women who had all suffered at the hands of misog-amist masculine energy. Odysseus had to learn to listen to the suffer-ing of women and, symbolically therefore, to his own soul. Our Spirit must always maintain its link to the suffering soul, both within us and in our neighbor, or our spirituality will remain phony and superficial. Only the suffering of the soul and feminine energy can reach past the masculine one-sided heroics of ego-conscious control, which violence actualizes and symbolizes.

This is confirmed by Odysseus's next encounters that is with men of power and notoriety. He meets King Agamemnon, leader of the Greek siege of Troy and who used his brother's loss of Helen as ratio-nale to conquer Troy and expand his notoriety, power, and wealth. He died at the hands of his wife, which symbolizes the end of a masculine ego-consciousness devoid of the balance of feminine energy. This is also emphasized in his counsel to Odysseus to not trust any woman. Agamemnon has yet even in death to integrate feminine energy. He also meets Achilles, who has learned the heroic death of Greek masculine energy is not enough to bring peace. All the great men both blessed and cursed in the land of the dead Odysseus encountered: King Minos, Orion, Tityos, Tentalus, Sisyphus, and Hercules. All these Greek heroes suffer in Hades or are blessed, based on their abilities to live out spiritual principles.

Odysseus returns to the Island of Circe and buries his friend. He then talks with Circe, who warns him that he will have to suffer another death, again symbolic. First, he will have to pass the beautiful nymphs, the Sirens, who seduce every unconscious male with their songs promising wisdom. Odysseus is instructed by Circe to have his men bind him so only he can hear the songs of the Sirens but will be unable to act while his men are to put wax in the ears so they won't hear the seductive songs of the Sirens, which lure men in their ships to destruction. The first temptation is for Odysseus to become arrogant and inflated now that he has made contact with his and God's spirit. Though he hears the songs of the Sirens, he is able to pass by being bound to the mast by his men, symbolizing his willingness to remain humble and willing to face temptations to find wisdom through sexuality.

The next counsel of Circe is she cannot fully guide him as he has to make a choice between two equally dangerous alternatives. This symbolizes that the choices we make are made with our spirit and not with the soul, for the spirit is to be the counselor to the soul/psyche, which is subject to suffering and temptations. She goes on and warns him of numerous future dangers and temptations but that Odysseus will be up to the task. Sometimes he will face his enemy, other times he will flee; all the while he will have to face his inner life and the circumstances set before him as Tiresias, his spirit, has notified him. He will have to continue to remain conscious or be sucked down into oblivion by the whirlpool of Charybdis, which symbolizes unconsciousness. The task is to be conscious in the moment and willing to be mindful and locate the center, where we have some serenity and that ability to learn the tasks set before us and hence live out unlived aspects of our lives.

Odysseus will revert back to the control of his ego-consciousness and ignore the suffering of his psyche/soul and counsel of his spirit but will learn from his mistakes. The remainder of his Odyssey will be full of suffering, failings, and wisdom acquired as he learns to have faith in the wisdom of the gods, goddesses, and his own spirit while overcoming temptations to inflation, depression, and anxiety by facing his inner life. I end my commentary here but encourage you to read the entire *Odyssey* for yourselves.

> Do you know the warm progress under the stars?
> Do you know you exist?
> Have you forgotten the keys to the kingdom?
>
> Let's reinvent the gods, all the myths of the ages
> Celebrated symbols from deep elder forests
> (Have you forgotten the lessons of the ancient war) . . .
>
> —The Doors, "An American Prayer"

Fate's Companion

(a poem by yours truly)

Oh ye daughters of the night
Ladies bending toward my plight
Descending from mysteries abode
Bearing gifts of broken hearts untold
I cry, in time.

Atropos carries out God's unalterable will
While Lachesis serenades to pathos's fill
Clotho darns life's tapestry devoid of thought
Anguish and weariness in which I'm caught
I moan, in time.

The Fate's herald with wretched rasp
That certainty escapes my trembling grasp
These goddesses bear their vulgar tidings
Unmasked from ambiguous hidings
Will staggering, in time.

Endeavoring to regard their seductive laces
Embracing inscrutable feminine faces
From faith and will a new sword is fashioned
A warrior trained by disciplined passion
I wait, in time.

My gaze stirs quantum fire
Primordial rudiments accrue and conspire
Choice and destiny spiral into the night air
Until fire permeates my open lair
I am baptism in fire, in time.

Sisyphus counsels his heroic defiance
From the clutches of unhealthy reliance
While the war proceeds between the fates and will
Where only faith can still
I listen, in time.

Sown by Fates uncertain winds scattered
Seeds nurtured, matured, pruned, and battered
Wisdom and will unite and coalesce
In hearts experience of love and distress
Faith doth endure, in time.

The torments of the Fates withstood
Peace in conflict understood
Acceptance finds its sacred place
Where egocentricity had its face
I enter God's presence, in time.

The time has come to examine the book of Job and delve into this tour de force and catch a glimpse of many hidden treasures, which will enlighten us to the dynamics of suffering and evil and enlightenment.

The Evolution of God Consciousness and Being in the Book of Job

When you think you have lost everything you find out you can lose a little more, I'm just going down the road feeling bad, trying to get to Heaven before they close the door.

—Bob Dylan, " Trying to Get to Heaven"

Introduction

I lost my money and I lost my wife,
Them things don't matter much
to me now.

Tonight I'll be on that hill 'cause I can't
Stop,
I'll be on that hill with everything I got,
Lives on the line where dreams are found

And lost,
I'll be there on time and I'll pay the cost,
For wanting things that can only be found
In the darkness on the edge of town.

—Bruce Springsteen,
"Darkness on the Edge of Town"

This work is a prime example within the Western tradition of a man of faith who surrenders to the will of God but simultaneously lives out an encounter with God where it can be said that of Job that he examines his life is the spirit of Socrates and Kierkegaard, where to "know thyself" and "be thyself" are the main tasks of life. Job's struggle is indicative of an individual with sensing as his superior function, unlike Odysseus's projected masculine Greek heroism of thinking and action. These two works therefore are good examples of Joseph Campbell's point that these two contrary beliefs stand side by side in our Western traditions. Taken together, they provide a glimpse at the delicate balance that we must achieve in holding these pairs of opposites together, that is the Greek emphasis on the thinking function and the spiritual traditions that emphasize surrender to God's will and the feelings-values function. True and mature faith itself is nurtured in the intuitive function as we will explore with Job but cannot be separated from a strong feelings-values function. Job's is stripped of all external crutches, and his valor departs from the Greek genus. From Job's suffering arises a direct struggle within the context of his need to integrate his inferior function; that is intuition into his consciousness. There are no external monsters to kill and destroy. Job's struggles lie within his psyche directly as he undertakes an expansion of his consciousness within the experience of his internal sufferings brought about through natural disasters and calamities, which stripped Job of almost everything within the world of his senses and precious to him. He was highly successful, rich, well thought of, healthy, and firmly lodged in the world with a large family. His suffering is caused by losses in the context of his material goods, his family, beliefs, motivations, values, attitudes, and *especially his status and physical health.* Job also seems to have a well-developed thinking and feeling function developed as he wrestles with

God directly through his encounters with sufferings and fate. However, it is only after he has lost his physical health does his anguish and inner transformations really begin. God's will and purposes are revealed in the context of all of Job's grief, but above all over his physical sufferings, which transform his beliefs, motivations, attitudes, values, but most importantly, *his experience with God in the context of his enduring faith.* Job's transformation occurs within his intuitive conscious function, which is the function we all have that links us to faith and God most intimately. Job maintains his faith throughout, but as we shall witness, his experience with God grows into an approach toward wholeness when his intuitive function is integrated.

There is widespread disagreement concerning the historical background to this work by most biblical scholars. For me, the most likely scenario is this ancient epic folktale made its appearance in the period of transition between the late Bronze Age and or early Iron Age, sometime in the second millennium BCE, and it was transferred from oral to written tradition around the sixth century during the Babylonian exile. The second millennium BCE was the same time the oral traditions for the *Iliad* and *Odyssey* were circulating. And like its Greek counterparts, it seems there are also poetic elements within the story or folktale that seems likely it was orally circulated by bards and sages. However, this tale was of Mesopotamia origin, and therefore, the book of Job is of not of Greek or Jewish origin. We know Job was not Jewish as he hailed from Mesopotamia in the land of Uz (Job 1:1). In addition, it seems likely that it was written down and edited during the exile when Jewish priestly scribes were in Babylon (Mesopotamia) as they were editing the Hebrew scriptures from Babylon after Jerusalem was sacked and the temple destroyed in the sixth century BCE. Therefore, the context for the editing lies during the Iron Age where patriarchal attitudes predominated. However, the roots of the folktale go back to the Bronze Age. The Jewish faith was in crisis and may have disappeared had not the exiled Jews maintained their traditions via adapting their worship without the temple and edited their written material. Their guiding traditions were transferred to the synagogues and written scriptures. It therefore makes sense that the epic fable would have particular significance to the upper classes and educated Jews during the exile. They most likely viewed themselves as righteous sufferers in the archetypal mold of Job, though the prophets of the exile held that the upper classes were responsible for the injustices committed against the poor and needy and therefore were the main *cause* of the exile.

This scenario seems credible because the epic is apparently on the surface about a righteous man's suffering, and we can assume the scribes who came across this epic in oral form would have identified themselves with Job's suffering while as I will elucidate throughout my commentary, this almost universal misunderstanding of the meaning of the text continues to survive. Human nature seems to naturally put itself in the place of the righteous victims and rarely demonstrates an ability to see itself as a protagonist who is guilty of self-deception, self-righteousness, and injustice. It's also evident that the oral traditions contained elements of the Bronze Age where the feminine archetypal characteristics were predominate, although the written text offers little evidence. We will have to read between the lines to extract its hidden wisdom. It's possible this epic would have been lost if Jewish priestly scribes failed to identify themselves with Job. Regardless, the work is of great philosophical and existential significance as it wrestles with the truths about suffering! I do not believe the epic tale's message is about a righteous man's sufferings; this is only so interpreted when viewed from a surface patriarchic perspective, and therefore, if I am correct, this universal defective interpretation also contributed to its survival.

Rather than being an ambiguous tale about a righteous man's sufferings, the book of Job is rather about one man's archetypal experience and *total* encounter with God. Job is a man of faith from beginning to end, and he therefore accepts the supposition—God's will is being accomplished no matter how incomprehensible it may seem on the surface, and all that occurs is for some benefit and good. Feminine archetypal elements have always included suffering, pain, and death in its mythologies. Job is not the innocent sufferer he appears upon superficial examination (Job 30:1–8), but *he is the quintessential* sufferer! Job is a rich patriarchal male and, as we shall see, inflated in relation to others (Job 30:1–8) and is tempted to inflate himself in the presence of God. Job has everything of value stripped from him by catastrophes and natural disasters. Due to his losses and his intense experiences of suffering, Job is being tempted to become further inflated by cursing God. He can curse God of he can maintain his faith that recognizes all things that occur in the life of a man of faith is for good, due to the loving nature of God (Edinger, p. 80). If he chooses not to curse God, he must make sense of his suffering and find God within the totality of his experience.

Many scholars believe this work contains little or no rational account or reasons for Job's suffering and again that he was a righteous man. The text does indicate he is a righteous man at its inception, and this assumption is made through much of the work by the editors as well. Therefore, I can sympathize with most scholars' views. But if we examine this work with an open mind and in more detail, in my opinion, we can come to some other conclusions. I will be arguing from the text that Job will have an authentic encounter with God through his intuition along with the other three conscious functions. I will also argue that this encounter with Job and God is one where the nature and character of God is thrust out of its patriarchic distortions of punishment and rewards into the realms of agape love and sufferings shared with Her creatures. Job can either embrace the process of individuation we discussed in the beginning of the section or curse God. He does embrace the individuation process and thereby discovers the true nature of God, which also resides within himself. Job is a work of major import as it grapples with the greatest archetypal dynamics within us all—that is the quest for meaning, wholeness, faith and relationship with God, purpose, worth, and security within the context of *guilt, suffering, and evil.* Coming to grips with Job's experience is so much more than an intellectual process, and the struggle toward authentic faith is fashioned out of the choices that include the dirty and real experiences of sleeplessness, fear, confusion, loneliness, guilt, dying, etc. Anyone practiced, trained, and a veteran of suffering *knows* that no intellectual anodynes can completely mitigate their anguish. The leap of faith and an encounter with God does not eliminate suffering; on the contrary, those of faith are exhorted to rejoice in their suffering (Romans 5:3–5). This paradox and contradiction will be examined in more depth later. *The need for understanding is vitally important for healing—but only in the context of real, unmitigated, dirty, grubby experience.* Filled with anguish and disorientation as his security and self-worth is stripped and plundered, Job is every man who has lost his way, where all his illusions are swept away or surrendered. *This includes all of us who suffer with self-deceptions that we are innocent and righteous before God.*

Commentary on the Book of Job

By the rivers dark
I wandered on.
I lived my life
In Babylon . . .

By the rivers dark
Where I could not see
Who was waiting there
Who was hunting me.

And he cut my lip
And he cut my heart.
So I could not drink
From the rivers dark.

And he covered me,
And I saw within . . .

Then he struck my heart
With a deadly force.
And he said, 'This heart:
It is not yours.'

And he gave the wind
My wedding ring;
And he circled us
With everything.

By the rivers dark,
In a wounded dawn,
I live my life
In Babylon.

Though I take my song
From a withered lip,
Both song and tree,
They sing for him . . .

—L. Cohen "By the Rivers Dark"

I use the Revised Standard Version.

There was a man in the land of Uz, whose name was Job; and that man was blameless and upright, one who feared God, and turned away from evil

There were born to him seven sons and three daughters. He had seven thousand sheep, three thousand camels, five hundred yoke of oxen, and five hundred she-asses, and very many servants; so that this man was the greatest of all the people of the east.

His sons used to go and hold a feast in the house of each on his day; and they would send and invite their three sisters to eat and drink with them.

And when the days of the feast had run their course, Job would send and sanctify them, and he would rise early in the morning and offer burnt offerings according to the number of them all; for Job said, "It may be that my sons have sinned, and cursed God in their hearts." Thus Job did continually. Now there was a day when the sons of God came to present themselves before the LORD, and Satan also came among them.

The LORD said to Satan, "Whence have you come?" Satan answered the LORD, "From going to and fro on the earth, and from walking up and down on it."

And the LORD said to Satan, "Have you considered my servant Job, that there is none like him on the earth, a blameless and upright man, who fears God and turns away from evil?"

Then Satan answered the LORD, "Does Job fear God for naught?

Hast thou not put a hedge about him and his house and all that he has, on every side? Thou hast blessed the work of his hands, and his possessions have increased in the land. But put forth thy hand now, and touch all that he has, and he will curse thee to thy face."

And the LORD said to Satan, "Behold, all that he has is in your power; only upon himself do not put forth your hand." So Satan went forth from the presence of the LORD.

Now there was a day when his sons and daughters were eating and drinking wine in their eldest brother's house; and there came a messenger to Job, and said, "The oxen were plowing and the asses feeding beside them; and the Sabe'ans fell upon them and took them, and slew the servants with the edge of the sword; and I alone have escaped to tell you."

While he was yet speaking, there came another, and said, "The fire of God fell from heaven and burned up the sheep and the servants, and consumed them; and I alone have escaped to tell you."

While he was yet speaking, there came another, and said, "The Chalde'ans formed three companies, and made a raid upon the camels and took them, and slew the servants with the edge of the sword; and I alone have escaped to tell you."

While he was yet speaking, there came another, and said, "Your sons and daughters were eating and drinking wine in their eldest brother's house; and behold, a great wind came across the wilderness, and struck the four corners of the house, and it fell upon the young people, and they are dead; and I alone have escaped to tell you."

Then Job arose, and rent his robe, and shaved his head, and fell upon the ground, and worshiped. (Job 1:1–20)

Commentary

The folktale begins as Job is described as blameless, and he has exceeded all the tasks an individual needs to complete by midlife. That is to say he has accomplished expectations for adulthood within the first thirty-five years of life—a distinct character with a solid ego-body- consciousness, able to handle most problems without undo damage to his ego; independence and autonomy; a marriage and a family; and a career. Job has a *reputation* for being a good guy who cares for others. Job is the consummate successful member of society with added prestige due to his wealth and power. Job is at the top of the cultural pecking order. All cultures are latent with class distinctions. Job was rich and successful. Job had a strong ego and achieved the normal illusionary sense of security and worth commensurate with his status. Job had achieved what life requires for a mature adult, plus additional status and power. It is within the context of his privileged status and reputation that his entire life is turned upside down as Job encounters God in the context of losing everything he prized.

The first act begins with God praising his servant Job before Satan (the word *Satan* means "adversary") because he was upright and blameless. It is important to distinguish Satan in differing manifestations and developments in the context of the Hebrew Bible with the Christian Bible's Satan. This figure was in the heavenly court, and his function was to be an adversary—that is one who challenges and takes the opposite position currently in conscious vogue. God even referred to Himself as a Satan when taking up an adversarial stance. I consider the role of Satan in the book of Job *as the adversarial unconscious counter position* to bring about a compensation for the one-sided conscious attitudes and beliefs of Job. It is also likely that this role of Satan was associated with the Serpent Lord and his relation with his bride in the tree of life myths in the Neolithic era. This myth associated the serpent with his bride as they both tested the initiate, attempting to coax some form of rebirth.

Is this adversary really a part of God? To answer this question, we must ask the question, can we associate the unconscious mind with God? What I have found confirms this hypothesis for when we bring unconscious contents into consciousness, I have discovered the unconscious mind has an unrelenting commitment to truth. The unconscious mind seems to sponsor the truth and then ask the conscious mind to make the proper adaptations. Therefore, my own belief is we can associate the Satan in Job as symbolically a part of God Himself. *God as the hidden treasure truly is found within us!* An adversarial position confronts us with an opposite position that requires we reconsider our beliefs, attitudes, and behaviors. I do believe God manifests His being through the pairs of opposites.

The adversary accuses Job of being good only because he was rich with material goods and a large family so that this man was the greatest of all the people of the east (Job 1:3b). These were all symbolically and literally associated with blessings of God. There is also no question that Job was a good man, often caring and thoughtful toward others.

Satan accuses Job of turning away from evil because of all the blessings bestowed upon him and offers a wager that if he is allowed to "touch all that he has" (Job 1:11), Job would curse God to his face. God accepts the wager and then allows Satan to visit Job with all forms of sufferings and calamities and tragedies (the renting of our attachments to the temporal) minus one: Satan was not allowed to take his life. Consequently, Job was stripped of his possessions, children, and servants except those who lived to inform Job of his losses.

There's Nothing Left Here For ME
It's Washed Away . . .

I Watch It Crush Me
And I Die . . .

—Moby, "The Sky Is Broken"

Job 1:21 states: "And he said, 'Naked I came from my mother's womb, and naked shall I return; the LORD gave, and the LORD has taken away; blessed be the name of the LORD.'"

Commentary

Psychologically speaking, Job weathers the initial losses with the use of denial and intellectualization. He utters profound truths and seems a man of mature experiences, but nobody can endure so many losses and possibly come to an acceptance so quickly. The text will validate this conclusion as Job's inner life is torn apart as he processes his suffering in the coming days. His denial and intellectual response is reasonable and attests to his highly developed thinking function. He acknowledges we come into this world naked, and naked we shall return. Material objects are temporary, and earth is not our home, and everyone we know will die. Though these insights are accurate and right on the money, his response seems too good to be true. He appears to be intellectualizing his grief, and this will become evident as we proceed. How can anyone respond to so many losses without true grief? Remarkable wisdom, when spoken by someone immature, is noticeably contrary than to that which is spoken from the depth of a mature personality. We have all meet people of immature and mature personalities who say the same things, but somehow the meanings and effects are different.

I can see through your walls
And I know you are hurting
Sorrow covers you like a cape . . .

—Bob Dylan,
"When the Night Comes Falling from the Sky"

Again there was a day when the sons of God came to present themselves before the LORD, and Satan also came among them to present himself before the LORD.

And the LORD said to Satan, "Whence have you come?" Satan answered the LORD, "From going to and fro on the earth, and from walking up and down on it."

And the LORD said to Satan, "Have you considered my servant Job, that there is none like him on the earth, a blameless and upright man, who fears God and turns away from evil? He still holds fast his integrity, although you moved me against him, to destroy him without cause."

Then Satan answered the LORD, "Skin for skin! All that a man has he will give for his life.

But put forth thy hand now, and touch his bone and his flesh, and he will curse thee to thy face."

And the LORD said to Satan, "Behold, he is in your power; only spare his life."

So Satan went forth from the presence of the Lord, and afflicted Job with loathsome sores from the sole of his foot to the crown of his head. (Job 2:1–7)

In addition to everything else, Job is now pilfered of his physical health. Job is struck down in his superior function, which now becomes within the realm of his five senses, and so Job's divine encounter begins in weakness (2 Corinthians 12:9). When the superior function goes, and his personality as we shall see will be thrown into a period of dis-orientation and titanic suffering and pain. The worst of it, as it is in this case, is that the sufferer does not know if it will ever end or the state is permanent. The text also doesn't say whether Job knew he would live; therefore, we should assume he did not know if his condition was fatal. We all are in fact living on borrowed time, and each day could be our last. Will Job live, ever recover his physical health or his status in the community or his wealth and security in the world? Will he die from his illness? We all know how physical pain disturbs our emotions while our thinking becomes easily distorted. Job is a man of faith, and this he holds firm throughout the entire text. He is a remarkable man in that he struggles with his faith and understanding throughout in the context of his suffering, disillusionment, and incompressibility at his fate. He delves deeper and deeper within himself and therefore wrestles with God within. It would be human nature to give up after suffering such tragedies and calamities, especially when one recognizes that God is part and parcel of these horrific experiences.

How can anyone not feel pity for Job? We have all suffered grief from losses in our lives. Few have suffered to this degree, and the reality of Job's experience is frightening and incomprehensible to our rational minds. It is only through the text that we can begin to come to grips with Job's personal anguish and the horror of his experience.

> You always got to be prepared
> But you never know for what.
>
> —Bob Dylan, "Sugar Baby"

> Then his wife said to him, "Do you still hold fast your integrity? Curse God and die."
> But he said to her, "You speak as one of the foolish women would speak. Shall we receive well at the hand of God, and shall we not receive evil?" In this entire Job did not sin with his lips. (Job 2:9–10)

Commentary

Job and his wife are in a state of shock, a normal reaction to such grief. She counsels him to curse God and die. Her response is one of anger at God, and in her anger she gives up. Prior to her losses, she had everything a rich and successful individual could want—with the false trappings of earthly security and status with material wealth and children. She is just as grounded in false security and worth as Job is. With the experience of all these losses, both Job and his wife are flung out of there illusions and into despair. It appears their losses are too much for Job's wife to bear, and she responds in one archetypal fashion, with self-pity and resentments. It is easy to become stubborn and stuck in bitterness and self-pity and unable to accept new situations. Unless or until any of us can learn to *eventually* accept our situations and let go, we will all get stuck in our illusions and distractions (i.e., whatever habits and patterns each of us has developed to avoid reality). This process of facing our pain and accepting reality is so very difficult that sympathizing with Job's wife is easy to do. The text says nothing more of Job's wife, and we can only speculate as to her grieving process. I hope we find it within ourselves to learn to process our own grief and eventually let go of our resentments and self-pity, search for gratitude, and endure until we finally can accept the new situation. Regardless, Job's wife takes an inflated stance toward God, and she encourages Job to take it as well. That is to curse God and die. In other words, she remains entrenched in her inflation, supported by self-pity and resentments. I remember a wall poster in a detoxification center I once worked, which read, "The last great act of defiance" where a mouse was giving the finger to a hawk just inches away from making him it's dinner. However, in his state of shock, Job refuses to take this route of defiance and inflation born of self-pity and resentments.

I have seen many marriages destroyed when losses are visited upon a couple and they are unable to bear the grief together. They blame each other or get lost in their solitary grief. They either lose the ability to let each other in on their grief and accept support from one another, or they never had it to begin with. We never are told what kind of marriage they had prior to their tragedies; therefore, it becomes impossible to tell whether they were ever intimate or their sufferings and grief sealed an already dead marriage where trust and mutual respect never really existed. Regardless, Job has decided not accept his wife's inflated attitudes, embittered beliefs, and defiant behavior and seems to endure in his present state of faith.

> I wonder if there's no forever
> No walking hand in hand
> Down a yellow brick road
> To never-never land.

> —Mark Knopfler, "True Love Will Never Fade"

Now when Job's three friends heard of all this evil that had come upon him, they came each from his own place, Eli'phaz the Te'manite, Bildad the Shuhite, and Zophar the Na'amathite. They made an appointment together to come to condole with him and comfort him.

And when they saw him from afar, they did not recognize him; and they raised their voices and wept; and they rent their robes and sprinkled dust upon their heads toward heaven.

And they sat with him on the ground seven days and seven nights, and no one spoke a word to him, for they saw that his suffering was very great. (Job 2:11–13)

Commentary

Job's friends come to offer their comfort and support and are shocked at Job's condition. No one speaks for seven days and nights as Job needs to overcome his initial shock and denial by solitude and silence. He needs to be alone with his thoughts and God while his friends' silence displays their respect for Job's grief. Few value silence or are willing to be alone for any extended periods of time without talking or turning to some devise or distraction and so tune out God's frequency. We pursue distractions in the belief that they will help us get through our grief and suffering. The usual response to Job and his wife's losses by others would be rejection, awkwardness, or a showering of the mundane frenzy of disparate tasks and inane conversations. Job and his wife are also likely objects of sympathy *and* gossip. Everyone but his three friends would be asking, why is Job withdrawing from everybody? What's wrong with him? We came all the way to be with him to be ignored? However, Job meditates and reflects in silence. Taking a week of silence is laudable. His suffering and pain must be experienced without undo intellectualizing or escape. The only way to heal from emotional wounds is to begin by allowing oneself to be, to sit in silence with our pain and whirlwind of thoughts. Very few would attempt such a thing, for in silence there is no distraction. As Leonard Cohen put it in "Waiting for the Miracle," "You wouldn't like it baby. You wouldn't like it here. There's not much entertainment and the critics are severe."

There is great pressure to please everyone. Job is able to withstand these temptations and enter a secret place inside where he follows his heart and mind wherever they wander. Job is seeking solitude and silence, which are the most important of all the spiritual disciplines. Solitude and silence allows true inner experiences to surface and, in addition, offer opportunities to gain perspective and insight (sight from within). This is near impossible in the company of others. How can we share with ourselves and others the true nature of our inner thoughts if we don't take the time to allow them to surface? How can we change if we don't take the time to figure out what's going on inside our own skin? The gospels reveal Jesus took time to be alone in silence, once for forty days and forty nights, and on other occasions we are not afforded the time frame of his contemplative prayers and meditations. The Buddha sat in silent meditation prior to his enlightenment. All great heroes must have their desert experiences where they are visited in solitude and silence by the divine voice so soft it hurts from the strain to hear it. Those who influence society for good are usually those who have and use silence and solitude as regular disciplines. We all are capable of shutting out external distractions so that the inner still and quiet voice can be heard above the clamor and hand clapping of the world. This is often a long process and one that cannot be rushed. Sadly today, we can't ever go anywhere in public without the blare of background music intruding upon our inner life. I assume Job's spiritual disciplines included solitude and silence because this is the first thing he does after the argument with his wife. Job allows his reason to rest in its ignorance and allow confusion to bear fruit. During this time in silence, we can imagine Job's tears being plentiful. He finally gets to the place where *he begins the process of grieving his losses and making sense of his suffering through his intuition along with his other conscious functions.* Are you willing to patiently remain in pain and confusion, putting yourself in a position to simultaneously wait to heal and come to an understanding within the process of suffering itself?

> Tear the promise from my heart
> Tear my heart today . . .
> So Hang down your head
> For sorrow
> Hang down your head tomorrow
> Hang down your head for me.

> —Tom Waits, "Hang Down Your Head"

After this Job opened his mouth and cursed the day of his birth.

And Job said:

"Let the day perish wherein I was born, and the night which said, `A man-child is conceived.'

Let that day be darkness! May God above not seek it, nor light shine upon it.

Let gloom and deep darkness claim it. Let clouds dwell upon it; let the blackness of the day terrify it.

That night—let thick darkness seize it! Let it not rejoice among the days of the year; let it not come into the number of the months.

Yea, let that night be barren; let no joyful cry be heard in it. Let those curse it who curse the day, who are skilled to rouse up Leviathan.

Let the stars of its dawn be dark; let it hope for light, but have none, nor see the eyelids of the morning; because it did not shut the doors of my mother's womb, nor hide trouble from my eyes.

"Why did I not die at birth, come forth from the womb and expire?

Why did the knees receive me? Or why the breasts, that I should suck?

For then I should have lain down and been quiet; I should have slept; then I should have been at rest, with kings and counselors of the earth who rebuilt ruins for themselves, or with princes who had gold, which filled their houses with silver.

Or why was I not as a hidden untimely birth, as infants that never see the light?

There the wicked cease from troubling, and there the weary are at rest.

There the prisoners are at ease together; they hear not the voice of the taskmaster.

The small and the great are there, and the slave is free from his master.

"Why is light given to him that is in misery, and life to the bitter in soul, who long for death, but it comes not, and dig for it more than for hid treasures; who rejoice exceedingly, and are glad, when they find the grave?

Why is light given to a man whose way is hid, whom God has hedged in?

For my sighing comes as my bread, and my groaning are poured out like water. (Job: 3:1-24)

Commentary

During his solitude, the archetypal feelings and thoughts of self-pity have been exhumed from his unconsciousness and harried through Job's consciousness.

Everything has been torn from Job except his life. Here is what Job initially wrestles with during his seven days of silence and solitude: he wishes the only thing left from his losses would disappear— his birth. He is in such torment, he believes he would find rest in nonexistence, and it would have been better that he never was born. One can imagine these seven days and nights were filled with sleepless nights and a total disorientation of time and space. Kierkegaard's classic *Sickness unto Death* suggests that many wish to shirk from the responsibilities inherent in the human condition, and their hope is to die without consciousness. The sickness unto death is that we want to die to the responsibilities inherent in consciousness, but even death itself cannot destroy our inner life. Therefore, the truth is we can never run away from ourselves in life or death. There is no place to steer clear of our inner life, and our sickness is we want to die, shunning the pain and responsibilities that truth demands from our innermost selves. Kierkegaard believed as many do that we live on beyond death and that the choices and responsibilities of existence never end. Job also overcomes the temptation to commit suicide as a response to his suffering, although the text never discloses that he contemplates this choice. The fact remains this would certainly and has been a human response to such suffering, and it is an archetypal reality for all those who suffer. This act of suicide is one of the sicknesses unto death because it will ultimately fail for all who choose this alternative. We are stuck with ourselves, even in death, and even as some religious folks do who try to throw themselves away to God. We have to face our innermost being, whether pleasant or painful.

Job's reaction or response after he has worked through his initial shock is one of anger and grief as he curses the day he was born. The burden of life is too much for Job at this juncture in time. His reactions seem reasonable, honest, and real. Anger is a healthy and normal response to a wide variety of human experiences, especially grief and loss. Job is not repressing his disturbed inner state or the complexities of his inner life, but rather sharing his anger and grief with others. It is good to let out our feelings and perceptions and let others in with whom we trust. As we shall see, though he remains honest with his inner reactions, he does not become trapped nor stuck in these feelings of anguish, anger, and grief. The way of healing contains a patient endurance for each stage in the process—only then can wisdom and wholeness ever be approached.

However, all his losses have not shaken him out of his pre-thirty-five-year-old consciousness. His life is centered on his ego-body-consciousness that is all his attachments and beliefs, which protrude from his ego-self. Nothing has changed in his present understanding of faith. His faith is *unconsciously identified* with God, and therefore, he is inflated or full of hot air. This unconscious identification with God as object is like any other object where the ego attaches worth and security without proper separation between subject and object. A union with God can only occur after this separation has taken place, and the experience(s) of abandonment are part and parcel of this process. The subject (Job) must separate from the object (God) before the subject can approach faith from a new perspective, where humility and awe replaces inflation. When a human approaches the sacred and the numinous, it is essential to make this approach with fear and trembling. This fear is not of the kind that we usually associate it with but with awe and wonder at that which is beyond our finite and fundamental humanness. We are made in the image of God but are not God. God is not in any box that we construct, and we are not the judges as so many believers of all the faiths seem to think. Self-righteousness, rigidity, and putting God in boxes are litmus tests of sorts for those who are unconsciously identifying with God. When people get into judging others, there is always a shame base and lack of grace and love that has been experienced for self and all of God's creation. This is one reason for all the intermediaries between God and man throughout the ages in an attempt to shelter our vulnerability and humanness from the mystery and majesty of the numinous. Unfortunately, these forms have often become stuck in convention, self-righteousness, political and religious power, and finances as so lose their ability to intermediate between the sacred and the profane. The point is it is impossible to approach faith without identifying with God in some way for the ego-body-consciousness is bound up in identifying itself with all objects in its environment.

The question posed by Job's losses is this: is the external world of ten thousand things and God (external objects) set up to serve his ego, and is it proper for humans to attempt to control and manipulate the external world of things, *or rather*, is his/our ego to revolve around and serve the truth and so serve God? Job is unconscious of his inflation, and the temptation to curse God remains a real possibility as long as his ego remains at the center of his entire personality.

> The man who twirled with rose in teeth
> Has his tongue tied up in thorns.
> His once-expanded sense of time and
> Space all shot and torn . . .
>
> "Look at me, I'm so forlorn-
> Ask anyone who can recall,
> It's horrible to be born"
>
> Left like a shadow on the step
> Where the body was before
> Shipwrecked at the stable door.
>
> —Bruce Cockburn, "Shipwrecked at the Stable Door"

"For the thing that I fear comes upon me, and what I dread befalls me" (Job: 3:25).

Commentary

Job faces a truth he has *always harbored*—that is the fear of losing all he has accomplished, accumulated, and acquired. This fear has been a part of human nature since time immemorial. Hence, throughout history, humankind has constructed walls, fences, security forces, barns, security systems, bank accounts, locks, and land where we live in an illusionary effort to protect ourselves. But inevitably, at death we take nothing external to ourselves. Fear often consumes us. As Job's attachments increased, so did his fears as he admits in the text. These fears haunt all of us, even those who have little to lose. This existential fear is real and must be faced and overcome if he will be able to live free of the fear of life's extensive possibilities and be open and relaxed, to be present and attentive to each moment, to be at peace, and to channel God's power with its mighty possibilities. Our attachments to ten thousand things are treasures that moths and rust corrodes and thieves can break in and steal. But alas, to gain this kind of joy that no man can take away, we have to struggle, make sacrifices, submit to discipline that is long and hard, experience loneliness and self-effacement, and choose obedience to and love of God's will. Most turn away in horror from these grueling and challenging tasks. Problematically, this turning away comes with it none of the privileges and treasures of God's Kingdom.

> Dragon of good fortune struggles with the trickster fox
> Energy and patience and the power of the buck
> Tonight I'm flying headlong
> To meet the dark red edge of dawn
> I know somebody will be crying
> And somebody will be gone.
> Oh Tokyo—I never could sleep in your arms . . .
>
> —Bruce Cockburn, "Tokyo"

"I am not at ease, nor am I quiet; I have no rest; but trouble comes" (Job 3:26).

Commentary

Job has entered the dark night of the soul where his ego is unable to cope with all his losses. It's only after all his natural modes of competence have been cut off from the ego—the senses, intuition, memory, will, emotions, imagination (everything we discussed in the first section) that the dark night of the soul commences. Job's ego is being broken and stripped of all its attachments, whether to the glitter and glitz of the five senses and/or intellectual logic, philosophy, etc. St. John of the Cross discusses this dark night as entering a secret place where everything becomes empty for a time and where disorientation, dissolution, confusion, and anguish are all that's left behind. Job is beginning to recognize his ego-body-consciousness has no *real* control over existential reality, and his beliefs and attitudes are breaking down and, with them, all his illusions. These losses leave Job with disquiet, anxiety, anguish, restlessness, and dread. The dark night of the soul is a death experience where the ego is left helpless and frightened. The mind swirls with thoughts unedited as feelings shroud consciousness with weariness and pain while the will is strangled in a temporary state of suspended animation. This state is described by contemplatives as true emptiness and nothingness. Darkness surrounds all the senses as well, and the individual loses all sense of space-time, balance, hope, intellectual abilities, beliefs, and sense of purpose—in effect, the whole lot! It's no wonder individuals are forced by circumstances into the dark night and why merely a handful of individuals have been willing to venture on their own into such a place of silence and solitude and what seems like total inner chaos. However, in letting go and staying with our emptiness and nothingness, there is a sense of relief that comes with not having to hang on to the pretense of control, of clinging to attachments, of getting our way, of appearing strong. Emptiness and nothingness usually come with it feelings of humiliation as well. But this state like suffering itself is not an end in itself, but only a means to a deeper and more enlightened experience of the five senses, mind, will, feeling, values, intuition, and memory where all these aspects of *being* are purified in the fire of the dark night. All of creation can then be experienced in its perfected state as it were, and human kind can again be freed to experience the original intention of God in creating everything in the first place! Emptiness is only a means of renewal and regeneration of our minds and hearts. Only an empty glass can be filled by God.

> Well my nerves are exploding
> And my bodies tense

I feel like the whole world
Got me pinned up against the fence
I've been hit too hard
Seen too much
Nothing can heal me now
Except your touch.

—Bob Dylan, "'Til I Fell In Love with You"

Behold, you have instructed many, and you have strengthened the weak hands.

Your words have upheld him who was stumbling, and you have made firm the feeble knees.

But now it has come to you, and you are impatient; it touches you, and you are dismayed. (Job 4:3–5)

Commentary

Job is confronted by his friends with his need to accept and adapt to his own advice. This is hard as our own counsel seems reasonable when we are not in the middle of the emotional torrents, but hollow when we are under the charge of the furies. It's easy to dispense advice and counsel when everything is going smoothly in our own lives. There are so many levels to the truths we dispense and verbalize, and so often it does not come from the wisdom of the heart where compassion lies, but rather we shower others with platitudes that fall on deaf ears precisely because these truths have not been integrated properly into our deepest selves. All the turmoil in my own life has only been a blessing over the long haul and enhanced my ability to counsel others.

I don't do that much talking these days . . .

Now if I seem to be afraid to live the life I have made in song
Well it's just I've been losing so long . . .

Please don't confront me with my failures . . .

—Jackson Browne, "These Days"

"Now a word was brought to me stealthily, my ear received the whisper of it.

Amid thoughts from visions of the night, when deep sleep falls on men, dread came upon me, and trembling, which made all my bones shake.

A spirit glided past my face; the hair of my flesh stood up.

It stood still, but I could not discern its appearance. A form was before my eyes; there was silence, then I heard a voice: Can mortal man be righteous before God? Can a man be pure before his Maker? (Job 4:12–17)

Commentary

This is the first mention of dreams and visions. Dreams and visions are numinous gateways of the unconscious mind and avail us of opportunities to catch God's spirit in the act! Hearing an authoritative voice during dreams and/or visions is common and indicative of straightforward wisdom. The voice compensates for Job's inflation by pointing out through a rhetorical question that before God, none is capable of purity and righteousness. The unconscious is aware of Job's arrogance unconscious identification with God and bluntly confronts him. There is nothing in the dream/vision that is threatening outside its numinous quality, and therefore, it is a direct compensation for Job's present attitude. It is here most commentaries miss the boat when interpreting Job's experience. Job's righteousness is based on a *public image* while his inner life harbors darker attitudes and motives. His inflation and arrogance are not hidden from the secret wisdom of the unconscious as the dream plainly states. The text goes on to disclose this inflation in the context of his attitudes toward others as we will discover and discuss.

Just thinking of a series of dreams . . .

And there's no exit in any direction
Except the ones that you can't see with your eyes
Wasn't making any great connection . . .

And the cards that you're holding
Are no good unless there
From another world . . .

Just thinking of a series of dreams.

—Bob Dylan, "Series of Dreams"

"In truth I have no help in me, and any resource is driven from me" (Job: 6:13).

Commentary

Exactly the point! Job's natural resources are inadequate and exhausted. His own strengths and abilities no longer can overcome or make sense of these new experiences. His suffering has leveraged his ego away from identifying itself with God, and his inflation is transformed into its opposite, alienation. His ego-body-consciousness, the center of his consciousness, is now in the process of a death and rebirth. The death of a strong ego and its rebirth is the primary archetype found in mythology. This is the journey of the hero. Every hero goes through a transformation where their ego is rendered useless and broken and then given the choice to consciously submit and surrender to a death prior to a rebirth. However, this is a long, drawn-out process and occurs over long periods of time where the ego alternates between inflation and alienation. It is only where the ego is weakest that God is truly encountered *holistically*. It is only in those precincts of weakness and brokenness that new possibilities, powers, perceptions, and experiences with the Living God occur.

The Apostle Paul shares an intimate moment he had with Jesus when he discloses some form of conversation with Jesus that "God's grace is sufficient for you, for my power is made perfect in weakness"(2 Corinthians 12:9). God's power is displayed in weakness as the ego is no longer damming the flow and power of God's spirit. In our weaknesses, obstacles are overcome, secrets and mysteries of God's Kingdom are revealed, and consciousness is infused with differing degrees of divine energies. The channel we are to be becomes unblocked, and we then are open to receiving joy, peace, and wholeness. God's will and protection are revealed in the secret place where man's and God's spirit's dwell together. God's healing power is made visible through the lives of his followers. Job's experience of tribulation is gradually moving him closer to that place where God can work as a channel through him. However, humiliation, shame, and alienation have appointments with Job before his transformation is completed and accomplished. When a strong and healthy ego is broken *and submits to its own death*, we no longer obstruct streams of God's Spirit in and through us.

As we proceed in the text, we will observe a continuing fluctuation within Job between inflation and alienation. Job will return to this place of total weakness and powerlessness over and over again until he internalizes this truth in his attitudes, beliefs, and behaviors. Like Job, we all are inclined to identify with *the source* prior to being alienated from it. The ego writhes back and forth from experiencing the power of God's energy, to identifying with it, to being shot back into alienation. The goal is the Tao, to reach that middle road that enables us to be intimate with God while accepting the vast chasm between our natures.

I can't stand up by myself
Don't you know I need your help
You're a friend of mine . . .

Some people say you can make it on your own
Oh you can make it if you try
I know better now
You can't stand up alone.

—Van Morrison, "Real Real Gone"

"Such you have now become to me; you see my calamity, and are afraid" (Job: 6:21).

Commentary

Job references his friends in an earlier passage in chapter 6 that they have become "treacherous, withholding kindness, and rejecting." Job is able to discern that beneath his friends' reprehensible behavior is fear that Job's fate could be their own. In point of fact, Job's fate is everyone's, for in losses and psychological deaths, all are wrenched from our ego-body-consciousness and ego-attachments. Job's friends are withdrawing from the truth; it is too painful for them, and they use typical defense mechanisms by blaming the victim! If they were to remain close to Job throughout his sufferings, they would have to be capable of identifying with Job by contemplating their own potential losses and need to die a thousand deaths themselves. Compassion only occurs when we learn to suffer ourselves.

> I'm on the fringes of the night
> Fighting back tears that I can't control
> Some people they ain't human
> They got no heart or soul.

—Bob Dylan, "Cry a While"

"Turn, I pray, let no wrong be done. Turn now, my vindication is at stake. Is there any wrong on my tongue?" (Job 6: 29–30a).

Commentary

Job asks his friends to refrain from condemning him before they commit any more wrongs against him. All relationships contain some forms of neurosis, and there is nothing we can do about it. Most emotional ties seem to contain some mixture of projections and ties, which contaminate and bind us to each other in ways that are unhealthy. These wrongs we do to each other seem endless and can be anything from jumping on others' misfortune while they are down to shaming, rejecting, belittling, gossiping, and judging based on his external circumstances—all of which Job's so-called friends do. When one's inner life is not well developed, judging superficially results. When we judge others, compassion vanishes like yesterday's weather.

Kierkegaard made the point that most of us are objective with others and subjective with ourselves, and the goal of anyone well versed in the inner life is to act in the exact opposite way; that is, learn how to suffer from within ourselves (i.e., to be subjective with others and be objective with oneself). Job's friends are only able to focus on what they understand via externals as they lack self-awareness, humility, and compassion.

Job says his vindication is at stake, which seems to reflect his concerns with what others think and say. I certainly understand Job's reaction, but it nevertheless steers him off the course of silence and solitude, contemplation and reflection. Rather than taking heed of his dreams and visions and thus turning inward toward the meaning of his dream, he is bothering about what wrongs may be done him, his vindication, and with his third comment, self-justification. His question concerning what wrongs may his tongue have committed seems reasonable as his suffering begs the question, is my suffering due to judgments by God, and if so, what have I said or done? In addition, he is asking his friends if they are annoyed with what he is saying. He's obviously holding out hope he also will not have to go on alone. In addition, he seems to be seeking to expand his consciousness. We observe disparate thoughts, motives, and longings that have been evoked by Job's experiences. Like gold, the human character must be purified by bringing the impurities to the surface so they can be dispensed with.

Oh, I listening to that conversation
Judge and jury in my head
It's coloring everything
All we did and said.

—Peter Gabriel, "In Your Eyes"

"Has not man a hard service upon earth, and are not his days like the days of a hireling?

Like a slave who longs for the shadow, and like a hireling who looks for his wages, so I am allotted months of emptiness, and nights of misery are apportioned to me.

When I lie down I say, 'When shall I arise?' But the night is long, and I am full of tossing till the dawn.

My flesh is clothed with worms and dirt; my skin hardens, and then breaks out afresh.

My days are swifter than a weaver's shuttle, and come to their end without hope.

"Remember that my life is a breath; my eye will never again see well.

The eye of him who sees me will behold me no more; while thy eyes are upon me, I shall be gone.

As the cloud fades and vanishes, so he who goes down to Sheol does not come up; he returns no more to his house, nor does his place know him any more. (Job: 7:1–10)

Commentary

Job expresses himself well, he tosses all night, and his body is in great torment as his sores open anew. His days go by without hope, believes death may be near, and he identifies with hirelings. Job is learning what it is like to be poor, sick, sleepless with anxiety, and an outcast. This is an initiation in compassion. Only when we experience pain and anguish ourselves can we begin to identify with others' sufferings. All passion includes suffering; by definition, friendship and compassion is putting ourselves in someone else's shoes to viscerally relate and bond. War veterans make their closest friendships during war because each knows exactly what the other has gone through and felt, thought, struggled with, and overcome. New attitudes and beliefs are fashioned from shared experiences. When a person can actually relate to another, the friendship extends beyond blood. If we all would allow ourselves to suffer legitimate pain, then hatred towards our fellows would be wiped away by shared sorrows. When we internalize our pain and suffering, violence and hatred will be forgotten like last year's fads. Job's insight and consciousness into the nature of things is expanding, though; as we shall see, it takes repeated experiences before Job, as for any of us, is capable of internalizing true love for our fellow sojourners through this mystery of life and death.

Job also experiences misery and emptiness within the context of death and the possibility there is no life beyond it. In Judaism, Sheol is the place of the dead, the great unknown where no expectations come for life after death. Within Judaism and by the time of Jesus, the belief in life after death is debated and believed by some religious groups and denied by others. Job's consciousness continues to expand as he begins to wrestle with the possibility of life after death. Job is examining his life in the Socratic spirit and continues to do so in spectacular ways as we proceed in the text.

> Every moment of existence
> Seems like some dirty trick
> Happiness can come suddenly and
> Leave just as quick.
>
> —Bob Dylan, "Sugar Baby"

"Therefore I will not restrain my mouth; I will speak in the anguish of my spirit; I will complain in the bitterness of my soul.

Am I the sea, or a sea monster, that thou set
test a guard over me?

When I say, 'My bed will comfort me, my
couch will ease my complaint,' then thou dost scare
me with dreams and terrify me with visions, so that
I would choose strangling and death rather than
my bones.

I loathe my life; I would not live for ever. Let
me alone, for my days are a breath.

What is man, that thou dost make so much
of him, and that thou dost set thy mind upon him,
dost visit him every morning, and test him every
moment?

How long wilt thou not look away from me,
nor let me alone till I swallow my spittle?

If I sin, what do I do to thee, thou watcher
of men? Why hast thou made me thy mark? Why
have I become a burden to thee?

Why dost thou not pardon my transgression
and take away my iniquity? For now I shall lie in
the earth; thou wilt seek me, but I shall not be."
(Job 7:11–21)

Commentary

Job is now sharing directly with God. Job is letting God in on his
anger and anguish. This is a very healthy choice, which is to talk to
God about all that lies within us. Intimacy develops from sharing and
letting others in regarding our inner life, and this is especially true with
God. God longs for us to share our inner torments and struggles, successes and achievements, and longs to share with us what's within the
very heart and mind of God. So few of us take the time to share and
then be silent and listen to God and thereby miss out on an intimate

relationship that God longs to have with us. Any of us is capable and invited to share everything with God and listen to God's reply.

In addition, Job is also being honest with himself about his inner experiences. Job is now able to step back and observe his experiences and make them conscious. Another way to express this is that Job is observing the observer (himself) and thereby becoming conscious of his own consciousness.

Ken Wilber argues this is one way we experience spirit for it allows us to gain a certain degree of objectivity and with it an ability to detach. I agree, and when we can detach while simultaneously holding on to the opposite pathos that comes from compassion, we have dialectic of spirit. I experience and express spirit when passionately forgiving, laughing, confessing, accepting, challenging, speaking the truth in love with others, and in detaching from my experience enough to be conscious of what I am experiencing in the first palace! Like every other truth, it is a double-edged sword where detachment and pathos coexist in an intricate tension and nearly impossible to delineate and differentiate in language.

Job seems to be meditating about God's activity in the lives of human souls: "Why are you so involved in our pathetic lives? Why don't you just direct your energies elsewhere because when you do, so much testing and burdens and judgment seem to accompany our relationships? Can't you put your mind on something, anything else?" Job then wonders what he has done to deserve his fate and why does God not pardon his incomprehensible sins. How has he missed the mark? Job does not consciously understand what he has done to deserve his fate. Job now wonders if he sinned, what that is to God. Great existential questions that need some play in the minds and hearts of anyone who wishes to "know thyself." There are many times I wished God or others would back off and just let go after I have missed the mark. I know when I am feeling full of anguish, I have often wished God would just leave me alone as I would be better off without all the trials and tribulations that seem to come my way. There is a hint of self-pity in this attitude, and there seems to be no harm intrinsically in this as long as we don't linger there too long. It seems we must taste humiliation and weakness before we are prepared to enter upon intimacy with God.

Job makes his second reference to his dreams and visions, and that is God scares and terrifies him with them. Job has yet to welcome his dreams and visions and therefore is wrestling with the truth that they are trying to teach. This is one of the ways we can say God lives in the soul or psyche of men and women. The psyche produces these dreams and visions from the mind of God as one of many ways God communicates to us. In the Hebrew Scriptures, dream interpretation was done by Joseph and Ezekiel, yet religious people today for the most part ignore these opportunities to grasp God's specific mode of communication and will for them. It's easier to settle for following general commandments than intimacy with God will only occur when we learn to grasp God's will for us in each moment and set of circumstances. God wants to speak truth to our hearts through many means and in each day of our lives if we have ears to hear. Learning to interpret my own dreams has been one of the most rewarding endeavors of my life. Job has not learned to interpret his dreams and visions as directed by God to help him recognize the power of God within and that his ego needs to be willing to go along for the ride.

> And yes here's to the few who forgive what you do
> And to the fewer who don't even care.

> —Leonard Cohen, "Night Comes On"

Then Bildad the Shuhite answered: "How long will you say these things, and the words of your mouth are a great wind?

Does God pervert justice? Or does the Almighty pervert the right?

If your children have sinned against him, he has delivered them into the power of their transgression.

If you will seek God and make supplication to the Almighty, if you are pure and upright, surely then he will rouse himself for you and reward you with a rightful habitation.

And though your beginning was small, your latter days will be very great.

"For inquire, I pray you, of bygone ages, and consider what the fathers have found; for we are but of yesterday, and know nothing, for our days on earth are a shadow.

Will they not teach you, and tell you, and utter words out of their understanding?

"Can papyrus grow where there is no marsh? Can reeds flourish where there is no water?

While yet in flower and not cut down, they wither before any other plant.

Such are the paths of all who forget God; the hope of the godless man shall perish.

His confidence breaks in sunder, and his trust is a spider's web.

He leans against his house, but it does not stand; he lays hold of it, but it does not endure.

He thrives before the sun, and his shoots spread over his garden.

His roots twine about the stone heap; he lives among the rocks.

If he is destroyed from his place, then it will deny him, saying, `I have never seen you.'

Behold, this is the joy of his way; and out of the earth others will spring.

"Behold, God will not reject a blameless man, nor take the hand of evildoers.

He will yet fill your mouth with laughter, and your lips with shouting.

Those who hate you will be clothed with shame, and the tent of the wicked will be no more." (Job: 8: 1–22)

Commentary

Job's friends make the case that God blesses the pure of heart and He a just judge, and therefore, your sons and daughters must have sinned against God in some ways you are not aware. They also make the arguments that we are to be rooted in God, and He will not take the hand of the wicked. They parrot one of the most accepted beliefs in Judaism at the time, that is if you are suffering, you or someone in the family sinned and made God angry, and punishment soon will follow. The concept of an angry and punishing God persists today as God is perceived like an angry father who cares only for the letter of the law. Job is progressing beyond these limited, narrow, trite, distorted, and projected images of God.

> In the cold light of day
> There in the midst of it,
> So alive and alone
> Words support like bone
> Dreaming of mercy street.

—Peter Gabriel, "Mercy Street"

Then Job answered:

"Truly I know that it is so: But how can a man be just before God?

If one wished to contend with him, one could not answer him once in a thousand times.

He is wise in heart, and mighty in strength -- who has hardened himself against him, and succeeded? -- he who removes mountains, and they know it not, when he overturns them in his anger; who shakes the earth out of its place, and its pillars tremble; who commands the sun, and it does not rise; who seals up the stars; who alone stretched out the heavens, and trampled the waves of the sea; who made the Bear and Orion, the Pleiades' and the chambers of the south; who does great things

beyond understanding, and marvelous things without number. (Job: 9:1–10)

Commentary

Job's sharing his inner life with God is interrupted by more human
dialogue. Job agrees with most of this counsel except he offers a rhetorical question, that is, how can we ever be just before God? None of us
are *always* just. This must be a self-deception. We hurt those closest to
us and are incapable of purity and wholeness at all times. However, so
often we hear some believers of all faiths make spurious claims about
how special they are while the rest of us are infidels and backsliders who
deserve to burn in hell. We all have fears and doubts and want to be in
the right. It is easy to adopt a mind-set of us against them rather than
live with insecurities and uncertainties. Better to cling to our beliefs no
matter how rigid and self-righteous they may be. But Job is struggling
with doubts about himself and his ability to perceive the truth within
himself and in his relationship with God. Mature faith allows for
doubts and uncertainties as these individuals are able to trust in God
that their difficulties and doubts will be resolved in time. Can you trust
all your beliefs and perceptions and *know* you are always in the right?
*Job adopts a cautious attitude toward his beliefs about himself and God,
recognizing he is limited and could be/probably is wrong in some ways or
another.* What courage and faith Job exhibits in this most difficult of
times! Can a believer trust that God will correct us with gentle understanding? In the realm of the unseen, there are circumstances that let
us know if we are on the right track or not. However, direction comes
with a willingness to question ourselves (beliefs, motivations, attitudes,
behaviors) as we continue to mature and change. Job correctly *distinguishes* his self-awareness from God's *truths*. Job has by no means given
up his quest for understanding and wisdom, but this period of disorientation and self-doubt needs to replace the false security of his past
faith. Job has the courage to question his past beliefs about himself and
the true nature of faith and God. As he does so, he is opening himself

up for new revelations. The skeptic is always farther along the road to truth than those religious believers who think they know God and his will through rigid laws, rules, and dogma The Hebrew, Islamic, and Christian Scriptures *are not books of rules*; but rather they are meant to be interpreted in their overall context and are a help to understanding the truth about ourselves, God, our neighbor, and our relationships to each other and to God. This is no easy task, and the desire to believe hard and fast rules seems too great a temptation for many people.

> We were Lot on the mountain
> We were Noah on the Ark
> Flying hand in hand
> From the doghowl dark
>
> Going up against chaos . . .
>
> —Bruce Cockburn, "Going Up Against Chaos"

"Though I am innocent, I cannot answer him; I must appeal for mercy to my accuser" (Job 9: 15).

Commentary

Job still believes he is innocent of any wrongdoing that he is consciously aware of and would justify his fate, but simultaneously, he appeals for mercy for any lack of self-awareness on his part. As we move on in the text, it becomes clear Job is suffering from significant self-deception related to a number of truths, including his ego-attachments and inflation. His sufferings are a crucible, which is burning off the dross in his character. Job also demonstrates respect for God in the midst of his losses, lack of self-awareness, and uncertainty. Job is open-minded yet willing to stand upon his present understanding until and at which time his consciousness is expanded, and he is able to get some conscious awareness to his plight. Job seeks no desperate, quick, or impetuous solutions. Job is learning patient endurance as he waits in the valley of uncertainty and the unknown. No clear skies, no mountain panoramas here, but rather weariness and anguish as he moves forward in the valley one step at a time. He does so with a faith that is both laudable yet lacking in the most important quality that sustains us, that is in conjunction with union/intimacy with God. This makes Job's present state all the more remarkable because he is holding on to his faith in the midst of his struggles and weariness with patient endurance without any real conscious intimacy with God as of yet. He is indeed on the road but doesn't even know his destination, yet he ferries forward nevertheless with a faith and perseverance beyond my limited comprehension.

> Dreaming of mercy street
> Wear your inside out.

> —Peter Gabriel, "Mercy Street"

If I say, 'I will forget my complaint, I will put off my sad countenance, and be of good cheer,' I become afraid of all my suffering, for I know thou wilt not hold me innocent.

I shall be condemned; why then do I labor in vain? (Job 9: 27–29)

Commentary

Job perceives that if he represses his sadness and anguish while putting on a pretense, this will set him up for self-deception, guilt, and fear of additional sufferings. What an insight for humanity around four thousand years ago! When we repress, avoid, and deny painful truths, we become phony and afraid. We cannot fake good cheer if we wish to court courage and honesty. This will always invite future disaster. Repression also procures fears of further sufferings. Our fears and anxieties only multiply and eventually cause neurotic symptoms in those even remotely sensitive to the truth. A neurotic suffers exponentially to the degree they are incapable of facing the truth, yet they demonstrate a certain degree of health as they cannot tolerate *falsehoods*. This inner tension between the truth and falsehoods sets us up for neurotic symptoms. Their sufferings create opportunities to adjust attitudes, beliefs, and subsequently, behaviors. Job offers us a glimpse into the depths of a maturing character as he chooses to face his sufferings and struggles rather than avoid and repress what is inside of him. In Greek mythology, Hercules had a choice early in his life to choose between three female goddesses, each promising different experiences if he chose one as the most beautiful. He did not choose ease or vanity, but rather the thorny path and, like Job, benefited in the long run.

> I don't cheat on myself I don't run and hide
> Hide from the feelings that are buried inside . . .
> Most of the time.

> —Bob Dylan, "Most of the Time"

> For he is not a man, as I am, that I might answer him, that we should come to trial together.
> There is no umpire between us, who might lay his hand upon us both.
> Let him take his rod away from me, and let not dread of him terrify me.
> Then I would speak without fear of him, for I am not so in myself. (Job 9:32–35)

Commentary

Job knows he cannot appeal to an arbiter in his clash with God. Job is therefore one of first persons this early in recorded history to endeavor to face God one-on-one in such an intimate way. Job has embarked upon the difficult task of individuation by leaving the herd and group consciousness behind and listening to the inner voice within himself that is God speaking through his unconscious mind. Job is grappling with God and his fears to generate self-knowledge and in an attempt to forge a faith, which includes speaking with God and which therefore has the potential to stand the trials and tribulations of life. Outer circumstances have conspired to provoke latent inner tensions within Job. However, it is easier to blame the external circumstances rather than internalize the conflicts. Before we face God, one need to know thyself as much as possible, but knowing thyself knows God to some extent, and we can add this to the multitude of seemingly contradictions and paradoxes we are discussing. The point is what lies within does so, whether we like it or not. The inner landscapes and land mines must explode to unveil the latent wars that lie within and are shaped by the clashes of the opposites. Can we become, like Job, our own prosecuting and defense attorneys while these inner conflicts shred the fabric of our souls and threaten to tear us apart? And what we find there is none other than God within us!

Working with our unconscious mind discloses that inner and outer circumstances have an underlying unity. How else can we account for common incidences of synchronicity? *I can't count the times* I have shared with clients the need to do what is required and trust the outcome to God and hear sometimes within the next few sessions that their internal needs were met by external circumstances just in the nick of time. External and inner circumstances seem as complementary as matter is with its positive/negative charges and wave/particles functions. Like Job, each is responsible to discern the correspondence of the inner and outer circumstances and/or learn to trust the mysterious will of God. There is no way our finite minds can comprehensibly integrate God's totality in all His/Her truths/will. Job's war is our own; how do we make sense of our fate or accept the mystery of God's will while maintaining trust that God loves us? Should we continue to push for answers, or let go and trust? Can we entertain both simultaneously?

Job goes on to recognize that to traffic with God, he needs to do so without fear. The opposite of fear is love. Like every man, woman, and child, the experience of love is fundamental and vital for life, let alone for a relationship to develop. This presupposes Job is presently in terror of God due to his earlier dream/vision and his perception that God is wrathful. In other words, Job needs an *experience* of God as loving before he will be able to get past his terror. How does God accomplish this in Job will be unveiled as we proceed.

Job also acknowledges the great gulf that exists between God and man. This is why in Judaism, the rituals and laws were so highly developed for to approach God, humans must be clean and demonstrate respect for God. These rituals and laws act like a shield and mediate our relations with God. In themselves, these rituals and traditions are symbols, the means of communicating the intimacy and distance between God and human beings, and therefore can be excellent representations of respect, awe, wonder, and adoration. However, the problem all rituals, laws, codes, traditions, or liturgies come up against is they become substitutes for first-hand experiences with God. Our traditions, laws, and rituals can never duplicate a first-hand experience, nor are they intended to substitute for a direct encounter with God. When this is attempted, they become human traditions and usually take on a life of their own and are mistaken and substituted for the real thing. The church, synagogue, temple, and mosque assume this role for many, and thereby, these institutions can become obstacles to first-hand experiences of faith. When this occurs, the traditions become idolatrous. It appears to me both the institutions and individuals create idolatry by mutual consent, allowing their insecurities and need for power and prestige to trump personal experience with God. On the other hand, when individuals and institutions recognizes their frailties, limitations, unworthiness, and inabilities to truly reflect God, they begin to reflect their original propose, that is to be a true intermediary of grace and God's power to those who have yet to experience these wonders for themselves. These institutions need always be pointing the individual toward personal experiences with God, whether through proclamation, teaching, rituals, sacraments, dogma, etc. We are privileged to have this inner experience of Job to help us gain a more intimate understanding of a divine encounter between one man and God. This process of individuation is not for everyone, and the intermediate stage of the collective path is proper and enough for some of us. But there are some who have an inner destiny, which must be heeded and followed, which does not include any previous paths followed by others, and which leads to a loneliness and joy no other way can achieve. Recollection is one of the great gifts of God's spirit. This is one solitary place where God meets us in our limited consciousness. Symbols, rituals, prayers, sacraments, etc., are also helpful and excellent and concrete gatherings where God and humans can commune together. These institutions can facilitate the incorporation of God's truths within us, or they can become stumbling blocks of the worst order, *skewing truth to the point where it can no longer be found. Religious institutions have become the most horrible vehicles of evil when human traditions are used to cultivate power and hate in the name of God. Our religions have been used to unleashed evil beyond comprehension, and by far, the greatest amount of evil leveled against the human race has been done in the name of God.* The wisdom hidden within Job's painful experiences furnish a path of individuation far from the collective paths of religion or any other cultural nexus between himself and God. That path is one of inner conflict and turmoil where the opposites threaten to tear us apart, and the law is one of truth and love that must come from within each person and cannot be provided for by any institution period.

But to live outside the law, you must be honest.

—Bob Dylan, "Absolutely Sweet Marie"

"I loathe my life; I will give free utterance to my complaint; I will speak in the bitterness of my soul.

I will say to God, Do not condemn me; let me know why thou dost contend against me.

Does it seem good to thee to oppress, to despise the work of thy hands and favor the designs of the wicked?

Hast thou eyes of flesh? Dost thou see as man sees?

Are thy days as the days of man, or thy years as man's years, that thou dost seek out my iniquity and search for my sin, although thou knowest that I am not guilty, and there is none to deliver out of thy hand?

Thy hands fashioned and made me; and now thou dost turn about and destroy me.

Remember that thou hast made me of clay; and wilt thou turn me to dust again?

Didst thou not pour me out like milk and curdle me like cheese?

Thou didst clothe me with skin and flesh, and knit me together with bones and sinews.

Thou hast granted me life and steadfast love; and thy care has preserved my spirit.

Yet these things thou didst hide in thy heart; I know that this was thy purpose.

If I sin, thou dost mark me, and dost not acquit me of my iniquity.

If I am wicked, woe to me! If I am righteous, I cannot lift up my head, for I am filled with disgrace and look upon my affliction.

And if I lift myself up, thou dost hunt me like a lion, and again work wonders against me; thou dost renew thy witnesses against me, and increase thy vexation toward me; thou dost bring fresh hosts against me.

"Why didst thou bring me forth from the womb? Would that I had died before any eye had seen me, and were as though I had not been, carried from the womb to the grave.

Are not the days of my life few? Let me alone, that I may find a little comfort before I go whence I shall not return, to the land of gloom and deep darkness, the land of gloom and chaos, where light is as darkness." (Job: 10:1–22)

Commentary

Again Job's lamentations are directed toward God. Job believes prior to his losses, he was cared for; post losses, he loathes his life, and he is full of complaints. His faith is being tested as he struggles to make sense of his fate in the context of whether God loves him or not and why he has been so oppressed. He does not see any iniquity within himself and wonders why God is destroying him. In addition, he again wishes he never lived. It seems he believes God not only does not love him but is full of wrath. Job is experiencing feelings of abandonment and the anguish that goes with it. It seems any real intimate encounter with God includes this most horrific of experiences. Even Jesus had to endure this on the cross when he felt abandoned by God the Father, and he did say during his ministry that his servants are not above their master and that his disciples are expected to go through many of the same trials and tribulations he did. I know that in any intimate relationship, we share with the significant other similar experiences, and it is in this sharing that intimacy develops.

Job is in need of new experiences with God, or he will continue to project this negative image onto God. That is exactly what he is getting! As we shall see, *his sufferings are essential* to his experiences of God as loving. The feminine side of our natures always has valued the pain and compassion intrinsic in the human condition, and I believe the misogynous beliefs of the Hebrews and all mid-Eastern traditions in general contribute to this incredible distortion that God is full of wrath and judgment. If these traditions would have experienced God as feminine as well as masculine a little more, perhaps this falsification and distortion would never have arisen in the first place!

Job goes on to complain that life is short; therefore, could he be left in peace so he can experience some comfort during the limited time he has left? Job is being subjected to God's touch of futility and mortality—the great equalizers to all hubris. For all those schooled in futility, anguish is consequently immense. Therefore, we wish pain would flee even if it means they were never born, or we could just die and be done with all this ineffable suffering. It becomes difficult to remain patient and endure until the confusion and sufferings lift as inevitably it will and does within those who are patient enough to endure it. Joy can only be appreciated when we becomes veterans of sorrow.

It's a wonder to me—
I still don't understand
Why I ever survived to be old
With a heart full of holes.

—Mark Knopfler, "Heart Full of Holes"

Then Zophar the Na'amathite answered:

"Should a multitude of words go unanswered, and a man full of talk be vindicated?

Should your babble silence men, and when you mock, shall no one shame you?

For you say, 'My doctrine is pure, and I am clean in God's eyes.'

But oh, that God would speak, and open his lips to you, and that he would tell you the secrets of wisdom! For he is manifold in understanding. Know then that God exacts of you less than your guilt deserves.

"Can you find out the deep things of God? Can you find out the limit of the Almighty?

It is higher than heaven—what can you do? Deeper than Sheol—what can you know?

Its measure is longer than the earth, and broader than the sea.

If he passes through, and imprisons, and calls to judgment, which can hinder him?

For he knows worthless men; when he sees iniquity, will he not consider it?

But a stupid man will understand when a wild ass's colt is born a man.

"If you set your heart aright, you will stretch out your hands toward him.

If iniquity is in your hand, put it far away, and let not wickedness dwell in your tents.

Surely then you will lift up your face without blemish; you will be secure, and will not fear.

You will forget your misery; you will remember it as waters that have passed away.

And your life will be brighter than the noonday; its darkness will be like the morning.

And you will have confidence, because there is hope; you will be protected and take your rest in safety.

You will lie down, and none will make you afraid; many will entreat your favor.

But the eyes of the wicked will fail; all way of escape will be lost to them, and their hope is to breathe their last." (Job: 11:1–20)

Commentary

Job's two friends interrupt his conversing with God. How often do we seek or permit these interruptions? Let us count the ways. Why does Job remain with them? They could not interrupt him if he withdrew from their presence. Perhaps it is due to his need for human companionship despite the fact they are interfering with his relationship with God. We all make these same mistakes, seeking support at times when we need to be alone and choosing to be alone when we need to reach out to others. As with everything, when living in the moment, there are no codified rules or laws that are universal except for a few, including love, mercy, justice, and humility. As we will see from the text, Job is gradually drifting away from human companionship so that he can experience a real understanding of his own and God's nature and so pave the way for true intimacy with himself and God. These are the prerequisites for intimacy with our fellow men and women.

To summarize their counsel, Job deserves *more* suffering because he is talking too much, he will never understand God, and if Job turns from his iniquity, he will be forgiven and experience peace! But Job does not know what his faults are, so is he to just mimic some general and phony repentance? With friends like these, who needs, well . . . you know. Job seems consciously to be expressing his pain, distress, and confusion in a manner worthy of praise. Job is reaching out from within his innermost being and sharing his travail, and his friends believe he is not suffering enough! Wow!

> Somebody's going to take the fall
> There's your quid pro quo
> They'll punish the monkey
> And let the organ grinder go.

> —Mark Knopfler, "Punish the Monkey"

Then Job answered:

"No doubt you are the people, and wisdom will die with you.

But I have understanding as well as you; I am not inferior to you. Who does not know such things as these?

I am a laughingstock to my friends; I, who called upon God and he answered me, a just and blameless man, am a laughingstock.

In the thought of one who is at ease there is contempt for misfortune; it is ready for those whose feet slip.

The tents of robbers are at peace, and those who provoke God are secure, who bring their God in their hand . . .

As for you, you whitewash with lies; worthless physicians are you all.

Oh that you would keep silent, and it would be your wisdom!

Hear now my reasoning, and listen to the pleadings of my lips.

Will you speak falsely for God, and speak deceitfully for him?

Will you show partiality toward him, will you plead the case for God?

Will it be well with you when he searches you out? Or can you deceive him, as one deceives a man?

He will surely rebuke you if in secret you show partiality.

Will not his majesty terrify you, and the dread of him fall upon you?

Your maxims are proverbs of ashes; your defenses are defenses of clay.

"Let me have silence, and I will speak, and let come on me what may. (Job: 12:1–6, 13:4–13)

Commentary

Job rejects his friend's dissertation on tradition and accuses his friends of self-deception and patronizing God! Job confronts his friends with what he perceives as self-righteousness and the audacity to speak for God. All his friends have done is mastered the social norms, traditions, and beliefs by following the beaten path. Once one has located this path, there is no need for expanding of consciousness. Job's friends are fundamentalists, trotting around judgmental attitudes like those shirts with some emblem or advertisement or another. There is fundamentalism in all religions as they all are judgmental and intolerant of anything that is not black and white. Many respectable folks follow the beaten path, glancing only at superficial behavior and its outcomes while the inner life and its intrinsic conflicts are ignored. There are factors and variables that make up each unique person, and no black-and-white vistas are capable of detecting the particular from the general. These guardians of tradition often spout the party line, proclaiming platitudes rather than thinking for themselves. Job also recognizes a certain degree of peace and security for those that attempt to put God in a box. Fundamentalist aims appear righteous on the surface and in control, and therefore they peddle their distorted beliefs around with them to justify their selfish and self-righteous intentions. Religious individuals who sponsor nationalism and violence have perverted the truth as they have long forgotten Jesus's imperative to *love* our enemies, pray for those who persecute us, and offer the other cheek not already smitten. In contrast, the archetype of the suffering servant will always reflect authentic faith.

By contrast, Job has set out on his own path. He ventures into the unknown by expanding consciousness, as all the heroes in mythology do. Heroes have already grasped and integrated social norms, but they reject those paths that have become full of mold and mildew. We are being offered a rare glimpse into someone on the road to genuine enlightenment. Job is in the mist of his own first-hand experience with God. This path is full of confusion and slippery slopes. These archetypal adventures lead Job to inner experiences, which will sustain him with an enduring faith capable of suspending judgments until circumstances unfold some of God's glorious and painful mysteries. Job is gradually gathering pearls of wisdom, experiencing healing, and being transformed into wholeness or God's image. This path is also leading him to becoming a powerful channel of God's healing wisdom. There is an important spiritual principle involved; that is, the more one integrates and becomes whole, the more efficacious one becomes as a channel of love in its mercy, justice, and humility. Alas, the harvest is abundant, but the laborers are few.

Job realizes he is really alone in his ordeal, and he must press on without the benefit of others sharing his unique journey. Though his friends continue milling around, they no longer provide any support or comfort for the lonely and abandoned Job. For anyone following their unique path, there are crucial periods when human comfort must vanish and we are left bereft of friends. For those willing, their path leads to experiencing God as their closest comrade. God's voice is crying out in the wilderness, waiting for ears to hear His anguished, sad, and yet persistently tender voice. His voice is still and quiet, yet constant, and only those willing to nurture their inner life as Job is doing will ever reach the depth of shared suffering with God that is required not only for intimacy, but for the work of locating the lost and promoting healing to this broken world. Those few who have found their deepest friend in God work with God in keeping the universe from a cosmic meltdown. I wish I could say I was one of these chosen few, but in truth, I am still stumbling and stuttering somewhere along the way. There is always more that we know than we can demonstrate. This truth helps me to let go of yesterday's failures and start anew each day on my own quest to be counted as one of His true and intimate friends.

> And the dealer wants you thinking
> It's either black or white
> Thank G-d it's not that simple
> In my secret life.

> —Leonard Cohen, "In My Secret Life"

> Bless the continuous stutter
> Of the word being made into flesh.

> —Leonard Cohen, "The Window"

But I would speak to the Almighty, and I desire to argue my case with God.

Behold, he will slay me; I have no hope; yet I will defend my ways to his face.

This will be my salvation that a godless man shall not come before him.

Listen carefully to my words, and let my declaration be in your ears.

Behold, I have prepared my case; I know that I shall be vindicated.

Who is there that will contend with me? For then I would be silent and die.

Only grant two things to me, then I will not hide myself from thy face:

withdraw thy hand far from me, and let not dread of thee terrify me.

Then call and I will answer; or let me speak, and do thou reply to me.

How many are my iniquities and my sins? Make me know my transgression and my sin.

Why dost thou hide thy face, and count me as thy enemy?

Wilt thou frighten a driven leaf and pursue dry chaff? (Job: 13:3, 15–25)

Commentary

Job is truly on his own and seeking an audience with God. Job seeks a direct and personal relationship and understanding with God while he asks that God would withdraw his hand from him and so remove his fear. To withdraw God's hand seems like the opposite of asking for the opportunity to "defend my ways to his face." Later he asks why God hides His face. He appears stuck in the wrathful concept of God's presence, and this seems logical based on his attitude toward his dream/ vision. He then asks for God to remove his dread so they can have a dialogue, and he can defend himself as he has prepared his case with the primary question, what is my iniquity? His seems grounded in his desire that God withdraw and that he cannot go forward in his relating to God without overcoming his dread/fear.

He recognizes the need to be alone so he can establish a dialogue and come to some kind of understanding with God. He is seeking truth that can only be found within him and where God is waiting! Thus, Job has now become a true contemplative as he seeks a union with God in the secret places of his heart. God exists in our soul and spirit, and nothing exists without God's presence. All energy and matter in all the universes not only were created by God but are sustained and alive with God's energy and capable of fulfilling their unique purpose.

Job seems simultaneously assertive and humble as he recognizes God being omnipotent while maintaining his own ways. Job needs to make sense of his fate. If he has transgressed, what has he done? If not, where does that leave him? Job is not cursing God but rather seeking an expansion of consciousness, *meaning to his sufferings*. All of Job's grief at his losses have shaken him out of his normal egocentric consciousness and confronted him with God's true existence. He is developing a God consciousness. Job is living out a difficult paradox in that he is combining audacity with humility. He is walking the razor's edge. All the while, he is feeling abandoned, totally confused, and scared of God's fury. To offer a context to this passage, God sought Ezekiel and asked him to stand up on his own feet so He may have a word with him. This seems like a show of respect from God toward humankind and God's wish to converse with man, almost as an equal. Standing up to face another has certain implications socially. It could be interpreted as threat or mutually respect. In the case with Ezekiel, it is obvious a show of respect. In Job's case, the situation is reversed, however, as Job seeks to stand up for himself and defend his ways before God. This is a complete reversal of the normal ordering where God is far above his creation, humankind. Ezekiel first encountered God with God asking him to stand up that they may talk, thereby honoring that man; in contrast, Job honors himself within the context of his faith. What makes Job's request arrogant and/or what makes it assertive? I believe it is both. Made in God's image, here is a man who is in the process of developing a trusting relationship with his Creator, and only his suffering avails him of the humility to pursue God in such a fashion. We must keep in mind, for his part he never questions God's existence nor defies or curses God. However, there seems to be a quantity of inflation in that Job fails to fully differentiate God from his ego. This kind of contradiction is in us all and needs to be accepted as part of our maturation process. To be able to identify these contradictions within ourselves without self-deception and learn how to gradually resolve them in the tension the opposites occasion is using the transcendent function we discussed earlier. We are getting a glimpse of Job being right smack in the middle of this within the text.

Job's assertiveness cultivates a new dynamic between God and humans and one God does not rebuff. In fact, I believe God yearns for and rejoices in the possibility of his created beings offering back to Him friendship and to be co-creators with Him. *What an honor.* God has chosen to be in relationship with human beings. God does not need relationship with His creation but rather has chosen to empty Himself, thereby making Himself vulnerable. He has given us free will, thus limiting His own power out of respect for His creation and love for each of us. He wants real friendships with us even at the risk of losing us if we so chose.

My experience tells me when any of us chooses to reject God, this causes God great sorrow. The compassion and vulnerability of God far outweighs the conception that God is wrathful and angry. Rather than a wrathful and angry God, He is stern with those attempting to manipulate, deceive, and desecrate the truth. It seems to me God wants us to stand on our own feet and make a stand for the truth and even at times make some decisions on our own within the context of faith and trust in God's love and grace. Specific guidance is not always so clear, and we are asked to fulfill our responsibilities and stand up and be counted. It also appears at other times, we are given specific guidance, and as we mature in our faith, it becomes easier and more joyful to surrender to God's will precisely because our will becomes more and more one with God's as we grow in love.

As we shall observe in God's response to later in the text to Job, in all of Job's attitudes and anguished sharing with God, he is never condemned. This leads me to the conclusion that God knows Job is speaking from a place of faith and that God wants a true friendship with him. Job has not experienced this aspect of God as loving. Job's actions seem to be opening new doors with the potential for new depths in relationship with God. However, Job has some additional humble pie to taste before the proper balance between audacity and humility is established within the psyche of Job. But it is important to notice God is honoring the process of individuation in Job and is slowing down His steps to coincide with Job's.

Any healthy relationship necessitates honesty, trust, assertiveness, and openness. Job has exhibited these dynamics in his communications with God. Intimacy requires trust and respect for the other. God and Job are in the process of establishing a safe place for each other with an intention of establishing intimacy and healthy communication. Job remains afraid of God, and therefore this safe place of intimacy has yet to be established. As anyone in a healthy relationship knows, creating a safe place for your mate or friend has to be done in the spirit of love with a willingness to yield one to the other. Each person must take responsibility for their feelings and actions while sharing them without expecting their friend to assume more responsibility for the relationship or to carry the other. When honest communication does occur, there is movement and sensitivity in the relationship. It is essential for a healthy relationship to let the other in without expectations, and when this is achieved, intimacy is created naturally. Each partner needs to have already established autonomy while willing to be vulnerable. We are witnesses of Job and his transformation within this very context. God longs for us as a lover and desires to embrace us as companions and friends. Friendship with God entails all that we experience in the best of our human friendships that is in its caring teasing, intimate favoritism, tender understanding, mutual acceptance and appreciation, shared confidences, and more. In fact, the more we share with God, the more God shares with us. God does not barge in and demand a relationship; it is our responsibility to let God into our lives. As we let God into the secret places of our inner life, God reciprocates with His joy, power, grace, healings, serenity, blessings, and knowledge of some of his mysteries and secrets. To let another in who has similar interests, passions, depths of character, insights, and integrity creates a bond nothing can obliterate. God encompasses all our nature as we are created in His image. Have you not ever been with a close friend among acquaintances when a mutual understanding arises between you and its acknowledgement is punctuated by a discreet smile? This does not diminish others but rather belies an intimacy between yourself and your close friend. This is the kind of relationship God desires with us! This is what God is after with Job. However, there are a few more bumps in the road before this intimacy is established.

If it be your will
That a voice be true . . .

—Leonard Cohen, "If It Be Your Will"

"For thou writest bitter things against me, and makest me inherit the iniquities of my youth" (Job 13:26).

Commentary

It seems Job has been taking a moral inventory as he wracks his memory to figure out what transgressions he committed in his youth. Taking a weekly if not daily inventory is critical to the life of any contemplative. Self-deception is so subtle and universal that God shows his mercy by revealing our delusions gradually and gently. As we shall see in the upcoming passages, Job is deluded as to the real dynamics of his self-deception but remembers the mistakes of his youth and wonders if this could have provoked his present sufferings. Job is willing to revisit his past. This is essential to anyone working through the healing process (salvation means healing). The goal is to revisit our past but not to live there. The purpose of revisiting our past is to integrate and resolve what has been left behind. Self-knowledge does not come without its complement of self-reflection. When we repress something from our past, we are in need of a new adult perspective on past foibles, experiences, embarrassments, and mistakes. We may need to die to false pride and accept some painful and humiliating truths. We may need to forgive ourselves. We also may need to forgive others, recognizing that they had no idea what it was that they did that wounded us in the way it did as they probably were immature and impetuous as we were/are. Without this courage, we will never change. Whatever is not resolved from our past is destined to repeat itself until we face the issues head-on. Many of our character defects were survival techniques we needed to survive during our youth but now have to be seen for what they are and then surrendered and overcome. If left unresolved, these issues get projected into our present beliefs, relationships, and circumstances. When we find ourselves overreacting to a situation or person, some inner archetypes or unresolved issues from our past have obviously become activated.

In the present case, Job is revisiting his past. Sometimes we make mountains out of molehills. At other times there are real issues back there that need to be resolved. Like Job, we need to resolve these dynamics if we are to live in the present unfettered by the past. By resolving the past, we are able to pay attention to the present with relaxed openness and grateful expectation. We will react less and live with mindfulness in the present more. I think one of the reasons we have perceived God as wrathful and full of judgments is we continue to project experiences with each other (especially our dads) onto God. This conception of God seems to have grown to epidemic proportions in the present age. There is a universal projection that God is full of wrath, and some use this to justify not having anything to do with God. The fact is God is trying to get through to us all—with communications from many quadrants in our lives that He yearns and suffers with us in every experience we have, whether inner or outer. Many have borne the brunt of our parents' wrath at one time or another, and this gets projected onto the God image that exists in our psyche. I have been guilty of this projected distortion. What's sad is these distortions spurn God's grace and loving-kindness. Job seems to be stuck in such projections as he continues to rail against God and his fate. Another reason we may mistakenly believe God is full of wrath is the process of being transformed is so very painful that it seems as if God is angry with us. This process can be seen very clearly in Job and his transformations in relationship with God throughout the text.

Job infers God writes bitter things against him. I have no idea what to make of this except to say it must be some form of a metaphor.

> By the rivers dark
> I wandered on.
> I lived my life in Babylon . . .

By the rivers dark
Where I could not see
Who was waiting there
Who was hunting me.

—Leonard Cohen, "By the Rivers Dark"

"Man that is born of a woman is of few days, and full of trouble.

He comes forth like a flower, and withers; he flees like a shadow, and continues not.

And dost thou open thy eyes upon such a one and bring him into judgment with thee? (Job 14: 1–3)

Commentary

An existential problem (that which is universal in existence) arises with Job's new insights (verses 1–2). Job grieves over our collective mortality and the troubles life brings and continues to project onto God a wrathful nature while wondering if there is a life after death, and if there is, are we judged? I doubt Job gave death much thought prior to his losses as his sufferings seem to be generating an insightful personality. When we meditate, reflect, and learn to accept our death, it often has the effect of refining our purposes and aims, helps us focus on what matters and reject the superfluous. It also helps us live one day at a time with more openness and gratitude.

Is there life after death, and if not, does anything matter? Are we justified in living out our lives in enlightened hedonism, or is there meaning to our existence, and does this place any expectations upon how we live and treat others? Whether we like it or not, we are all philosophers and have to answer these questions for ourselves. Whatever answers we come up with have enormous consequences. Job is struggling with doubts as we all do. This is an aspect of faith, not an indication of its absence! All people of faith have to go through periods of doubt as they wrestle with our impending death. Many who believe there is no life after death become hedonists as this seems to be a logical conclusion, yet others like Albert Camus and my friend Kevin O'Grady in his reworking of the Sisyphus myth have found value in life without this belief in an afterlife. At same time, many who do believe in the afterlife use it as an excuse not to live fully in the here and now, and I would like to point out that those who are believers also believe we are already living eternally in the new life of the spirit of truth, and death is just a portal to another life—life after life, so to speak. This perspective brings with it the full obligations of living in the present with attention to love and duty to this world and not shirking from responsibilities for some pie in the sky afterlife that somehow is different from the tasks of facing the truth at all times, whether in the body or out of it in a new body! For the Christian at least, the Kingdom of God is both present in our ego-body-consciousness and as a future hope.

I respect Job in his seeming willingness to throw out his previous beliefs and start over. He is stuck in the nether lands where anything is possible and nothing is actualized. He is lost in the nadir of anguish and the unknown, where darkness is lived and breathed. He is not giving up with self-pity despite being abandoned by his wife, losing all of his earthly and material goods, the deaths of his children, the ignorance of his friends, and doubts about God's judgment and the afterlife. Job is an extraordinary man.

> I get so lost sometimes
> Days pass and this emptiness fills my heart.
>
> —Peter Gabriel, "In Your Eyes"

> Tell me again when I'm clean and I'm sober
> Tell me again when I've seen through the horror
> Tell me again over and over
> Tell me that you love me them
> Amen.
>
> —Leonard Cohen, "Amen"

"Who can bring a clean thing out of an unclean?
There is not one" (Job 14:4).

Commentary

Job seems to be referencing inherited sin and is aware he is incapable of perfection. Prior to Christ's life, death, and resurrection, all of creation was subjected to futility and without hope. Since no one is perfect or capable of fulfilling all the law's requirements, there is a huge amount of futility, sorrow, and hopelessness by merely existing. After Jesus's life, death, and resurrection, creation is still subject to futility, but now with hope (Romans 8: 19–21). What makes Job so remarkable is that his quest for intimacy with God continues unabated despite the scars of inherited sin and without the presence of the Holy Spirit, who confers hope and grace to the person of faith. No one is clean and pure before God, and Job perceives this reality despite maintaining his own ways before God, even with the knowledge he is not perfect. There is a growing humility in Job that is reflected in these verses. This stand before God is remarkable in that futility, resentment, self-pity, hopelessness, and hubris are all standard archetypal reactions toward a perceived wrathful deity.

> You carry the weight of inherited
> Sorrow
> From the first day till you die
>
> —Bruce Cockburn, "The Rose Above the Sky"

Since his days are determined, and the number of
his months is with thee, and thou hast appointed
his bounds that he cannot pass, look away from
him, and desist, that he may enjoy, like a hireling,
his day.

"For there is hope for a tree, if it be cut down, that it will sprout again, and that its shoots will not cease.

Though its root grow old in the earth, and its stump die in the ground, yet at the scent of water it will bud and put forth branches like a young plant.

But man dies, and is laid low; man breathes his last, and where is he?

As waters fail from a lake, and a river wastes away and dries up, so man lies down and rises not again; till the heavens are no more he will not awake, or be roused out of his sleep.

Oh that thou wouldest hide me in Sheol, that thou wouldest conceal me until thy wrath be past, that thou wouldest appoint me a set time, and remember me!

If a man die, shall he live again? All the days of my service I would wait, till my release should come.

Thou wouldest call, and I would answer thee; thou wouldest long for the work of thy hands.

For then thou wouldest number my steps, thou wouldest not keep watch over my sin; my transgression would be sealed up in a bag, and thou wouldest cover over my iniquity.

"But the mountain falls and crumbles away, and the rock is removed from its place; the waters wear away the stones; the torrents wash away the soil of the earth; so thou destroyest the hope of man.

Thou prevailest for ever against him, and he passes; thou changest his countenance, and sendest him away.

His sons come to honor, and he does not know it; they are brought low, and he perceives it not.

He feels only the pain of his own body, and he
mourns only for himself." (Job 14:5–22)

Commentary

Again Job ruminates over mortality, that is we have only so many days
on earth, and he would like to at least live without the fear of death,
judgment, and/or annihilation, which has a stranglehold on his mind,
heart, and body. Honesty demands we live with consciousness of death
within the context of our longings for hope and meaning. The desires
for security, worth, meaning, and purpose go on in Job. In addition,
Job continues to display the outlook of a once-born person, where the
ego is the measure of all things. He is in the process of becoming a
twice-born individual where the ego serves the powers greater than
itself by adapting to the truth, which lies outside the scope of the ego,
but this will not occur until he gets past the belief that God is wrathful.

Job goes on to recount how even trees that are cut down have
shoots, which bring at least a remnant back to life while humans are
not so fortunate unless God would release, remembers, and sets a time
for him (i.e., there is life after death). Job speculates and hopes for life
after death if it is a place of acceptance and affirmation for his weary
soul. Before his suffering, these inner conflicts were probably not even
in his conscious awareness. Now reality of the human predicament is
falling in like a sinking anchor in the sea. Without his suffering, we
can assume Job would never have gone to such depths and seen behind
the veil of denial and distraction. The questions of death, life's meaning, good, evil, consciousness, and truth all occupy those who have the
courage to struggle with their sufferings and the feelings these conflicts
occasion. Job is no longer one of the majority who are seduced by the
glitz and superficiality of the world of ten thousand things. Job is being
honest about his aspirations and longings, which demonstrate his progress as his conception of and experience with God is gradually shifting
and expanding in his consciousness. Job is longing for forgiveness and
grace, and his consciousness of a loving God is expanding as he hopes

not only for God's wrath to pass, but for his transgressions to be sealed in a bag to cover over his iniquity. But alas, he comes to the conclusion at this juncture that when a person dies, they have no perception of the outcome of his sons' lives, but they only feel pain in his own body and mourns for himself. Job is wrestling with depression and the sense of hopelessness in the context of his broken body and his knowledge of death. Yet he endures, remains open to his vast and anguished inner life, and he shares it all with God. Remarkable!

I'd like to pause and mention that Job is wrestling with many dialectics and pairs of opposites at this juncture: life/death, eternal/temporal, necessity/possibility, despair/hope, fear/longing, truth/falsehood, pain/joy, although he is unaware of many of these consciously. This is the transcendent function in action as we are witnesses to the incredible and incomprehensible process of transformation and individuation discussed earlier. If you find this work vague and confusing at times, welcome to human condition and the quest for truth and enlightenment!

> You must blaze a trail of your own, unknown, alone . . .
> You're old and disillusioned now as you realize at last,
> That all you have accomplished here will have all soon turned to dust.
> You dream of a future after life, well that's as maybe,
> I don't know.
> But you can't take what you left behind,
> You're all alone.
> So keep in mind
> Don't live today for tomorrow like you were immortal.
>
> —Genesis, "Burning Rope"

> Then Eli'phaz the Te'manite answered: "Should a wise man answer with windy knowledge, and fill himself with the east wind?
>
> Should he argue in unprofitable talk, or in words with which he can do no good?
>
> But you are doing away with the fear of God, and hindering meditation before God.

For your iniquity teaches your mouth, and you choose the tongue of the crafty.

Your own mouth condemns you, and not I; your own lips testify against you.

"Are you the first man that was born? Or were you brought forth before the hills?

Have you listened in the council of God? And do you limit wisdom to yourself?

What do you know that we do not know? What do you understand that is not clear to us?

Both the gray-haired and the aged are among us, older than your father.

Are the consolations of God too small for you, or the word that deals gently with you?

Why does your heart carry you away, and why do your eyes flash, that you turn your spirit against God, and let such words go out of your mouth?

What is man, that he can be clean? Or he that is born of a woman, that he can be righteous?

Behold, God puts no trust in his holy ones, and the heavens are not clean in his sight; how much less one who is abominable and corrupt, a man who drinks iniquity like water!

"I will show you, hear me; and what I have seen I will declare (what wise men have told, and their fathers have not hidden, to whom alone the land was given, and no stranger passed among them).

The wicked man writhes in pain all his days, through all the years that are laid up for the ruthless.

Terrifying sounds are in his ears; in prosperity the destroyer will come upon him.

He does not believe that he will return out of darkness, and he is destined for the sword.

He wanders abroad for bread, saying, 'Where is it?' He knows that a day of darkness is ready at his hand; distress and anguish terrify him; they prevail against him, like a king prepared for battle.

Because he has stretched forth his hand against God, and bids defiance to the Almighty, running stubbornly against him with a thick-bossed shield; because he has covered his face with his fat, and gathered fat upon his loins, and has lived in desolate cities, in houses which no man should inhabit, which were destined to become heaps of ruins; he will not be rich, and his wealth will not endure, nor will he strike root in the earth; he will not escape from darkness; the flame will dry up his shoots, and his blossom will be swept away by the wind. Let him not trust in emptiness, deceiving himself; for emptiness will be his recompense.

It will be paid in full before his time, and his branch will not be green. He will shake off his unripe grape, like the vine, and cast off his blossom, like the olive tree.

For the company of the godless is barren, and fire consumes the tents of bribery. They conceive mischief and bring forth evil and their heart prepares deceit." (Job 15: 1–35)

Commentary

The simplistic thinking of Job's friends never gets at the essence of what is really going on, but rather, they always make matters worse. First they fail to hear Job's gradual humbling of himself and the depth of his inner life as it expands and reaches out to God. Secondly, they are parroting the beliefs of the times. As in Jesus's day, some asked Jesus if a blind person they encountered was blind due to his or his family's sins. Jesus *spent much of his teaching ministry* trying to rout these simplistic, distorted, and accepted beliefs. He proclaimed that this man's malady offered an opportunity for God's power to be made manifest through his weaknesses, and he then proceeded to heal him. In addition, God's power is also manifested through the patient endurance of maladies whereby one is sanctified through their weaknesses and sufferings. Thirdly, Job's friends are unwilling and/or unable to put themselves in Job's shoes and open themselves up to an expansion of their own consciousness. They believe Job is guilty of some iniquity or another. Everyone misses the mark sometimes; to be human is to make mistakes. The letter of the law is concerned with externals and judgment. This is the attitude taken by Job's friends and most religious people today. In contrast, the spirit of the law fixes its emphasis on wholeness in attitudes, beliefs, and motives while nurturing compassion, love, and mercy in common experience. What we do springs from what and who we are on the inside. Consciousness of our actions is the key to unlocking the truth and, therefore, to our inner freedom.

The Apostle Paul discussed his freedoms in the context of the letter of the law (in the context of eating food sacrificed to pagan gods) when he wrote, "All things are lawful, but not all things are helpful" (1 Corinthians 10:23). Spirit is bound only by one law, the law of love, and when love is the guiding principle, all things are lawful, but not all things are helpful to others; and sometimes we are asked to restrict our personal freedoms for the sake of others. This kind of freedom is too much for most to handle, and therefore, all sorts of restrictions and taboos are constructed to offer counterfeit security. As we discussed in the chapter on addictions, attachments to false securities constricts freedom to the metaphorical penitentiary. Freedom demands conscious awareness. However, with conscious awareness comes responsibility, and therefore, it is easy to understand why it is hard to become self-aware. The strict adherence to the letter of the law is valid only for those so trapped in unconsciousness. With consciousness comes freedom and responsibility to think and act consciously, and with it, more is required, and therefore, few seek the uncertainty, insecurity, and responsibility that consciousness begets. Jesus said the heart of the law is *mercy* and the spirit of the law is *love*. Jesus confronted the prevailing focus on the letter of the law, with its emphasis on external rituals and behaviors. Many examples of this are found in the authentic saying of Jesus, including his understanding that the Sabbath was made for man (Spirit of the law), not man for the Sabbath (letter of the law). The Spirit of the law recognizes that all fall short of the truth and that the truth is complex, and it requires wisdom to delve and probe and scrutinize truth in self-knowledge and consciousness. As we overcome freedom from fear, we are free to love and show mercy. Pursuing love and mercy sets the stage for lasting transformations of our motives and inclinations. We must sift through our shadowy side of our psyche to be transformed into the image of our Maker. That image is whole, pure, and the complete/whole/holy. God is the Spirit of Truth. The goal of every Christian is to be like Christ. Fourthly, Job's friends take up a condescending tone and posture with Job.

Job is not giving up or willing to accept the trite answers of his friends. He is going to keep on keeping on as he seeks greater heights of consciousness/wisdom.

> And from the center of the circle.
> And he taught us more about living
> Then we ever cared to know
> We came to know the secret
> And we never let it go
> And it was more than being holy
> But it was less than being free.

—Neil Diamond, "Dry Your Eyes"

Then Job answered:

"I have heard many such things; miserable comforters are you all.

Shall windy words have an end? Or what provokes you that you answer?

I also could speak as you do, if you were in my place; I could join words together against you, and shake my head at you.

I could strengthen you with my mouth, and the solace of my lips would assuage your pain.

"If I speak, my pain is not assuaged, and if I forbear, how much of it leaves me?

Surely now God has worn me out; he has made desolate all my company.

And he has shriveled me up, which is a witness against me; and my leanness has risen up against me, it testifies to my face.

He has torn me in his wrath, and hated me; he has gnashed his teeth at me; my adversary sharpens his eyes against me.

Men have gaped at me with their mouth, they have struck me insolently upon the cheek, they mass themselves together against me.

God gives me up to the ungodly, and casts me into the hands of the wicked.

I was at ease, and he broke me asunder; he seized me by the neck and dashed me to pieces; he set me up as his target, his archers surround me. He slashes open my kidneys, and does not spare; he pours out my gall on the ground.

He breaks me with breach upon breach; he runs upon me like a warrior.

I have sewed sackcloth upon my skin, and have laid my strength in the dust.

My face is red with weeping, and on my eyelids is deep darkness; although there is no violence in my hands, and my prayer is pure.

"O earth cover not my blood, and let my cry find no resting place.

Even now, behold, my witness is in heaven, and he that vouches for me is on high.

My friends scorn me; my eye pours out tears to God, that he would maintain the right of a man with God, like that of a man with his neighbor.

For when a few years have come I shall go the way whence I shall not return. (Job 16: 1–22)

My spirit is broken, my days are extinct, the grave is ready for me.

Surely there are mockers about me, and my eye dwells on their provocation.

"Lay down a pledge for me with thyself; who is there that will give surety for me?

Since thou hast closed their minds to understanding, therefore thou wilt not let them triumph.

He who informs against his friends to get a share of their property, the eyes of his children will fail.

"He has made me a byword of the peoples, and I am one before whom men spit.

My eye has grown dim from grief, and all my members are like a shadow.

Upright men are appalled at this, and the innocent stirs himself up against the godless.

Yet the righteous holds to his way, and he that has clean hands grows stronger and stronger.

But you, come on again, all of you, and I shall not find a wise man among you.

My days are past, my plans are broken off, the desires of my heart.

They make night into day; 'The light,' they say, 'is near to the darkness.'

If I look for Sheol as my house, if I spread my couch in darkness, if I say to the pit, 'You are my father,' and to the worm, 'My mother,' or 'My sister,' where then is my hope? Who will see my hope?

Will it go down to the bars of Sheol? Shall we descend together into the dust?" (Job 17:1–16)

Commentary

Job complains to his friends that they have become judgmental and lacking in compassion for his losses and grief. Job confronts his friends with what it would be like for them if they were in his shoes. If only his friends wound go back to those splendid seven days of silence! Job then complains that God has worn him out and forsaken him to ungodly men. His tears are plentiful.

Finally it seems Job has entered his grief as he states he was once at ease, and now God has broken him. He is ready for the grave. He feels rejected not only by his friends but by God as well. Abandoned and forsaken, he is more and more disappointed and at the brink of hopelessness. He goes on to use some humor to express his friends' lack of comfort and some creative metaphors to express God's apparent attack. One of the major problems for Job and all of us is when we are at ease, we become full of compromises, complacency, and laziness. Job's pain and suffering has shaken him out of his life of ease and has broken him of his delusions about his capacities of being in control. It seems without pain, there is no gain—and being at ease seems to invoke indolence where we remain stuck in safe and comfortable routines. Few seem to nurture asceticism and self-discipline on their own, and only after being roused out of our sloth by pain are we stirred to change. Job is caught in the dilemma we all find ourselves in; that is, we usually seek comfort from each other before seeking intimacy with God in the secret places of the heart where solitude and silence can hear the still and quiet voice of God. We can get stuck in social networks where we avoid God. Some of us share too much with others and allow shame and fear to cut us off from God. Of course, some of us share too little with others and get stuck in not reaching out in humility to others and therefore not loving others enough. Living the balance is extremely difficult to navigate. In Job's case, he is wasting his time talking to his friends and would be better served by taking his entire inner life to God in that secret place of his heart or soul.

Let us take an inventory of Job's anguish. Job's children are dead, his career and material security have vanished, his marriage is in shambles, his friends have turned on him, and his body has become full of sores and is a seat of misery. In addition, his faith is in a state of crisis as he feels abandoned by God. He is being tempted to curse God and die, and he has taken an inventory of his past while being visited with dreams that terrify him and that he does not understand. He not only does not understand why God has left him to this horrific fate, he feels attacked by God. He is broken. Yet Job also seems tethered to hope by a tiny thread as he maintains his faith while going through a remarkable expansion of his consciousness. He is closing in on not only on the truth of the human condition but also in on an inner transformations where he becomes one counted as experiencing a second birth. Yet he is unaware of this and is enduring beyond the capacities of any normal person. The stress level and tears are beyond measure, and it really no wonder he wants to die for that would seem the easier way out of all this pain and suffering. He is ready for the grave, and who wouldn't be?

> Tried and tested
> By the tears I've cried
> By the lure of false pride
> By the weight of the choice
> By the still small voice
> By what I haven't met yet.

> —Bruce Cockburn, "Tried and Tested"

Then Job answered:

"How long will you torment me, and break me in pieces with words?

These ten times you have cast reproach upon me; are you not ashamed to wrong me?

And even if it be true that I have erred, my error remains with myself.

If indeed you magnify yourselves against me, and make my humiliation an argument against me, know then that God has put me in the wrong, and closed his net about me.

Behold, I cry out, 'Violence!' but I am not answered; I call aloud, but there is no justice.

He has walled up my way, so that I cannot pass, and he has set darkness upon my paths.

He has stripped from me my glory, and taken the crown from my head.

He breaks me down on every side, and I am gone, and my hope has he pulled up like a tree.

He has kindled his wrath against me, and counts me as his adversary.

His troops come on together; they have cast up siege works against me, and encamp round about my tent.

"He has put my brethren far from me, and my acquaintances are wholly estranged from me.

My kinsfolk and my close friends have failed me; the guests in my house have forgotten me; my maidservants count me as a stranger; I have become an alien in their eyes.

I call to my servant, but he gives me no answer; I must beseech him with my mouth.

I am repulsive to my wife, loathsome to the sons of my own mother.

Even young children despise me; when I rise they talk against me.

All my intimate friends abhor me, and those whom I loved have turned against me.

My bones cleave to my skin and to my flesh, and I have escaped by the skin of my teeth.

Have pity on me, have pity on me, O you my friends, for the hand of God has touched me!

Why do you, like God, pursue me? Why are you not satisfied with my flesh?

"Oh that my words were written! Oh that they were inscribed in a book!

Oh that with an iron pen and lead they were graven in the rock forever!

For I know that my Redeemer lives, and at last he will stand upon the earth; and after my skin has been thus destroyed, then from my flesh I shall see God, whom I shall see on my side, and my eyes shall behold, and not another. My heart faints within me!

If you say, `How we will pursue him!' and, `The root of the matter is found in him'; be afraid of the sword, for wrath brings the punishment of the sword, that you may know there is a judgment." (Job 19:1–29)

Commentary

Verses 1–5

His friends not only are unable to have any compassion, but they scorn, judge, and torment him with their superficial and idle words. If he had erred, then it is his to face and overcome. No one can judge another because none of us has a working understanding of the experiences, motives, pain, and capabilities of another, let alone ourselves! There are so many subtle variations that give form to each complex individual being. We are all an alchemist's mixture of histories: archetypal weaknesses, strengths, feelings, desires, etc. No one who gives this a moment of thought would realize they can put themselves in a position to judge another.

Verses 8–9

Job is left to struggle on alone while being stripped of all earthly glory and attachments. This is characteristic of all contemplatives on their journey toward intimacy, friendship, and union with God. Job has been stripped one cord at a time of all he had previously relied upon, and that is the world's treasures and acclaim. All the cords that have imprisoned him to the world have been cut away, leaving him feeling pilfered and full of grief and confusion. This is as it must be for we cannot serve two masters.

Verses 10–18

Job finally realizes he is utterly alone, rejected, abandoned, and forsaken by his friends, wife, family, acquaintances, servants, guests, and even young children! The saddest truth is many people thrive on others' misfortunes as it takes the focus off them. Hence, so many are interested in sensationalistic journalism, gossip, and any distraction rather than face the painful work of self-knowledge and transformation. It is easy to gossip and hard to steer clear of this poisonous endeavor. We need to make specific choices not to gossip and let that be known when others attempt to draw us into their poisonous intrigues. Job is hurting from others' judgments and abandonment, and we hurt others when we make superficial and impetuous comments about them. There are few things I despise more than gossip. Job is betrayed by everyone. Others are abandoning or sticking it to him. Job is now at the bottom of the proverbial pecking order. We can now add betrayal to the loneliness Job experiences from those of his clan.

Job has also grown beyond his friends and wife. There seems to be a lonely path set aside for those who enter the unknown, whether by choice or circumstance. We all have a unique journey. There seems to be periods in everyone's life who is on the road to enlightenment when no human help or support is there to interfere when God wants to traffic with us alone. This is a lonely and painful path. Job feels abandoned and attacked by God. Jesus was abandoned by everyone and, when on the cross, felt forsaken by God the Father as well. These experiences seem destined for those who seek intimacy with God and are meant to be shared with God alone. Only God can relate to all our needs, pain, feelings, aspirations, etc. Only in companionship with God will we ever be able to reach the deepest recesses of our true inner self and achieve wholeness and union with the divine. However, all suffering is efficacious only when our suffering leads us to an experience with God. Suffering is therefore not an end in itself, but only a means. Suffering opens us up to sharing with God, and this escorts us toward intimacy.

Verses 25–27

Job is desperate and either is grabbing at straws, or he seems to have made a *quantum leap* of faith as he appears to affirm his trust in life after death and the resurrection of the body! *Job's inner life has either been transformed by a personal experience of God's presence and love* (which is the only way Job could have found such assurance that he could make such proclamations of faith), or he is suffering from some self-deceptions and delusions borne from his frantic state of mind. I believe it is some of both as we will see in the continuing text. It seems our consciousness is apt to overcompensate for our pain and panic by grabbing onto whatever hopes it can cling to, yet at the same time, there is real authenticity is this quest out of the anguish of despair. Let there be no mistaking Job's state; he is full of anguish, panic, despair, and whatever other adjectives you want to place here that speak to your heart of Job's present state. The problem with words is they fail to convey the true experiences of the heart, and to try to put ourselves in Job's place is near impossible except for those who have made pain a friend. The fact remains that all contemplatives experience God's presence and love in that secret place of the heart or soul within their inner life in a silence and an aloneness that is ineffable. Job's consciousness and experience has expanded into areas few are even willing to venture. Most of us remain like the initial states of Thomas and Peter after the resurrection; Thomas doubted the proclamation from women and the frightened and ashamed Peter after his denial of Jesus. Both Peter and Thomas were able to overcome their doubts and shame after experiencing God's loving presence. It seems Job is in the process of being transformed by his experience with God in that secret place where God dwells in our psyche.

Some strains of Judaism and Christianity affirm the body while others diminish the flesh. In the purity system, the body is a major detriment to our relationship with God while the gift system recognizes everything that is made is created by God and, therefore, good and a gift. This includes the body and the material universe. Job's sufferings and experiences with God have obviously shifted his values to the more holistic gift system in the context of his body and psyche in his affirmation of life after life.

Some scholars have divided up Judaism and Christianity within two main camps, one the purity system concerned with the law and the separation of God and humans, and two the gift system concerned with love, intimacy, and reconciliation (see Kurt Greenhalgh's *Christian Idolatry/Christian Revival.*

> On the turning away
> From the pale and the downtrodden
> And the words they say
> Which we don't understand
> "Don't accept that what happens
> Is just a case of others suffering
> Or you'll find that you're joining in
> The turning away.
>
> —Pink Floyd, "On the Turning Away"

Then Job answered:

"Listen carefully to my words, and let this be your consolation.

Bear with me, and I will speak, and after I have spoken, mock on.

As for me, is my complaint against man? Why should I not be impatient?

Look at me, and be appalled, and lay your hand upon your mouth.

When I think of it I am dismayed, and shuddering seizes my flesh.

Why do the wicked live, reach old age, and grow mighty in power?

Their children are established in their presence, and their offspring before their eyes.

Their houses are safe from fear, and no rod of God is upon them.

Their bull breeds without fail; their cow calves, and does not cast her calf.

They send forth their little ones like a flock, and their children dance.

They sing to the tambourine and the lyre, and rejoice to the sound of the pipe.

They spend their days in prosperity, and in peace they go down to Sheol.

They say to God, `Depart from us! We do not desire the knowledge of thy ways.

What is the Almighty that we should serve him? And what profit do we get if we pray to him?'

Behold, is not their prosperity in their hand? The counsel of the wicked is far from me.

"How often is it that the lamp of the wicked is put out? That their calamity comes upon them? That God distributes pains in his anger?

That they are like straw before the wind, and like chaff that the storm carries away?

You say, `God stores up their iniquity for their sons.' Let him recompense it to themselves, that they may know it.

Let their own eyes see their destruction, and let them drink of the wrath of the Almighty.

For what do they care for their houses after them, when the number of their months is cut off?

Will any teach God knowledge, seeing that he judges those that are on high?

One dies in full prosperity, being wholly at ease and secure, his body full of fat and the marrow of his bones moist.

Another dies in bitterness of soul, never having tasted of good.

They lie down alike in the dust, and the worms cover them.

"Behold, I know your thoughts, and your schemes to wrong me.

For you say, `Where is the house of the prince? Where is the tent in which the wicked dwelt?'

Have you not asked those who travel the roads, and do you not accept their testimony that the wicked man is spared in the day of calamity, that he is rescued in the day of wrath?

Who declares his way to his face, and who requites him for what he has done?

When he is borne to the grave, watch is kept over his tomb.

The clods of the valley are sweet to him; all men follow after him, and those who go before him are innumerable.

How then will you comfort me with empty nothings? There is nothing left of your answers but falsehood." (Job 21:1–34)

Commentary

Again Job is distracted by his friends, and for the sake of eschewing monotony, I have deleted Job's friends' usual input. Job seems to be temporarily regressing into self-pity and striving to justify himself. We all swing like a pendulum from one position to its opposite, from hope and affirmation to resentments and self-pity—in the blink of an eye. This is customary when accusations fly and explanations are needed and self-justifications rear their ugly heads. This shift in Job's gaze away from God and toward others moves him to self-pity and self-justification. Most of us would not have lasted this long and would have cursed God and be done with all the tension and struggles inherent in faith and suffering. Job questions God's justice in allowing evil to prosper while making him suffer. The question of evil withstanding, Job seems to be drifting into self-pity and resentments. There is nothing like self-pity to set us up to just throw in the towel and give up.

I worked with adolescents where hoop was the joy and passion of their lives and seen firsthand a transformation from attitudes where giving up and losing were tolerated and later rejected. The core group would not take certain players early until they proved their worth by playing hard no matter the score. I have never witnessed a relapse into whatever addictive behavior that was not preceded first by self-pity and her identical twin, resentment. Job's resentments and self-pity are an honest and healthy reaction only if we tarry along with them temporarily. Of course I have experienced the poisonous power of self-pity and resentments in my own life. It's easy to skid backward on the precipice, yet if we accept and take responsibility for this archetypal pattern, it will be less problematic to initiate once more the complex path of repentance, endurance, and acceptance. Regardless, God's grace offers us ample opportunities to face our self-pity and resentments and turn around and embark upon each novel day with a clean slate. The meaning of repentance is to turn around. The only mistakes are not learning from our mistakes for they are part of the bargain of freedom within the human predicament.

We find Job unable to detach from projecting onto God the judgmental, wrathful, and intolerant father archetype. It bears repeating, we have all perceived God from our limited and often infantile perspectives and which are born from negative experiences with the ogre masculine archetype. These infantile projections have nothing to do with God as I have come to understand Him/Her. It seems to me we need to take a more cautious approach to affirming any beliefs we have about God while conceding they will forever remain incomplete. Prepare yourself to be surprised that after death, many of our mistaken impressions will be lovingly corrected. We are often unable to peer outside the box constructed by our projected fears, insecurities, lack of experience, and indolence. However, our constricted worldviews can be expanded if we maintain openness to new experiences. The contemplatives call it having the beginner's mind. We all have assumptions from which we construct our worldviews; our boxes are full of assumptions, some accurate and others not. I believe it is advantageous to remain open to contradictory ideas. One aspect of my faith depends on trusting that God will reveal mysteries when and how She seems fit. This track makes many uncomfortable because faith is often based on the deluded certainty of one's beliefs rather than on God, who will reveal only to the poor in spirit the wisdom of His Kingdom. I've heard it said, "The mind is like a parachute, it only works when open."

> There's nothing here I can understand
> And no one cares I'm a lonely man . . .
>
> I have no name for each and every day
> Until the year is done and fades away . . .
>
> And I,
> I know I'll be all a
> Alone again, alone again tonight oh I'm
> Alone again . . .
>
> —Genesis, "Alone Tonight"

Then Job answered:

"Today also my complaint is bitter, his hand is heavy in spite of my groaning.

Oh, that I knew where I might find him, that I might come even to his seat!

I would lay my case before him and fill my mouth with arguments.

I would learn what he would answer me, and understand what he would say to me.

Would he contend with me in the greatness of his power? No; he would give heed to me.

There an upright man could reason with him, and I should be acquitted for ever by my judge.

"Behold, I go forward, but he is not there; and backward, but I cannot perceive him; on the left hand I seek him, but I cannot behold him; I turn to the right hand, but I cannot see him.

But he knows the way that I take; when he has tried me, I shall come forth as gold.

My foot has held fast to his steps; I have kept his way and have not turned aside.

I have not departed from the commandment of his lips; I have treasured in my bosom the words of his mouth.

But he is unchangeable and who can turn him? What he desires, that he does.

For he will complete what he appoints for me; and many such things are in his mind.

Therefore I am terrified at his presence; when I consider, I am in dread of him.

God has made my heart faint; the Almighty has terrified me; for I am hemmed in by darkness, and thick darkness covers my face. (Job 23: 1–17)

"Why are not times of judgment kept by the Almighty, and why do those who know him never see his days?

Men remove landmarks; they seize flocks and pasture them.

They drive away the ass of the fatherless; they take the widow's ox for a pledge.

They thrust the poor off the road; the poor of the earth all hide themselves.

Behold, like wild asses in the desert they go forth to their toil, seeking prey in the wilderness as food for their children.

They gather their fodder in the field and they glean the vineyard of the wicked man.

They lie all night naked, without clothing, and have no covering in the cold.

They are wet with the rain of the mountains, and cling to the rock for want of shelter.

(There are those who snatch the fatherless child from the breast, and take in pledge the infant of the poor.)

They go about naked, without clothing; hungry, they carry the sheaves; among the olive rows of the wicked they make oil; they tread the wine presses, but suffer thirst.

From out of the city the dying groan, and the soul of the wounded cries for help; yet God pays no attention to their prayer.

"There are those who rebel against the light, who are not acquainted with its ways, and do not stay in its paths.

The murderer rises in the dark, that he may kill the poor and needy; and in the night he is as a thief.

The eye of the adulterer also waits for the twilight, saying, 'No eye will see me'; and he disguises his face.

In the dark they dig through houses; by day they shut themselves up; they do not know the light.

For deep darkness is morning to all of them; for they are friends with the terrors of deep darkness.

"You say, "They are swiftly carried away upon the face of the waters; their portion is cursed in the land; no treader turns toward their vineyards.

Drought and heat snatch away the snow waters; so does Sheol those who have sinned.

The squares of the town forget them; their name is no longer remembered; so wickedness is broken like a tree.'

"They feed on the barren childless woman, and do no good to the widow.

Yet God prolongs the life of the mighty by his power; they rise up when they despair of life.

He gives them security, and they are supported; and his eyes are upon their ways.

They are exalted a little while, and then are
gone; they wither and fade like the mallow; they
are cut off like the heads of grain.

If it is not so, who will prove me a liar, and
show that there is nothing in what I say?" (Job 24:
1–25)

Commentary

I again spare you the monotonous ramblings of his friends. His friends
are like those teachers who repeat lessons by rote, who haven't thought
out the full implications of what they are saying and don't live what
they preach.

Job seems to be feeling incredibly abandoned. God seems to be
blessing the unjust. The experience of abandonment seems to me to be
the most painful and difficult to overcome. The lack of trust this experience occasions opens up like a yawning abyss. The sufferings presented
within the Psalms display wounds so deep it seems even the scars have
their own scars. I can testify to these inner struggles. I love the Psalms
and find so much comfort and shared experience therein. *Healing is a
long and precarious road, and only a few seem willing to do the painful
work that is necessary for the healing process to reach its end, which in
some ways may not even come until after death.* What makes it especially
difficult is abandonment is associated with some form of betrayal—
and if this occurs in childhood, the child naturally blames oneself for
being abandoned. The child is unable to differentiate between his parents and himself while lacking abstract thinking, and therefore, the
child is locked in its own egocentricity, only capable of blaming herself
for being abandoned and/or rejected. Shame then becomes attached
to the abandonment like stink to a monkey, and whenever anything
is perceived as vaguely threatening, the shame and fear of abandonment resurfaces. When this occurs, the person projects into the new

situation and thereby pushes others away—settings themselves up for more abandonment! This blueprint will continue to be drawn until the individual makes a conscious decision to work through it. This task is very difficult when someone believes they are inferior (shame) and deserving of abandonment. This attitude sets one up for additional rejection and blocks the ability to feel the pain and change within the archetypal possibilities. When you're needy, which these individuals inevitably are, it shows. How does one trust in others or God when they feels shame and worthy of abandonment? This becomes a catch-22 for to trust, one must feel loved, and to feel loved, one must trust. Where does one start, and where does it all end?

Job is also upset that the wicked prosper for a while, yet he knows they will not avoid the bitter fruit of their ways and eventually be punished and forgotten.

Job seems to be waiting for an audience with God. He endures painful feelings without giving in to desperate, impetuous, or resentful/self-pitying attitudes. Job is exhibiting the ability to wait and endure the ultimate tests of faith.

They turned their backs
I made it hard
Every place they touched me
Is a laceration now . . .

Derailed and desperate
How did I get here?
Hanging from this high wire
By the tatters of my faith
Sometimes the wind comes out of nowhere and
Knocks you off your feet and look-see my tears-
They fill the whole night sky

—Bruce Cockburn, "The Whole Night Sky"

O gather up the brokenness
And bring it to me now
The fragrance of those

Promises
You never dared to vow . . .

Behold the gates of mercy
In arbitrary space
And none of us deserving
The cruelty or the grace
O solitude of longing
Where love has been confined
Come healing of the body
Come healing of the mind

O see the darkness yielding
That tore the light apart
Come healing of the reason
Come healing of the heart

O troubled dust concealing
An undivided love
The Heart beneath is teaching
To the broken heart above

O let the heavens falter
And let the earth proclaim
Come healing of the Alter
Come healing of the Name.

—Leonard Cohen, "Come Healing"

And Job again took up his discourse, and said:

"As God lives, who has taken away my right, and
the Almighty, who has made my soul bitter; as long
as my breath is in me, and the spirit of God is in
my nostrils; my lips will not speak falsehood, and
my tongue will not utter deceit.

Far be it from me to say that you are right; till
I die I will not put away my integrity from me.

I hold fast my righteousness, and will not let it go; my heart does not reproach me for any of my days.

"Let my enemy be as the wicked, and let him that rises up against me be as the unrighteous. (Job 27:1–7)

Commentary

Job is unwilling to give up his personal struggle to grow in consciousness. Through his trials, he recognizes his need to maintain his integrity rather than feign guilt and end his torment by admitting to something he did wrong and to which he does not understand. The word *integrity* is rooted on the noun *integer*, which means wholeness or completion; therefore to have integrity is to be whole or complete. The word *integrate* comes from the same root. We integrate into the whole and so become individuals with integrity. We do so by knowing with consciousnesses as we talked about earlier and then putting it into practice through grace, obedience, and discipline.

> Oh help me in my weakness
> I heard the drifter say
> As they carried him from the courtroom
> And were taking him away
> My trip hasn't been a pleasant one
> And my time it isn't long
> And I still do not know
> What I have done wrong.
>
> —Bob Dylan, "Drifters Escape"

"But where shall wisdom be found? And where is the place of understanding?

Man does not know the way to it, and it is not found in the land of the living.

The deep says, 'It is not in me,' and the sea says, 'It is not with me.'

It cannot be gotten for gold, and silver cannot be weighed as its price.

It cannot be valued in the gold of Ophir, in precious onyx or sapphire.

Gold and glass cannot equal it, nor can it be exchanged for jewels of fine gold.

No mention shall be made of coral or of crystal; the price of wisdom is above pearls.

The topaz of Ethiopia cannot compare with it, nor can it be valued in pure gold.

"Whence then comes wisdom? And where is the place of understanding?

It is hid from the eyes of all living, and concealed from the birds of the air.

Abaddon and Death say, 'We have heard a rumor of it with our ears.'

"God understands the way to it, and he knows its place.

For he looks to the ends of the earth, and sees everything under the heavens.

When he gave to the wind its weight, and meted out the waters by measure; when he made a decree for the rain, and a way for the lightning of the thunder; then he saw it and declared it; he established it, and searched it out.

And he said to man, 'Behold, the fear of the Lord, that is wisdom; and to depart from evils understanding.'" (Job 28:12–28)

Commentary

Job is hungry and thirsty for wisdom and understanding. And *anyone who seeks sincerely will find!* He realizes it cannot be bought with material things nor is humankind naturally able to easily find it in the land of the living. Job recognizes wisdom is more precious than anything else this life has to offer. Job's thirst for wisdom and inner truth is setting the stage for a response from God that will add to his suffering yet simultaneously pave the way for his longings for wisdom to be satisfied. Job is wise because he seeks wisdom from the source of all wisdom, God. Wisdom is not found in the world of politics or the crowd. He then ends this discourse recognizing wisdom resides in the fear of the Lord and understanding in departing from evil.

> We live in a political world
> Wisdom is thrown into jail
> It rots in a cell
> Is misguided as hell
> Leaving no one to pick up a trail.

—Bob Dylan, "Political World"

And Job again took up his discourse, and said:

"Oh, that I were as in the months of old, as in the days when God watched over me; when his lamp shone upon my head, and by his light I walked through darkness; as I was in my autumn days, when the friendship of God was upon my tent; when the Almighty was yet with me, when my children were about me; when my steps were washed with milk, and the rock poured out for me streams of oil!

When I went out to the gate of the city, when I prepared my seat in the square, the young men saw me and withdrew, and the aged rose and stood; the princes refrained from talking, and laid

370

their hand on their mouth; the voice of the nobles was hushed, and their tongue cleaved to the roof of their mouth. When the ear heard, it called me blessed, and when the eye saw, it approved; because I delivered the poor who cried, and the fatherless who had none to help him.

The blessing of him who was about to perish came upon me, and I caused the widow's heart to sing for joy.

I put on righteousness, and it clothed me; my justice was like a robe and a turban.

I was eyes to the blind, and feet to the lame.

I was a father to the poor, and I searched out the cause of him whom I did not know.

I broke the fangs of the unrighteous, and made him drop his prey from his teeth.

Then I thought, 'I shall die in my nest, and I shall multiply my days as the sand, my roots spread out to the waters, with the dew all night on my branches, my glory fresh with me, and my bow ever new in my hand.'

"Men listened to me, and waited, and kept silence for my counsel.

After I spoke they did not speak again, and my word dropped upon them.

They waited for me as for the rain; and they opened their mouths as for the spring rain.

I smiled on them when they had no confidence; and the light of my countenance they did not cast down.

I chose their way, and sat as chief, and I dwelt like a king among his troops, like one who comforts mourners. (Job 29:1–25)

"But now they make sport of me, men who are younger than I, whose fathers I would have disdained to set with the dogs of my flock.

What could I gain from the strength of their hands, men whose vigor is gone?

Through want and hard hunger they gnaw the dry and desolate ground; they pick mallow and the leaves of bushes, and to warm themselves the roots of the broom.

They are driven out from among men; they shout after them as after a thief.

In the gullies of the torrents they must dwell, in holes of the earth and of the rocks.

Among the bushes they bray; under the nettles they huddle together.

A senseless, a disreputable brood, they have been whipped out of the land.

"And now I have become their song, I am a byword to them.

They abhor me, they keep aloof from me; they do not hesitate to spit at the sight of me.

Because God has loosed my cord and humbled me, they have cast off restraint in my presence.

On my right hand the rabble rise, they drive me forth, they cast up against me their ways of destruction.

They break up my path, they promote my calamity; no one restrains them.

As through a wide breach they come; amid the crash they roll on.

Terrors are turned upon me; my honor is pursued as by the wind, and my prosperity has passed away like a cloud.

"And now my soul is poured out within me; days of affliction have taken hold of me.

The night racks my bones, and the pain that gnaws me takes no rest.

With violence it seizes my garment; it binds me about like the collar of my tunic.

God has cast me into the mire, and I have become like dust and ashes.

I cry to thee and thou dost not answer me; I stand, and thou dost not heed me.

Thou hast turned cruel to me; with the might of thy hand thou dost persecute me.

Thou liftest me up on the wind, thou makest me ride on it, and thou tossest me about in the roar of the storm.

Yea, I know that thou wilt bring me to death, and to the house appointed for all living.

"Yet does not one in a heap of ruins stretch out his hand, and in his disaster cry for help?

Did not I weep for him whose day was hard? Was not my soul grieved for the poor?

But when I looked for good, evil came; and when I waited for light, darkness came.

My heart is in turmoil, and is never still; days of affliction come to meet me.

I go about blackened, but not by the sun; I stand up in the assembly, and cry for help.

I am a brother of jackals, and a companion of ostriches.

My skin turns black and falls from me, and my bones burn with heat.

My lyre is turned to mourning, and my pipe to the voice of those who weep. (Job 30:1–31)

"I have made a covenant with my eyes; how then could I look upon a virgin?

What would be my portion from God above, and my heritage from the Almighty on high?

Does not calamity befall the unrighteous, and disaster the workers of iniquity?

Does not he see my ways, and number all my steps?

"If I have walked with falsehood, and my foot has hastened to deceit; (Let me be weighed in a just balance, and let God know my integrity!) if my step has turned aside from the way, and my heart has gone after my eyes, and if any spot has cleaved to my hands; then let me sow, and another eat; and let what grows for me be rooted out.

"If my heart has been enticed to a woman, and I have lain in wait at my neighbor's door; then let my wife grind for another, and let others bow down upon her.

For that would be a heinous crime; that would be an iniquity to be punished by the judges; for that would be a fire which consumes unto Abaddon, and it would burn to the root all my increase.

"If I have rejected the cause of my manservant or my maidservant, when they brought a complaint against me; what then shall I do when God rises up? When he makes inquiry, what shall I answer him?

Did not he who made me in the womb make him? And did not one fashion us in the womb?

"If I have withheld anything that the poor desired, or have caused the eyes of the widow to fail, or have eaten my morsel alone, and the fatherless has not eaten of it (for from his youth I reared him as a father, and from his mother's womb I guided him); if I have seen any one perish for lack of clothing, or a poor man without covering; if his loins have not blessed me, and if he was not warmed with the fleece of my sheep; if I have raised my hand against the fatherless, because I saw help in the gate; then let my shoulder blade fall from my shoulder, and let my arm be broken from its socket.

For I was in terror of calamity from God, and I could not have faced his majesty.

"If I have made gold my trust, or called fine gold my confidence; if I have rejoiced because my wealth was great, or because my hand had gotten much; if I have looked at the sun when it shone, or the moon moving in splendor, and my heart has been secretly enticed, and my mouth has kissed my hand; this also would be an iniquity to be punished by the judges, for I should have been false to God above.

"If I have rejoiced at the ruin of him that hated me, or exulted when evil overtook him (I have not let my mouth sin by asking for his life with a curse); if the men of my tent have not said, 'Who is there that has not been filled with his meat?' (the sojourner has not lodged in the street; I have opened my doors to the wayfarer); if I have concealed my transgressions from men, by hiding my iniquity in my bosom, because I stood in great fear of the multitude, and the contempt of families terrified me, so that I kept silence, and did not go out of doors—Oh, that I had one to hear me! (Here is my signature! let the Almighty answer me!) Oh, that I had the indictment written by my adversary! Surely I would carry it on my shoulder; I would bind it on me as a crown; I would give him an account of all my steps; like a prince I would approach him.

"If my land has cried out against me, and its furrows have wept together; if I have eaten its yield without payment, and caused the death of its owners; let thorns grow instead of wheat, and foul weeds instead of barley." The words of Job are ended. (Job: 31:1–40)

Commentary

Job begins this section longing for the days when he felt close to God in their friendship while his family was about him and his status secure as a compassionate and respected member of society. Job's tone changes as he seems to enter a period full of self-pity, resentment, and self-righteously justifying himself by listing off his good deeds and talking about his disdain for the fathers of some young people who spit at the sight of him. Job's suffering has evoked and exposed his ultimate self-deceptions and missing the mark, that is his arrogance and disdain for certain people. The dross in Job's character—a disdain toward others, which belies arrogance, is brought out in the open only through his suffering. Job's suffering has stoked the kiln that purges his character of his concealed arrogance and paves the way for a true humility, which is love's essential companion. All this is borne from his grief and losses, depression and despair, and perhaps if his friends had a touch of psychological acumen and spiritual maturity, they could have been God's agents of transformation. They theoretically could have had compassion for Job's pain and then confronted his self-concealed arrogance/disdain for others after it made its appearance. This presupposes his friends would have gone through enough experiential suffering of their own that they were free of an inordinate amount of self-deception and arrogance and capable of humility to confront first their own character defects and then Job's. However, his friends' self-deception and lack of wisdom/love prevent them from ferrying Job to the truth that he has a judgmental, arrogant side to his character. His friends have yet to take the log out of their own eyes so they could see the speck in Job's.

Job's self-image prior to encountering God is as follows: his life has been a book of virtues with integrity and compassion toward most of his fellows. It's worth saying it is easy to be magnanimous when you are rich and others respect, like, and value your contributions. Job is basically a sincere person who values integrity and truth. It is precisely these true qualities in Job that provide God with fertile ground to sow some really extraordinary seeds as Job's hidden defects are exposed, which will make him lead toward intimacy and union with God and wholeness.

The crux of Job's complaint seems very reasonable on the surface. However, Job's suffering manifests finally for the first time a negative aspect of his personality; he is full of judgments, self-righteousness, and inflation. All along, Job has harbored judgmental and arrogant attitudes toward certain people, and only now that he is suffering has he reached a pinnacle; they come to the surface. Job is scornful of those he believes are inferior to him. The reality is each and every one of us are at different levels of maturity and self-awareness, but the attitude that is required is humility and one of service, not disdain and scorn!

Job exhibits his inflation when he talks about how everyone used to be in awe of him and seek his counsel and how reliant he obviously became on this for him to *feel secure and self-worth.* His insecurity is evident in his feeling others and God have abandoned him. He seems to be externalizing or projecting evil in that it is residing in others but not himself! Evil resides in all of us, and it is in the projection of the evil within us onto our neighbors that circulates evil the world over. *None of us is perfect.* Job has become unconscious of a subtle inflation within himself as he continues to deny his shadow. As in Proverbs, pride comes before a fall, and now we are moving into the territory where Job will make his transformation from egocentric attitudes toward truth-centric attitudes. *If we ignore chapter 30, the crux of Job's complaint seems very reasonable.* However, Job in his egocentric state is focusing only his consciousness on his righteousness while ignoring his shadow. *We can see Job's shadow clearly when he talks about the children of individuals he would have disdained.* He also belittles these youth and calls them a disreputable brood—those with a bad reputation. Job is unconscious of his shadow. It will be interesting that in the next section, it is a youth that comes to ferry Job's life into wholeness. From the standpoint of his conscious attitudes uncovered in chapters 29 and 31, he only is aware of how he has helped the oppressed. However, chapter 30 displays an unconscious side that Job is totally unaware of. He is no longer compassionate but judgmental and arrogant toward a particular group and their "bad reputations." Therefore, his unconscious mind discloses a side to him, which is unrighteous. Everything temporal in nature casts shadows, whether we speak of external or internal realities. Job must integrate his shadow; that is accepting painful truths about himself that he has kept buried out of fear of facing these painful truths consciously. This is a very difficult process. Job is not righteous because no man is.

Psychologically, projecting our shadow also includes projecting godlike qualities onto others. When they inevitably fall short of these unrealistic projections and expectations, we often begin to dislike them. This is what is generally meant by transference. The latter is what is called negative transference and the former, positive transference. With positive transference, we need heroes (celebrities, parents, politicians, religious leaders, etc.) for the purpose of extracting security and self-worth; hence, the cults of personalities. It seems from our text, Job was an object of positive transference reflected in chapter 29. When we turn on our heroes, we simply transfer the positive transference to a negative one. People indeed turn on Job following his personal losses. Job becomes the archetype of the scapegoat and mocked hero as he is a precursor to Jesus's experience of the passion. Both Jesus and Job are examples of positive and negative transference in the collective psyches of the world.

When Jesus came into Jerusalem on Palm Sunday, he was greeted with praise and a lot of hoopla, but not unlike Job, it took only a week later before he was turned on, mocked, and ridiculed and crucified. Jesus knew men's hearts too well to be seduced by man's double-mindedness while Job laments his lost status. We talked earlier of manna personalities, and these folks are always going to be a lightning rod to others for positive and negative transference as long as others project their inner psyche onto the external world.

As I discussed earlier, God is taking the adversarial position with Job and exposing the other side to Job's character hidden from him. Jacob Boehme expounded the notion that God wrestles with the opposites within His being as well (*Science, Meaning, and Evolution: The Cosmology of Jacob Boehme* by Basarab Nicolescu). God and Satan represent an opposite or adversarial position within Job. Therefore, God is exposing Job to all his suffering with the intent to guide Job to a greater wholeness. God is aware and wrestles with the inner struggle of *all* the opposites. God is both prosecutor and defense attorney. This is surely speculative, yet it has a ring of truth for me due to the fact God shares in all our struggles and experiences.

Meister Eckhart discusses God's sharing with us everything in *The Talks of Instruction* when he says, "However great your suffering may be, if it passes through God, then he must first endure it." If God must endure everything we go through, then surely God must know of the inner tension and struggle we go through when we wrestle with any and all the pairs of opposites. Therefore, God exposes Job to God's own experiences, the experiences of contrasts. There is no joy without sadness, no heat without cold, etc. Job is the reluctant recipient of experiencing life's contrasts; in Job's case, he went from having everything to nothing and had to face and endure a look into his nature and find out about his character defects before experiencing healing and oneness with God.

One more note on positive and negative transference. Job is no longer carrying in his personality all the power the average person needs to feel worth and security by being somehow associated with a cult and/or charismatic figure. Human nature is such that we will seek a new hero or have the present hero reestablished. The awe and deference we pay to celebrities continue the dynamic where we hide behind someone rather than take on the responsibility for ourselves and seek the only being capable of fulfilling our needs for security and worth— that is God within ourselves. Hero worship is so prevalent; whenever a celebrity brushes our experience, most of us run to tell everyone who will listen about our encounter, as if the very sight of someone has any real significance in its own right. In addition, the sort of people we make into celebrities these days is pathetic! With a moment's thought, we would never in our right mind admire many of these figures, but rather pity them. This entire dynamic speaks of our need for a *higher power*.

The few creative types who confront convention often become their own higher power. They need to defend their theories/creations because they have become their own higher powers; this is the ultimate inflation of ego-consciousness. We long to be connected to a higher purpose from which we gain security, meaning, and a sense of worth. From this standpoint, the need itself is legitimate and normal. It seems to me the problem is we often venture into all the wrong places *for our aims are temporal.*

As we discussed in chapter 7, any temporal attachment that becomes a source of worth and security and passes away is a living lie that we are living unfortunately. It is also usually a sincere delusion; that is the person believes the lie and often is not even aware of this! Self-deception runs deep in our psyche and culture (chapter 8). The desire for the eternal is projected onto temporal objects or ideologies. We can recognize this when individuals become fanatical with some cause or another. A fanatic is someone who projects their spiritual needs onto a temporal aim. It's as if the spiritual portion of their souls is activated and seeks a release. Unfortunately, these temporal aims become more and more dysfunctional as the person continues to avoid their spiritual natures by projecting them onto these temporal aims. The reason they are so fanatical is their spiritual energy builds while becoming focused on theses temporal ideologies or objects (aims). They have the psychological need of their beliefs and values to be true so they can be justified and secure in their aims. These aims provide meaning and purpose. The more fanatical, the less secure the individual feels with these temporal aims. In other words, their spirituality is activated and seeks integration in something truly higher than themselves. When spirituality is activated and then responded to appropriately, its integration is born out in the fruits of openness, true humility, and inner peace.

Over many years, I have shared with my clients that the measure of what they are living for is authentic to the degree it opens them up to the complexities of life and where all things are valued. This includes the positive and negative energies: pain and joy, life and death, beauty and the ugly, strength and weakness, power and powerlessness, adequacy and inadequacy, wisdom and mystery, confusion and insight, etc.

In contrast to the dynamics of self-justification, defensiveness, self-deception, temporal aims, and projecting evil onto others, I am reminded of one of my favorite Greek myths, that is the one concerning Orestes. He was caught in a paradox of morality. Orestes was a tragic figure who chose not to project his own evil onto others. His mother and her new lover killed his father (Agamemnon), and he was wedged between two conflicting moral imperatives. On the one hand, for the Greeks, justice is served in that one is required to avenge the death by killing the perpetrator if someone murders either of your parents. In addition, for the Greeks, everyone is forbidden to commit matricide. In Orestes's situation, his father is murdered by his mother and her lover. What is he to do? He is put in an impossible situation like we all are with the endless pairs of opposites hidden within our psyches where we are required to choose to maintain both pairs within us while choosing one pair at a certain stages in our development. He chooses to kill his mother and her lover. I would always choose the opposite myself for I believe committing violence upon another, especially killing another human being, is wrong, and his decision seems erroneous. Love is the sacred code by which I live by, and I don't see murder and killing and violence as loving acts.

This begs the question of what to do with Hitler, who rose to so much power to obliterate others and the truth on a massive scale and who authored one of the worst periods in human history. I believe I would have been willing to participate in a plan to kidnap him if the opportunity presented itself and try to render his power impotent. That would assume I had those kinds of skills, which I don't. I do believe in rendering violent people unable to perpetrate their violence on others, and this does include some forms of force. Where I draw the line between force and violence is one I can't answer adequately at this juncture. I don't put myself in situations that are likely to produce violence, but I have been in work situations where I was required to use force to restrain those who could harm themselves or others. However, I believe this use of force must be used with great care and thoughtfulness and is easily abused.

But I'd like to get back to what I think are the meanings and implications of the myth. After Orestes is accused of his guilt of matricide, he unpredictably does not defend himself to the gods but accepts responsibility. Eventually, the gods were so impressed with his willingness to face the consequences of his actions, he was immortalized and taken in to live with them on Mount Olympus. This myth demonstrates a complex truth; that is whenever we make a decision, we choose half the truth while the other is neglected in the choice. The choice that we reject also demands to be integrated. Orestes may have spared his mother in a different set of circumstances. The evil is when we make out of a particular choice a one-sided universal. The only way out of this dilemma is to hold up in painful awareness the paradox and be willing to choose both possibilities. A given situation will dictate the proper choice. I try to nurture an ability to hold the pair of opposites together in their natural tension, suspending the decision until the last possible moment. If this can be integrated, it encompasses courage of the highest order. There are universal principles that dictate given choices; that is love/compassion. Loving compassion enjoins us to place the other person's spiritual needs and ours above all else, no matter what the cost. This is one of the incremental steps we have to take toward wholeness. It is worth noting no one will ever achieve complete wholeness or completeness in this temporal world of space and time. That does not deter us from plowing forward, ever pursuing perfection while knowing it is impossible to achieve. As I discussed in the introduction and chapter 10, the pairs of opposites are the breath of life within us and seem to be what anchors the psyche together. Orestes exhibits an attitude of wholeness when assuming responsibility regardless of the paradox, eschewing the defensiveness displayed by Job in his projections, self-justifications, self-pity. Orestes accepted his fate as part and parcel of his true self. We are our fate combined with the choices we ultimately formulate.

> When the secrets are all told
> And the pedals unfold
> When there was no dream of mine
> You dreamed of me.

—Grateful Dead, "Attics of My Life"

So these three men ceased to answer Job, because he was righteous in his own eyes.
Then Eli'hu the son of Bar'achel the Buzite, of the family of Ram, became angry. He was angry at Job because he justified himself rather than God; he was angry also at Job's three friends because they had found no answer, although they had declared Job to be in the wrong.

Now Eli'hu had waited to speak to Job because they were older than he.

And when Eli'hu saw that there was no answer in the mouth of these three men, he became angry.

And Eli'hu the son of Bar'achel the Buzite answered: "I am young in years, and you are aged; therefore I was timid and afraid to declare my opinion to you.

I said, `let days speak, and many years teach wisdom.'

But it is the spirit in a man, the breath of the Almighty, that makes him understand.

It is not the old that are wise, nor the aged that understand what is right.

Therefore I say, `Listen to me; let me also declare my opinion.'

"Behold, I waited for your words, I listened for your wise sayings, while you searched out what to say.

I gave you my attention, and, behold, there was none that confuted Job, or that answered his words, among you.

Beware lest you say, `We have found wisdom; God may vanquish him, not man.'

He has not directed his words against me, and I will not answer him with your speeches.

"They are discomfited, they answer no more; they have not a word to say.

And shall I wait, because they do not speak, because they stand there, and answer no more?

I also will give my answer; I also will declare my opinion.

For I am full of words, the spirit within me constrains me.

Behold, my heart is like wine that has no vent; like new wineskins, it is ready to burst.

I must speak, that I may find relief; I must open my lips and answer.

I will not show partiality to any person or use flattery toward any man.

For I do not know how to flatter, else would my Maker soon put an end to me. (Job 32:1–22)

"But now, hear my speech, O Job, and listen to all my words.

Behold, I open my mouth; the tongue in my mouth speaks.

My words declare the uprightness of my heart, and what my lips know they speak sincerely.

The spirit of God has made me, and the breath of the Almighty gives me life.

Answer me, if you can; set your words in order before me; take your stand.

Behold, I am toward God as you are; I too was formed from a piece of clay.

Behold, no fear of me need terrify you; my pressure will not be heavy upon you.

"Surely, you have spoken in my hearing, and I have heard the sound of your words.

You say, `I am clean, without transgression; I am pure, and there is no iniquity in me.

Behold, he finds occasions against me, he counts me as his enemy; he puts my feet in the stocks, and watches all my paths.'

"Behold, in this you are not right. I will answer you. God is greater than man.

Why do you contend against him, saying, `He will answer none of my words'?

For God speaks in one way, and in two, though man does not perceive it.

In a dream, in a vision of the night, when deep sleep falls upon men, while they slumber on their beds, then he opens the ears of men, and terrifies them with warnings, that he may turn man aside from his deed, and cut off pride from man; he keeps back his soul from the Pit, his life from perishing by the sword.

"Man is also chastened with pain upon his bed, and with continual strife in his bones; so that his life loathes bread, and his appetite dainty food.

His flesh is so wasted away that it cannot be seen; and his bones which were not seen stick out.

His soul draws near the Pit, and his life to those who bring death.

If there be for him an angel, a mediator, one of the thousand, to declare to man what is right for him; and he is gracious to him, and says, `Deliver him from going down into the Pit, I have found a ransom; let his flesh become fresh with youth; let him return to the days of his youthful vigor'; then man prays to God, and he accepts him, he comes into his presence with joy. He recounts to men his salvation, and he sings before men, and says: `I sinned and perverted what was right, and it was not requited to me.

He has redeemed my soul from going down into the Pit, and my life shall see the light.'

"Behold, God does all these things, twice, three times, with a man, to bring back his soul from the Pit, that he may see the light of life.

Give heed, O Job, listen to me; be silent, and I will speak.

If you have anything to say, answer me; speak, for I desire to justify you.

If not, listen to me; be silent, and I will teach you wisdom." (Job 33:1–33)

Then Eli'hu said:

"Hear my words, you wise men, and give ear to me, you who know; for the ear tests words as the palate tastes food.

Let us choose what is right; let us determine among ourselves what is good.

For Job has said, `I am innocent, and God has taken away my right; in spite of my right I am counted a liar; my wound is incurable, though I am without transgression.'

What man is like Job, who drinks up scoffing like water, who goes in company with evildoers and walks with wicked men?

For he has said, `It profits a man nothing that he should take delight in God.'

"Therefore, hear me, you men of understanding, far be it from God that he should do wickedness, and from the Almighty that he should do wrong.

For according to the work of a man he will requite him, and according to his ways he will make it befall him.

Of a truth, God will not do wickedly, and the Almighty will not pervert justice.

Who gave him charge over the earth and who laid on him the whole world?

If he should take back his spirit to himself, and gather to himself his breath, all flesh would perish together, and man would return to dust.

"If you have understanding, hear this; listen to what I say.

Shall one who hates justice govern? Will you condemn him who is righteous and mighty, who says to a king, `Worthless one,' and to nobles, `Wicked man'; who shows no partiality to princes, nor regards the rich more than the poor, for they are all the work of his hands?

In a moment they die; at midnight the people are shaken and pass away, and the mighty are taken away by no human hand.

"For his eyes are upon the ways of a man, and he sees all his steps.

There is no gloom or deep darkness where evildoers may hide themselves.

For he has not appointed a time for any man to go before God in judgment.

He shatters the mighty without investigation, and sets others in their place.

Thus, knowing their works, he overturns them in the night, and they are crushed.

He strikes them for their wickedness in the sight of men, because they turned aside from following him, and had no regard for any of his ways, so that they caused the cry of the poor to come to him, and he heard the cry of the afflicted— When he is quiet, who can condemn? When he hides his face, who can behold him, whether it be a nation or a man? that a godless man should not reign, that he should not ensnare the people.

"For has any one said to God, `I have borne chastisement; I will not offend any more; teach me what I do not see; if I have done iniquity, I will do it no more'?

Will he then make requital to suit you, because you reject it? For you must choose, and not I; therefore declare what you know.

Men of understanding will say to me, and the wise man who hears me will say: `Job speaks without knowledge, his words are without insight.'

Would that Job were tried to the end, because he answers like wicked men.

For he adds rebellion to his sin; he claps his hands among us, and multiplies his words against God." (Job 34:1–37)

And Eli'hu said:

"Do you think this to be just? Do you say, `It is my right before God,' that you ask, `What advantage have I? How am I better off than if I had sinned?'

I will answer you and your friends with you. Look at the heavens, and see; and behold the clouds, which are higher than you.

If you have sinned, what do you accomplish against him? And if your transgressions are multiplied, what do you do to him?

If you are righteous, what do you give to him; or what does he receive from your hand?

Your wickedness concerns a man like yourself, and your righteousness a son of man.

"Because of the multitude of oppressions people cry out; they call for help because of the arm of the mighty.

But none says, `Where is God my Maker, who gives songs in the night, who teaches us more than the beasts of the earth, and makes us wiser than the birds of the air?'

There they cry out, but he does not answer, because of the pride of evil men.

Surely God does not hear an empty cry, nor does the Almighty regard it.

How much less when you say that you do not see him, that the case is before him, and you are waiting for him!

And now, because his anger does not punish, and he does not greatly heed transgression, Job opens his mouth in empty talk, he multiplies words without knowledge." (Job 35:1–16)

And Eli'hu continued, and said:

"Bear with me a little, and I will show you, for I have yet something to say on God's behalf.

I will fetch my knowledge from afar, and ascribe righteousness to my Maker.

For truly my words are not false; one who is perfect in knowledge is with you.

"Behold, God is mighty, and does not despise any; he is mighty in strength of understanding.

He does not keep the wicked alive, but gives the afflicted their right.

He does not withdraw his eyes from the righteous, but with kings upon the throne he sets them for ever, and they are exalted.

And if they are bound in fetters and caught in the cords of affliction, then he declares to them their work and their transgressions, that they are behaving arrogantly.

He opens their ears to instruction, and commands that they return from iniquity.

If they hearken and serve him, they complete their days in prosperity, and their years in pleasantness.

But if they do not hearken, they perish by the sword, and die without knowledge.

"The godless in heart cherish anger; they do not cry for help when he binds them.

They die in youth, and their life ends in shame.

He delivers the afflicted by their affliction, and opens their ear by adversity.

He also allured you out of distress into a broad place where there was no cramping, and what was set on your table was full of fatness.

"But you are full of the judgment on the wicked; judgment and justice seize you.

Beware lest wrath entice you into scoffing; and let not the greatness of the ransom turn you aside.

Will your cry avail to keep you from distress, or all the force of your strength?

Do not long for the night, when peoples are cut off in their place.

Take heed, do not turn to iniquity, for this you have chosen rather than affliction.

Behold, God is exalted in his power; who is a teacher like him?

Who has prescribed for him his way, or who can say, 'Thou hast done wrong'?

"Remember to extol his work, of which men have sung.

All men have looked on it; man beholds it from afar.

Behold, God is great, and we know him not; the number of his years is unsearchable.

For he draws up the drops of water, he distils his mist in rain which the skies pour down, and drop upon man abundantly.

Can any one understand the spreading of the clouds, the thunderings of his pavilion?

Behold, he scatters his lightning about him, and covers the roots of the sea.

For by these he judges peoples; he gives food in abundance.

He covers his hands with the lightning, and commands it to strike the mark.

Its crashing declares concerning him, who is jealous with anger against iniquity. (Job 36:1–33)

"At this also my heart trembles, and leaps out of its place.

Hearken to the thunder of his voice and the rumbling that comes from his mouth.

Under the whole heaven he lets it go, and his lightning to the corners of the earth.

After it his voice roars; he thunders with his majestic voice and he does not restrain the lightnings when his voice is heard.

God thunders wondrously with his voice; he does great things which we cannot comprehend.

For to the snow he says, `Fall on the earth'; and to the shower and the rain, `Be strong.'

He seals up the hand of every man, that all men may know his work.

Then the beasts go into their lairs, and remain in their dens.

From its chamber comes the whirlwind, and cold from the scattering winds.

By the breath of God ice is given, and the broad waters are frozen fast.

He loads the thick cloud with moisture; the clouds scatter his lightning.

They turn round and round by his guidance, to accomplish all that he commands them on the face of the habitable world.

Whether for correction, or for his land, or for love, he causes it to happen.

"Hear this, O Job; stop and consider the wondrous works of God.

Do you know how God lays his command upon them, and causes the lightning of his cloud to shine?

Do you know the balancings of the clouds, the wondrous works of him who is perfect in knowledge, you whose garments are hot when the earth is still because of the south wind?

Can you, like him, spread out the skies, hard as a molten mirror?

Teach us what we shall say to him; we cannot draw up our case because of darkness.

Shall it be told him that I would speak? Did a man ever wish that he would be swallowed up?

"And now men cannot look on the light when it is bright in the skies, when the wind has passed and cleared them.

Out of the north comes golden splendor; God is clothed with terrible majesty.

The Almighty—we cannot find him; he is great in power and justice, and abundant righteousness he will not violate.

Therefore men fear him; he does not regard any who are wise in their own conceit." (Job 37:1–24)

Commentary

Prior to Job meeting God, there is a fourth friend who makes an appearance, Eli'hu. Edward F. Edinger makes a solid case that Job's fourth friend is his fourth function, in which, "Job's totality has finally been constellated" (Edward F. Edinger, *Ego and Archetype*).

Here is a brief review from chapter 3. Jung identified the four conscious functions as follows: sensing (tells us something is there), thinking (tells us what it is), feeling (tells us what its value is), and intuition (tells us about possibility and gives us a sense of where something was, is, and is headed). The four functions are set up as two pairs of opposites with one being thinking/feeling and the other sensing/intuition. In addition, we are born with one superior function in which we usually make our living, and the opposite function is our inferior function. Further, he believed we integrate the auxiliary functions (the pair of opposites that do not contain our superior or inferior ones) before we are in a position to integrate our inferior function. The few who reach this level of maturity do not necessarily integrate the fourth function, but the possibility exists that we may bring the inferior function into actuality and therefore moves closer to wholeness. However, this is very rare.

But Job is just such a person, and we are allowed a unique peek into this process—from something that had its roots three to four thousand years ago! The fourth function evokes our totality, but it arrives in the form of exacerbating weakness, inadequacy, and humiliation. This is the main reason it makes its appearance in the suffering of the individual and in the manifestation of a youth or some other unlikely source, anything which evokes disgust and ridicule within us. This fourth friend, Eli'hu, is indeed young. Percival was also one such character in the myths of King Arthur; he was ridiculed when he first sought knighthood, but after attaining knighthood, he was the only knight to find the Holy Grail and therefore restore wholeness, health, and peace to the kingdom. My premise is Job's inferior function is intuition.

The appearance of Eli'hu and therefore Job's fourth function is a prelude to God's direct contact in the next section and exhibits itself as a warning to Job's consciousness by compensation for his *inflation* (Job 37:23–24). Job is full of judgment toward the wicked, which he presumes to know who they are (36:17). He also seems to long for the night, when peoples are cut off in their place (36:20). Where there is a lack of mercy toward others, there is always some form of inflation. Job's fourth function of intuition is his connection to God par excellence as it is for all of us. And God is aware of Job's conceit, and his fourth function contains a maze of perplexity, embarrassment, uncertainty, awkwardness, inadequacy, failure, and suffering precisely because this function is outside conscious control. Few ever are able to integrate this into their psyche's economy due to the suffering and anguish it entails. Job is in the process of this very Sisyphean labor, which is to bring forth this fourth function into consciousness. It is the inferior function, and in Job's case, intuition, which brings out the worst in him because it is firmly entrenched in the unconscious. Job must be humbled by being taken out of his self-deception and inflation in his attitudes toward others for an essential part of him lacks compassion and mercy for others on a fundamental level. The ego is stripped of all illusions as to its power and emptied *so God can fill with it with the light of his truths.* This is exactly what is happening to Job. These unconscious contents also express themselves in his night dreams and visions. It is with the activation of the fourth function that God confronts us/Job with the darkest and central weaknesses intrinsic in our ego-consciousness. These are all the unlived aspects in our personality and, in Job's case, the subtle inflation within Job's ego-consciousness. It seems to me everyone's fourth function will evoke a reckoning with some aspect of inflation because it is here where all control is lost, and we are emptied of all the illusions of the ego's ability to stand alone.

This young friend recounts how dreams/visions compensate for Job's/our lack of wholeness. His main message to Job is that no one can set himself up with arrogance before the majesty and power of God and judge our fellows. As I alluded to earlier, the inferior function always comes in the guise of something or someone who is a fool, young, inexperienced, etc. This is because the fourth function appears as a weak figure in comparison to our normal ego-body-consciousness with all its illusions of control. The activation of the fourth function only occurs in those who have integrated the first three conscious functions. The appearance of the fourth function never appears prior to midlife and often much later. It can remain with us for the remainder of our lives, depending on whether we succeed in integrating this inferior function. We are subject to all sorts of humiliating desires and behaviors, attitudes, and beliefs during this time period. We, along with Job, are lost and completely inadequate and unable to integrate the inferior function without outside aid. Job's journey is that of the heroes' journey, and it is within hero myths the world over that a wise man in the guise of a fool comes and guides him at that precise moment after one is humbled and left inadequate. The time is ripe for self-emptying so God can fill the vacuum. Only then can inner peace, joy, and wholeness ever be achieved. This pattern is contained in all the mystical aspects within each wisdom tradition where intimacy and union with God is achieved.

This is precisely what is in the process of occurring within Job. Unlived aspects of Job's nature are being experienced in his struggle with God! Job is being initiated into God's being with intimacy, friendship, and real union where humans become one with God through affliction and adversity (Job 36:15). This initiation seems crazy and unjust to the rational mind and the other three conscious functions that have been brought under our control by our ego. This is, in my opinion, why the book of Job has been so misinterpreted by so many who has taken the time to read it. Most believe Job was a righteous man. *He was on the surface and is when judged from the perspective of the first three conscious functions* but hidden within his nature, and these three conscious functions are crucial shortcoming and self-deceptions and inflations, which only his afflictions and adversity could evoke within his self-awareness and consciousness. When we integrate the truths that we are all dying and suffering in this earthly existence, the inclinations toward judging another disappear and are replaced with compassion born of the passion of suffering within the psyche of the individual.

Job's egocentric state of consciousness must die, and a new one must be born. A second birth is occurring right before our eyes as we work our way through the text of Job. There is a fundamental disparity between human's psyche (soul) and spirit and God's Spirit. While human's spirit is made in God's image, our soul is often at odds with our and God's Spirit precisely because it assumes it is the center of our entire personality. The essence of this union is our spirit, and God's becoming *one while the soul (psyche) is the middle precinct where the war is fought. The soul stands between Spirit and the flesh/body.* The psyche is then the receptacle of this union with God *and* the active agent in its transformation. *Psyche or soul is therefore the nexus of being and both a noun and verb.* Job's and our soul is where the war is fought, won or lost. The soul can experience wholeness in a balance of spirit and flesh—our spirit and God's. The soul is redeemed and transformed where God's Spirit and our spirit come to the surface through the window of the soul. This process takes discipline and failure, struggle and success, pain and much adversity and affliction!

Job's fourth friend is a prelude to God's disciplining Job due to Job's inflated consciousness. Henceforth, a new set of priorities and values that provide meaning heretofore unknown to his conscious ego will come to the surface and take over Job's consciousness. This fourth function is Job's intuition and, when integrated, is humble, meek, sincere, merciful/compassionate/, and direct in sharing the truth (32:6–8, 21–22). As painful as the fourth function is in its relationship to ego-consciousness, it speaks the truth in love. Job must digest some humble pie before *the truth sets him free!* It is the inexperience and weakness of our fourth function that speaks true wisdom (32:6–10). Again, the fourth function in Job is intuition speaking through this fourth friend and is affirming that weakness is essential for God's power to be made manifest: "My grace is sufficient for you, for my power is made perfect in weakness" (2 Corinthians 12:9). Job will need to live these new truths before the truth ultimately sets him free from all fear and fantasy and move him toward that place where all peace and wholeness/holiness and joy intersect.

God speaks through many forms, and Job's fourth friend emphasizes that God speaks directly through the unconscious in the forms of dreams and visions. Dreams are a direct way to hear the wisdom of God. God sends dreams to warn us of misguided attitudes, beliefs, and behaviors. God disciplines us in grace through pain and strife, redeeming us and keeping us from falling into the pit (33:19–24, 28). We are instructed, and a portion of discipline is always painful. God instructs and wishes to see truth in the inner being of his creatures. This is stated quite elegantly by the Psalmist in Psalm 139: 23–24: "Search me, O God, and know my heart! Try me and know my thought! And see if there is any wicked way in me, and lead me in the way of everlasting!" Or again in Psalm 51: 9–10, 16-17: "Behold thou desires truth in the inward being; therefore teach me wisdom in my secret heart. For though hast no delight in sacrifice; were I to give a burnt offering, thou wouldst not be pleased. The sacrifice acceptable to God is a broken spirit; a humble and contrite heart."

The text goes on, and the fourth friend talks about how God responds to those that seek him in prayer by visiting upon us His presence with joy (33:26). This joy comes in two different forms and times. Initially, when a person experiences an encounter with God's love and mercy, joy and gratitude results from the realization that God exists. The second type of joy comes only after a long period of discipline, adversity, and affliction accompanied with feelings of abandonment.

However, with it also comes with a sense of serenity, security, and worth no man can take away.

In addition, Job's fourth function/friend proclaims God is just, demonstrating no partiality toward the rich and famous; in fact, God hears the voices of those afflicted (34:17–33). His fourth friend also confronts Job's self-pity (35:1–16). God confronts evil because he loves each of us unconditionally with the caveat that he rejects the evil within us. He attempts to humble us for the purpose of drawing us back from our iniquity (36:5–12).

Job's fourth friend also discusses how God delivers the afflicted by their affliction and adversity. All who are to experience God intimately must trust God to the end where they have nothing left to rely upon but God alone. This accomplishes something in us; that is, we are drawn out of our cramped consciousness and world while being brought to a broad place where they will be satisfied (36:15–16). What kind of truth is this? We are delivered and rescued by the very adversity that puts each in need of being rescued and delivered! This truth certainly gives us pause to reflect! It seems to me hope comes through like rays of sun in the midst of a cloudy day. The pain of adversity can be so overwhelming, hope appears only a mirage. Yet the fourth conscious function of our personality shatters our "logical" beliefs. Only in the veil of tears we call this life could such a concept enlighten the darkness of hopelessness and anguish and ferry us to safety and true enlightenment. *God therefore disciplines us through our pain and suffering as all lesser values must be surrendered to the supreme value of pursuing a union with God.*

Eli'hu also states there are times when God's will is incompressible (37:5). In that space where understanding is only a pipe dream and the ineffable is all that is left stand two contrasting attitudes, one of self-pity/resentment and the other of faith. During the dark night of the soul where nothing makes sense to our rational minds, gratuitous transformations occur within the secret places within us. Spiritual metamorphosis occurs in that shadowy world of the irrational. If everything was nice and neat without mystery and the unknown, life would be boring and insipid. Mystery and wonder have a place in the economy of our psyche. The unknown and mystery gives life its spice and sense of adventure. God is so much more than our conceptions and rational explanations! There is a place for wonder and horror, mystery and wisdom, wherever the fourth function tarries a while (37:14–18). When we were young, wonder was our constant bedfellow. When the fourth function is integrated, it takes us by the hand and brings us back to this experience of wonder and awe at the miracle world we live in. Everything is miracle! Who else but God could have conceived of such beauty of the world and soul, spirit and flesh, mind and body, memory and will, emotions of many forms and variations? The glory of God (holiness/wholeness) is truly expressed in time and actuality through the lives of his followers.

Job has been initiated through his fourth function and now prepared for a direct experience with God.

> Oh bless the continuous stutter
> Of the word being made into flesh.

> —Leonard Cohen, "The Window"

Then the LORD answered Job out of the whirlwind:

"Who is this that darkens counsel by words without knowledge?

Gird up your loins like a man, I will question you, and you shall declare to me.

"Where were you when I laid the foundation of the earth? Tell me, if you have understanding.

Who determined its measurements -- surely you know! Or who stretched the line upon it?

On what were its bases sunk, or who laid its cornerstone, when the morning stars sang together, and all the sons of God shouted for joy?

"Or who shut in the sea with doors, when it burst forth from the womb; when I made clouds its garment, and thick darkness its swaddling band, and prescribed bounds for it, and set bars and doors, and said, `Thus far shall you come, and no farther, and here shall your proud waves be stayed'?

"Have you commanded the morning since your days began, and caused the dawn to know its place, that it might take hold of the skirts of the earth, and the wicked be shaken out of it?

It is changed like clay under the seal, and it is dyed like a garment.

From the wicked their light is withheld, and their uplifted arm is broken.

"Have you entered into the springs of the sea, or walked in the recesses of the deep?

Have the gates of death been revealed to you, or have you seen the gates of deep darkness?

Have you comprehended the expanse of the earth? Declare, if you know all this.

"Where is the way to the dwelling of light, and where is the place of darkness, that you may take it to its territory and that you may discern the paths to its home?

You know, for you were born then, and the number of your days is great!

"Have you entered the storehouses of the snow, or have you seen the storehouses of the hail, which I have reserved for the time of trouble, for the day of battle and war?

What is the way to the place where the light is distributed, or where the east wind is scattered upon the earth?

"Who has cleft a channel for the torrents of rain, and a way for the thunderbolt, to bring rain on a land where no man is, on the desert in which there is no man; to satisfy the waste and desolate land, and to make the ground put forth grass?

"Has the rain a father, or who has begotten the drops of dew?

From whose womb did the ice come forth, and who has given birth to the hoarfrost of heaven?

The waters become hard like stone, and the face of the deep is frozen.

"Can you bind the chains of the Plei'ades, or loose the cords of Orion?

Can you lead forth the Maz'zaroth in their season, or can you guide the Bear with its children?

Do you know the ordinances of the heavens? Can you establish their rule on the earth?

"Can you lift up your voice to the clouds, that a flood of waters may cover you?

Can you send forth lightnings, that they may go and say to you, `Here we are'?

Who has put wisdom in the clouds, or given understanding to the mists?

Who can number the clouds by wisdom? Or who can tilt the waterskins of the heavens, when the dust runs into a mass and the clods cleave fast together?

"Can you hunt the prey for the lion, or satisfy the appetite of the young lions, when they crouch in their dens, or lie in wait in their covert?

Who provides for the raven its prey, when its young ones cry to God, and wander about for lack of food? (Job 38:1–41)

"Do you know when the mountain goats bring forth? Do you observe the calving of the hinds?

Can you number the months that they fulfill, and do you know the time when they bring forth, when they crouch, bring forth their offspring, and are delivered of their young?

Their young ones become strong, they grow up in the open; they go forth, and do not return to them.

"Who has let the wild ass go free? Who has loosed the bonds of the swift ass, to whom I have given the steppe for his home, and the salt land for his dwelling place?

He scorns the tumult of the city; he hears not the shouts of the driver.

He ranges the mountains as his pasture, and he searches after every green thing.

"Is the wild ox willing to serve you? Will he spend the night at your crib?

Can you bind him in the furrow with ropes, or will he harrow the valleys after you?

Will you depend on him because his strength is great, and will you leave to him your labor?

Do you have faith in him that he will return, and bring your grain to your threshing floor?

"The wings of the ostrich wave proudly; but are they the pinions and plumage of love?

For she leaves her eggs to the earth, and lets them be warmed on the ground, forgetting that a foot may crush them, and that the wild beast may trample them.

She deals cruelly with her young, as if they were not hers; though her labor be in vain, yet she has no fear; because God has made her forget wisdom, and given her no share in understanding.

When she rouses herself to flee, she laughs at the horse and his rider.

"Do you give the horse his might? Do you clothe his neck with strength?

Do you make him leap like the locust? His majestic snorting is terrible.

He paws in the valley, and exults in his strength; he goes out to meet the weapons.

He laughs at fear, and is not dismayed; he does not turn back from the sword.

Upon him rattle the quiver, the flashing spear and the javelin.

With fierceness and rage he swallows the ground; he cannot stand still at the sound of the trumpet.

When the trumpet sounds, he says `Aha!' He smells the battle from afar, the thunder of the captains, and the shouting.

"Is it by your wisdom that the hawk soars, and spreads his wings toward the south?

Is it at your command that the eagle mounts up and makes his nest on high?

On the rock he dwells and makes his home in the fastness of the rocky crag.

Thence he spies out the prey; his eyes behold it afar off.

His young ones suck up blood; and where the slain are, there is he." (Job 39:1–30)

And the LORD said to Job:

"Shall a faultfinder contend with the Almighty? He who argues with God, let him answer it."

Then Job answered the LORD:

"Behold, I am of small account; what shall I answer thee? I lay my hand on my mouth.

I have spoken once, and I will not answer; twice, but I will proceed no further."

Then the LORD answered Job out of the whirlwind:

"Gird up your loins like a man; I will question you, and you declare to me.

Will you even put me in the wrong? Will you condemn me that you may be justified?

Have you an arm like God, and can you thunder with a voice like his?

"Deck yourself with majesty and dignity; clothe yourself with glory and splendor.

Pour forth the overflowings of your anger, and look on every one that is proud, and abase him.

Look on every one that is proud, and bring him low; and tread down the wicked where they stand.

Hide them all in the dust together; bind their faces in the world below.

Then will I also acknowledge to you, that your own right hand can give you victory.

"Behold, Be'hemoth, which I made as I made you; he eats grass like an ox.

Behold, his strength in his loins, and his power in the muscles of his belly.

He makes his tail stiff like a cedar; the sinews of his thighs are knit together.

His bones are tubes of bronze, his limbs like bars of iron.

"He is the first of the works of God; let him who made him bring near his sword!

For the mountains yield food for him where all the wild beasts play.

Under the lotus plants he lies, in the covert of the reeds and in the marsh.

For his shade the lotus trees cover him; the willows of the brook surround him.

Behold, if the river is turbulent he is not frightened; he is confident though Jordan rushes against his mouth.

Can one take him with hooks, or pierce his nose with a snare? (Job 40:1–24)

"Can you draw out Levi'athan with a fishhook, or press down his tongue with a cord?

Can you put a rope in his nose, or pierce his jaw with a hook?

Will he make many supplications to you? Will he speak to you soft words?

Will he make a covenant with you to take him for your servant for ever?

Will you play with him as with a bird, or will you put him on leash for your maidens?

Will traders bargain over him? Will they divide him up among the merchants?

Can you fill his skin with harpoons, or his head with fishing spears?

Lay hands on him; think of the battle; you will not do it again!

Behold, the hope of a man is disappointed; he is laid low even at the sight of him.

No one is so fierce that he dares to stir him up. Who then is he that can stand before me?

Who has given to me, that I should repay him? Whatever is under the whole heaven is mine.

"I will not keep silence concerning his limbs, or his mighty strength, or his goodly frame.

Who can strip off his outer garment? Who can penetrate his double coat of mail?

Who can open the doors of his face? Round about his teeth is terror.

His back is made of rows of shields, shut up closely as with a seal.

One is so near to another that no air can come between them.

They are joined one to another; they clasp each other and cannot be separated.

His sneezings flash forth light, and his eyes are like the eyelids of the dawn.

Out of his mouth go flaming torches; sparks of fire leap forth.

Out of his nostrils comes forth smoke, as from a boiling pot and burning rushes.

His breath kindles coals, and a flame comes forth from his mouth.

In his neck abides strength, and terror dances before him.

The folds of his flesh cleave together, firmly cast upon him and immovable.

His heart is hard as a stone, hard as the nether millstone.

When he raises himself up the mighty are afraid; at the crashing they are beside themselves.

Though the sword reaches him, it does not avail; nor the spear, the dart, or the javelin.

He counts iron as straw, and bronze as rotten wood.

The arrow cannot make him flee; for him slingstones are turned to stubble.

Clubs are counted as stubble; he laughs at the rattle of javelins.

His underparts are like sharp potsherds; he spreads himself like a threshing sledge on the mire.

He makes the deep boil like a pot; he makes the sea like a pot of ointment.

Behind him he leaves a shining wake; one would think the deep to be hoary.

Upon earth there is not his like, a creature without fear.

He beholds everything that is high; he is king over all the sons of pride." (Job 41:1–34)

Commentary

Job's *patient endurance and openness to share with God has been rewarded with a mystical encounter and dialogue with God.* What kind of mystical experience Job had, we cannot say for sure except to say he had some form of mystical experience. Mystical experiences by their very nature are ineffable and are not subject to rational concepts. Out of a whirlwind, God tells Job to "gird up your loins like a man, I will question you and you shall declare to me" (Job 38:1–3). The amount of respect God exhibits toward Job is enormous, and it appears he indeed delivers humans out of their adversity through their affliction!

William James described many mystical experiences in his monumental lectures and work, *The Varieties of Religious Experience.* In *Apparitions*, Kevin Johnson describes the spectrum of mystical experience in three phases. They are briefly where (1) the soul reaches out to God through ascetic practices, (2) the illuminative or communion where God reaches back mystically, and (3) union where both draw together in intimacy.

The specifics of how we reach out to God and how God reaches back to us are unique to each individual. Dallas Willard has a good introduction into spiritual disciplines in different ways to reach out to God in *The Spirit of the Disciplines.* To gain a further grasp of the final two stages, I refer the reader to Thomas Merton's *Contemplative Prayer* and *New Seeds of Contemplation*, Meister Eckhart's *Talks of Instruction* and *The Book of Divine Consolation*, St. John of the Cross's *The Ascent of Mount Carmel*, St. Ignatius's *The Spiritual Exercises*, and St. Teresa of Avila's *Interior Castle*—all offer variations on this process. These works are a repository of wisdom from which to reach out to God and wait upon God for truth and love (intimacy). What is important is not so much method as sincerity and openness along with a willingness to nurture silence and solitude with patient endurance.

The text reveals Job reaching out to God in silence and solitude while sharing that which he discovered inside of him as he ventured through his dark night of the soul. God reaches back to Job through his afflictions, dreams, visions, and finally through this mystical experience "out of the whirlwind." While most think mystical experience is bizarre and frightening and some of it seems so to the outsider, yet God visits us each in ways that we can handle. What we need is the openness and patience and not to worry about how God communicates with us and the forms that intimacy takes. We need to make ourselves open to whatever kind of intimacy that is of God's own choosing. This is not in our control. We open up to God by obedience and trust through action, meditation, asceticism, silence, and contemplation, and God communes with us through many different means. I will have much more to say about this later. Now let's get back to the text.

What does God say to Job? God answers Job in a way that is both rational and yet beyond rationality. First, God is full of mystery, majesty, and creativity. Second, the dynamics of their relationship cannot take the form of some rational response devoid of pathos, which will only feed Job's inflation further. Rather, God wills a union with Job's *whole being*, which includes his faith, spirit, emotions, body, will, mind, and intuition. *His all must be engaged in their relationship.* God treats Job with respect ("Gird up your loins like a man, I will question you, and you will declare to me" [Job 38:3]). The more we share with God, the more God shares with us. God does not force Himself on anyone. His power, joy, grace, love, and the secrets of His Kingdom all become manifest in their time. Like Job, any of us can choose to disclose everything that is within to God with all our conflicts, failures, disappointments, triumphs, feelings, longings, etc., and we too will be recipients of God's companionship! While many failures will pile up, many ambitions die, and many desires will have to be relinquished. God's companionship of love and joy will also be shared with any willing to go the distance. Like with Job, the difficulty lies in waiting and patient endurance for God to respond to our cries.

God's response is, in effect, that Job's ego is puny, and he will never grasp all the mystery and wonder inherent in creation or in God's being. God's response is direct and annihilating in comparison to Job's ego-body-consciousness. This is why an individual must develop a healthy ego-strength prior to this ordeal of suffering and wrestling blessings away from the Living God. What appears on the surface abusive, rigid, and/or unjust from the standpoint of ego-consciousness is in point of fact *salvation/healing* for our entire personality. Those who fail to make this distinction are looking at God's response from the outlook of their bound, inflated, and imprisoned ego-consciousness. From the standpoint of God-consciousness, the response is liberating and full of grace and truth! It becomes a matter of perspective. Death always must come first; it is only afterward that abundant life can manifest itself. The ego is asked to die, not remain wounded. In fact, a wounded ego, like an injured animal, is much more dangerous! Wounded, they each cling to life more ferociously. Selfishness actually becomes much more pronounced when the ego is wounded but refuses to die. As we have seen with Job, this transition in time takes colossal sufferings and breaking down of all self-sufficiency.

God and each individual have a potential relationship, which is both unique and secretive. There are times God speaks to us in the quiet of our inner consciousness, and it is meant for us alone. Likewise, there are aspects within us only meant for God alone. There must be a degree of openness, which is reserved for God and no one else. What we have in the text is this: God speaks to Job out of the whirlwind and confronts Job and his ego inflation by recounting his mystery and power in a variety of ways. All humans' ego- consciousness has its foundation in God's spirit! Human psyche is in fact already grounded in God because we are created in God's own image.

What is Job's primary experience from his encounter and new relationship with God? To get a handle on this question, let us look at Job's response to God in the text just ahead.

You're the ocean ringing in my brain
Fireflies around you like a crown of sparks
You blow me a kiss that blurs by vision
Blurs the human condition

It's your eyes I want to see
Looking into mine
Got you live on my mind
All the time.
—Bruce Cockburn, "Live on My Mind"

Then Job answered the LORD:

"I know that thou canst do all things, and that no purpose of thine can be thwarted.

`Who is this that hides counsel without knowledge?' Therefore I have uttered what I did not understand, things too wonderful for me, which I did not know.

`Hear, and I will speak; I will question you, and you declare to me.'

I had heard of thee by the hearing of the ear, but now my eye sees thee; therefore I despise myself, and repent in dust and ashes." (Job 42:1–6)

Commentary

Job's reply to his mystical experience is thus: "I have heard of thee by the hearing of the ear, but now my eye sees thee; therefore I despise myself, and repent in dust and ashes" (Job 42:5–6). Job finally recognizes his ego for what it is, puny and limited and its need to repent of its primary position as the center of the personality. Job also demonstrates a heroic acceptance of his suffering in the context of his opening up and sharing with God all he discovered *within himself* during his adversity and within the context of the opposites within him. Therefore, a friendship and relationship with God was forged through Job's immense grief and sufferings. Job's encounter with God presupposes much more than just a rational meeting of the minds. Job earlier said to God, "Hear and I will speak. I will question you and you declare to me." This is not a response of a frightened animal with its tail between its legs, but rather of one secure enough in the relationship to exhibit some audacity inherent in this aspect of his reply. He is able to speak from a position of another paradox and pair of opposites, one of *audacity and humility.* Job's humility is demonstrated in the rest of his response: "Therefore I repent in dust and ashes." Job has begun experiencing the effects of the integration of the fourth function through his intimate union with God. Mutual intimacy, acceptance, and understanding are now established in a safe and loving space between both God and Job.

Heretofore, their relationship was occupied by Job's distorted beliefs and attitudes. *Job's enlightenment is secured because Job was willing, honest, and open with his ego-consciousness, and then he surrendered his ego to revolve around the power of God and to allow God, the author of his psyche, to be the transpersonal center of his entire personality with God's consciousness directing but not bullying his ego-consciousness.* The transformation includes expanded consciousness and the rest of his being impacted through his emotions, will, and body in equal measure.

Our mind does come to understanding, but only through experiences that have taken their course and then joined to our will, emotions, and body. There becomes a harmony/ oneness/wholeness in a union with God. The blessing Job receives at the conclusion of the book of Job is a confirmation to the reader that the union between God and man has been accomplished. Job has succeeded as a contemplative. Job sought God through silence, solitude, prayer and meditation in the spirit of a contemplative and God reciprocated by inaugurating an new intimacy with Job.

The result of Job's encounter with God in which his suffering drove him is power to be a channel of God to a suffering world that comes with this relationship, exhibited in growing in holiness/wholeness and wisdom/truth. This is what results when anyone moves closer to union with God. The point is God has infused Job with his positive energy in response to Job opening up and dying to the selfish ego as the center of existence as we will see demonstrated in his willingness to pray for his friends indicated in the text further on. God can only fill an empty cup. Job's forced asceticism (when he lost everything) and his choice to contemplate (share with God his thoughts and feelings and reflect/ meditate) combined to allow Job to experience God's touch as he was infused with His grace and power to be transformed. God blesses Job's effort with grace, strength, healing, and power. He did have to wait and wrestle with God and his inner life (all that God evoked) in the process. The person of faith recognizes the eventual fruits of this process that only come with patient endurance, which far outweigh the suffering inherent within it. It also appears to me the wager God made with himself was whether Job could become an intimate friend of God's. In Job 42 1-6, it appears God has won his wager and Job has succeeded in becoming an intimate with God.

Each one alone yet not alone
Behind the pain, fear
Etched on the faces
Something is shinning
Like gold but better
Rumours of glory

You see the extreme
Of what humans can be?
In that distance between tensions born
You plunge your hand in
You draw it back scorched
Beneath its shining like
Gold but better
Rumours of glory.

—Bruce Cockburn, "Rumours of Glory"

After the LORD had spoken these words to Job, the LORD said to Eli'phaz the Te'manite: "My wrath is kindled against you and against your two friends; for you have not spoken of me what is right, as my servant Job has.

Now therefore take seven bulls and seven rams, and go to my servant Job, and offer up for yourselves a burnt offering; and my servant Job shall pray for you, for I will accept his prayer not to deal with you according to your folly; for you have not spoken of me what is right, as my servant Job has."

So Eli'phaz the Te'manite and Bildad the Shuhite and Zophar the Na'amathite went and did what the LORD had told them; and the LORD accepted Job's prayer.

And the LORD restored the fortunes of Job, when he had prayed for his friends; and the LORD gave Job twice as much as he had before.

Then came to him all his brothers and sisters
and all who had known him before, and ate bread
with him in his house; and they showed him sympathy and comforted him for all the evil that the
LORD had brought upon him; and each of them
gave him a piece of money and a ring of gold.

And the LORD blessed the latter days of Job
more than his beginning; and he had fourteen
thousand sheep, six thousand camels, a thousand
yoke of oxen, and a thousand she-asses.

He had also seven sons and three daughters.

And he called the name of the first Jemi'mah;
and the name of the second Kezi'ah; and the name
of the third Ker'en-hap'puch.

And in all the land there were no women so
fair as Job's daughters; and their father gave them
inheritance among their brothers.

And after this Job lived a hundred and forty
years, and saw his sons, and his sons' sons, four
generations.

And Job died, an old man, and full of days.
(Job 42:7–17)

This last section (42:7–17) seems to be a later addition, and therefore, it is obvious the book of Job is a composite composition. First,
notice how verse 7 reads, "After the Lord had spoken these words to
Job." The problem is Job had just finished talking with the Lord about
what he had learned, and God had not spoken. Second, the text says
Job received twice what he had lost, yet his children were dead in the
initial wager. Job's material compensations could never replace his children; therefore, this seems like a hastily added addition at that. Third,
this ending brings us back to the wealth theme and how one is only
blessed by wealth to enjoy God's favor. Fourth, in verse 11, he was
comforted by his siblings and all who had known him, and each gave
him money and a ring of gold. Thanks, my fair-weather family and
friends; by the way, your material gifts and words of comfort definitely
makes up for your rejection, abandonment, gossip, and judgmental

attitudes. On top of all this, they comforted Job for all the evil done by God. Let's see, hmm, I think I will comfort and give you material gifts because God is to blame for your problems and for our unfaithful and pathetic behavior.

Job was not the first, nor will he be the last to lose everything. Jesus came into the world as a nothing and then sacrificed his life after he had sacrificed everything else to follow his Father's will. The poor, the outcasts, the widowed, the imprisoned, the orphaned, and all the lost, unappreciated, and unwanted by our culture have more opportunities for intimacy and friendship from the Lord (for the first shall be last, and the last first) than do the rest of us. This last section seems contrived, superficial, and totally inconsistent with all the transformations Job achieved through his suffering and endurance. Like the later additions to the end of the gospel of Mark, it seems likely to me a later redactor was ill at ease with the ending of this folktale because it did not agree with his retrograde sensibilities that justice had to include a restoration of his material objects and acceptance by others while his children remained in their graves! The only other possibility is that this last section was a poor metaphor for the truth that once Job/we have surrendered to God all that we have or are, we are then able to enjoy our friendships and interests in their proper place, and we are given all that we need when we first seek the Kingdom of God. Regardless, this ending is pathetic theology as everyone else except Job comes out as phony as a three dollar bill.

However, there seems two redeeming qualities to this last section. First, Job seems to have accepted his grief over the loss of his children in the greater purpose of God's will. This does not include an absence of grief and pain! Healing the wounds of grief never implies that pain or suffering dissipates like the morning dew. The sun sometimes shines only upon the top of the clouds. The reconciliation that occurs with one's acceptance of the truth of our grief does makes some sense of our grief, and it becomes less overwhelming.

Secondly, Job exhibits love and grace/forgiveness toward his three friends. If taken as real people, this is love in action. Taken as metaphor for his first three conscious functions, it reflects an important psychological truth, which is when the fourth function is integrated, the other three functions, which were useless during his trials by fire of the fourth function, are restored and then redeemed; now the potential is for all four conscious functions to navigate around and serve the truth rather than the ego-consciousness. Nevertheless, Job prays for his friends, loving them despite being abandoned and belittled by them, thereby forgiving them because he must have recognized he was as arrogant and judgmental of others as they were.

If it be your will
That I speak no more
And my voice be still
As it was before
I will speak no more
I shall abide until
I'm spoken for
If it be your will
If it be your will
That a voice be true
From this broken hill
I will sing to you
From this broken hill
All your praises shall ring . . .

—Leonard Cohen, "If It Be Your Will"

Across the concrete fields of man
Sun ray like a camera lens
Some will run and some will stand
Everything is bullshit but the open hand.
—Bruce Cockburn, "Strange Waters"

Now, this is the blues.
There was a white man had the blues,
For nothing to worry about,
Now you laid down at night,
You row from one side of the bed to the other all night long,
You can't sleep,

What's the matter?
The blues has got cha.
You get up and sit on the side your bed in the morning,
You may have a sister and a brother, mother and father around cha,
But you don't want no talk out of em.
What's the matter"?
The blues has got cha.
Well, you go put your foot under the table,
Look down on your plate,
You got everything you want to eat,
But you shake you head, you get up,
You say Lord, I can't eat and I can't sleep.
What's the matter?
The blues got cha
Wanna talk to ya.
Here's what you gotta tell 'em.

—Leadbelly, "Good Morning Blues"

Conclusions on Job and *The Odyssey*

Behold the gates of mercy
In arbitrary space
And none of us deserving
The cruelty or the grace
O solitude of longing
Where love has been confined
Come healing of the body
Come healing of the mind . . .

O troubled dust concealing
An undivided love

The Heart beneath is teaching
To the broken Heart above

O let the heavens falter
And let the earth proclaim:
Come healing of the Alter
Come healing of the Name . . .

And let the heavens hear it
The penitential hymn
Come healing of the spirit
Come healing of the limb

—Leonard Cohen, "Come Healing"

The wheel is turning and you can't slow it down,
You can't let go,
And you can't hold on,
You can't go back and
You can't stand still,
If the thunder don't get 'cha,
The lightning will.

The small wheel turns by the fire and the rod,
The big wheel turns by the grace of God,
Every time that wheel turns around,
It's bound to cover just a little more ground.

—Jerry Garcia, "The Wheel"

From the annals of *The Odyssey* and the book of Job, we are left with a terrible and mysterious paradox that begs the question, is the contrast and clash between good and evil and suffering and joy justified? We are brought up from infancy to experience a thousand deaths at the hand's loss and suffering. The wheel keeps turning, both by judgment and grace, whether we choose to move forward or not. Do we deserve our fate, and are we in part cocreators of it? Where is the line between our responsibility for our suffering and God's? How does God suffer with each conscious sufferer? Each will have to answer these questions for themselves. The answers can only be found in those mysterious precincts, which lie within each individual psyche.

The messages of these great and seminal works seem to guide us to the brink of an abyss where only grace, love, and faith can rescue us. Shall we remain infantile and rebel against our common and individual fate(s), or travel along the road to individuation and authenticity? Will love, peace, joy, and wholeness eventually be reflected within our soul, or will we remain compartmentalized, self-centered, lazy, full of self-deception, and wounded? The possibilities of suffering, alienation, inflation, excess, greed, wholeness, and joy flash before us like those psychedelic lights of the '60s and '70s. In the following chapters, I will share with you my speculations on many of these questions posed by *The Odyssey* and the book of Job. Presently, I think it comes down the

417

two primary *spiritual* archetypes and dialectics the universe seems to have set up within the confines of it energy; that is *fear and love and truth and falsehood.* I see both at play within me and induce it from the behaviors and attitudes of others around me. I think the crucial question is, *which of these two life forces do we align ourselves with? The attitudes we take towards each and the actions from which they spring will determine our ultimate fate. As I said earlier, I believe love and truth are one, and their measure is suffering. I also believe evil and fear are one, and falsehood and desecration are its measure. These themes, along with the fact our ego-consciousness needs to revolve around love and truth while we accept suffering with courage, seems to be the real meanings of these two great works.* It is essential to be aware that none of us will be perfect in our struggles to overcome fear and lies with love and the truth. What is of crucial import is *we align ourselves with love and the truth* as we become aware of how fear and falsehood and self-deception creep into our lives. As I talked about earlier, the meaning of the word *repentance* is to turn around, and we are always offered the opportunity do so when we recognize we have been waylaid by fear and lies. And make no mistake, we will inevitably get lost in our fears and lies throughout our lives as the human condition is fraught with so many temptations to avoid truth and get bogged down in fear. The whys must never cloud our vision of the reality of the human condition in its inherent weaknesses and finitude. We grow through the pain occasioned by our experience of suffering as it offers us not only the possibility of expanding our consciousness but opportunities to develop an intimacy with God, others, and ourselves. Only when we face what is will it be possible to experience any true form of detachment and enlightenment. What is, is—horrific and full of anguish as life can be at times. Life also unveils love, beauty, and truth.

These two heroes were living sacrifices unto the truth and God within them as they were pilfered and stripped of all their attachments to the temporal while eventually they each in their own way sacrificed these attachments with their own free will. This is in part what I think it means to exist as a living sacrifice unto the *truth.* Odysseus and Job demonstrated both a willingness to face their fears and the truth as they proceeded through their individual struggles toward enlightenment and an authentic life. They were both heroes in the true sense of the word as each in his own way was able to face death and God hidden within their psyches while surrendering and sacrificing all that stood in the way of the truth within them.

Kierkegaard believed suffering and anxiety offer each of us a gift and, by its work, pilfers all our attachments to temporal objects and aims from our ego, thus opening the door to freeing us to add the infinite to our experience. Freedom is only possible when we wrestle with suffering and the anxiety and anguish it occasions; by pain we are flung from temporal aims into the vast and inscrutable realms of God. Where our treasures are, their heart will be also. If our life has substance by seeking love and truth, we will eventually experience some measure of each along with peace and wholeness in our personal journeys through this life and onto death. Seeds are sown in darkness and death and flowers bloom at night. Deep in the soil, the seed must grow downward to establish strong roots while simultaneously, it grows upward toward the sun. Down into the darkness of the soil, wonder and terror lurk across the borderlines of familiarity and false security. Few are willing to venture there where they surrender and grow in death. It is only in the depths of darkness where we are lost and disoriented can we be found. The process takes the courage to face oneself and the truths of the human condition while abiding in the residence where unknown and ineffable suffering dwells. God also dwells there for anyone able to perceive Him/Her. Only then can we really bear healthy fruit for God. Sadly, it seems only sufferings are latent with strong-enough medicinal qualities to shake us out of our illusions and initiate heroic growth.

As we delve further into my conclusions on these commentaries on Job and Odysseus, it is interesting to note another distinction between the Hebraism and Hellenism (Greek). William Barrett discusses how the Hebrews were concerned primarily with doing, practice, and conduct while the Greeks were focused on knowing (*Irrational Man*). Barrett goes on to discuss how the law is not at the center of the Hebrew legacy but rather "the man of faith in his wholeness," as delineated by Job's encounter with God (ibid., p.77). Each of these heroes was able to integrate the inferior function of their respective cultures and bring together the pairs of opposites within the ethos of their civilizations. Odysseus's sufferings revolutionized the thinking function *to include feeling values*. Odysseus's thinking became filled with proper values. Job's senses and doing becomes conscious of God. The word *conscious* comes from the Latin *con-scire*, which means "to know with." Odysseus becomes conscious or knows with the guidance of feminine feeling values.

W. S. Peck suggested to know with someone else and specifically with God (*The Road Less Traveled and Beyond*). Job's consciousness knows with God. Odysseus faces his spirit in his encounter with Tiresias, thereby unveiling God within his/our spirit. Job has a mystical experience and comes to know God with an open intimacy. When anyone uncovers these treasures hidden in the field of their soul, an initial excitement begins with accompanying transformations, the truth turns our world upside down, and finally we are inspired and required to reverse our attitudes and act upon our new understanding!

John Crossan wrote a wonderful piece on the parables of Jesus entitled *In Parables*, where he describes these three chief messages of the parables of Jesus. As we will explore in chapter 23, all pairs of opposites are finally unified in the wisdom and practices of Jesus.

Job's and Odysseus's fates have been discussed endlessly and for good reason. The problem with many of these commentaries is that few in academia have explored their personal sufferings enough for their interpretations to hit us where we live and have our being. Platitudes are hurled about like pregame baseballs. It seems often when academia gets its hands on any given text, detached intellectualizing overshadows human experience, and the real impact such monumental texts such as the book of Job and *The Odyssey* can have when they reach individuals who really choose, suffer and face their finitude and mortality. Anyone who is attempting to live an authentic existence and is in the midst of some form of suffering knows that no intellectual anodynes can mitigate their anguish. Rather, for a time, we are confused and in darkness. A willingness to be so is laudable as it is the only response that is genuine. The need for understanding is vitally important, but only in the context of real unmitigated and grubby experience where we sacrifice our creature comforts and wait for God's timing and healing touch. We are so impatient that it usually takes external circumstances to evoke the suffering necessary for our soul's healing. Job's and Odysseus's experiences are filled with external losses and circumstances where doubts, depression, anxiety, confusion, loneliness, and sadness are evoked. Their security and self-worth were stripped and plundered, and in their place, disorientation proceeded remarkable transformations. Job eventually experiences an inner serenity and peace within the context of his wrestling with God rather than some detached intellectual formulations extracted from endless mental masturbation. Odysseus finally reaches home, but only after suffering and learning much related to letting go and embracing new feeling values his patriarchal thinking function denied.

Socrates is quoted by Plato in his dialogues that philosophy's chief aim is learning how to die. This aptly describes the demands of the second half of life. Job and Odysseus are traumatized out of complacent attitudes and beliefs and offered possibilities for new and dynamic visions of what humans can become and be as we are headed inexorably toward our death. All their suffering is within the context of loss, death, and mortality. We are finite beings who are responsible and must find meaning and purpose to carry on and learn how to love. Both these classic works offer a radical glimpse of a new stage in our collective conscious development. In the second half of life, we are no longer to expand our world in the external sense, but rather open ourselves to the unconscious (God's direction). This will lead us toward the contents and substance of the inner life hidden within the unconscious. This compensates for the body's inevitable decline. The inner life's latent potential now is displayed in new possibilities and where new territory of the psyche can be traversed. These new territories prepare us for letting go of life itself and accepting our death. Our ego-consciousness was correctly the only center in the first half of life. However, the position shifts in the second half where ego-consciousness becomes secondary; it is to become a satellite revolving around that secret place where truth and creativity reside and where your true inner self abides. This secret place is nothing less than the image of God within you!

There are many powers greater than us, and for many of us, a realization occurs at some juncture that this is God. If we are able and willing to sacrifice and embrace the unconscious, we can get to the hidden depths and roots; that is *God's being within us.* Our ego-consciousness *must* revolve around the Spirit of Truth if we are to accomplish the tasks set for the second half of life. However, the spirit of untruth or falsehood also abides within us as well. The fact is it will take more than a lifetime to entirely extricate ourselves from this phony self. Yet the unconscious mind continues to compensate and manifests the truth, and it is there where we find the substance and depth of our potential character. Can we muster up the courage as Job and Odysseus did and let go of control with our cramped consciousness while embracing our personal odyssey? Can we also be led into the unknown where we are broken and stripped of our attachments to the temporal? For in the empty space left where our attachment once found refuge, occasions are uncovered within our unique center; where purpose, quiet strength, equanimity, joy, wisdom, and wholeness reside. In other words, our psyche needs to shift inwardly. If we fail to do so, we fashion within ourselves grumpy old men. The movie *Grumpy Old Men*, though hilarious, maintains the fiction that blessings come externally. The problem in America at least is our country is full of grumpy old men instead of mentors who can model serenity and teach our young the wisdom, depth of character, and an acceptance of life and death they crave.

Job and Odysseus became wise and moved closer to wholeness though their weaknesses. A second birth was recast by the first death, a psychological death. They faced their shadows, which cannot be done without the midwifery of suffering. They learned to accept the world on its terms for we are part and parcel of it. Faith and hope are not contained or experienced in what we witness with our five senses. It seems to me individuals of faith locate their security and worth in God's mysterious will. God's will is revealed day by day and within each new opportunity in life. In other words, the mystery of God's will unfolds to those of faith (trust), whereby it's extracted in the daily circumstances of our life. These circumstances can never be controlled nor predicted. The etymological root of happiness is "to happen"; therefore, happiness is to be experienced inwardly in the happenings of our lives. What is certain is uncertainty; we have no idea what is around the corner. As my friend Kevin O'Grady once said to me, God does not stop the world of the believer so they can pass by unscathed (I have paraphrased). The essence of faith or trust is that one trusts God's will within the context of everyday circumstances. This does not mean we are victims of the circumstances of life; rather the hidden treasure of God's will and activity and transformative power is often hidden within these circumstances.

As Gai Eaton said,

> There is no radical distinction to be made between what a man is given in the way of mind, emotional make-up and body on the one hand and, on the other, what he is given in the way of outward circumstances and environment. Together they form a significant whole and are aspects of a particular individual life. The being between birth and death scrawls-in matter and in events-a pattern which, taken as a whole, expresses his unique identity. This man so and so is not a sealed personality moving through an alien environment. He is the sum total of all that he does and all that happens to him and all that comes within his range, spread out (from our point of view) in time and space, but a single, timeless fact in the mind of God. What we are and where we are cannot ultimately be divided. And to accept our destiny is part of our nature-in the widest sense-as the most intimate contours of our selfhood . . . In the last resort, a man looks at the love or anger or fears within himself and says, so this is me. Looks at his withered and or wounded foot and days, So this is me . . . Looks finally on his enemy and upon his death and says, So this is me. But in saying this he bears witness to the fact that he is also incomparably more than an itemized list of the elements that make up his individuality and its inseparable field of action. (H. Smith, *Forgotten Truth: The Primordial Tradition*, Harper & Row,

Publishers, New York, Hagerstown, San Francisco, London, 1977)

Job and Odysseus learned to value their sufferings. However, suffering is not an end in itself but rather a means to a greater end, that is enlightenment and wholeness, which we will explore in depth in chapter 23. It seems to me if suffering or any experience leads us into the arms of God can we say it has real purpose or meaning. Specially, Job opened up and shared all that he discovered in his consciousness and his inner life, so God opened up and shared all that is His to the degree Job's soul could receive Him: of God's love, power, grace, joy, secrets, and blessings. All of Job's suffering brought him into an intimate relationship with his creator. Both Job and Odysseus were imprisoned in their ego-body-consciousness and its inherent selfishness, dishonesty and self-deception, cowardice, and laziness. Job and Odysseus were led and followed that lonely road where all saints and heroes have to tread. They uncovered a second birth by approaching a balance of everything that existed within their respective ego-consciousnesses. And so they eventually accepted God's purpose in all that is within the mystery of their unique destinies. So too any person, who by the grace of God becomes the ruler of himself, also becomes whole and holy. These two are inexorably linked; you cannot have real power without God's power. The one establishes the other. *We are only channels of God's love and power and beauty and truth.*

Some of us hunger for the finer things
Some of us lust for power like the ancient kings
Some have to leave everything behind everything
They thought they knew
Some people don't know how much
Trouble they can brew

Some take the burden of another's pain
Some spend forever for a moment's gain
Everybody's got to find their
Way through

But if you love love, then love love's
You too

—B. Cockburn, "Love Loves You Too"

Amid the rumors and the expectations
And all the stories dreamt and lived
Amid the clamor and dislocation
And things to fear and forgive . . .

Though you find yourself alone and stranded
With no friend to take your side
On the endless road afoot and empty handed
Where the wide eyed Cossacks ride

Don't forget about delight

—Bruce Cockburn, "Don't Forget about Delight"

The Problem of Evil: Its Nature and Origins

Terrible deeds done in the name
Of tunnel vision and the fear of change
Surely are expressions of
A soul that's turned its back on love

—Bruce Cockburn, "Put It in Your Heart"

Introduction

Deliver us, Lord from this golden calf
People only want what they cannot have
Forbidden fruit
That's the fruit you'd better not taste
Forbidden fruit . . .

How did I walk with this ball and chain?
How can I land in this hurricane?
Or is this part of man's evolution
To be torn between truth and illusion?

Just watch out for the sign of the snake . . .

—The Band, "Forbidden Fruit"

The predicament of human suffering inexorably leads us to the problem of evil. There is so much suffering in the world that would not exist if it were not for evil. Would there be suffering in the universe if evil did not exist? How do we know the good if there is nothing to contrast it with? Some philosophies, religions and individuals deny the reality of evil. I think this rejection has its roots in the denial of malevolence from within the psyche. The shadow is by its nature repressed for it contains unwanted aspects of the personality we wish to deny. It is our denial and the subtle and negative energy of evil that leaves us so vulnerable to its power and influence.

Evil has wreaked havoc on the human condition from seemingly the foundations of human experience. It seems negative energy pervades our universe along with positive energy. Individual and collective neurosis, with its needs for security and worth, have driven all of us to commit acts of falsehood, self-deception, false pride, insolence, and violence upon ourselves and each other. Our motives are often hidden from ourselves. None of us are immune from the grip of our shadow, and we hurt ourselves and others in a myriad of ways that are both intentional and unintentional. We are subject to all kinds of conflicting impulses, desires, and fears, which coerce our motives and behaviors in many directions at once and stem from the archetypes of the unconscious.

I wish now to speculate on the *nature and origins* of evil. I then will share my own thoughts and beliefs about evil. I don't assume I have all the answers on such a mystery that has baffled our species to the degree most of us would rather ignored the subject altogether. The universe is full of enigmas and riddles. Nevertheless, I feel inclined to speculate all the same while recognizing much of the reality of evil will remain in obscurity throughout my earthly life.

The Nature of Evil

Much of what I have to say about the nature of evil has come from my experience and five works: *Evil: The shadow Side of Reality* by John

Sanford, *People of the Lie: The Hope for Healing Human Evil* by M. Scott Peck, *Hostage to the Devil* By Malachi Martin, *My Descent into Death* by Howard Storm, and *The Denial of Death* by Earnest Becker.

Give me back my broken night
My secret room, my secret life
It's lonely here,
With no one left to torture
Give me absolute control
Over every living soul
And lie beside me baby,
That's an order!

Give me back the Berlin wall
Give me Stalin . . .

—Leonard Cohen, "The Future"

Any discussion on the nature of evil has to begin with the unconscious mind, for within it contains our motives and projections. We must remember from our earlier discussion that the unconscious mind predates the conscious mind and is therefore the template for our entire nature with its motives, desires, fears, and behaviors. This inevitably must include our capacity for evil. The shadow is often where evil lies hidden within the human psyche, and it is here where we must begin. To sum up, it is the archetype within the unconscious, which contains all the discarded aspects of our personality that the conscious mind rejects. The fact that we have a need to discard aspects of our personality leads us to motives and negative energy, which we are prone toward. There would be no Ten Commandments if there we no propensity to commit these acts. But before behaviors comes motives, and it is here where the nature of evil must be initially recognized. We are all in fact capable of every motive and behavior that has existed within our species from the beginning of our existence to the present. We carry with us the collective memory of our ancestors in our very cells, brain, and psyche and share with them in our collective motives, intuitions, capacities, emotions, and behaviors. It is imperative we recognize this from the start and stop projecting evil onto our neighbor if there is any hope of adequately overcoming it. The imperative in facing our shadow is both not acting it out while not denying these motives and urges, that is to live out the tension between the two.

Another aspect of evil resides in our denial. When we deny our weaknesses and defects and mortality, we project these onto our neighbor. This denial and projection takes what is inside us and pushes it outward onto our environment. Hence, we have hatred and a multitude of superstitions. If we can manage to blame something outside ourselves, we then avoid the alien, which resides within.

The New World Dictionary uses the following adjectives to describe evil: *depraved, wicked, wrong, injurious, offensive, disgusting, disastrous, misery, unlucky, unfortunate, sin*—all relating to morality, pain, or Satan. This only proves the definition is very difficult. Now I'd like to continue with a working definition of evil. I subscribe to W. Scott Pecks definition of evil, that is "as the exercise of political power—that is, the imposition of one's will upon others by covert or overt coercion—in order to avoid . . .spiritual growth" (*People of the Lie*, Simon & Schuster,1983, p.74).

From my experience and perspective, evil is about using denial and inflated and negative energy to propagate falsehood, cruelty, fear, confusion, blame, untruth, selfishness, false pride, and all forms of deception onto others while avoiding all forms of spiritual growth/positive energy. There is a perversity and intent that follows evil wherever it casts it net. We experience evil when negative energy is used to harm others in some way and twist the truth. Evil is narcissistic in its selfish concentration; it lacks understanding of anything outside its myopic orbit. True evil will *never face truths of any kind*. Evil is also subtle and highly strategic in aspiring to destroy everything about truth/wholeness. Evil cannot stand or survive on its own but only exists to destroy the good. Evil compartmentalizes; it divides and destroys while maintaining self-deceptions and deceiving others to hide from truth. Evil attempts to profane and desecrate beauty and truth. Evil cannot stand the truth and will shrink away whenever and wherever holiness/wholeness takes a stand. Evil's belief is that it is superior to everything and will never bow down willingly to any sort of powers greater than itself.

In contrast, good is always dedicated to truth and reality, no matter where it is found or what the cost. Evil is about dominance and power and using fear to control those within its range. As I discussed earlier, organized evil is the worst category of evil as it has been expressed in institutions like slavery, nation states (especially totalitarian states), and large corporations. Organized evil is set up in hierarchical patterns where power is centralized and strict adherence to its structures and intentions are required for those within the system. Those at the top use their power and fear to dominate and control those beneath them in horrific and manipulative strategies, which govern the strict adherence to its aims. These aims are selfish and dishonest with its bend toward destruction, domination, and control.

There is positive and negative energy in the universe, and both are indispensable for growth. Examples of negative energy are fear, hatred, jealousy, despair, deception, selfishness, intolerance, unkindness, arrogance, etc. Examples of positive energy are love, kindness, patience, humility, mercy, hope, etc. Evil takes negative energy and uses it for the purpose of opposing truth. Evil attempts to distort truth and beauty. Evil will not tolerate truth and will do everything in its power to run away and hide form truth. Evil is separation from all truth in its choices to disrupt, deform, and destroy genuineness, integrity, and truth.

Ironically, the presence of evil seems to help develop the feeling function/values and to promote consciousness in some individuals. The snake in the myth of the fall told Eve she would have the knowledge of good and evil if she ate from the tree of life but left out the truth that when this new self-consciousness is left unto itself, it is capable of only evil. So this negative energy seems to be one more contradiction and paradox with which we must face and deal with; we all live on a razor's edge by accepting the fruits of negative energy (consciousness) without succumbing to its power. We are all subject to negative energy, both from within and without. However, we have the choice whether we nurture and identify with it or not.

When evil comes to call, you will feel totally shamed and belittled to the extent that you will want to hide away, feeling like something is challenging, accusing, and devouring your very essence. Evil is opposed to life while Jesus said he came to bring abundant life. Evil is not intrinsic to the body or the instincts, and therefore, the present preoccupation of many religions on the sins of the flesh are a product of repression. This belief says more about the fear of life and experiencing all of God's creativity than it does about evil. These only appear evil when they are repressed because they become split off from the psyche and produce negative energy. Therefore, as I spoke of earlier, negative energy can work for our good and is certainly not intrinsically evil—it appears so only to those who nurture it and become caught in its grip. In fact, this negative energy and the suffering it causes is often the very instrument of our salvation (healing). Our ego builds walls of denial, which imprison us in defenses—the more rigid the defenses, the more prone we become to being instruments of evil. Redemption is in part reclaiming lost aspects of ourselves. But evil uses negative energy to its own ends, which is to distort truth and its beauty.

Natural evil includes events like famine, earthquakes, floods, disease, pandemic, etc. I will be speculating on the possible function and dynamics of natural evil later in this chapter.

Origins of Evil

Gotta serve somebody
It may be the devil or it may be the Lord
But you gotta serve somebody.

—Bob Dylan, "Gotta Serve Somebody"

The blizzard of the world
Has crossed the threshold
And it's overturned
The order of the soul
When they said Repent
I wonder what they meant . . .

—Leonard Cohen, "The Future"

Before I share my beliefs on the origins of evil, I'd like to review opposing views to my own that have been offered in mythology and other religions.

What of the philosophy of evil, that is why is there evil in the universe? What follows is a canvass of the different beliefs about the origins of evil that I have run across. I'd like to *briefly* explore wisdom traditions and beliefs to get a bird's-eye view of their perspectives on suffering and evil.

First, there is the belief evil and suffering are illusions. This is found in the Hindu and Buddhist traditions. External reality and matter are illusions. Therefore, suffering and evil are created by our attachments to nouns. Buddhism makes this leap through the belief that reality is unified and whole, and it is only through enlightenment that an individual will overcome the illusions of desire and no longer suffer. If we work at it, we can achieve a state of transcendence and nirvana where no disunity exists. There is no personal God in Buddhism. The latest incarnation of the Buddha was Siddhartha. While he was a prince, he chooses to leave the safety of his palace against his parents' wishes, and then he came across the three types of sufferings, that of old age, disease, and death. He was shaken out of his innocence and decided to try to make sense of these sufferings in the hopes of discovering authentic being. After dislodging himself from parental protection and his privileged status, he embraced an extreme asceticism and poverty with a capital *P*. He became sick and recognized in this weakened physical condition that he could experience little in the way of authentic enlightenment. He therefore embraced a more temperate asceticism. Extremism in any form is always destructive and will only lead to additional suffering. He eventually achieved enlightenment after overcoming attacks from evil. I'm not sure how he was attacked by evil if evil is an illusion. He taught his three noble truths that to overcome suffering, one had to eliminate all desires since desire is the cause of all sufferings. If we can quench desire, we will be set free from the cycle of life and become enlightened, reaching nirvana at death. Though I disagree with the notion we are to eliminate desires, there is much to respect in Siddhartha, sacrificing as he did his privileged existence and embraced the unknown as he searched for truth and enlightenment. I believe our desires and longings are intrinsic to our human condition, and therefore, they need to be integrated, not denied or eliminated. Whatever value and purpose we place on suffering, it is within our collective experience and therefore needs to be accepted as opportunities to learn and grow. We cannot love without desires, risks, and yes, attachments. Attachments are necessary though fraught with the temptations toward addictions. The pain and suffering these attachments occasion is a sign of health. We need to be willing to surrender these attachments at a moment's notice, but a philosophy that denies them and desire seems to me to miss one aspect of being really human. Love itself is in part a desire and part action.

Hinduism also believes suffering and evil are illusions; Maya or all matter is a transient realm where we are deceived. Hindus believe personal suffering has to do with an individual's karma. Karma is a balancing of the scales, so to speak. For instance, a person is born in the lower castes because of negative karma created in previous lifetimes. Reincarnation and the transmigration of souls guarantees all energy in the universe will eventually balance itself out. There are many gods in Hinduism with Brahman, the earthly representatives of Vishnu, who dreams, and out of his navel all that comes that we recognize as matter. This is not reality, but only a dream of Vishnu. If you were born in some form of negative circumstances, you're karma in a previous incarnation is the culprit. I do believe there is a balancing that occurs in the universe, and we reap what we sow; the problem I have with this belief system is it justifies treating individuals unequally and leaves little room for much compassion. Nor can I accept physical reality is all an illusion; to be whole we must embrace all in life with the exception of pure evil.

Both of these eastern faiths believe evil is an illusion. I see evil within myself and in others around me, and every day I look at the news. It is what it is, and denying it only gives it more power. I have much to say about the reality of evil as the chapter unfolds.

Another belief system is that the universe is polytheistic, that is with many gods. Within this belief system, there is often a dualism, with two primary gods, one good and the other evil. Evil is therefore consigned to an evil God. This belief system is found in the Egyptian gods Osiris and Set. It is also found in the Gnostics who believed that the lesser God is the deity of the Hebrew Bible, a God who is punishing and negative, while another God is good and enlightens man through secret knowledge. This dualism is also found in Persian myths and Zoroastrianism, a Persian religion predating Islam, which believed there were two equal gods, a God of light and truth and one of darkness and deception. Like the Gnostics, Zoroastrianism believed the world of spirit engulfed the world of good while the material world imprisoned humankind in the world of evil. Evil and suffering are therefore caused by these evil deities. This belief makes logical sense for the existence of evil, but I take issue with the conception that good and evil have equal energy and the material world is evil. Love and truth are infinitely more powerful than evil. I also believe the world of the five senses was created out of the stunning imagination of God and is a reflection in space-time of the beauty of God's glory.

Deism is of the belief that some God created everything, but he is too busy to bother about the trivial lives of individuals, and therefore, we suffer the inevitable pain of fate. This is hard to reconcile for me in that some maker would go to all the trouble of creating everything out of nothing with such mathematical and imaginative precision and then ignore the results. Consciousness and the inner life seem so personal and intimate to those who have ventured into her depths that to believe some deity with consciousness would create and then disregard everything is too great a leap. Love exists, and where else could it stem but from the creator who loves?

The Greek heroes and culture embodied a quest for wholeness and balance in body, mind, and spirit through its diverse pursuits of philosophy, politics, myths, science, tragedy, mathematics, astronomy, astrology, and spirituality. The Greeks taught that we must come to terms with suffering, anxiety, desire, despair, terror, and tragedy rather that run marathons in the other direction. Their heroes include Hercules, Odysseus, Ajax, Perseus, Achilles, and Theseus, who were able to overcome the debilitating nature of suffering and bring back wisdom and truth to the rest of humankind. All had to face their sufferings and tests. This included courage, faith, intelligence, acceptance, etc. The Greek myths are strewn with those who failed to face legitimate suffering like King Midas and Minos, Ecco, Icarus, and Creon. They suffered because of the "Fates," who were Zeus's daughters and who were assumed to be just. The gods themselves took on the entire landscape of human that is with deception, cruelty, arrogance, falsehood, indolence, selfishness, etc. How much one could sway the gods is unclear.

The Greek tragedies took a different approach. Since suffering and evil was humankind's lot, generally the tragedies etch out a portrait of compassion in this most difficult of our collective experiences. Greek philosophy has many divergent responses to human suffering and evil, generally teaching the importance of personal integrity of some fashion or another. In this emphasis on personal integrity, Greek and Judeo-Christian philosophies are similar.

In the Hebrew Bible, there seems to be conflicting views of the origins of evil. Satan is referenced four times in the Hebrew Bible, all post-exilic (John A. Sanford, *Evil: The Shadow Side of Reality*). In the first three references, Satan appears as a personification of evil, and the fourth is in the book of Job, where as we discussed earlier, Satan is a separate being, but one who dwells in God's court.

The Hebrew Bible also references Yahweh as being responsible for evil (Amos 3:6, Isaiah 45:5–7, Isaiah 54:16, 1 Samuel 18:10), all pre-exilic (ibid.). All scriptures must be read critically as they were written by men full of weakness and finitude with their accompanied neurosis, self-deceptions, and delusions. God is also purported to have the Israelites kill women and children in their assimilation of the Promised Land. In the parts of Christian Bible, women are denied the right of leadership and teaching. These infantile beliefs I reject categorically and have nothing to do with the God I have come to understand and worship. *Each of us is responsible to filter through the lens of love and mercy* the nonsense in the scriptures of whatever faith we may belong and recognize the overriding principles that more accurately reflect the God of the universe. Love and mercy are such overriding principles and the lens I use to filter all truth.

Christianity initially was another branch within Judaism (and still is to some, including myself), and its philosophy was similar if not exactly consistent. For the most part, these Western traditions believe God is perfect, whole, and good while evil came from Lucifer's rebellion. God chose to allow for the possibility of evil due to instilling all of his creation with free will. God, however, does transform evil and creates good out of it. Humankind did not create evil but through the fall of humankind in the Garden of Eden, now tainted by it; and we are now capable to becoming pawns of evil if we so choose. I'd like to go into this in much more depth.

Personal Beliefs and Thoughts

In front of the house I'm supposed to be born
I don't think I'm ready to walk through that door
Just yet
To be one more voice in the human choir
Rising like smoke from the mystical fire
Of the heart

—Bruce Cockburn, "Messenger Wind"

First, I'd like to share some experiences with evil I have encountered as a counselor and friend to some trustworthy people. I have two close friends who claim to have personal experiences with demons. I also had a number of previous clients who relayed experiences where they purported seeing demons, angels, and Jesus. I had little reason to doubt my friends or these self-reports. I found all these individuals completely credible and lucid. One past client told me he had a negative near-death experience (NDE), where he left his body when he OD'd. He further told me he was going down into the darkness and was escorted by horrific creatures. He seemed to have no motives for sharing this that I could see outside of needing to get this off his chest to someone whom he thought understood and would empathize. Another client told me a relative of hers reported during her dying process that she saw demons and angels in a battle right in her hospital room. Another client had a vision of Christ in his jail. He said Christ came into his jail cell with open arms after he had killed someone. He put his head under the covers and waited until Christ left.

I subscribe to the Christian belief system as I have described it above. Some of what I have to share is tentative and therefore not essential to my Christian faith. Where I am in error, I will gladly be corrected on the other side. Nothing can be proven, and we must take leaps of faith. Some beliefs are more essential to my faith than others, and I will try to differentiate these as I move forward.

As I said earlier, I think much of the evil we experience is of the moral or psychological kind, which we perpetrated on each other and ourselves. This does not, however, have anything to say about God's possible purpose in allowing evil.

First, I want to review Christian doctrine on the matter in more detail and of which I believe. Chief among the angels God created was Lucifer, the greatest among the angels. It seems the role set out for this being was to augment the spiritual growth of human beings as an adversary, using tests and temptations. At some juncture, Lucifer blasphemed against God due to pride and made false claims. Many angels joined in this rebellion. Therefore, Satan is the originator and source of all evil in the world. Lucifer and the other rebellious angels were cast out into hell, and Lucifer became the Father of Lies and the head of this rebellion. This demonic host wages war again God's plan, and their role is one in its own purpose, which is to destroy God's plan by battling for the souls of individuals. Therefore, God did not create the darkness and evil but did create free will, which presupposes the possibility for rebellion and evil. All I shared about the nature of evil has its roots in Lucifer and the rebellion. How exactly this took/takes place and why God allows evil to perpetuate itself is difficult to decipher. There seems to be no easy answers. Before I speculate on a possible answer, I can say God transforms good out of evil. This can be seen in the story of Jacob's sons in Genesis where Joseph is sold into slavery by his brothers into Egypt. He is eventually responsible for saving the world from starvation by becoming a central figure in Pharaoh's house. Howard Storm put it thus in his recounting of his NDE, and I'd like to quote him at length:

> In my conversations with Jesus and the angels, they
> told me about God. I asked them about God and
> they told me this. God knows everything that will

happen and, more important, God knows everything that could happen. From one moment to the next, God is aware of every possible variable of every event and each outcome. God doesn't control or dictate the outcome of every event, which would be a violation of God's creation. This is because every bit of energy and matter has its own integrity and course to fulfill. Every living creature has its own will that must be expressed. God created all things to be what they are and knows the ultimate outcome is part of the Creator's design. Every action serves God's purpose by fulfilling its nature, including the total range of activity from negative to positive. The outcome will always serve God's ultimate purpose, no matter how long or how impossible it appears to us.

Whether we humans understand why is unimportant because we are not in control of creation. Creatures are not the Creator, and this is not our world to control. Our job is to discover how we can be part of the divine plan. God has given humans a divine image and likeness in order to comprehend our role in the divine plan. God has endowed humans with the divine ability to conceptualize the past and future in order that we may adjust our behavior to further or frustrate the divine will toward ultimate good. God sees our mistakes and allows them to happen, knowing we will suffer the consequences of our mistakes. The Supreme Being sees our right decisions and enjoys the knowledge that we have taken another step closer to God.

They explained to me that people experience God's emotions as we participate in the creation just as God participated in the creation and feels our emotions. The world that we live in and our ability to affect the world is governed by God's

> design. The principle of cause and effect governs
> our life experiences. God wants us to know this to
> the very core of our being. Our every thought and
> every deed has an effect on our sphere of influence.
> Negative thoughts produce negative actions just
> as positive thoughts result in positive outcomes.
> (Howard Storm, *My Descent into Death*)

It seems clear to me God allows evil to exist due to the gift of free will. At the same time, God fashions good out of all the negative energy built up within the universe. God shares all with us and yearns for us to learn and grow through experience, becoming more whole/holy and therefore closer to God. Somewhere along the way, humankind also committed some sort of disobedience or something to that effect. God did not create evil for God is perfect in wisdom and wholeness/holiness. God provides all creation with intelligence and free will, and therefore, the possibility existed for any of God's creatures to reject God. When Lucifer and his minions rebelled, they somehow created evil in the context of that rebellion and therefore separated from all that God is. This rebellion created evil in the forms I discussed earlier in this chapter. Satan personifies the entire ego's narcissistic urges toward pride and falsehood. Evil is the opposite of good, which is wholeness. Evil would not exist if wholeness/goodness did not exist for evil only exists to destroy the good. God does not intervene unless we ask; ask for His/Her help and seek to follow or become a disciple of the truth. The separation was and still is voluntary. We can choose our own will to be done, and we therefore become an instrument of Satan's evil. When we choose evil, we are emulating Satan in some way for that is the source of all evil.

Again it appears to me that Satan is the leader of all rebellion and all who separate from God in this particular segment of creation. Satan rules over this world. It appears from the five exorcisms documented by Malachi Martin in his work "*Hostage to the Devil*" that Satin also demands complete control over all who rebel against God while coercing total servitude and allegiance to its intelligence and absolute power. To quote from Martin,

This difference of spirits from one another on the basis of intelligence seems to culminate in the servile, almost wooden allegiance of all to "the Lord of Knowledge" as Tortoise called him . . . This servility and allegiance to Lucifer among evil spirits is matched in constancy and overshadowed in intensity only by their craven fear and of hatred for Jesus, freely and undisguised displayed at any mention of his name or at the sight of objects and people associated with Jesus.

The misuse of domination and power is personified in the personality of Lucifer, and all I talked about of the nature of evil has its origins in Lucifer. When men and women use political, religious, military, cooperate, etc., power and use fear and domination to control others, they are simply copying and mirroring Lucifer's present state and nature.

The good news is God has won the battle against evil. Though evil remains in effect upon this earth for the time being, it has already lost the war when Jesus conquered death at His resurrection. I have much more to about this in the next chapter on wholeness.

I will now share some further speculations but are not without their own difficulties of which I will also discuss. The following is not an essential part of my faith, but it satisfies me in ways that's hard to illustrate. *I have come to believe all human beings were created before we came upon the earth, and our coming to earth is a choice we made. I also believe we had a part in the dynamics of creation and how this universe was constructed.* I first came across this notion when I read Betty Eadie's *Embraced by the Light* in the early 1990s. She shared a revelation from Jesus during an NDE that we all exist prior to being born as referenced in the epigraph by Bruce Cockburn at the beginning of this section. She goes on to say a veil of forgetfulness masks our true identity as spiritual beings. This implies we also choose to take the risk inherent in this decision to come to earth. We all agreed and had a say to the laws or principles that limit experiences here on earth. The general idea is we all agreed to these limitations that are necessary for our greater growth that can be achieved in our souls and spirits in this earthly life. Since we decided to become human beings, we choose with God the specifics regarding our personal circumstances, abilities, attributes, friends, parents, strengths and weaknesses, body types, the historical period we would live out our lives, etc. I also believe some of us do reincarnate. There seems to be many personal testimonies from most every culture that reincarnation and prebirth planning occurs and much evidence to support many of these claims (see Robert Schwartz's *Courageous Souls* and Brian Weiss, MD's *Many Masters*). If we live in a spiritual state prior to becoming human, and many of our circumstances and life experiences are planned beforehand, this can account for the suffering we incur because it implies a choice on our part. This includes natural evil of which I spoke of earlier in that if we are included in the plans for creation and in some of the specific details of our life's circumstances, then we are no longer victims of natural evil but rather participants in our destiny. If it turns out that I am all wrong on this score, I will have no problem with it because I do know that on many levels, my finite rational mind is limited and can never grasp the eternal by any method or system while I'm on earth. God's ways are often inscrutable to human understanding, yet I believe we are to delve inward and outward nonetheless in an attempt to make sense of our experiences. My faith is strong on this point; that God works for good in all circumstances and is full of more love/compassion and understanding than most of us can ever imagine. God also yearns for a personal relationship with all his creatures while sharing in our angst and joys while longing for us to share in God's.

A major problem with this belief is why would anyone choose some of the horrors that occur from within the landscape of the human condition? Does this mean some of us choose to be raped and murdered, and how does this square with other individuals' free will? I would suspect we have some agreements with others prior to becoming human, but this does not take into account the evil that we commit upon one another as a choice that is opposed to God's will. I know in my case I question my sanity in choosing many of my circumstances in some type of prebirth session! In addition, have I experienced some circumstances because they we preplanned or natural consequences for my indolence, blindness, and missing the mark. I can't answer these obvious objections and conundrums yet find somewhere within the walls of these beliefs something that satisfies me in a profound and essential way. Perhaps in our prebirth state, we are privy to a perspective on the circumstances and events in our lives, which provide the opportunities for us to grow in ways that otherwise we would be unable to accomplish. *Regardless, I have chosen to personally delve deep into all my experiences on a practical and rational level.* I have found meaning in most of my circumstances and occurrences through my faith and rational abilities where I glimpse God's love and grace shining through the horror and anguish of these life events. But I must confess, there are others where my faith has had to stand alone and accept the things that have occurred without any rational understanding whatsoever. The fact that I have experienced God's presence is enough for me, and although this rarely takes the form of comfort on an emotion level, it does bring a certain sort of joy—that all is well and I am cared for and guided through this life no matter what the outward circumstances. Whether I made some choices before I was born has no impact on my faith that God is working in all things for my good, and nothing can separate me from God's love (Romans 8).

I also believe that all come to God through Christ, but that this choice is offered beyond our death; that is we can choose God through Christ no matter what circumstances we come from, be it another faith or from skepticism and even after becoming instruments of evil.

> You may come to me in your deepest faith
> Or you may come in disbelief

> —Leonard Cohen, "Lover, Lover, Lover"

Enlightenment and Wholeness

I asked my Father
I said Father change my name
The one I'm using now is covered up with
Fear and filth and cowardice and shame . . .

You may come to me in happiness
Or in you may come to me in deepest grief
You may come to me in deepest faith
Or you may come in disbelief

Yes and lover, lover, lover, lover, lover,
Lover, lover come back to me . . .

—Leonard Cohen, "Lover, Lover, Lover"

Introduction

Whenever God shines a light on me
Opens up my eyes so I can see . . .

Reach out for Him, He'll be there
With Him your troubles you can share
If you live the life you love
You get the blessings from above.

He heals the sick and heals the lame
Says you can do it too in Jesus name.

He'll lift you up and turn you around
And put your feet on higher ground.

—Van Morrison, "Whenever God Shines His Light"

I want to acknowledge my debt to Ken Wilber's *A Brief History of Everything*, Thomas Merton's *The Inner Experience: Notes on Contemplation* and *New Seeds of Contemplation*, John A. Sanford's *The Kingdom Within: The Inner Meaning Of Jesus' Sayings*, *Ego and Archetype* by Edward F. Edinger, and Howard Storm's *My Descent into Death*. I refer the reader these and other individuals who have achieved a much greater degree of enlightenment than I. Although what I wish to share I believe and/or have experienced for myself, the fact of the matter is I am very inconsistent in my own living out these truths of wholeness and enlightenment. Many of these viewpoints and perspectives—which all seem to coincide with what we know from quantum physics, psychology, anthropology, history, etc.—have grown within me, and it is impossible to say what the exact influence each of these writers has had upon my own maturation and perspectives. I do know the ability of these writers to elucidate and articulate these principles of truth has gripped me, and I gratefully acknowledge their influence and inspiration and encourage you, reader, to familiarize yourselves with these works as well as all the music that goes with the lyrics found throughout this work.

I wish to discuss enlightenment/wholeness in a general sense before discussing Jesus of Nazareth, who I believe exhibited what an enlightened individual looks like before going on to discuss the nature of the contemplative life, which is the means in my opinion to achieve wholeness and enlightenment. I have chosen to live alone these last years and pursue the life of a contemplative in much silence and solitude. I share all that I discover within myself with God alone but realize I don't need to share everything with others any longer because something's are only meant for God. I also have found myself defending or justifying some actions or motives at times when it was better that I remain silent and allow God to be my prosecutor and defender. I know I have many defects of character, and it is only God that has the infinite patience to forgive and listen to the entire inner life that abides within me. I wish I was more constant and unswerving in all I am about to share, but alas, I am what I am, no more and no less.

I feel this is an appropriate juncture to be more specific about my personal faith. *I am a disciple of Christ and believe Jesus demonstrated through his earthly life, teachings, and death and proved via his resurrection that he houses within himself all truth. There are many roads to God, and all the spiritual traditions have validity and truth that have led some of their followers to enlightenment and into the essence of God.* Though I'm a follower of Jesus, I do not feel compelled to convert others to my beliefs. I don't believe pushing one's spirituality onto others is motivated by love. The spirit of truth will speak for itself in the hearts and minds of others. Though I believe everyone eventually comes to God through Christ, the path that this takes within each individual is unique, and I dare not assume to know the workings of God in another's psyche. Nor am I willing to judge anyone or their path to God. Neither am I ashamed of my faith as I attempt to channel God's truth to others. I pray that others may see Christ in me. I do know that others care little of my claims to be a follower of Jesus and that it is of much more significance as to how I live my life and whether I reflect His poise, peace, joy, and love. This, it seems to me, is what people are longing for.

When will I ever learn to live in God
When will I ever learn
He gives me everything I need and more
When will I ever learn

Whatever it takes to fulfill His mission
That's the way we must go
But you've got to do it in your own way
Tear down the old bring up the new.

—Van Morrison, "When Will I Ever Learn to Live in God"

Enlightenment and Wholeness

Chop that wood
Carry water
What's the sound of one hand clapping
Enlightenment, don't know what it is

Every second, every minute
It keeps changing to something different . . .

It says its non attachment, non attachment

I'm in the here and now, and I'm meditating
And still I'm suffering but that's my problem
Enlightenment, don't know what it is

—Van Morrison, "Enlightenment"

For me, enlightenment is living freely in the moment with a relaxed openness and grateful expectation in God's presence. It is a depth of faith and knowledge that is ineffable but can only be hinted at in symbols. Yet it is a living, breathing consciousness of God, which lives in and through us. Since this changes and cannot be put into words, and so we get profound proverbs like it's the sound of one hand clapping from the great Zen Buddhist tradition. Hence, an enlightened individual lives in the real world of duty and responsibility but also in eternity via the unique type of mindful consciousness that is indicative of the contemplative. The past needs to be forgiven and worked through so it can be forgotten, except for the wisdom we have gained from it. The anxiety of the future must be turned over in faith in nonattachment to a higher consciousness that we somehow know is guiding and *directing our lives out of love and for our good.* There is a clear summons to *experience* God's gifts of love and recollection where God already exists within us and fills our consciousness with truths and loving energy in the moment. This is accompanied with differing degrees of peace and joy in the midst of our sufferings. Through this gift of recollection, God shares His/Her thoughts with us in the moment, which keeps changing as moments give way to new moments. Of course, other intrusions invade our consciousness all the time, including life's pleasures and temptations, to distract us from the real inner work of the psyche and spirit. The work of self-discipline is lengthy and harsh to those who choose to be trained by it.

Our ego-body-consciousness is designed to circle and revolve around God's will and not its selfish desires and longings. Our individual lives are meant to be a satellite of the truth, which God personifies in His/Her infinite mystery. There is no more important truth! This truth is present deep within us all but often forgotten in the clamor and noise of everyday ego-body-consciousness.

From this truth, enlightenment it to recognize everything fits in and belongs in the great web of being. "For everything there is a season, and a time for every matter under heaven" (Ecclesiastes 3:1). There truly is a time to experience whatever comes to pass and learn to recognize God's presence in all that is. In addition, the writer of Ecclesiastes goes on to say, "I have seen the business that God has given to the sons of men to be busy with. He made everything beautiful in its time; also he has put eternity into man's mind, yet so that he cannot find out what God has done from the beginning to the end" (Ecclesiastes 3:10–11). God's presence lies within everything and every experience, but the entire purpose and plan remains a mystery. Faith in and intimate friendship with God is what can enter the breach between knowledge of eternity and the mysteries that encompass it.

Truth and love is the pinnacle of everything. Truth and love are one and measured by suffering. We do not choose love and truth, but they choose us through the mystery of God's wholeness/holiness. The only place to begin to grasp, encounter, and demonstrate the unity of truth and love is through our capacity to endure and learn from our sufferings. All suffering is beneficial to us and others and therefore vicarious by its very nature. All suffering is redemptive as it teaches us eternal truths and is used by fate to help others. This is where all enlightenment begins. That is why it is imperative we come to befriend and accept all our experiences, especially that of suffering. I know these are dark and foreboding assertions. I have come to embrace and delight in most paradoxes, losses, deaths, and contradictions, but there are many that remain a complete mystery to me. So be it.

This life of faith specifically entails the life of the mystical contemplative and is found in all the major faiths. Most of the traditions *include prayer as an essential aspect of mystical contemplation.* I will have much more to say about the contemplative later in this chapter as it seems to me the essential process by which we humans achieve enlightenment. I believe reality and truth are unfolding via God's creative consciousness through energy, matter, and space- time. All the higher forms in existence that have evolved—including consciousness, emotions, free will, the ability to reason, and love—emanate from God's nature through His Holy Spirit to all of creation. Everything has the potential to continue to evolve. We humans and the universe are still evolving! In one way or another, everything emanates from and returns to God, with the exception of evil. Evil will not be forced to return to God as God does not impose Her will upon any of Her creature or creations. Whether evil repents and returns to God is up to evil itself. All of creation, including evil, has its own integrity and purpose to fulfill. All of us have the choice to become nothing and arrogant and regress endlessly backward into less depth, substance, and complexity. The process that separates the sheep from the goats is experiential learning and the choices we make when confronted with our experiences. Everything created is allowed to act and to fulfill its nature. Even evil is permitted to fulfill its nature and is miraculously transformed in some mysterious ways and used to serve God's ultimate purposes. This does not mean evil is good or to justify its horrific nature. *We must all be on our guard and not become the instruments of evil.* All living creatures have a will that seeks expression, and the most complex of all living creatures, human beings, are capable of growing into the likeness of God or Satan.

We have a choice to cooperate with God's creative will and purpose as it has and continues to unfold by growing in more depth and complexity through intimacy, contact, and knowledge of God. This process inherently exposes us to a growing understanding of ourselves and others as God reveals His/Her nature to us. We know God when we experience what God experiences through His/Her wholeness in the unfolding archetypes, which are overflowing and loaded with positive and negative energies.

Meister Eckhart recognized that God's shares directly with us—in all our experiences. In fact, I believe God becomes more conscious through our consciousness and delights in our experiences and uniqueness. This is a truth few have grasped in its complexity and depth. Everything we experience, God experiences as well. The bond and intimate friendship with God that is a product of this reality and truth has the potential to transform anyone who internalizes it. By nurturing the inner life of the soul and spirit, we find God dwells within us wherever we are and whatever we have done. In addition, we will be given the privilege and honor to experience what God experiences. Wonder of wonders that the creator and God of the universe wants to share with us, his creatures, His/Her own will, pain and pathos, joy, designs, creativity, glory, peace, intimate thoughts, compassion, understanding, acceptance, mercy, and so much more than any of us can imagine! Much more of this sharing and intimacy will occur beyond the second death when we are free from the limitations of space-time. (The first death is where some of us die to our ego as the center of our personality and will.)

The Spirit of God is the Spirit of Truth, which guides the willing into enlightenment and wholeness, which is consciousness and awareness of God at each and every moment. We become conscious of God at each moment by surrendering each moment to God. This is a spiritual law or truth very few have recognized and fewer have achieved. We are fragile, dying, and full of contradictions and weaknesses. Fulfilling our needs for self-worth and security can only be achieved through God's presence in the struggle of faith. It is in the struggle of faith where we wrestle with the tensions inherent within the pairs of opposites. Wholeness begins by accepting and surrendering to these truths. In this universe, God houses and exalts love, freedom of the will, and creativity. Our purpose is to uncover God and His will within us and follow God's great adventure as His will weaves in and through each and every momentary experience. Principles and laws—physical, psychological, spiritual—were created to frame our experience and allow opportunities to grow into the image and likeness of God. I wish to quote Howard Storm, who also emphasizes the link between God-loving consciousness and our consciousness:

The creation is entirely in the *now* to God. God's consciousness is the entire creation. Everything that was, and everything that will be, is *this moment to God*. God is incomprehensible to us except in the ways that he has chosen to reveal the true nature of himself to us. We have been given the ability to know God by being made in "the image and likeness of God." The prime characteristics that allows us to know something about God is love. Love is to care intensely about something. We say we love chocolate, fishing, history, a person, cars, gardening, flying, sewing, music, and so on. The passion we experience is sharing in God's passion for everything. Our love is from God. When we love, we experience God. God loves everything passionately. Love is infinitely complex because there are so many variables. We were created to learn how to love. It takes more than a lifetime of experience to learn to live lovingly. Each person will be given all the experiences one needs to learn how to love.

Everything is now to God while *Homo sapiens* live within this fabric of space-time and experience everything sequentially. In this universe, reality is spread out, so to speak, affording us opportunities to integrate truth. *Love is the key to unlocking the mystery of God and overcoming of all fear, guilt, shame, grief, self-deception, and the illusion of separateness.* Negative energy and evil seeks to separate and destroy wholeness as it seeks to control us. *We are capable of surrendering to God's will or rebelling.* Ignoring God is another form of rebellion and is deeply wounding to God. We need to allow ourselves to love, grieve, accept, surrender our attachments, and come to the realization that everything is connected to God, including our innermost selves. Whenever we open ourselves up to the depths of our inner life, we will unearth emotions, rational concepts, beliefs, and attitudes that merge with God's will to form being. *It is at this point in self-awareness that we need to share intimately with God all that we find hidden by letting God into our innermost selves. We will then be prepared to experience God sharing His/ Her nature with us.*

Everybody knows the secret,
Everybody knows the score,
I have finally found a place to live
In the presence of the Lord.

—Blind Faith, "Presence of the Lord"

The best definition of enlightenment I have come across was expressed by Howard Storm which I quote here: "Enlightenment is to see God working in every moment." *That is to say, to be enlightened is to be conscious of God's presence in each moment.* From what I have gathered to date, what this is in actual practice is both an active and passive process, an active seeking of God's presence by surrendering each moment to God and by practicing the spiritual disciplines, which put to death the ego's selfish ways and surrendering to God's will while simultaneously experiencing infused grace from God. God brings to our thoughts recollections of truths through a variety of channels. Our task is to tune in to God's frequency and follow His/Her directions.

As I declared in the introduction, I defined truth as the convergence and integration of understanding/wisdom and holiness/wholeness in the context of the archetypal pairs of opposites. It is interesting that the root for *integrity* is *integer*, which means wholeness and completeness (from W. Scott Peck's *The Road Less Traveled and Beyond*). Therefore, to have integrity is to integrate and be whole and complete through understanding and praxis. We are to incorporate truth into our soul or psyche through the cooperating of our soul/sprit and God's Spirit. Becoming whole and enlightened is a process whereby a harmony of body, psyche, and spirit is approached. We must embrace every aspect of being and celebrate being as it expresses itself in wholeness. There are so many unlived aspects of life that we must learn to live through experience. *To accomplish these tasks, we need to surrender each moment to God's will. We therefore seek a personal relationship with God through obedience, faith, and contemplation. All the spiritual traditions include mystical and contemplative elements, which are very similar.*

These are the days of the endless summer
These are the days, the time is now . . .

There's only here, there's only now

Oh you're smiling face, your gracious presence
By the fires of spring are kindling bright
On the radiant heart and the song of glory
Cry of freedom in the night.

These are the days of the sparking river
His timely grace is a treasured thing
This is the love of the one magician
Turn the water into wine

—Van Morrison, "These Are the Days"

Soul and Spirit

I swept the marble chambers,
But you sent me down below,
You kept me from believing
Until you let me know;

That I am not the one who loves—
It's love who chooses me.

—Leonard Cohen, "You Have Loved Enough"

God is Spirit, and Spirit is perfect truth where all wisdom, pure and perfect knowledge, love, creativeness, and holiness/wholeness are ubiquitously present and eternal. Human spirit, though created in God's image, lacks the perfection and wholeness of God. However, pure truth exists potentially in the human spirit because we are created in God's image. Though rarely is it completely manifested in the lives of human beings, this perfection is an extension, if you will, of God's Spirit. Our spirit can only reach toward pure truth by worshiping God in spirit and in truth as God infuses us with His/Her nature. However, all truth is filtered through our perceptions in our brains where analyzing, rationalizing, etc., often distorts our experience of pure truth. Human spirit is capable of a union with God's Spirit in a perfect harmony through the work of the soul and all the dialectical pairs of opposites shaped by God's extraordinary imaginative creativity. This union with God automatically unites us with every other created being, human and nonhuman. We will never know the depths of God's creative imagination nor perfection while on earth. We aspire toward perfection through faith. Our spirit can join with God's Spirit and approach oneness with God by our psyche's participation in both our and God's Spirit by aligning ourselves with the laws and principles inherent in creation. Since we have discussed the psyche/soul in depth, I'd like to take a shot at spirit.

What makes up spirit? What I believe is first our spirit is filled with differing degrees and portions of pure love and truth, which is initially forgotten upon our birth. Our spirit's deepest desire is to love God, others, and ourselves. Therefore, spirit contains passion. Love does not exist without the emotional glue, which binds love to its objects. We accomplish these tasks to the degree we participate in adapting and integrating God's love. Our spirit can accept and surrender to the Spirit of Truth (God's Spirit) and internalize—another important component of Spirit. Spirit is receptive and internalizes the truths from life's experiences. When our psyche or soul becomes a satellite of God's Spirit of Truth, we become transformed into God's likeness more and more. Our will is gradually transformed to love and obey God's will until our will and God's become one and the same. Our spirit contains different degrees of love and knowledge and wisdom at birth, though a veil of forgetfulness shields our understanding of our true spiritual nature and all its capabilities for wisdom and holiness/wholeness. Spirit longs to be one with the unconditional love of God and is capable of offering love back to God. Each spirit is created uniquely with different capacities, as is our psyche's. Our spirits essence is hidden like the treasure in a field of the unconscious as Jesus shared in his famous parable (Matthew 13:44).

As we explored in the chapter on evil, our spirit can digress and be harmed through the negative energies of fear, hatred, self-deception, etc., which are used by evil spirit to distort the truth. We can recharge our spirits, so to speak, by worshiping God through contemplative prayer, serving others, faith, and locating the truth and the positive in so-called negative experiences.

Truth or wisdom involves finding a synthesis of understanding and will, knowledge and actions, insight and behavior. Wisdom takes knowledge and integrates it with the cooperation of the will, which is that aspect of our souls that makes choices. It is here a healthy balance is achieved where priorities are fashioned and truth is lived and valued. Thought and life must be wedded. Perhaps some have achieved this, but I don't think I've ever met anyone who has accomplished these ideals; however, this must not deter us. Strive for perfection, and yet we shall never accomplish this perfection on earth.

Here is a paradox and dialectic of the first order. We need to maintain the tension this particular pair of opposites occasion while passionately pursuing both sides of these opposites. Both the pursuit of perfection and the impossibility in its achievement are simultaneously believed and valued. Because paradox goes beyond the rational, it is often termed irrational. However, the irrational is rational, yet beyond the confines of the rational mind. The great oracle at Delphi had two temples, one to Apollo, the God of the consciousness and rationality, and Dionysus, the God of the unconscious and irrational. The Greeks myths and philosophy celebrated all elements found within the human psyche; that is soul (mind, emotion, will) along with the body and spirit, while also attempting to develop and live them. Out of such balance comes inner peace and love. All truth emanates from God, from the Spirit of Truth, which Christians call the Holy Spirit. God's Spirit animates our human spirit, and both God's and our spirit stand behind the unconscious mind or psyche/soul, informing and animating it, just as the soul animates the body. Whether we seek a union with God is up to us. It is the only way to wholeness and holiness and the joys it engenders. All joy emanates from the beauty inherent in the holiness/wholeness with God's character. True joy is recognizing the Spirit of Christ in everyone and everything we come across. Laughter is the outward expression of joy.

The inner torments that are occasioned by our wrestling with each pair of opposites are difficult to bear. As we grow closer to wholeness, our own faults and weaknesses will haunt us as new revelations of defects and weaknesses cascade across consciousness. Behaviors and attitudes about which we never gave a second thought now cause ineffable heartache as we recognize our selfishness and the pain we cause others. We will need to sacrifice much that is bent on security and acceptance from others and built on illusions. Our relationships, careers, material goods, and pursuits will all be subject to scrutiny and perhaps discarded along life's trail because they stand in the way of growth. We need be willing to surrender all our ego attachments to temporal objects. Some will be swept away by fate. It is usually the case in the course of a healthy life that both occur.

In this life, achieving complete wholeness is impossible. However, we need to make the endeavor! It is also true that this hard work will take different shapes and is unique for each person. Therefore, it is imperative we not judge one another along the way. However, as we have explored throughout this book, there are some principles and universal truths and reality that form a guide toward wholeness. We are created in God's image and have therefore a spirit, soul, and body. All three aspects of being must be harmonized and brought to completeness or wholeness. We must leave everything that binds us to this world with our defenses and temporal aims so we can be free to grow toward wholeness, which is another way to say toward God. What I hope to illustrate in this chapter is what emerges as we approach the dynamics of wholeness and enlightenment. Neither I nor anyone will be able to live or express this completely. However, while it varies with each personality, we are able to catch a glimpse of spirit in action as the Spirit of Truth expresses itself in our world of space-time. We will be exploring the personality of Jesus that comes through the gospels and how he uncovers, represents, and contains wholeness. In addition, we will explore contemplation and the what and how they manifest themselves within the enlightened knight of faith.

I also believe the physical universe was created out of a unity of God. The evolution of the universe has been a painstaking process from chaos to order over the course of billions of years to finally culminate in consciousness. Consciousness itself seems to be growing and developing throughout human history and, in some individuals, into more and more wholeness. Each of us is a unique center in which God experiences reality through us as we experience reality through God! I am now going to look what I believe is a unique personality and how he exhibited wholeness unlike any other.

Enlightenment and Wholeness in Jesus of Nazareth

Jesus of Nazareth

He is the way, He is the truth, He is the light.
Put your feet back on higher ground.

—Van Morrison, "Whenever God Shines His Light"

The question remains, what does a whole and enlightened individual look like? The question is not completely answered in the text of Job or in the life of Odysseus. What does the individuation process consist of and look like in the concrete life of the individual? From my perspective, Jesus is Whole and Holy, Perfect and One with God and having been created as having life within Himself as God's only begotten Son. Jesus of Nazareth chose to empty himself of his Godhead and become human in order to demonstrate and illustrate what union with God is and looks like and how to achieve wholeness and holiness through faith and communion with God. When Jesus conquered death, he conquered it along with all fears and guilt for the persons of faith. Likewise, each can find security and worth in Christ. Like Job, Jesus accepted suffering and took his strong individuated ego and surrendered it to the transpersonal center of all—God the Father/Mother. He went beyond Job by embracing his suffering, living out every aspect of wholeness, conquering evil, sin, and even death.

The authentic teachings and practices of Jesus in the gospels within the Christian Bible expose a personality unlike any other and contain a repository of truth that has scarcely been comprehended, appreciated, or actualized. Nobody could have created or imagined the personality of Jesus; it is so striking and beyond all convention. The wisdom and holiness/wholeness reflected and neglected in these traditions contains seeds for further explorations and interpretations (see John Dominic Crossan's *Cliffs of Fall: Paradox and Polyvalence it the Parables of Jesus*).

The seeds of contemplation, of silence and solitude, are scattered all over the teaching and practices of Jesus and his disciples. There are many treasures yet to be uncovered and fashioned by any wishing to grow in spiritual ways. However, no one book, no any one individual's experience can contain the height, depth, length, and width of what it means to be intimate with God in each moment. It seems God experiences Himself through the billions of individuals created in His/Her image. We need each other for this ongoing journey.

To be all we are meant to be—whole and unified with God in Christ—we must pursue the individuation process. This process of individuation is making conscious that uniqueness, which is buried within our unconscious, where God dwells in the secret place of our mysterious being and specific to each individual. I believe Jesus is the perfect example of individuation, so we will look into his life in more depth.

Jesus is the perfect example of what is possible to achieve in wholeness—living and reflecting God's reality. The coming of God's Kingdom is the coming of redemption, salvation (healing), and wholeness for all who are willing to follow Jesus. I think Jesus both taught and lived what completeness means; there were no aspects of an unlived life within Jesus as the Kingdom of God dawned upon his arrival. What did Jesus live that was developmental and whole?

First, Jesus surrendered his ego-body-consciousness to God the Father/Mother and lived a wholeness and union with God, which we can only strive for. The purpose for a disciple is to be like Christ. In the presence of God, self died away, and Jesus was able to embrace his mission and purpose. It is the same for us. We must die a thousand deaths if we are to be reborn a thousand times.

Secondly, Jesus perfected and made conscious all four conscious functions in perfect harmony. (see John Sanford's chapter 1, "The Personality of Jesus," in his work *The Kingdom Within*). Jesus's personality was whole with the thinking and feeling, sensing and intuiting functions all expressed in various authentic teachings and actions of Jesus throughout the gospels. Let me try to sum up some of Sanford's insights.

Jesus's sensing function was obviously well developed as he was not only purported to be a stone mason/carpenter; but also his use of metaphors were brimming with images from the natural world. He also went to a wedding, turning water into wine, thus affirming sex in marriage and alcohol as a celebratory substance. His intuitive function was also equally developed as he has insights into men's being and knew what was within each man's soul (John 2:23–4; also see *The Kingdom Within* by John Sanford.) His thinking function was also uncovered in his teachings and dealings with the religious leaders of his day. His was wisdom personified as anyone who has tried to take in the Sermon on the Mount can verify and in the numerous retorts he had to challenges from the myopic religious leaders of his day. An example of his keen intellect and intuition is located in Matthew 22:15–23 when he tells the Pharisees to render unto Caesar what is Caesar's and to God what is God's. His feeling function expressed itself in his tears, the incredible compassion he had for all but the completely phony and self-righteous, his cleansing of the temple, and among many other examples, his emphasis on mercy, justice, and loving God, neighbor, and self and so fulfilling the entire law.

Thirdly, his sense of meaning and purpose, security and worth, were linked to God the Father/Mother in heaven. Jesus was also able to synthesize the archetypes the universe contains: femininity with masculinity, life with death, independence with intimacy, introversion with extroversion, possibility with necessity, laughter and joy with sorrow, etc. This is with the exception towards evil for God the Father/Mother and Jesus are perfect in all the qualities of truth. Jesus took a firm and uncompromising stance against evil and injustice.

Fourthly, He had no false or external self (persona) that he hid behind, but only the interior self—the Spirit of Truth. The external self is where ego-body-consciousness is in the position of superiority; the exterior and false self is in charge of its full regalia of selfishness, dishonesty, and laziness. This false or exterior self puts barriers or walls of objects between the inner man and experience. The real and immediate experience is what the mystics call recollection; that is where God speaks to the soul intimately in awakening the inner self or our spirit. Nevertheless, he knew when to put up his walls and not trust himself to certain individuals while maintaining love for all. In contrast, the once born are concerned with temporal aims and building monuments to their ego, which is concerned with power and control. The once born do not even recognize the selfish pursuit of wealth as a problem; rather, they have mutated it into a virtue!

Finally, Jesus rose from the dead and is in our midst! His historical life and living personality discloses wholeness in the sphere of God's perspective. His death and resurrection proclaims and publicizes God's power and love and redemption to bring humans back to God and into a completion or wholeness in anyone willing to partake in the good news of His Kingdom. Jesus rose from the dead and not only is in our midst, but in addition, His poise and complete oneness with the Father was validated by His resurrection and is extended for all who follow Him (John 17:20–26). His death and resurrection proclaims and publicizes God's power and love and redemption to bring humans back to God and into a union with God for those willing to genuinely pursue God in His Truth. Jesus prayed for his followers to be sanctified in the truth (John 17:17).

> And I owe my heart to you
> And that's saying it true
> And I'll be with you when the deal goes down.
>
> —Bob Dylan, "When the Deal Goes Down"

The Contemplative

No Guru, no method, no teacher
Just you and I and nature
And the Father and the
Son and the Holy Ghost . . .

—Van Morrison, "In the Garden"

How do we become contemplatives and fulfill our unique purpose and so return to God and cultivate a union with God? Above all else, the contemplative both actively seeks and passively receives an intuitive union with God. External circumstances are vital in this process, yet the contemplative actively seeks and willingly chooses to experience the painful and excruciation light of God's love in silence and solitude.

Active or Meditative Contemplation

Active contemplation begins by our efforts/willingness to seek, detect, and adapt our life to the will of God. Contemplation is a combination of meditation, study, and prayer. This prepares us for infused contemplation, which we will explore in the next segment. Prayer is on the whole chiefly significant and the key to unlocking the mysteries of our union with God because it prompts a mindfulness of God in every thought, activity, and circumstance within our life. And union with God is the aim of the contemplative. Union with God is integrating His truths into our characters. To be one with God, we need to be like Him. There are many methods used by contemplatives, but many seem to get in the way of experiencing communion with God. However, some structure to prayer is efficacious, and I'd like to offer an example of contemplative prayer that I have come to employ.

I begin by becoming still in God's presence through deep breathing (deep breathing is a universal meditative technique, which stills the soul in preparation to experience consciously God's presence). I breathe in by saying the simple prayer "Father, come to my aid" and breathe out with "Jesus, have mercy." These two simple but powerful prayers help me center and become conscious of God's presence. I can't remember where I read these prayers, but I know they were in my books on contemplation. I then share all that is in my heart with God. This sharing leads to supplication for others' needs, the earth, guidance, holiness/wholeness, peace, the church, etc., and any problems in the world that crosses my radar. When I pray for myself, I try to limit my prayers to the sanctification of my soul by repentance and then empty myself by turning everything over to God. At times I also am led to claim certain things and then wait upon God's activity to take place in His manner and timing. My supplications often capture and mirror the Psalms. The Psalms contain a storehouse of truths about what goes on within the hearts and minds of my inner life. I then empty myself and seek God's presence in silence and solitude. I try to quiet my mind and wait in silence and solitude before God. Sometimes nothing occurs but a struggle to lay aside distractions of my mind; at other times I hear specific words in my mind; at others I hear nothing but know that resting in God's presence is where real transformation occurs. Ironically, the dry times in prayer when I feel nothing are usually more efficacious where change is concerned. Why this is I do not know but am aware that the dry times are a testing of my willingness to trust and obey God without feeling Her presence. I cling to God in my weaknesses, and this very contact flows into my being, reviving my fervor for all the *truth* that God is.

At other times, tears of anguish and joy coexist during times of silent meditation and communion. Any work is fruitless without contact with God's presence. Whatever I notice within me, I try to be mindful and discern whether it is from God or myself in its selfishness, false pride, indolence, etc., or the evil one. I attempt to nurture God's presence and truth while turning aside those thoughts or desires that stem from self or the evil one. My active meditations usually are upon Jesus's teachings or practices or the Psalms. Finally, I praise and thank God for all that is—the trials and suffering that I incur as well as the successes and blessings. I adore God and appreciate the sun or rain, the pain or joy, obscurity or enlightenment. I recognize the contemplative is not to get hung up on how we feel or whether I receive anything tangible; these are unimportant in the grand scheme of contemplative prayer. At times I find myself just resting in the love of God's presence while offering my friendship and presence to God. I adore Jesus and the Father and want to be like them. Silence in prayer is where we become aware of that secret place where our spirit and God's dwell together.

Meditation is of two types, the silent and directed. Both are essential and eventually become different forms of prayer themselves. Meditation is providing an opening for God to commune with us. To do the work of a contemplative, one must naturally detach and surrender the attachments of the exterior self or persona via the spiritual disciplines. For an excellent description and study of these, see Dallas Willard's *The Spirit of the Disciplines: Understanding How God Changes Lives.*

The two most important of the disciplines are silence and solitude where a prayerfulness and mindfulness of God's presence is nurtured. Active contemplation begins with prayerful silence and solitude and is scattered all over the teaching and practices of Jesus. To seek solitude and silence, one must naturally detach and surrender our attachments to temporal objects and aims. In silence and solitude, we are able to grow in self-knowledge and learn the art of living within our own skin. Only within the context of an active awareness of God's presence can we hope to reach out to others with acts of love, which channel God's healing love to the specific needs of another. God's wisdom knows the needs of each person, and the contemplative is one channel in ferrying others toward their truths, which are contained in their uniqueness, whether assisting them in recognizing where they are stuck, locating their abilities and talents, and in general providing wisdom where their needs may crave friendship, understanding, forgiveness, acceptance, etc. Nurturing the inner life is the beginning of the process of becoming enlightened, being cognizant of and infused with God's presence in each and every moment. God's creative energy of love begins to stir in the contemplative and where true freedom begins. Active contemplation is preparing our souls to receive the infused love of God.

The twice born are those whose inner life is willing to surrender and die a thousand deaths. We die to among other things, to the senses, external objects, others' opinions of us, our modes of experiencing the world, old beliefs, controlling others and situations, our selfish desires, laziness, self-deceptions, etc. The death of the ego precedes any lasting freedom and maturity; where integrity, honesty, health, love, egalitarianism, courage, and *wisdom/truth* can abide in our psyche. The contemplative never stands above anyone, but rather is a humble servant of all. The contemplative also understands the human condition from the inside out because God gradually reveals all truths that the contemplative is capable of understanding. There is no show, no phoniness, no arrogance in the mature contemplative; they nurture a death of the ego-consciousness as the center of their personality and, in all things, submit their ego-consciousness wishes, desires, interests, abilities, weaknesses, failures, successes; and all their experiences are gratefully accepted as God's will. They are thereby transformed and become capable of transforming the world.

Contemplation itself is the intuition of God's presence in us. This intuition is insight or sight that comes from within. Contemplatives have also described it as knowing without knowing. His grace, direction, love, mercy, joy, and peace—all wisdom and holiness/wholeness is potentially in us all. However, we receive these blessing passively; it is God's work in our body, soul, and spirit. This process is theologically called sanctification where the individual becomes holy/whole. We put forth the effort by withdrawing all projection and living the tension of the clash of opposites within us while accepting our shadow, anima or animus, and reconciling the opposites. Traditional characteristics of sanctity are all based on *love*, whether it is courage, honesty, meekness, gentleness, faithfulness, patience, kindness, humility, sacrificial, merciful endurance, trust, hope, mystery, etc. These characteristics must be balanced with a connection to the world, and the forms it takes must be concrete and practical.

Too often, weak-minded individuals seek holiness at the cost of wholeness. I want to clarify what perfection means. When Jesus said, "You must be perfect our heavenly Father is perfect (Matthew 5:48), John A. Sanford said the following about the Greek word translated perfect: "The difficulty for the English reader hinges on the word perfect. This implies to the modern mind the idea of a one-sided pureness; that is, a person without any kind of thought or emotion that could be regarded as in any way sinful or wrong. The Greek word, however, means 'brought to completion' or 'brought to the end state'" (*The Kingdom Within*).

If we understand the word this way, we see that Jesus is urging us to be brought to the end state for which we were created and that is brought about through the unfolding of the inner self. The exterior self will still exist and always put pressure upon our inner life. The inner life contains our psyche and spirit. We will always need to cooperate with God's power. In fact, all change and growth will not stick unless we wait and enter into God's holy presence, for only there will we experience all the power to be transformed into His image.

Blessed are those who mourn. Ours is a baptism of water, spirit, and fire. If we value and embrace the fires of sufferings, it will befriend us. The Kingdom of God is taken by force, that is by effort and struggle. Let us bid good-bye to all that is superficial. Let the still small voice find its companion in our minds and will. Yes, the world and our psyche are subject to futility, but not the human spirit! Let us loosen the cords that imprisons us to what the five senses measure but rather bind our psyche to all that is true, pure, and courageous. Let the sweet smell of mercy, justice, and humility reign within. The meek will inherited the earth. Those who have suffered and endured this transformation process are the salt of the earth, able to empathize and weep with those who weep and rejoice with those who rejoice.

There are secrets of what is the part we play in overcoming temptations that I'd like to share with you. Each of these exercises must be practiced until the time comes when you will know which one(s) are to be applied to any particular temptation. First, we must thank God for all that comes our way, whether viewed by our ego as positive or negative. That is to say we are to express our gratitude and thanks for what is. Secondly, we are to empty ourselves of everything and sit alone in silence and, therefore thirdly, remain in God's presence. Only in the presence of God' glory can change ultimately and permanently occur. Finally, we are to claim His power.

I'd like to summarize with a quote from Thomas Merton concerning the disciplines within the interior self:

> All we can do with any spiritual discipline is to
> produce within ourselves something of the silence,

the humility, the detachment, the purity of heart, and the indifference which are required if the inner self is to make some shy, unpredictable manifestation of His presence. At the same time, however, every deeply spiritual experience, whether religious, moral, or even artistic, tends to have in it something of the presence of the interior self. Only from the inner self does any spiritual experience gain depth, reality, and certain incommunicability. Nevertheless, a certain cultural and spiritual atmosphere favors the secret development of the inner self. The ancient cultural traditions, both of the East and West, having indeed transmitted certain common materials in the form of archetypal symbols, liturgical notes, art, poetry, philosophy, and myth, which nourished the inner self from childhood to maturity. In such a cultural setting no one needs to be self-conscious about his interior life, and subjectivity does not run the risk of being deviated into morbidity and excess. Unfortunately such a cultural setting no longer exists in the West or is no longer common property. It is something that has to be laboriously recovered by an educated and enlightened minority. (*The Inner Experience*, Harper San Francisco, 2003, p. 7).

It is here, in God's presence that we now turn to infused contemplation.

Infused Contemplation

You know who I am
You've stared at the sun
Well I'm the one who loves

Changing from nothing to one.

If you should ever track me down
I will surrender there
And I will leave you one broken man
Whom I will teach to repair,

You know who I am . . .

—Leonard Cohen, "You Know Who I Am"

Infused contemplation is the work of God, and the contemplative can only receive it passively. The intense love that is God's light blinds the contemplative at this stage, and therefore, St. John of the Cross called it the dark night of the soul. Here, though the contemplative is being carried by God's light and love, this love and light annihilates the ego as it becomes helpless, bitter, incapacitated, and full of anguish, loneliness, depression, anxiety, and despair. We traced this very process through the experience of Job and His encounter with God. This process takes us out of all our comfort zones and into realms of pain and suffering at times, which seems unbearable. The pain God inflicts is due to the impurity of our psyche, and his light literally blinds all the faculties of our ego-consciousness, our senses, the intellect, our values, emotions, and intuitions, etc.

This process is the same one described by Jung when he discussed the integration of the fourth function and which we traced in the experience of Job. We go through an experience where everything is turned upside down, and all our preconceived notions of who God is and our false concepts of self are destroyed along with our pursuits of security, worth, and meaning, which no longer are valid for the healthy functioning of the personality. We will become embittered toward everything, and love will seem to be completely dissipated. It will feel like an attack without mercy or reconciliation; it is the baptism of fire Jesus referred to. Everything within our psyches is filled with darkness, anguish, obscurity, and lifelessness; our prayers and silent meditations, relationships, work, interests, everything is systematically placed before the blinding light and obliterated and exterminated. Like Job, if you enter this stage of contemplation, you will think you are being punished. Our natural self will want to rebel; we want to depend upon ourselves and want to know what's going on, know where we are going, and experience the security in our knowing. Our ego-consciousness naturally wants to mutiny against these experiences, and this reaction is an expected and standard response. When stripped bare and emptied of all illusory supports, it will seem God has conspired against us. The contemplative must go through the valleys of humiliation where rejection, despair, depression, anxiety, anguish, and failure will become your companions. God leads us out into the desert where no human friendship or help will be accessible; we will be alone and forsaken, abandoned, disorientated, befuddled, and lost. Evil will attempt to exploit every weakness that lies within. We shall suffer as Job did—with sufferings indescribable. Jesus said his followers will suffer and be persecuted as he was. The world is full of tribulation, yet he has overcome the world.

Paul took Job's experience a step further when he proclaims, "We rejoice in our sufferings, knowing that suffering produces endurance, and endurance produces character, and character produces hope" (Romans 5:3–4). Paul also experienced God to the degree he could make this seemingly masochistic statement of faith. This attitude led him to learn the secret of contentment as he can do all things through God who strengthens him (Philippians 4:11–14). I have yet to meet anyone so capable, including myself. This seemed only a pipe dream to me until recently. However, I see the initial step is to accept what is and that we are not so special as to be exempt from whatever sufferings come our way and in whatever form it may take. Men and women have been struggling with indescribable sufferings since *Homo sapiens* came in the scene some 150,000 years ago. "Why me?" is replaced by "Why not me?"

Secondly, we need to seek something positive in each and every painful situation while maintaining gratitude for what we do have. Our response to experience holds the key that will unlock the truth, which sets us free.

Edinger quotes from Ecclesiastes 4:11–12 when discussing wisdom:

Wisdom brings up her sons,

and cares for those who seek her . . .

for though she take him first through winding ways,
bringing fear and faintness on him,
plaguing him with her discipline until she can trust him,
and testing him with her ordeals,
in the end she will lead him back to the straight road,
and reveal her secrets to him.

Only when we have endured the dark night of the soul do we hit upon new beliefs and attitudes that make transformations substantive. Only after we struggle to accept our sufferings and endure them long enough can we finally grasp the blessings inherent in these experiences. Jesus said blessed are those who mourn, for they shall be comforted, and it is with this comfort we in turn can comfort others. These are difficult tasks indeed! However, the alternative is worse! Avoiding the truth of suffering and blaming externals for our pain is the easy way out. No matter how painful our suffering may be, they will never measure up on the misery index that is created when we remain stuck in all those negative attitudes and patterns that repeat themselves continually.

However, the contemplative recognizes that this is God's touch and work in us, and therefore, the contemplative empties themselves by imitating Jesus, who emptied Himself of His divinity; and forgetting ourselves, we begin to learn what real faith is, which trusts His love and guidance through this period of darkness. The contemplative, like Job and every true hero, will eventually experience the dynamics where we wrestle with and from God his blessings of intimacy and thereby share in His peace, joy, love, hope, and truth. It is essential we realize we are on the right path during these experiences, and now is the time for patient faith and obedience, which is willing to endure the darkness and accept the weaknesses that rip us apart and strip us of all our false crutches.

Your love for God will grow. Your experience of God's love will also become more apparent, though in the obscurity of faith, we will know without knowing. The contemplative will experience inner freedom and be unfettered by lifelong attachments, which bound us like Sisyphus to his boulder. In fact, the contemplative will be willing to sacrifice even spiritual gifts and experiences; she will, on some levels, become detached from everything. There is a definite quantity of detachment that can be achieved where a nontemporal state of wholeness is experienced with God in these higher levels of consciousness. Though this does not eliminate suffering, desires, emotion, etc., it is a state of consciousness where we catch a glimpse of wholeness in our ability to not worry and let go of all needs to control our inner life, outcomes of situations, and people. Jung called it objective cognitions. This state is not, however, immune to suffering in any way. The difference seems to be that when one achieves this high level of consciousness, one is not overwhelmed in pain and fear anymore; rather, a serenity and acceptance permeate these experiences. We observe ourselves from a detached perspective. The experience of God's love and presence, in faith, seems to afford an undeniable amount of detachment from the temporal world's torrents, yet our pathos and love for God and ourselves will mature, as will our abilities to heal and love others with the true compassion of God. Your very concern for others will bless them, and whatever you ask will be granted as your will and God's will be one, for you will only wish for what is efficacious in furthering the truth.

This is completely the work of God in our soul as we become like Him. It will be true that it will no longer be us who lives, but Christ living in and through us (1 Corinthians). Though we are afflicted, perplexed, persecuted, and struck down, we will never be forsaken, crushed, driven to despair nor destroyed (2 Corinthians 4:7–9) because we will have learned the secret of being content in all things (Philippians 4:11–12, 2 Corinthians 12:10) and are able to do all thing through Him who strengthens us (Philippians 4:13). We know that we exist in this body of death, yet we know without knowing that all thing work for our good (Romans 8:28), that the Spirit helps us in our weaknesses (Romans 8:26). His grace is sufficient as His power is made perfect in our weaknesses (2 Corinthians 12:9), and that when we are weak, then we are strong (2 Corinthians 12:10).

A love for God will overwhelm your soul, and your desires will be to count everything as loss for the sake of God and, with gratitude and joy, accept and share in His suffering (Philippians 3: 8–11), knowing that friendship with God is the only treasure worth striving for. I can't emphasize enough, your ego will never be able to achieve this maturity and depths of contemplation, and it is infused and done by God alone and in His time. As I said, all we can do is to empty ourselves and endure as Job and Jesus did and patiently wait for God to accomplish His work in and through us. Waiting is one of the hardest tasks set before us, and there is much need for patient endurance with infused contemplation. However, eventually, if we hang in there with whatever degree of faith we have, our spirit in us will rejoice simultaneously with a wholeness and enlightenment bestowed upon us beyond our wildest imaginations to conceive. In fact, in Christ, there is no longer any divisions between any men and women (Galatians 3:28) or God and man (John 17:23). And this is the secret wisdom and "the mystery of His will, according to His purpose that he set forth in Christ as a plan for the fullness of time, to unites all things in Him, things in heaven and things on earth" (Ephesians 1:9–10).

Whenever we unearth traces of wholeness and enlightenment within a human psyche, we will also come across within its mystery, joy, serenity, and power to be transformed into God's likeness and image. These blessings not only leave scars, but come with no special exemption from ongoing suffering and grief, loss and pain. The blessings that approach wholeness come at the end of the track; they are fashioned within the psyche only after the desert experiences. As I discussed earlier, the difference is a security and peace proliferated amid the sufferings and the intuitive understanding that we are safe and protected, guided and directed, and where no evil nor anything can separate us from the love of God (Romans 8: 31–39).

Now, I'd like to explore contemplation and how it is manifested within the enlightened knight of faith'

The Knight of Faith

On the road with my
Sword

And my shield in my hand
Pressing on to the new
Day
This love will surely last
Forever
This love will surely last
Always

In the valley I see
Horseman pass . . .
There's a battle for the throne

And it's raging down in
Your soul . . .

I've been accused
Of truth and alchemy . . .

Here comes horsemen
Through the pass
They cast a cold eye
On life on death
There's a battle for the truth
And it means to thine
Own self be true.

—Van Morrison, "Here Comes the Knight"

Now we can turn to the true nature of faith. First, knowledge and beliefs precede faith. We must seek the truth and find her before we can begin the long journey of faith. God reaches out to *most intimately* around the age of thirty-five. Grace opens our eyes to the eternal paradox of faith. Kierkegaard proclaimed faith as a paradox precisely because we trust in an objective uncertainty. Faith is a risk, and we take the leap into the absurd. Faith is a risk because we are never certain in an objective sense in anything that has to do with our physical existence/the five senses. We seek the eternal truth is time with a faith wrought by God's initiative love/grace. Our authentic response can only begin with our beliefs and risks we take with our faith that God is in control and to be trusted no matter what human nature is, no matter what external circumstances may be, no matter how incomprehensible life is. The leap of faith is into the unknown, an objective uncertainty, and as we hold fast onto God, like children. Are you willing to trust and develop a relationship in existence with God?

I want to quote from Earnest Becker's opus *The Denial of Death* as he describes a personality using Kierkegaard's knight of faith as the perfect example of enlightenment. I need to quote it here because I could never describe this personality any better:

> This is the man who lives in faith, who has given over the meaning of his life to his Creator, and who lives centered on the energies of his Maker. He accepts whatever happens in this visible dimension without complaint, lives his life as a duty, and faces his death without a qualm. No pettiness is so petty that it threatens his meanings; no task too frightening to be beyond his courage. He is fully in the world on its terms and wholly beyond the world in his trust in the invisible dimension. It is very much the old pietistic ideal that was lived by Kant' parents. The great strength of such an ideal is that it allows one to be open, generous, and courageous, to touch others' lives and enrich them and open them in turn. As the knight of faith has no fear-of-life-and –death trip to lay onto others, he does not cause them to shrink back upon themselves, he does not coerce or manipulate them. The knight of faith, then, represents what we may call as ideal of mental health, the continuing openness of life out of the death throes of dread. (*The Denial of Death*, the Free Press, a division of the Macmillan Publishing Co., Inc., New York, 1973)

What does this person look like in her day-to-day operation? I think a female patient of Dr. Jung's says it best:

By being quiet, repressing nothing, remaining attentive, and by accepting reality-taking things as they are, and not as I wanted them to be-by doing all this, unusual knowledge has come to me, and unusual powers as well, such as I could never have imagined before. I always thought when we accepted things they overpowered us in some way or other. This turns out not to be true at all, and it is only by accepting them that one can assume an attitude towards them. So now I intend to play the game of life, being receptive to whatever comes to me, good and bad, sun and shadow that are forever alternating, and, in this way, also accepting my own nature with its positive and negative sides. Thus everything becomes more alive to me. What a fool I was! How I tried to force everything to go according to the way I thought it ought to! (*The Secret of the Golden Flower*)

I would have treasured the opportunity to meet her! These two quotes summarize what I believe and think God is trying to convey to all of us in the context of a true relationship with Him/Her. The knight of faith is the one who finds the Holy Grail because he/she can say, "Oh well" without trying to control anything, but rather allow the truth to come to the surface in her own time. All the needs for worth and security are met, and the knight of faith can rest in the protection and guidance of God's will.

What does enlightenment have to say about the meaning of our mortal life? To begin with, we are here to glorify God by approaching wholeness and thereby glorifying Him by furthering His Kingdom. We are His ambassadors. We approach perfection/holiness and wholeness/enlightenment by becoming intimate with God. In humility, we need to allow love by opening the door of our hearts to everything that is from God. By so doing, wisdom and enlightenment, wholeness and holiness, penetrate us to the degree we empty ourselves within the context of our unique abilities and destiny. God lives and acts through us, and we are the channels from which the very essence of God is expressed to this world. In those obscure alleys is the dance called life. I believe we are not what we appear; we are limited by certain strengths and weaknesses from personality traits from the get-go, some because they are intrinsic to our true self and some given for the purpose of teaching some valuable lessons. Whether our weaknesses are in our true self or not is hard to say, but in either case, we need to face and overcome our weaknesses while using our strengths for the benefit of others. Job and Jesus refused to deceive themselves, and we can make the same choice by discovering what lies within.

In Jung's study of alchemy, he believed the philosopher's stone symbolized a detachment of spirit from matter. The philosopher's stone is easily located but not easily utilized. The philosopher's stone is our daily dance of experience, and it's everywhere built into our duty to adapt to the truth as it is. This symbolism transforms the frog into a prince, lead into gold, spiritual gold, refined and manufactured into its pure form. It is no symbolism but a literal truth that one day the believer will be transformed into a resurrected body. All of God's creation needs to be valued and integrated.

I am grateful for the suffering this fourth function has evoked in me but know there is much that is expected from me, and I know that like the Apostle Paul,

> Not that I am already perfect; but I press on to make it my own. Brethren, I do not consider that I have made it my own; but one thing I do, forgetting what lies behind and straining for what lies ahead, I press on toward the goal for the prize of the upward call of God in Christ Jesus. (Philippians 3:12–14).

We all are required to take seriously how to glorify God in our unique way. May you be blessed in your struggle, and remember to dance and take your sword and shield with you!

Are we growing in *wholeness* or not, up or down or all round? Are we *centered* on self or God/Truth? These two questions and the answers our lives compose are really all that matters. We are either growing toward wholeness and intimacy with God or we are not—there's no middle ground. Evolution is in a constant state of movement toward wholeness and the truth. De-evolution is the opposite direction. Along the journey and sojourn our lives take, we will fail and make numerous mistakes. You will wonder whether all the failures and pains can be endured, whether you can nurture confusion and the unknown until the darkness gradually recedes and the light heals and enlightens you. These mistakes will become more apparent as you approach wholeness and cause immense suffering as you reach higher and higher to seek, find, and then adapt to the truth. Can you start over with each failure, eschewing falsehood and affirming the truth as you go? We can never ultimately judge another ourselves, but we can forgive and forget. Yet we need to separate the truth from lies and affirm it in the way we live our lives—in our speech, actions, mannerisms, and when we are alone.

My final word on the matter of our collective purpose is summed up by prophet Micah: "He has shown you, O man what is good; and what does the Lord require of you, but to do justice, love mercy, and walk humbly with your God" (Micah 6:8).

To follow these three injunctions, you will experience your unique purpose and unite with the living God.

> In the ebb and flow of dying and birth
> In wounded streets and whispered prayer
> The dance is the truth and it's everywhere.
>
> —Bruce Cockburn, "Everywhere Dance"

Apotheosis

> There's something I'm watching
> Means a lot to me
> It's a broken banjo bobbing
> On the dark infested sea . . .
>
> It's coming for me darling
> No matter where I go

Its duty is to harm me
My duty is to know . . .

—Leonard Cohen, "Banjo"

The goal or apotheosis of existence is to accumulate as much wisdom/ truth and holiness/wholeness as possible while in this temporal and fallible frame. We take only our experiences and the knowledge we have acquired in this life into the next with love, wholeness/holiness, and wisdom at our side as light to guide our way. Our inner and outer experiences are cut from the same cloth as our soul, and these along with the truth/wisdom we accumulate *in God* sustain us in the great beyond. All else will fall away and be lost. All that love does not author will be set ablaze.

In the epitaph, the sea is a metaphor for the unconscious/life, and the banjo is a metaphor for ego-consciousness. The duty of the unconscious is to make us suffer in order that ego-consciousness dies as the center of the personality, and we therefore are able to grow through spiritual-knowledge and love. In addition, we're required to integrate these truths into our psyche or soul, making our spirits whole.

Oh that love that was
Within me
You know it carried me
Through
Well it lifted me up and it
Filled me
Meditation
Contemplation too

Oh we got to go back . . .

For the healing go on
With the dreaming.

—Van Morrison, "Got to Go Back"

Laughing at the hands I hold out
Only air within their grasp
all you can do is praise the razor
For the fineness of the slash

You carry the weight of inherited sorrow
From your first day until you die
Toward that hilltop where the road
Forever becomes one with the sky

Got me thinking of the sea
And the currents that brought
Me to you and you to me
And in the silence at the heart of things
Where all true meetings come to be

I see the rose above the sky
Opens
And the light behind the sun
Takes all

—B. Cockburn, "The Rose Above the Sky"

Appendices

Appendix I

Community

For the millions in the prison,
That wealth has set apart—
For the Christ who has not risen,
From the caverns of the heart-

For the innermost decision,
That we cannot but obey—
For what's left of our religion,
I lift up my voice and pray;
May the lights in The Land of Plenty
Shine on the truth some day.

I know I said I'd meet you,
I'd meet you at the store,
But I can't but it, baby.
I can't buy it anymore.

—Leonard Cohen, "The Land of Plenty"

There must be more . . .more
More songs more warmth

More love more life
Not more fear not more fame
Not more money not more games

There-you coming through the crowd
Blue light silhouettes your head
I want to shout your name out loud
But I shout inside instead

There must be more . . . more
More current more spark
More touch deep in the heart
Not more thoughtless cruelty
Not more being this lonely

Don't I hear them talking
Don't I know what they say?
I'm a fool for thinking
Things could be better than they
Were today

There must be more . . . more
More growth more truth
More chains more loose
Not more pain not more walls
Not more living human voodoo dolls

—B. Cockburn, "More, Not More"

But everything is not the way it seems—
Tears can sing and joy sheds tears
You can take the wisdom of this world
And give it to the ones who think it all ends here!

—B. Cockburn, "Hills of Morning"

This is too big for anger,
It's too big for blame.
We stumble through history so

Humanly lame
So I bow down my head
Say a prayer for us all
That we don't fear the spirit
When it comes to call

—Bruce Cockburn, "Postcards from Cambodia"

Our communities have suffered greatly from a lack of truth and the illusion of separateness. We have an obvious society that is built on different classes and caste systems, with some rich and privileged while others poor and oppressed. The exterior or false self dominates our culture and the psyche in its natural state. We are enslaved by transient, exterior, and superficial objects. As I have already talked about, monuments are built to the ego to that false exterior self, which manipulates and accumulates material objects. Some of us see people as objects as well, and not just in the sexual sense. Political power has come to dominate much that can be said about community and comes in all shapes and sizes but has common threads, which always destroy the spirit.

White-collar crime is insidious and odious; wealth and privilege is accumulated surreptitiously and often upon the backs of the poor while politicians and the famous often accept gratuities without a second thought. Too often, wisdom atrophies like a dead conscience, and the only measure of worth and value is found in what others think of us or in the bank. Courage is lost and replaced by training in taking the easy way out. Systemic evil and ignorance breed like rabbits and is already stacked against the oppressed in each society. Whoever has capital increases it without working for it, just stick it in some account and watch it grow! Peace is extracted from the poor like those abscessed teeth.

By far, the worst of all and the greatest abomination of all is where God is used to justify hatred, violence, and fear. This is often couched in nationalism, and I am reminded of a verse by Dylan where he sings in a moment of pith, "Patriotism is the last refuge to which a scoundrel clings." Some use religion for political ends and seek superficial worldly power. The grave awaits us all, and we will reap what we sow. Military regimes that are politically brutal and where the selfish and dishonest egocentric individuals justify murder, torture, oppression, and injustice of every fathomable kind, whether in the first, second, or third world.

A friend of mine, Tom Varno, has spent many years in Africa building facilities and faith. I'll never forget what he told me after his first journey was complete; he said something to the effect that most of the local folks he had encountered were selfish, always looking for a handout, and materialism was bought into hook, line, and sinker. What's become normal is the accumulation of material things and the construction of walls and weapons that endeavor to protect these things and which all inevitably avoid true community, reality, and truth. We so often propagate suffering a millionfold upon nature and each other. False security binds us to fears like flies to dung. We have, as a society in the West, created and tolerate abuses and evil within our prison walls, church structures, VA hospitals, old people's homes, corporations, and every other institution swaying unhindered under our national flags, where we all too often store and hide our greed and dishonesty from view. America has been the primary proliferators of wars around the world as we manufacture more weapons, many of which are crimes against international law. If only a few more who work in these and other institutional death traps would stand up and proclaim to the world the truths of what goes on behind the normal ruses that institutions use, though they would be attacked for being disloyal and whistle-blowers, they would be creating justice.

Evil and falsehood cannot stand the light of truth, and they wither in the winds of truth faster than you think. Many of the rich and powerful have presently fallen asleep at the ethical wheel and need a rousing from the malaise that afflicts humankind. The so-called common man is often in complicity with the rich and powerful, often seeking material things and its own versions of power in the guise of self-worth and security rather than justice. How naïve have we become as new revelations of impropriety and illegal activity show up in the daily newspapers while few question the moral crisis our distorted values have created. We pollute our planet and place a heavy boot upon the neck of the poor and the outcast, destroy relationships with anyone not us, and project untold negative energy into the universe at large. Meanwhile, we hear regularly about some new scandal where those in power abuse that power, taking advantage of our children while gaining all sorts of perks, which expose their lack of understanding and compassion. I think a suit and tie give the wrong symbolic messages where everything below the head is repressed. I stand ashamed of my masculine white skin, knowing what evil has been manufactured in the name of God, America, and respectability. Am I the only one nauseated by the status quo? The institutional church has become an empty shell in the Western world. The secular world has taken inflation and arrogance to a new level of absurdity, and the institutional church has been in complicity with for too long.

Hope for true community lies within a willingness to face the truths that are within us. The little decisions we make every day is what matters, how we treat each other and our responsibilities. The truth contains more than enough power to transform and unify the entire world. We are capable of transforming the world with each seemingly insignificant decision with more effectiveness than billions of politicians and other elected officials. We are all interconnected, and I share with many others a vision that reflects wholeness/holiness and the actions these engender. I think individually, any of us can identify a passion in at least one area where injustice and oppression have taken a toll upon the oppressed and the unheralded of this world. Most of us have a calling and passion to change the world—choose that area wherever your passions lie as you do not have the time to be involved in everything. However, every bit of injustice and evil I run across, I can pray and so add positive energy to a negative situation. I know that I must always attempt to speak the truth in love and know there is time for any of us to turn our values and lives around. Justice must be served and eaten if any kind of wholeness and union with God is real.

As an alternative, I would like to share a particular vision of worldwide small communities that resist the values of violence, economic inequity, oppression, or inequality and move toward egalitarianism. This ideal community will be small as individuals choose to live together, where equality and justice is promoted and valued. This ideal community will also engage in a real confrontation with the values of the world in which they are situated, simply by a lifestyle that opposes the current values that surround them. There have been many such communities attempted throughout history. To name a few, a Jewish sect called the Essences existed in both a small community near the Dead Sea and also one that was in rural communities of different households; another was the Cynics as they were itinerant and wandering philosophers whose lifestyle challenged the world of material values; and the early church in Jerusalem was also a community where radical values of equalitarianism were proclaimed in conjunction with the good news of the Kingdom of God preached initially by Jesus and carried on by the early Jewish church where everything was held in common. As a Christian myself, I want to advocate and share with you some additional readings that go into depth in ways that are outside the scope of this book. I encourage the reader to become familiar with the works of Kurt Greenhalgh. Kurt Greenhalgh's works are self-published and only available through mail. Send requests for his books and donations to Kurt Greenhalgh, 1828 Superior, Duluth, MN 55812. He has written three that are interrelated and are very challenging and enlightening.

For any community, the union with God must always remain integrated with suffering, community, and the reality of evil. William James could just as easily have been describing the knight of faith in the context of community when he spoke of Bunyan and Tolstoy:

> Each of them realized a good which broke the effective edge of his sadness; yet the sadness was preserved as a minor ingredient in the heart of the faith by which it was overcome. The fact of interest for us is that as a matter of fact they could and did find something welling up in the inner reaches of their consciousness, by which such extreme sadness could be overcome. Tolstoy does well to talk of it as that bay which men live; for that is exactly what it is, a stimulus, an excitement, a faith, a force that re-infuses the positive willingness to live, even in full presence of the evil perceptions that erewhile made life seem unbearable. For Tolstoy's perceptions of evil appear within their sphere to have remained unmodified. His later works show him

implacable to the whole system of official values: the ignobility of fashionable life; the infamies of empire; the spuriousness of the church, the vain conceit of the professions; the meanness and cruelties that go with great success; and every other pompous crime and lying institution of the world. To all patience with such things his experience has been for him a permanent misery of death. (*The Varieties of Religious Experience*)

None of us can do or change everything. However, each can choose some sufferings and injustices that our thoughts, creativity, time, and other resources can begin to orchestrate change. We can at first chip away at injustice and evil before it gains the momentum of truth, and eventually, we will overcome. The reality of evil is it will shrink and slink away where a humble boldness is fostered from the light of truth and faith and prayer!

It seems to me we must begin by agreeing on the problem and its causes. I have attempted to delineate each of these the best I can. I know grace is bountiful, and we need to begin by facing our errors and begin to turn around (repentance). From here, are there those like Job, willing to let go of their ego and all the attachments, thus beginning their journey into the insecurity of the unknown? Can we not banish fear by the faith that will trust truth as the only belongings we need for our unique journey through life?

I exhort you to slow down; reflect upon what is going on within and around you; separate right from wrong, truth from falsehood, and good from evil; choose the truth and try it on. It will blind you for a while, but it will create the light within to ferry you onto justice and the pursuit of healthy community.

From bitter searching of the heart,
Quickened with passion and with pain
We rise to play a greater part.
This is the faith from which we start:
Men shall know commonwealth again . . .

The lesser loyalties depart.
Neither race nor creed remain . . .

Reshaping narrow law and art
Whose symbols are the millions slain,
From bitter searching of the heart
We rise to play a greater part.

—Leonard Cohen, "Villanelle for Our Time"

These shoes have walked some strange streets
Stranger still to come
Sometimes the prayers of strangers
Are all that keeps them from
Trying to stay static
Something even death can't do
Everything in motion
Let the motion be true

In this cold commodity culture
Where you lay your money down
It's hard to even notice
That all this earth is hallowed ground—
Harder still to feel
Basic as a breath
Love is stronger than darkness
Love is stronger than death

Hackles rise in anger
Heat waves rise in sex
The gift moves on regardless
Tying this world to the next
May you never tire of waiting
Never feel that life is cheap
May your life be filed with light . . .

The gift
Keeps moving—

Never know
Where it' going to land
You must stand
Back and let it
Keep on changing hands

—Bruce Cockburn, "The Gift"

Appendix II

For Those Who Labor

There's an evening haze settling over town,
Star light by the edge of the creek,
The buying power of the proletariats gone down,
Money's getting shallow and weak . . .

Meet me at the bottom, don't lag behind,
Bring me my boots and shoes,
You can hang back or fight your best on the front lines,
Sing a little of bit of these working man's blues . . .

I'm a trying to feed my soul with thought,
Going to sleep off the rest of the day,
Sometimes no one walks with you God
Sometimes you can't give it away . . .

Well, they burned my barn,
And they stole my horse,
I can't save a dime,
I got to be careful;
I don't want to be forced into a life of continued crime.

—Bob Dylan, "Working Man Blues"

I have had the privilege of working with blue-collar men and women for most of my adult life. Herein I applaud all the hardworking men and women who carry the burden of our economic system upon their aching backs. I have worked with tens of thousands over the years and have been witness to the love, courage, patience, endurance, and perseverance within these laborers as their bodies break down. Their bodies break down well before the rest of us, and some literally have been carried into the hospital to get them to recognize the seriousness of their condition. They often chafe at the limitations in their bodies, and because of their physical pain and newfound sobriety, many have found new careers. After a certain point, the pain in their body and the work they do become triggers for continued drug use.

Most blue-collar types work outside and can appreciate the sights, sounds, temperatures, tastes, and feel of the land contrasted against every sky imaginable. They wrestle and fight on the front line, yet are not appreciated for their contribution. They often don't seem to prize what they do, and I have to remind them that Jesus was a carpenter/mason. They often end up misunderstood, judged, and in jail or prison. The working man's blues couple physical pain with a sacrificial attitude that is often trampled upon. Their anger is all the uninitiated can see, especially intellectuals who don't have the slightest idea what these men and women go through. Their defenses do set many up for continued conflict and illegal behavior. Some are alcohol and drug addicts as they struggle with people-pleasing more often than abusive behavior. Of course, they explode and set themselves up for continued life of crime, not premeditated but rather impetuous. I've seen many extremely sincere and honest, only to watch them self-destruct as their resentments and self-pity get the best of them. They fight on the front lines daily for their life often becomes a struggle to get by. When sleep comes, it is usually deep. My respect for these folks is without limits.

I stumbled out of bed
I got ready for the struggle
I smoked a cigarette
And I tightened up my gut

I said this can't be me
Must be my double
And I can't forget
Can't forget
Can't forget
But don't remember what.

—Leonard Cohen, "I Can't Forget"

Acknowledgments

Heavens perfect alchemy
Put you with me and me with you
Come on put it in your heart
Come on put it in your heart

—Bruce Cockburn, "Put in Your Heart"

Pangs of love
That's the price you pay
When you give your love
But don't give it all the way
Pangs of love
Won't let me go

—Bruce Cockburn, "Pangs of Love"

I want to thank the mother of my three children, Trina and my four children Carin, Ava, Sophie, and Isaac for your love, grace, and patience with me. Though we no longer live together, you have all stuck by me in your own ways in the midst of my personal contradictions, health issues, and my numerous defects of character. My love speaks sometimes only softly, and your adherence to the truth has always inspired me in ways you will understand only after we have reached the other side. You have all helped me to remain tethered to the real world, which has been essential is my search for the truth and for exploring the mysteries of life. I thank you all for providing a grounding, without which the mysteries and truths inherent in creation would always remain obscure and out of reach of my intuition.

I also want to thank Kevin O'Grady for all your support and input for me and this book through the years. You have truly been a great friend and fellow journeyman in the apprenticeship of life.

I also want to thank you Kurt Greenhalgh for your editing, my brother, whose own leap of faith has and continues to inspire and challenge me to face my compromises and contradictions as I struggle within the context of faith and grace.

In addition, thank you, Lynn Savage and Scott Beaumont, for your friendships have been an unmitigated blessing to me all these many years.

Thanks to my men's Al-Anon group, without whose support and love this final revision would have been impossible.

I also thank all my Strat-O-Matic friends who have I have shared the joy of play and camaraderie over these last thirty or so years.

Thanks also to family, especially to my brother Dave and his wife Linda for all your support.

And my heartfelt thanks to all my clients over these many years; ten thousand books could not contain all the gifts of wisdom, mutual understanding, courage, and truth we have shared. This work is, in part, a dedication to you all.

Finally, I have learned to ignore what others say and think of me. I've had to take all my experiences and follow its leadings wherever it has taken me. I have left many a friend along the way and regret not a moment with anyone I have shared time with under the sun. I've never tried to hurt anyone, though I know I have done so many times over. Shalom to you all.

I pray that all may give and receive love through this world and into the next.

> Blessed are you poor, for yours is the Kingdom of God.
>
> Blessed are you that hunger now, for you shall be satisfied.
>
> Blessed are you that weep now, for you shall laugh.

Blessed are you when men hate you, and when they exclude you and revile you

and cast out your name as evil, on account of The Son of Man!

Rejoice in that day, and leap for joy, for behold, you reward is great in heaven; for so their fathers did to the prophets.

But woe to you that are rich, for you have received your consolation.

Woe to you that are full now, for you shall hunger.

Woe to you that laugh now, for you shall mourn and weep.

Woe to you, when all men speak well of you, for so their fathers did to the false prophets.

But I say to you that hear, Love your enemies, do good to those who hate you, bless those who curse you, pray for those who abuse you. To him who strikes you on the cheek, offer the other also; and from him who takes away your coat do not even withhold your shirt. Give to everyone who begs from you; and of him who takes away your goods do not ask them again. And as you wish that men would do to you, do so to them. (Luke 6:20b–31)

> I've change my name so often
> I've lost my wife and children
> But I've many friends.
>
> —Leonard Cohen, "The Partisan"

May God bless and keep you always . . .

> May you grow up to be righteous
> May you grow up to be true
> May you always know the truth

May you always see the light surrounding you . . .

May you stay forever young.

—Bob Dylan, "Forever Young"

Tell me again
We're alone & I'm listening
I'm listening so hard it hurts
Tell me again
When I'm clean and sober
Tell me again
When I've seen through the horror
Tell me again
Tell me over and over
Tell me you want me then
Amen . . .

—Leonard Cohen "Amen"

For the millions in a prison,
That wealth has set apart
For the Christ who has not risen,
From the caverns of the heart—

For what's left of our religion
I lift my voice and pray;
May the lights in The Land of Plenty
Shine on the truth some day.

—Leonard Cohen, "The Land of Plenty"

The lights are all on
The world is watching now
People looking for truth
We must not fail them now . . .

To see both sides . . .

—Phil Collins, "Both Sides of the Story"

About the Author

Will Barno has spent the better part of thirty years working as a chemical dependency counselor while writing throughout. Will has been a student of the inner life and human condition since his late teens, and he continues to wrestle with many of the issues and problems outlined in his book. Will has four children and lives alone in Mora, Minnesota.